AN ANTHOLOGY OF RESPECT

The Pullman Porters National Historic Registry

of

African-American Railroad Employees®

By Lyn Hughes

Preface By Lerone Bennett, Jr.
With Excerpts From "Train Rides" By Nikki Giovanni
And Contributions From
Beth Tompkins Bates & Christopher R. Reed PhD

An Anthology Of Respect
The Pullman Porters National Historic Registry Of African American Railroad Employees
All Rights Reserved
Copyright © 2009 Lyn Hughes
V4.0R2.5(2)

By Lyn Hughes

Cover images: The Chicago History Museum and
The A. Philip Randolph Pullman Porter Museum

Cover layout and design by Kim E. Lovely
Edited by Lyn Hughes
Audra Akins
Interior layout and design by:
ef Design Group

ISBN-13: 978-0-9793941-2-6

Library of Congress Control Number: 2007927155

Printed in the United States of America

For My Children

Crystal
Alita and
David

Special Thanks To

The A Philip Randolph Pullman Porter Museum

Beth Tompkins-Bates Associate Professor
African Studies, Wayne State University

Lerone Bennett, Jr.

Chicago History Museum

Christopher R. Reed PhD, Professor Emeritus
Dept of History, Art History, and Philosophy
Roosevelt University

Nikki Giovanni Author, Poet

Printed in the United States of America

Cover images: The Chicago History Museum and
The A. Philip Randolph Pullman Porter Museum

Cover layout and design by Kim E. Lovely

Interior layout and design by:
ef Design Group
Outskirts Press

Page one graphic, is a photo of the original art mural commissioned by
the now defunct Historic North Pullman corporation, with the Chicago
Public Art Group, Lead Artist Bernard Williams with a grant from the
Morrison Knudsen corporation through the city of Chicago's Department
of Cultural Affairs and Gallery 37 Satellite program.

Contents

Acknowledgment

The registry was an undertaking that began in 2000. Inspired by God and the ancestors, with the help of Amtrak, this research project was launched and continued in phases along the years. Special individuals such as Dr. Phyllis M. Cunningham, Distinguished Teaching Professor Emeritus, Northern Illinois University, encouraged me and helped to find the resources to help me continue the work. Dr. Phyllis Ham-Garth and Dr. Paul ILsley, of Northern Illinois University, provided enthusiastic encouragement. I would not have been able to amass the research in one place without the technical support and expertise of Design Teck One of Chicago, Illinois. Thanks also to American Family Insurance for underwriting the national advertising campaign of 2002. Special thanks to Northern Illinois University doctoral candidates Lametra Curry, and Sikson, and Audra M. Akins for retrieving and repairing an enormous amount of data, Illinois Institute Of Technology's Digital Media Center, and to Kevin Glover without whom I would never have been able to get this project to print. Finally, a heartfelt thank you to three very special people for whom the label "friend" just doesn't seem adequate: Regina Curry, ABD, Northern Illinois University, Dr. Georges Germain, and once again to Dr. Phyllis Cunningham, a person for whom a separate category should be created. For me, she was an educator, a friend, and a constant source of encouragement like no one else could. To all mentioned here, who offered support at the right time and in the right places during the various phases of the project, a huge thank you is in order.

Introduction

By Lyn Hughes

Pullman Porters were a driving force in African-American labor history following the Civil War, for they represented a rich cultural and intellectual resource of the African-American community (Perata, 1996). The well-educated and socially cultivated African-American male could no more find work than his uneducated, unsophisticated cousin could. However, when George M. Pullman decided to provide well-mannered servants for the well-to-do clientele that rode his elegantly furnished Pullman Palace Sleeping Cars, he turned to this pool of able workers to become the Pullman Porters. These men (and to a lesser degree the Pullman maids) were the pride of the African-American community. Though they were poorly paid, they were employed in a white-collar job and were well dressed, and quite urbane because they were well traveled. Accordingly, this group of men assumed much historical significance for the African-American community and historians in general. For it is within this group where the first black union was formed, the idea of the march on Washington was hatched, and the second civil rights movement was accelerated. The means was found for distributing the *Chicago_Defender* by dropping it off as the porters traveled their runs nationwide, fostering the Great Migration and setting the stage for the documentation of lynching (Grossman, 1991; Reef, 2001). Today much of that history has been lost to the African-American community. There has been a renaissance of sorts according to Arnesen (2001) in African-American history in the general public and academia, but the availability of resources for the community historian, the family genealogist, or popular educators is rare. It is this concern that I have sought to address.

Preface

By Lerone Bennett, Jr.

The name was right. It was more than a union, more than a group focused solely on the grievances of workers in one sector of the economy. Although it could picket with the best of them, and although it defeated the powerful Pullman Company in a bitter twelve-year struggle that made it the first Black union recognized by the AFL, it was always, as its name said, a Brotherhood organized to make the world better for union and non-union people everywhere.

Lyn Hughes, the founder-director of Chicago's A. Philip Randolph Pullman Porter Museum, knows this story as well as anyone, and she reminds us in *Anthology of Respect* of a labor milestone that helped create the new world of Black and White America.

Driven by a cruel history that required them to smile *and* fight, and shaped by a racist system that ignored their personal qualities and made them Sleeping Car *Porters* instead of Sleeping Car *Guests*, the heroes of this story labored in one of history's hard places to maintain the dignity of labor and the "manhood rights" of African-Americans. And you have to read between the lines and above and below the lines to understand how they transformed themselves and the situation, smiling the many-faceted smiles that reversed signs and codes, making minuses plusses and plusses minuses. That's what my Morehouse college professor, Brailsford R. Brazeal, meant when he told us in 1946 (*The Brotherhood of Sleeping Car Porters*] that the Pullman Porters redefined themselves and their adversaries.

There was poetry and power in this "congregation of Black men"—see poet Nikki Giovanni on page 6—and it foreshadowed the real-life reversals of the sixties.

Dr. Christopher R. Reed is very good on this point. "[W] earing their uniforms as symbols of knightly authority," he writes (23) in Chapter 3, "Pullman Porters assumed unto themselves a power never envisioned by their employers and customers and recognizable all too clearly in the black community." In a fine phrase, he adds, "Adorned in their distinguished Pullman blue uniforms (27) and with a brass 'Pullman' emblem on his cap, African-Americans registered their employment into more of a sign of internal dignity than company ownership over labor." They were, as he and others have said, soldiers in the labor trenches, "czars of the sleeping car," men with flair and style and an air of responsibility and authority.

And let it be said, as Lyn Hughes says, that the Brotherhood was also a Brotherhood-Sisterhood of men and women, husbands and wives, sons and daughters, communities and villages, like the village of Harlem and the village of the South Side. Beth Tompkins-Bates tells us in Chapter 4 that one of the early leaders of the Brotherhood Movement was Ida B. Wells-Barnett, who let Asa Philip Randolph speak in her house on what is now Dr. Martin Luther King Jr. Drive (43) when other Chicago spaces were closed to him because of fear of the powerful Pullman Company.

For all these reasons, and for others as well, Pullman Porters became a living presence in Black America. They bought homes, raised and educated families, led movements and lifted up communities from one end of this country to the other. They or at least most were de facto ambassadors for Black Americans on every train they rode, and they helped thousands of Blacks, especially Black students, to continue trips when money ran out or tickets were lost.

Some of the best-known names in Black America—Thurgood Marshall, Malcolm X, Gordon Parks—worked as Pullman Porters. Benjamin E. Mays, the great president of Morehouse College who has been called "The Schoolmaster of the Movement,"
recalled in his book, *Born to Rebel*, that he spent the summer of 1914 and "several more" working out of Grand Central Station in New York and South Station in Boston. He also tells a fascinating story of how two cool and endlessly inventive Pullman Porters outwitted the conductor and made it possible for him to travel several thousand miles and arrive in Chicago in time to meet the registration deadline at the University of Chicago. At the beginning of the trip, Dr. Mays and his Pullman Porter friend evaded the conductor by walking a car behind him as he collected tickets. Then the porter hid him in a vacant upper birth. The next

morning he stowed Mays in the linen closet, putting a cord on the door so it wouldn't slam and lock and suffocate the guest. To protect him further, he put a soiled linen bag between Mays and the door. By these means and others we need not reveal, Mays, who was down to his last forty-three dollars, arrived in Chicago at 8 a.m. on the last day for registration at the University of Chicago Divinity School. Thus, thanks to the Pullman Porter brigade, another great preacher—and the mentor of Martin Luther King Jr.—was saved for the race and the dream. It is scarcely necessary to underline here that the porters directly involved and every employee who knew what was happening risked their jobs to further the education of a young Black man who was not in their family but who was in their bond and their Brotherhood.

Still another great American, John H. Johnson, the legendary founder of *Ebony* and *Jet* magazines, said in his book (*Succeeding Against The Odds*) that he and millions of Blacks in the Jim Crow South, including this writer, were indebted to Pullman Porters who smuggled militant Black newspapers into towns in Arkansas, Alabama, Mississippi and other states in the first decades of this century.

Given this background, it is not surprising that Pullman Porters were among the pioneer leaders of the first stages of the Freedom Movement. To cite only one example, the unsung and virtually unknown father of the Montgomery, Alabama, movement was Pullman Porter E. D. Nixon. When, on December 1, 1955, Rosa Parks was jailed for refusing to give her seat to a White man, she was permitted only one phone call—and she called her mentor, E. D. Nixon, an active Pullman Porter who was also president of the Alabama chapter of the Brotherhood of Sleeping Car Porters. Nixon arranged bail and started mobilizing cadres for the Boycott that changed the dimensions of the Civil Rights Movement.

Finally, and most importantly, the Brotherhood produced and supported Asa Philip Randolph, one of the two or three most creative leaders of African-American protest movements. It was Randolph who founded the March on Washington Movement that forced Franklin Delano Roosevelt to issue in 1941 Executive Order 8802 ending discrimination in World War II defense industries. And although few media people know it, Randolph was the leader of the great March on Washington of 1963 and made the keynote address.

Forty-two years ago, in the foreword of my 1965 book, *Confrontation: Black and White*, Randolph anticipated the contemporary crises of the civil rights and labor movements, saying:

"Even if all racial barriers are abolished it is hardly possible for the Negro workforce to catch up with the white workforce and bridge the widening gap of the annual average median wage between the two groups. *Automation may mean that Negro workers as young as thirty years of age may never work again, especially those without skills, training, and education* (my emphasis)."

What was the solution?

"Negro civil rights organizations," he said, "must lead the war on poverty in the interest of developing a socioeconomic order which will bring about the humanization of the revolution of automation. To this end, Negroes must take the leadership in building a coalition of conscience to include the black poor and the white poor, the black unemployed and the white unemployed, the black worker and the white worker, civil rights organizations and organized labor, Negroes and Jews, Catholics and Protestants, liberal intellectuals and progressive businessmen, to create a national consensus which will prod, persuade, and support the federal government to build decent, low-costing housing for all, integrated quality schools for all, and jobs or a guaranteed decent income for all."

The shift from trains to planes marginalized the Pullman Car but it didn't, as Randolph's quote indicates, marginalize the Pullman Porter image, which is as current, relevant and challenging as tomorrow's headlines.

This *Anthology of Respect* is a reminder of a living legacy and a clarion call to continue what A. Philip Randolph and the Brotherhood defined as "the unfinished task of emancipation."

Lerone Bennett Jr.

July 2007

Excerpt From Train Rides

By Nikki Giovanni

So when you find yourself on the first day of fall which is not actually the first day but simply early October and because it has been such a dry hot summer the leaves aren't really turning so it looks enough like late spring to make you think back to when you and your sister used to catch the train from Cincinnati to Knoxville to go spend the summer with your grandparents and you thought you were pretty well grown because Mommy didn't have to travel with you and the two of you were given money which is not exactly true because your sister was given money and you were told to ask her if you wanted something and we couldn't wait to get to Jellico Tennessee because the man came on the train with ham sandwiches which were made with butter instead of mayonnaise and ice cold little cokes in a bottle and we had enough for that though we always shared the potato chips and we didn't have a care that the world was not a warm and welcoming place but we didn't realize that all up and down the line there was a congregation of Black men looking out for us that no one said or did anything to disturb our sense of well-being and what a loss that more Black men are in prison than on the trains which no longer exist protecting two little girls from the horrors of this world allowing them to grow up thinking people are kind and so even though we lived in a segregated world and even though everybody knows that was wrong that band of brothers put their arms around us and got us from our mother to our grandmother seamlessly and this poem recognizes that.

CHAPTER 1

By Lyn Hughes

In the early 1990s, I was a recent divorcé with three children, all of whom were enrolled in private schools with expensive tuition. I did not face destitution, however, like most people in America I was only one, maybe two pay-checks away. Therefore welfare was not an option. I searched for a way to continue to pay their tuition. I thought that perhaps real estate projects might be a good way to accomplish my goal. Specifically, I might be able to acquire and rehab properties. One day, while watching an early morning talk show, I saw an interview with Dempsey M. Travis, a prominent Chicago real estate developer and author. He offered a comment during the interview that stayed with me. "The best real estate investments are those in communities that have bottomed out or in an historic district."

Since I had lived in Chicago for only a short time at that point, and was not all that familiar with the communities, I wasn't really sure of where to start. I began searching for real-estate opportunities. Someone gave me a referral to a woman who was interested in working with me. I spoke with her on the telephone and made an appointment to meet her at a property. To make this part of the story short, I got lost and did not keep the appointment; however, I wound up in the community of Pullman on the far south side of Chicago. I was intrigued by the housing stock because it was similar in appearance to a community in my hometown of Cincinnati, Mount Auburn. I remember thinking to myself, *wow, this looks pretty bad. I just might be able to get something here.* I left, and over the next few days I began seeking advice concerning the prospects of the area.

Primarily, I needed an overview about the community, so I began my research. I learned that it was also an historic district, and I decided to begin a little due diligence before investing. I took the tour offered at the south end of the community. As docents usually are, the one who led the

1

tour was very informative about the historic nature of the Pullman community, about George Pullman, its founder, and about the railroad sleeping cars that made him famous. In a group of about 20 people, I was the only African-American. During the tour, my own self-interest prompted me to ask the question, "What role did African-Americans play in the Pullman story and in the Pullman Company?" After I asked the question, there was a silence. After a long pause, the docent responded by saying, "Well, they worked on the trains." It was that response that piqued my curiosity. After the tour I went to the local library and asked the librarian what she could give me that I could read that would tell me about Blacks and the Pullman Company. She gave me a children's book that was written at about the sixth- or seventh-grade reading level. The title of the book was *A Long Hard Journey*. Reading the book literally changed the direction of my life. After I read the book, I wept.

As I was reading the book, something happened to me that changed who I was forever. The book told the story of the Brotherhood of the Sleeping Car Porters. It was the story of ordinary men who in the beginning were the recently freed slaves who were hired as the onboard crew to work on the legendary Pullman sleeping cars. The book told the story of how these men took a job that by today's standard would be considered menial, and made it into a job of prestige in the Black community. Essentially, it was a job that set the standard for the hospitality industry. Beyond that, however, and without knowing it, their very existence changed the lives of African-Americans. In their struggle for dignity and fairness, the right to decent and fair wages, they made history by forming the first black labor union in America to be chartered under the American Federation of Labor. What they did to form the first Black union was to win a collective bargaining agreement with a major U.S. corporation, paving the way to improved labor practices in the country. Their actions opened the doors for African-Americans for generations to come.

During the peak of America's railroad industry, in the 1920s and '30s, there were an estimated 20,000 black Pullman porters, maids, and other railroad personnel, making this the largest category of African-American labor in the United States and Canada at that time. For years, the Pullman Porters worked aboard the Pullman Palace luxury train cars, attending to the needs of the train passengers, They worked under conditions that would never be tolerated today. However, under the leadership and determination of A. Philip Randolph, the BSCP union was established.

2

The BSCP made enormous sacrifices to gain the right to unite; they struggled together for 12 years to become the first African-American labor union to successfully negotiate a collective bargaining agreement with a major U.S. corporation. In other words, it was the first African-American labor union established in the U.S. (Bates, 2001).

After reading the book *A Long Hard Journey*, I could not stop thinking why didn't I know about this history. Why had I not been taught in school about these men and their contributions? More importantly, why was it that my children were not being taught this history as well? I was very angry at this situation. I kept saying it was terrible; why wasn't there some representation about these men? Someone ought to do something.

I started on this journey, which ironically ended up being like the Brotherhood, one that also lasted 12 years. It was one that I thought was to develop real estate. But God had another plan. When I began what I call *Cultural Economic development* in the Historic North Pullman community, founding a museum wasn't even an idea. After introducing the idea of Cultural Heritage tourism to the community, I was forced by a power greater than mine to focus on developing the museum.

To make a long story a little shorter, in February of 1995, I founded the A. Philip Randolph Pullman Porter (APRPP) Museum. It is the first museum in the nation dedicated to these men, and honors their contribution to their community, organized labor, and civil rights. The museum is a privately independently operated non-profit institution that is not funded by city, state, or federal funds. Private contributions, fund-raisers, and memberships generate its *operational budget.*

Establishing the museum in their honor was not something that I planned. I had absolutely no expertise whatsoever in operating a museum. But it was something that had to be done. In 2000 I began thinking, wouldn't it be interesting to know about the descendants of these? The Porters were such strong men of character, I thought it would be educative and worthwhile to know how they lived their lives, what impact their example had on their families. I then started to collect data on, and from, their descendants. It was through that process that the concept of developing this book, The Pullman Porters National Historic Registry of African-American Railroad Employees, came to fruition.

Annually, during Black History Month, particular individuals are singled out and paraded across America in a top-down fashion. But it is usually for only one month. In the APRPP Museum, we want to acknowledge and honor these men 365 days a year. Over the years of the museum's existence there have been many individuals who have come, called, or written to ask and have received our assistance in documenting this important history. Though neither credited nor given recognition from most, clearly the APRPP museum has been the impetus of newfound interest and research of both A. Philip Randolph and the Brotherhood of Sleeping Car Porters, aka Pullman Porters, and this grossly neglected component of America's history.

I have often said that the founding of the museum, which was the inspiration for this book, was not my idea. I truly believed then, as I do now, that this effort was divinely inspired. In 1995, on faith, I founded the museum. I know there is something greater than all of us that has made it possible; there has to be. There have been too many obstacles thrust in my path seemingly certain to stop the efforts of the museum and this National Registry Project. The concept of the registry was initially supposed to be a wall of honor in a property in which the museum was to be relocated. However, that plan was preempted. I believe that at this juncture it is important to explain to those reading this book what I mean.

Simultaneously, at the onset of my efforts to fulfill a culturally significant journey from which the inspiration for this project emerged, a plan was also being formulated to in fact stop the cultural economic development work sparked by the excavation of this important history. Five years later, the plan incorporated a strategy to stop the museum from reaching its full potential.

For many years I had heard the jokes about the ruthlessness of Chicago politics, but did not really understand. However, I now have a very clear understanding of the meaning behind the jokes about the Chicago style politics. Even if you are not involved in the political arena, it doesn't matter. If what you have is deemed something of value, and after you have been given an offer you can't refuse and do, as was the case with me, brace yourself for the storm, because it is coming.

In the year 2000, the A. Philip Randolph Pullman Porter Museum was scheduled to relocate as the anchor tenant to the proposed Pullman Firehouse Cultural Complex in Chicago. The not-for-profit North Pullman Development Corporation owned the firehouse property. The complex development plan was made possible through a successful two million dollar grant proposal, written and submitted by the not-for-profit to the federal government in 1994 under the Intermodal Surface Transportation Enhancement Act (ISTEA) program. Completion of such a project would have resulted in independence for the two non-profits, and would certainly guarantee a measure of success.

The property the museum was scheduled to move into, and where this National Registry was to occupy a wall, was literally taken by the city of Chicago. This act was spearheaded by the efforts of a local city of Chicago politician. But in spite of the unethical, vicious efforts to destroy the museum and to stop efforts to celebrate this neglected component of history, thus far they have not succeeded. The Pullman Porters National Historic Registry (first edition) will not occupy a wall as originally planned, but with this publication it is in existence. Many who have become aware of this plight have commented on what they perceive as my courage; however, I think of it as my strength through my faith. I felt compelled to share this story with you because there may be someone who may have an idea and is afraid to step out on that idea. I say to you, don't step out on the idea — step out on your faith with that idea.

Especially gratifying has it been that the 1995 founding of the A. Philip Randolph Pullman Porter Museum and its ongoing public education work has been the inspiration for and the spawning of several books, films, and documentaries. The most recent is from Larry Tye, author of the book *Rising from the Rails*. In the first paragraph of the preface he states:

> *The most influential black man in America for the hundred years following the Civil War was a figure that no one knew. He was not the educator Booker T. Washington or the sociologist W.E.B DuBois, although both were inspired by him. He was the one black man to appear in more movies than Harry Belafonte or Sidney Poitier. He discovered the North Pole alongside Admiral Peary and boycott that sparked the civil rights movement and tapped Martin Luther King Jr. to lead both. The most influential black man in America was a Pullman Porter.*

For decades, this special group of people, men of a powerful unspoken purpose, a strong-willed, unified, courageous, group of Black men, stood tall with pride and dignity, making sacrifices and creating change in communities across this country, and without knowing they were making history. There were no newspaper reporters or TV cameras documenting their every action. But those things were not contributing factors to their motivation. They were our fathers, grandfathers, great-grandfathers, uncles, and cousins. Quite simply, men...concentrating on how to provide for their families. They were ordinary men who unknowingly were doing an extraordinary thing. Making history. For that they deserved to be honored.

This book is basically the result of a five-year research project. I began the project to create a resource for the A. Philip Randolph Pullman Porter Museum, and to also satisfy my own curiosity. It is interesting to note that when research emanates from the community it is referred to as collecting stories. It is not accepted or respected as *research* unless a scholar completes it. Well, with me it seems you have a 2 for. I am a community person first, and also an individual who through academia has earned the title of scholar.

This registry is my way of honoring those unacknowledged sacrifices and documenting that informal and formal history, and the contributions made by thousands of men and women who worked on the railroad. The content of this book includes the names of former employees whose information was contributed in most cases by a descendant. While every attempt has been made to insure accuracy, we want to acknowledge that we are certain that some information may be missing.

However, it is my hope that this book will be a memento for many; Something that descendants will pick up and point out to other family members, friends, and others, the name, dates, and railroad line that they worked on, and if applicable a photograph. To honor with great pride their descendant who helped to make history.

CHAPTER 2

By Lyn Hughes

The Registry: In 2000, through the A. Philip Randolph Museum, I made the decision to establish a Pullman Porters National Historic Registry of African-American Railroad Employees. I wanted to determine the impact that being a railroad worker, a Pullman Porter, had on their family members. In the African-American community, men who were Pullman Porters were viewed as a special group of men. They have made an indelible mark in history that is not widely or openly discussed in any real detail.

In 2002, the national publicity and media promotion around the original SHOWTIME drama, *Ten Thousand Black Men Named George*, a film documenting the story of the Pullman Porters, encouraged public interest and enabled the research to be conducted on a broader scale, and this process is ongoing. African-Americans were encouraged to register their relatives and family members in the registry by mail, and online. Many of those who registered, would ultimately be interviewed by telephone. The publicity around this film documenting the story of the Pullman Porters not only encouraged interest in the community's history but in American history as well. The registry portion of this book consists of African-Americans who worked for the railroad between the years 1865–1969. With the renaissance of interest in African-American history in the general public and academia, we realized that while there are several repositories of certain information related to the Brotherhood of Sleeping Car Porters and Dining Car Waiters, there was no central source of this data. The availability of resources for the community historian, the family genealogist, or popular educators is rare. Therefore, the need to develop the Registry was revealed.

1. **What data are available within the Pullman Porters National Historic Registry?**

Through the establishment of the registry, the museum amassed a large amount of information that needed to be organized for use by community researchers. There were 2,000 entries made through the online registry, another 500 entries through the 800 number, and another 500 that came through the U.S. mail. For example, there were 1,967 entries for jobs held by those registered. While 73% were listed as porters, another 14% were firemen, 3% cooks, and 1% each redcaps, attendants, or trackmen. Over 40 other positions were listed, including maids and one nurse, representing the few Pullman maids registered. Of the 3,000 data entries, 1,500 were simply the name of the former employee, the route run, and the number of years worked. The remaining data, consisting of 1,500 entries, provided a few more details, and 1,000 data entries provided recollections of a story or impressions of their descendants the respondents felt compelled to share.

The task of entering and organizing the data into an accessible format has been completed. An offline database was set up with a table designed to provide the researcher with the ability to produce responses to any number of queries. The categories used were as follows: The registrant (the relative, i.e. the living relative of the Pullman employee) and their descendant's name (the former railroad employee, the job they held, their address, phone, city where they lived, the railroad line they worked for, the number of years they worked, and the state from which they came). The purpose was to establish a user-friendly data source containing pertinent information a researcher would seek; and to establish a database capable of being integrated and linked with other available data sources.

However, because of legal and privacy issues, not all of the data collected appears in this publication.

> 2. **What other major data sources are available that could be linked to this registry that would add to the people's stories of the Pullman Porter?**

There are numerous sources of content on this subject matter; however, none has been prepared in a form that makes the task of the researcher easy. The Newberry Library holds the most promise, as it has the complete collection of the Pullman Company's employee records. Our research information is being prepared in a manner that will provide direction to the employee records held at the Newberry. Our future efforts will be directed to computerizing those sources and linking them to the registry. In this way the community researcher will be assisted in obtaining additional genealogical information about his or her relative.

3. What did the subjective data provided by the descendents yield?

We read through the subjective data several times to illicit possible common themes. Five themes emerged, other than the ubiquitous one of racism. These themes were:

- Self-pride
- Belief in unity
- Self-imposed standard of excellence
- Dedication to the Union's cause and existence
- Commitment to family

These themes, combined with the personality traits and work experiences (observed and obtained by the relative either through direct observation or oral histories), were passed down from generation to generation and have lasted a lifetime. The most interesting fact from analyzing the data was how these men used their traveling experience as a means of informal education to further develop themselves and their family members. Their travels were lessons in geography and American history. We have included voices from the data to illustrate the themes:

Self-Pride

"John L. D—, my father, was active in the movement of The Brotherhood of Pullman Porters of Chicago until his death. He was a positive role model in family and community life. He always reminded us of the dignified role of The Brotherhood of Pullman Porters in the struggles of our community. He wore his uniform with pride for 'The Brotherhood.' He was the first person to tell me that The Brotherhood of Pullman Porters, under the leadership of A. Philip Randolph, was very active in the Civil Rights Movement. He said that Martin Luther King was drafted by 'The Brotherhood.' My dad also spoke about having to eat in kitchens or have food brought out to them (he and his coworkers) as they traveled though the segregated U.S. Those stories allowed me to grow up with a feeling of pride and determination because my dad was so positive on how he dealt with the times of the day as a Black man."

"My father was a Pullman Porter for Union Pacific Railroad. He held that position with great pride and distinction. He accepted every aspect of the job — realizing that the opportunity Union Pacific afforded him always outweighed the indignities that ignorant men and women chose to hurl at him."

"My father, James W. Mc—, was a member of the Sleeping Car Porters Union for years, and worked as a Pullman Porter from approximately 1924 –1960. Because of the teaching and foundation given to us by my father, we have achieved some degree of success in our careers. I am one of his seven children, which are all still alive. My father emphasized education and integrity to his children. He would have been proud to know that all of his children have went on to become professionals and, I believe, people of character. I am an attorney with licenses in Texas, Illinois, and several other federal venues, my two sisters both hold master's degrees, one brother previously served as assistant police chief in Centerville, Illinois, another brother retired from General Motors in Detroit, and a sister taught at Grambling University and currently works for the United States government at Redstone Arsenal, Huntsville, Alabama."

Belief in Unity

"Memories of my father and his friends who were Pullman Porters and their wives were so very positive. They were proud men. They had great pride related to their work and were supportive of one another. I have often tried to figure out why employees in organizations and companies today do not seem to be as supportive to one another. As I have pondered this question, I have come to believe they came together in such support for one another due to their work of their union and their union leader, A. Philip Randolph."

"My father was stationed in Atlanta, GA and did regular routes to New York, Washington, D.C. and New Orleans, LA. My father (born 1910) worked for 28 years on the railroad until he was furloughed — as did my father's older brother (born 1894) (my uncle) and my uncle's son. They both told stories of the fight to get the union started and of all the prejudice they faced. At one point they had to start their own laundry for the black workers just so they could get their uniforms cleaned; and even so they encountered a lot of resistance. It really was a brotherhood, as they had to stick together just to survive. My father, Lee O. W— Sr. and my uncle, Harold W—, are now deceased. My cousin, Herbert V. W— Sr., is in his 70s and lives outside of Kankakee, Illinois. He talked about how the Pullman Porters used their job as a type of 'underground railroad' for sharing Black political ideology. One Black porter or railroad worker would pass valuable information along to another Black railroad porter or worker and the 'news' would get to the other part of the country before it 'hit' the legitimate news establishments or papers. I don't remember the particulars now, but I do remember there was historical significance in the method of using the railroad as a messenger service for the Negro cause during the days before integration."

Self-Imposed Standard of Excellence

"My father worked during the years when Black people were treated as second-class citizens. He experienced prejudice every time he went to work. But he raised his girls to look beyond the color of a person's skin, to look at the color of one's character."

"As an African-American working for the Pullman Company in the early forties through the seventies, I considered myself fortunate to be able to have the numerous benefits that we fought for. In addition to the economic benefits, I enjoyed traveling across the country and meeting new people of all races and nationality. I believe Pullman Porters did a lot to promote race relations in this country. We always presented ourselves in a positive manner and therefore we were a positive representation of our race."

"McKinley F— and his brother Thomas F—, two country boys born in Courtland, Alabama, were Pullman porters out of Birmingham, Alabama for more than a quarter of a century. Blaine's major route was from Birmingham to New York. He also worked the Rose Bowl trips to California when Alabama was a major contingent. Blaine raised a family of six children, who all attended Black colleges. They all became teachers, lawyers, and engineers."

Commitment to Family

"My father, Spencer B. B—, was a proud, hardworking man, who instilled in his children a very positive work ethic. We graduated from college and reached high levels of achievement in our chosen fields. More importantly, my dad taught us how to negotiate through life's adversities and to meet each day in a positive manner. I contracted polio at five years of age and my parents were told I would never walk. My dad refused to accept that prognosis and found a specialist that was willing to perform experimental surgery on me. My dad's tenacity made it possible for me to walk and lead a normal life. Upon retiring I was one of the highest ranked Black women in my corporation. The Brotherhood of Pullman Porters gave my dad life choices that poor Black men seldom got, and he, in return, provided opportunities to his children."

"My father worked for the railroad during the Great Depression; he had a law degree and worked as a waiter in order to care for a wife and three children. His base was Chicago, even though he lived in Cincinnati, which meant he had to ride all the way to Chicago in order to begin a day's work and vice versa when he had the day off. He saw a lot of the United States and met a lot of interesting people. One thing I learned from my father that has lasted a lifetime, was that the tips that he earned as a waiter was the real money that kept his family afloat during the Depression. I keep that in mind when eating out, to this day. There really are too many experiences to write in this block—the derailments, snow jams, the floods, the recipes created by the individuals on the railroads that got no credit, hopping on and off the trains that could have caused injuries but most times didn't because the men got good at that. The kind of hotels and restaurants that those men had to live and eat in were unthinkable, even though they had the money to do better. In those days it was called 'Jim Crow,' out of bounds for Negroes."

Dedication to the Union

"My grandfather fought very hard for the porters to have a union. He was one of the first African-Americans to become a part of the union. Striking to become a union member was very costly for my grandfather. It cost him his marriage to my grandmother and seeing his two sons grow up. He almost lost the home he was buying in Long Island. He told me that back in the '20s and '30s, working conditions were very bad for African-Americans. African-Americans were not permitted to organize into unions. They worked with little benefits. They did not have pensions, vacation time, or sick time. They were expected to work overtime with no extra pay. My grandfather said that for the sake of the children he will continue to strike until the black porters had a union."

"I became a Pullman Porter in charge, which gave southern travelers the ability to see a BLACK MAN operate without white supervision, and resented being called *George* or *boy*. However, I enjoyed the job and took pride in my work. I gained great experience; I attended the meeting called by Randolph for the first MARCH ON WASHINGTON."

"After serving his country in WWII, M— was rehired by Pullman, and joined the Union to advocate equality and fair treatment of all men. He trained and counseled many Porters on work ethics and Porters' rights. His Porter travels and communications aboard presidential trains exposed M— to institutes of higher learning. M— assisted first-class passengers who transported their sons and daughters to Yale University and Mt. Holyoke College, and later, his own son was the recipient of the AMTRAK National Merit Scholarship to Yale University. Dave and Vinie's five children all attended college: a daughter graduated from Mt. Holyoke, all others, college and one law school graduate."

"There was a dignity and nobility in these men; my grandfather worked many long hours on the railroad. He took pride in his work because this is how he supported his family. Grandfather was kind, intelligent, politically astute, and humble."

Implications

Through this publication, I believe my intent to restate the point of a critical need for academia to relate to practice has been demonstrated. By encouraging research in the African-American community, we, as academicians, accomplish several things: (1) Through praxis we strengthen our own work; (2) we contribute to a more accurate history of our country for all Americans; (3) we build cultural and intellectual capital in the African-American community; and (4) through non-formal learning, we strengthen civil society.

This chapter was previously published in the 44th Annual Adult education research conference proceedings.

CHAPTER 3

PULLMAN PORTERS IN THE LATE 19TH AND EARLY 20TH CENTURIES BEFORE THE FORMATION OF THE BROTHERHOOD OF SLEEPING CAR PORTERS (1925)

By Christopher R. Reed

The Pullman Porters who provided hotel-type service on railroad coaches and on the luxurious Pullman Palace Cars were dubbed the "Ambassadors of Hospitality." This occupational group, along with their female counterparts working as maids, symbolized a labor segment with a unique status among African-Americans because of their elevation beyond their previous work experience, place in the burgeoning railroad industry, and expected workplace demeanor. As the era of industrialism went forward and performed its unique transformation of American society, a new economic opportunity evolved in 1867 for a nation becoming dependent on the rails for long-distance transportation and the expectation of luxury as its nonmaterial by-product. Barred nationally as conductors and engineers, and outside the South as trainmen and firemen, the jobs of porter and maid assumed importance as an immense opportunity beyond rural farm work. William H. Harris wrote: "The Pullman Palace Car Company of Chicago employed many blacks as porters and maids on sleeping cars to perform personal services for the increasing number of passengers who traveled across the country." But Pullman did even more than this. Blacks virtually monopolized this entire service sector.

Industrial magnate George M. Pullman sought a particular personality to satisfy his white customers, both in the North and in the South, so racial and class deference bordering on obsequiousness, whether feigned or ingrained, fit the bill. Pullman even went so far as to demand that porters smile on all occasions when encountering passengers. Matching previous disposition with a modern demand, his choice of a workforce predisposed him to recruit from the ranks of persons who previously held the status of slaves. In context, to this industrial magnate who made millions manufacturing his palace cars "which provided the needed link

14

between the sumptuous hotels that met the traveler in all of our great cities," servility was demanded and expected from all of his employees, whether in the shop, in the rolling hotel suites called "Palace Cars," or at his model, all-white employee town — appropriately named Pullman — located at the southernmost tip of Chicago. As to whether the specter of racism was at the core of Pullman's demands, that point is conjectural since African-American leaders such as Frederick Douglass often spoke effusively about the industrialist's beneficence with apparent knowledge or indifference to his demands as an employer. At the Congress on Africa held at the Columbian World's Exposition of 1893, even Bishop Henry McNeal Turner found occasion to praise Pullman.

Belying the sincerity of that smile, the Pullman Porter work schedule was especially grueling; it was becoming all too common to work 100 hours per week on train runs. In addition, the chances for promotion were virtually nonexistent. "If [a porter] enters the service at 18 he will likely be receiving the same pay at 48 if he stays in the service," reported Richard R. Wright, Jr. However, the wage level at times, bolstered by tips, could exceed that enjoyed by a waiter or porter in private hotel service, so this benefit resulted in an attractiveness ordinarily unimagined.

As a newer generation of workers succeeded the original pool of former slaves, the expectations of these employees rose without any appreciable change occurring in the employer's expected work demeanor. The image of the ubiquitous, sometimes overly courteous "George," with his obligatory smile still dominated this new service by the end of the century. Yet, for the later generation of porters coming into service around and after 1893, their public image belied their antithetical one of elevated status among African-Americans of all classes who knew all too well the intricacies of wearing the mask in a white-dominated society. To confirm this disparity between perception and actuality, one only has to reflect on the career of erstwhile porter Jesse Binga, who in the next century became the personification of African-American assertiveness and success in first entrepreneurial, and then business endeavors as a hard-nosed financier who could be broken only by a national economic depression.

In order to compensate for the drudgery and sometimes-excessive demands on their labor, the "Daddy Joe" stories evolved. While a real person, the exploits of this extraordinary figure outgrew reality and seemed appropriate remedies for all occasions when members of his race needed relief from the worst aspects of their economic and psychological oppression. According to stories told in private in off hours around the Baker heating stoves, Daddy Joe's stature was Bunyanesque. Not surprisingly, his height and hands were so imposing that he could "walk flat-footed down the aisle and let the upper berths down on each other." Whether encountering hostile red men on the Plains or malicious white men on the palace cars, Daddy Joe proved himself master of the situation. Through it all, his demeanor established the standard to which all Pullman Porters aspired: loyalty and dedication to the job regardless of the hardships and obstacles.

Renowned sociologist E. Franklin Frazier both legitimized and elevated the status of these workers when in 1932, his doctoral dissertation of the previous year was published. He maintained that "the occupational organization of the Negro community conform[ed] to the distribution of Pullman porters, who at one time represented on the whole the group that had a comparable good income and a high conception of his place in the community. 'Once in Chicago,' said a former Pullman porter, 'you weren't anybody unless you were a Pullman porter. We handled more money than most of the colored people, and led all the social life.'" This commentary had significance beyond the sphere of work and extended into the social realms of recreation and leadership.

Bolstering the popular belief held first by Chicagoans of successive generations and which has gained currency as to its authenticity nationally, was the demonstrated ability of Pullman Porters, waiters, and others to translate their experience in fine living into one that the greater community could enjoy. In a social realm dominated by camaraderie and an escape into leisure time activities, food and social interaction had the power to transform a people, especially members of the working class in the service areas. One example of how a supposedly dispirited group could use a menu to affirm self-esteem among persons accustomed to social and racial proscription required only a scan of the serving list at the third annual banquet of the Newport Hunting and Fishing Club (a working class club) on January 22, 1885. The menu featured Fillet of Beef Larded aux Champignon, Rabbit Braise, Stewed Bear with Jelly,

Squirrel Larded, Quail on Toast, Roast Venison, Baked Red Snapper, and other delicacies. The plethora of social clubs and fraternal orders that pervaded the city depended on these annual functions to ease the tensions of living in an increasingly hostile society. The desire to be left alone, free from white interference, to have "good times," much the same thing that the European immigrant groups wanted, makes too much sense not to have been accepted and examined by earlier social analysts on African-American behavior.

Moreover, wearing their uniforms as symbols of their knightly authority, Pullman Porters assumed unto themselves a power never envisioned by their employers and customers and recognizable all too clearly in the black community. On occasion, these men could be masters of any given situation. These "ambassadors" also expanded their horizons individually as well as collectively, gaining knowledge of how the nation and the world operated through travel, eavesdropping on the discussions of the nation's movers and shakers, and reflecting on what they said and heard in dialogues with compassionate whites. In 1883, one Pullman Porter, Floyd Thornhill, initially engaged in an informal conversation with a U.S. senator that soon transformed itself into a formal interview used in a senate hearing on labor conditions in the South. Perhaps with knowledge of the aforementioned, or of a similar episode on the rails, historian J.A. Rogers illustrated this newly emerging personality among the Pullman Porters through his use of a composite character, Dixon, who bettered his Southern "better" intellectually on a transcontinental train ride. On a westbound train heading to the Windy City, one World's Fair writer from New England expressed intense satisfaction at curbing the fake fawning of one obnoxious porter serving his car. The porter was a tyrant; "the un-resisted bully of the car" whose actions were stopped once "that dapper darkie's shoulder" was paralyzed by a firm grip. Quite reasonably, for an African-American to intimidate white passengers while simultaneously appearing to observe proper racial decorum demonstrated how well some of these men struggled to be masters of their work environment.

Moreover, another challenge to maintain the dignity of labor took place during the summer months of 1893, when the Pullman Company placed its famous Palace Cars on display at the World's Fair at the imposing Transportation Building. A rather servile "Mr. Fritsch" provided regular status reports to his "honored Mr. Pullman" on the number of visitors inspecting the cars, the number of important dignitaries who viewed the cars with a prospect of adding them to their railroads or personal travel accouterments, and the efficiency of his retinue of porters who kept the cars spotless. On one occasion, Fritsch proudly wrote to Pullman, "We had a fine train to show today. It was cleaned well inside and outside, as I had made it pretty lively for the [work] force yesterday and am determined to return a well-kept train to Pullman [town, on] Oct. 31." Porters on the rolling trains worked just as hard as this crew on the stationary exhibit, yet the prospects of decent wages never materialized for any of them, a feature all too typical for all employees of the Pullman Company.

In the early twentieth century, the legacy of Southern slavery that first emphasized near total black economic subordination, and then, post-emancipation wage exploitation, plagued black workers even when they sought employment in the North. Having succumbed to two centuries of bondage without successful resistance in the form of a revolution (which whites did not really want to experience in the likeness of the Haitian Revolution), blacks were subject to being condemned in the national mind to labor oblivion. America positioned its labor force into a caste-like arena. After having achieved these fixed statuses, one historian has described white America at the turn of the century as seeing black workers as indifferent and unreliable workers. Moreover, part of this image of black labor was defined by labor strife and worker vulnerability. When a government inquiry on industrial relations sought an explanation for the Pullman Company's attitude toward limited wages and a surplus labor supply, the reply was thus: "All I can say is that you can get all the men you require to do the work." The black worker who attempted to break the bonds of racial limitations met opposition when he took available work. In the teamster's strike of 1904, this was especially true.

As one major component of the twentieth century's contingent of black workers, the ranks of the Pullman Porters were comprised of the remnants of the original employees of the immediate post-Civil War era as well as those young men coming to age beyond the mentally stultifying confinements of the slavery experience. Such a generational difference implied a variance in mind-set toward both work and race relations. In the white mind, especially in the eyes of the riding public, where the only interracial contact whites had with blacks existed, the white perception served as the only valid image of these workers and of all African-Americans. While the original generation of porters might have acquiesced emphatically to the racist whims of a manipulative company as well as the white riding public, this new breed in the twentieth century accepted the demands of their employment status more begrudgingly and with a steady eye to self-transformation. Not that all porters resisted public obsequiousness as a part of their internal makeup, since enough were still in the dying psychological throngs of bondage that afflicted their parents and kin to be influenced by its insidious effects.

Overall, as reflective of the times with pervasive racism in the American workplace, the Pullman Company was seen even more as a good employer. Many black workers, therefore, perceived that they owed the company public recognition and workplace loyalty for providing steady, non-stultifying, nonagricultural employment. Given the climate in the nation toward black labor because of the slave legacy — blacks were supposed to work and not expect considerations of any sort, their having been unpaid minions for generations in all regions of the country — this sentiment is not surprising. Pullman shrewdly monopolized rail travel accommodations and the conditions of employment for all of its employees, equally oppressing white and black in what amounted to a buyers' market. The exploitation of white workers in the company town of Pullman, Illinois outside Chicago is well known. African-Americans faced other obstacles apart from their membership in an exploited labor pool. The Big Four railroad brotherhoods of white railroad workers deliberately excluded blacks from memberships and any benefits that would have accrued to organized labor.

The nature of the work regimen dictated an acceptance of near total control over the porters' lives while on the job, or as often referred, in service. When the Pullman Company conducted its business in the manner of a closed institution, demanding complete obedience to authority and the rules it instituted, it exceeded the demands on behavior and thinking of a antebellum plantation and a post-emancipation sharecropping arrangement. But with employment opportunities virtually nonexistent through the nation, the Pullman Company's offer of steady employment and stable wages seemed attractive. Wages were low and hours long and grueling.

Attitudinal and personality development among Pullman Porters varied, of course, as much as it did among the general American population. Some workers would always be obedient toward authority and persons with super ordinate status. This would relate to their experiences in the post-slavery South as well as the competitive North when they acted as other workers did in variance to their bosses' wishes. It was a trait that was evident as late as 1925 when the Brotherhood of Sleeping Car Porters organized among the ranks of the porters. Chicagoan and future Brotherhood leader Milton P. Webster exemplified this trait from his youth as leader of a neighborhood component of an Eighth Regiment youth group, the Marshall Chapter. Their opposites would have embraced anything from complete rejection of white authority, begrudgingly working in variance to their dreams because sustenance demanded it be so, to a partial accommodation to any authority. To the former, New Negro thinking to be sure, Bishop Turner's declaration that "God was Black" at the World's Columbian Exposition resounded as appropriately in the ears of these porters as did Ida B. Wells' uncompromising stance on Colored American day at the World's Fair, Chicago school segregation schemes, and Southern lynching.

In the middle of these clusters there existed persons able to respond to authority with an outward smile, which belied an inward seething at those parties taking advantage of black workers in America's caste-like labor arena. The story of those new men of the North who rejected conformance to expected deportment around whites runs parallel to the life experiences of the earliest group of porters, Chicagoan Rodney Long. Sergeant Long had reached the highest rank as a noncommissioned officer during the Civil War, commanding black men and seeing them at their best, while witnessing the myth of white superiority demolished against General Robert E. Lee's forces at Petersburg, Richmond and finally, Appomattox. Long saw the effects of defeat on the faces of a broken Army of Northern Virginia before he entered the Pullman service. Pride or even haughtiness on a palace car could be submerged with a show of feigned deference once comfort with its underlying essence was self-recognized. Beyond Long, there were the likes of black Chicago's giants in politics, business, and letters, such as banker and real estate broker Jesse Binga, Republican Party leader and Cook County Commissioner Edward H. Wright, and writer and historian Joel [J.]A. Rogers. All served on the rails but achieved mightily thereafter as molders of their race's future.

Within a generation, much to the surprise of many, turn-of-the-century "New Negro" thinking would evolve into an even more militant phase, and the Brotherhood of Sleeping Car Porters would emerge from the ranks of these workers in 1925. If not overtly occupationally courageous in the tradition of Chicago's firemen, policemen, and soldiers, porters still had a reason to be proud and assertive off the job. They possessed a quality that other workers could emulate because they had a national presence as essential service personnel. They were the face of black labor in the early twentieth century. Spero and Harris wrote: "To the general public, the Pullman porter is above all else a Negro. He is in effect the only contact, which thousands of white persons had with the race. His doings therefore assume an importance which extends beyond the confines of his own group..." However, they had many faces: obsequious and mask wearing; childlike and steadfastly manly; filled with wanderlust, and family-oriented and settled.

Clearly, their economic subordination as employees to the behemoth Pullman Company's wishes related solely to their workplace demeanor. While they worked the palace cars and sleepers that the Pullman Company manufactured and owned, their souls and bodies were never owned by the company. Their external demeanor masked internal strivings that bore seedlings in their limited individual resistance during these early days of the twentieth century but produced fruit by 1925 with the formal organization of an employees union. Company disciplinary records record the following repeated reasons given for dismissal, revealing subliminal white expectations of black attitudes and behavior: "insubordination and used insulting language;" or, "he is 'I'll see a lawyer' kind;" or, "refused to carry out instructions and maintained a very ugly and independent manner."

On its positive side, and generally, the American mind envisioned the average Pullman Porter based on an image of high character and gentlemanly demeanor. Adorned in their distinguished Pullman blue uniforms and with a brass "Pullman" emblem on his cap, African-Americans registered their employment into more of a sign of internal dignity than company ownership over labor. They were much like the best of soldiers of Civil War days, liberating a race through limited labor opportunities. One contemporary description in a northern publication reported the following as these workers made more out of the situation than whites could have ever imagined:

Not long ago the writer, who is anything but a Sherlock Holmes, entered a crowded street-car, and without the least difficulty picked out one of the passengers as a Pullman porter. The man was not in uniform, but he was Colored, he was immaculately clean and neat from his polished black shoes to his spotless linen, and he was unobtrusive and yet entirely at his ease. Now all people with these attributes are not porters, nor, alas, all porters possessed of these attributes, but there was about this man a certain air of cosmopolitanism — a poise that comes only to those that travel the earth and come into daily contact with men and women from all ranks of life — and, withal, the air of one who, in his own sphere, carries both responsibility and authority.

Being on the road and looked upon as being attractive because of who you can meet and what sights you can see, they wore well their 1904 sobriquet of "Tzar of the Sleeping Car" and later "Ambassadors of Hospitality."

A prominent Chicago physician and civic leader, Dr. M.A. Majors, remarked on porters, both good and bad. "There are hundreds of our porters and waiters whose human kindness and hospitable spirit make them seem Chesterfieldian [gentlemanly] at heart, who, whenever the opportunity allows, go to the extreme limit in showing the passenger of their own race every kind of attention due any other kind of passengers, and all ought to do this. Many of these gentlemen porters and waiters had rather leave their lucrative positions than to mistreat one of their own race."

Conversely, Majors had only scorn for the opposites of these Lord Chesterfields, who, in his estimation, acted as psychological extensions of persons holding sentiments of white racial supremacy. Any Pullman Porter, who laughed along with whites at the misgivings of migrants traveling north for the first time, who might clumsily handle their food, or luggage, or appear in rural dress, exemplified this racial pariah. If a porter went overboard in enforcing the rules, such as changing cars when a train crossed the Mason-Dixon Line, he also was a target for Majors' ire. In ideological terms, Majors categorized these men as virtual race traitors, writing, "and The Jew is for the Jew always, even in death. The Irish is for the Irish as far away as Killarney. The German is for the German, and so on through the category of races, until we reach Sambo, who 'is just here with the other fellows.'"

If Pullman service offered benefits to some, to others who were more ambitious, it served only as a stepping-stone for careers ranging from medicine to law to acting to business pursuits. This admirable characteristic found among these workers is well remembered among African-Americans of succeeding generations. More importantly, it has become the essence of urban myth surrounding the wholesale educational level of porters. In reality, educational levels varied among the porters, with the majority being undereducated consistent with the level of the black and white population during this period. Beyond their own limits and ambitions, these men could move others upward, as was the case with insurance businessman, and undertaker, Robert A. Cole, originally a native of Mount Carmel, Tennessee. He arrived in Chicago in 1905 with limited education, having completed only four years of elementary school. He applied himself immediately to an upward path toward success by working the service sector as a busboy. Driven to succeed, he then entered Pullman service as a porter where he recalled that he "compensated for his lack of formal education [by] talk [in] to business executives and observe [in] their actions." This began a 20-year personal crusade toward respectability and success, capped by his occupational elevation as porter-in-charge and a manager's position with prospering saloonkeeper, funeral home director, and politician Dan Jackson. In another case, poet Fenton Johnson, who was born in Chicago in 1888, grew up in a household influenced by the Pullman link. His father worked as a Pullman Porter, and his mother concentrated on sustaining a nurturing family life as a homemaker in their own home. Ambition in writing led Johnson to explore the hidden nuances of black life, with Johnson adopting a style in dialect that was reflective of Paul Lawrence Dunbar.

So, what appeared in urban folklore as an image of a well-educated man did have some semblance in reality. The main character, Dixon, who appeared in former Pullman Porter J.A. Rogers' *Superman to Man* (1917), represented the quintessential educated porter found among the intercontinental ambassadors of hospitality. Dixon carried on a transcontinental dialogue with a Southern senator about the virtues as well as the failings of African-Americans, in the end convincing the lawmaker that tolerance and inquisitiveness about others offered a benefit more fitting someone of his station than his original ignorance and racism.

Another image of the Pullman Porter emanated from the scholarly work of sociologist E. Franklin Frazier, one that was reiterated by fellow University of Chicago researchers St. Clair Drake and Horace R. Cayton in their classic study, *Black Metropolis* (1945). Using an unpublished manuscript entitled "Autobiography of a Physician," Frazier established the Pullman Porter as the prototype of black Chicago society during the early twentieth century. Reaching Chicago late in the nineteenth century, his informant freely reminisced about the historical transformation that he witnessed in black Chicago as he elevated his occupational status from service worker to physician. This account was, by necessity, skewed to reflect the interpretation the "physician" gave to his experience. It was one in which he saw and understood only a portion of what was transpiring in the "Black Belt." As a dilettante faced with examining and interpreting the social scene, nuances of social change and the emergence and disappearance of social influences escaped his attention. He saw life from the bottom up, emphasizing the role Pullman Porters, headwaiters, restaurant and hotel porters, and barbers played in an emerging social composition as black Chicago assumed a normative class structure, that is, one replicating that set of relationships that existed in mainstream America. Lacking the professional training and, thereby, professional commitment to national standards of a Daniel Williams or Charles E. Bentley, Frazier's informant displayed a limitation to his world view that produced restricted vision.

Serving, as an "everyman" among the historical ranks of the Pullman Porters was Walter J. Green, who arrived from Lexington, Kentucky shortly after the turn of the century. Green, an employee of the Baltimore and Ohio Railroad who made regular runs to and from Washington, D.C., could not reasonably be considered to have represented *every* porter in the rail service, but he surely approximated that heralded element in racial memory in character, ability, and influence in his community. Green sought expanded social and economic opportunities that would elevate his status and improve his life and that of his wife and family. Seeing the life of a laborer in the South as dead-in, Green moved north to gain employment of opportunity. Over generations once in the North, he was repeatedly described by family members years after his death as "a man's man," "family leader," "outstanding gentleman," and a man who possessed a "dominating and dynamic personality."

On the negative side of Pullman service, the porters were seen by many whites as part of the car and train itself, without an essence of humanity. This explains why whites would engage in outrageous behavior in front the men or make impossible requests of them. Despite disadvantages in a work world of inequalities and needed adjustments, porters remained on the job for life, for the most part. Then, there was the nature of the work itself. While it was steady work, with nothing of the vagaries of seasonal work, it also demanded long hours of service and travel without rest.

In 1900, among railroad workers, they received the lowest wages and were expected to pay for their meals and upkeep of their uniforms while on the road. "He was expected to polish passengers' shoes, but with polish and brushes purchased out of his own pocket. If he was found without polish, he was reported, and that alone was grounds for dismissal." Supplies for the sleeping cars required not only care but monitoring. The Pullman Company maintained a two million dollar inventory of nearly three and one-half million linen sheets and pillowcases of which "porters were responsible...[from their wages for] the cost of lost or stolen items."

Further, the traditional low wages of 20 dollars a month relegated the receipts of tips as important as wages. This condition necessitated a tendency toward fake obsequiousness at times toward passengers and the gesticulated outstretched empty hand awaiting coins or bills. It even encouraged the practice of hiding the exact amount of high tips from fellow workers, lest a particular train run be taken by someone with greater seniority. The reverse might prove beneficial, fooling someone with greater seniority into taking what is in effect a poor tipping run. Certain runs, such as those on the northeast lines' Twentieth Century Limited, the Broadway Limited, and the Santa Fe Chief, paid well. Certain groups did better than others in tipping; females better than males; foreign visitors, especially the English, were poor tippers, while national celebrities did well. The behavior of passengers differed occupationally; salesmen were steady, if not high tippers. Never a chance for promotion to conductor or higher, reserved for whites.

The behavior of the porter reflected the effectiveness of his training for service on these moving luxurious palace cars. The education of porters usually took place in larger cities where a stationary car acted as a classroom. The pressure on porters accompanying this training was tremendous, but it represented only a fraction of what awaited him once he assumed his actual duty station. With the responsibility of transforming a car filled with daytime seating into overnight sleeping berths, the neophyte porter learned the proper method used to fold and put away blankets, with the precision accorded the folding of the American flag. In pulling down the berth, the porter "made down" the bed, which required placing a curtain for privacy across each slumber bunk. Precise judgment was required to determine what items — towels, sheets, and pillowcases —were clean enough for use. He had to master awakening riders without a raised voice and physical touching — whispering melodiously and shaking the curtain gently was the rule. He had the responsibility of operating the heating system and had to suffer the harassing of certain women ringing bells for service constantly. Unlawful activities and untoward behavior by whites reflected directly on the porter, who in fact, under the nation's racial protocol, had no authority over their actions. Heavy smoking and gambling by some of the men made for a foul-smelling and unruly car that the porter had to ventilate and "regulate."

From veteran porters the newcomer learned how to assess the needs as well as regional eccentricities of passengers. A Southern lady or gentleman might be expected to act a certain way whether in the North or South, while a liberal, northern male or female college student seeking excitement might behave in another fashion. Sometimes the prospective porter received his recommendation from an already employed porter. Baggage had to be handled properly, requiring upper body strength and a strong back. Then, the porter incurred the expense of buying his own uniform and even shoe polish. He paid for his own food in the diner, with a modest discount, whenever time permitted for food. Recognition of these realities gave way to attempts at organizing along unionized lines in advance of the trade union push led by A. Philip Randolph nationally and Milton P. Webster locally during the 1920s.

Historically significant, years before the emergence in 1925 of the Brotherhood of Sleeping Car Porters, Pullman Porters organized consciously to protect their rights as workers in several ways. According to the authoritative Brailsford R. Brazeal, then of Morehouse College, "Approximately forty-two years after Negro porters entered Pullman service they made their first efforts to form a union. A restiveness among the porters at the beginning of the twentieth century did not lead to a direct organizing effort until 1909." That this boiling turmoil failed to result in effective organization could readily be traced to an unfamiliarity with the concept and efficacy of collective bargaining, the heavy influence of Southern mores that reinforced subordinate behavior and thinking, and white resistance from within unions. By 1909, porters in the Northwest who worked during the Alaska-Yukon-Pacific Exposition coalesced briefly into an organized body, only to have their energies dissipate shortly after the event. The next year, the locus of organizing was found in the St. Paul area with similar results to the previous year. Failed efforts could not dissuade further attempts at organizing, so by 1913, Chicago, along with Denver, Portland, Seattle, and St. Paul, experienced coordinated labor activities. But once again, it was a epoch event that stimulated the biggest boost to date toward collective organizing. With the beginning of the First World War in August 1914, more than demographic changes resulted, with labor affected also. In addition to black workers entering the industrial sphere, wartime congressional legislation positively affected all rail activities, including labor relations.

Importantly, the Pullman Porter lived in two worlds that divided his loyalties and attention toward life. There was the external world of smiling "Georges," seen as the pliant workers with whom white Americans felt most comfortable. This sphere of labor activity was one familiar to workers the world over as they assumed subordinate roles and personas to their employers. Deference did not mean surrender of one's soul. Yet, the conditions of work and expectations of the white passengers dictated an appearance of anonymity that led to the porter being the ubiquitous "George" or "porter" in the eyes of passengers. According to Larry Tye, in the South passengers continued the practice of referring to the servants of the plantation master by the latter's name. Hence, company president George M. Pullman's shadow cast wide over his thousands of "Georges."

The interior world of Pullman Porters existed outside the Pullman Company's reach and view. Away from home, the Baker Heater League developed, representing a fraternity of trainmen who lived together while between train runs. They told stories around the activities of larger than life figures, conveniently lumped together as Daddy Joe or Henry stories, which grow more interesting with time. Importantly, the porters' psyche always found satisfaction, with the porter emerging as the victorious "combatant" for safety or recipient of high tips, similar to the Brer

Rabbit tales in which the subordinate or weaker party emerges triumphant at the end. There were real heroes with exploits to explore. In 1908, a runaway train carried porter Johnson miles away from his rail yard and into possible death before he brought the two cars to a halt. Earlier during the great forest fires of 1894 in eastern Minnesota, one porter assumed leadership of his passengers and led scores to safety amidst raging fires.

Chicago was also the real home to many of the porters, and a look at home life for men such as Walter J. Green of the Baltimore and Ohio Railroad meant personal relief among wife, family, and friends. It meant the consolation of church and an abundant social life. Green developed his persona so that he became the embodiment of manliness and mentorship to males of several succeeding generations. What this meant on the job is conjectural, but no one could be so dynamic among his peers who internalized a subordinate sense of self.

The advent of war in 1914 directly affected Pullman Porters in a positive manner. Once the United States entered the war, these workers benefited from wartime legislation that authorized the U.S. government to virtually run the railroads for the duration of the conflict in Europe, "thus, through governmental action, Pullman's anti-union policies were definitely challenged fifty-one years after its incorporation." The U.S. Railroad Administration exerted its authority under General Order 27, which gave it control over all Pullman operations. Higher wages and overall better working conditions resulted, as the porters now received equal treatment because of the demands of war on the nation's productive capacities.

Importantly, the porters claimed their right to organize collectively. Several bodies were formed — the Brotherhood of Sleeping Car Porters Protective Union, the Railway Men's International Benevolent Industrial Association, and at least two locals, which had membership in the American Federation of Labor as units of the Hotel Workers Alliance, one in St. Louis and the other in Chicago.

To the benefit of railroad workers, direct government intervention meant that congressional investigations on labor conditions followed. Any disruption, real or threatened, raised consternation in Washington because of its possible effect on the war effort and war production. In 1917, the U.S. Senate "released a report stating that 'the employees of the Pullman Company are unable to improve their conditions through organizations.... Workers known to be members of labor unions are promptly discharged...

A system of espionage caused black workers to be fearful of affiliating with unions of any sort.'" As to pursuing grievances, the Railway Men's Benevolent Industrial Association, now a thousand strong, did take its complaints before an arbitration commission in Washington in February 1918 and was able to win a pay increase.

The other major body, the Brotherhood of Sleeping Car Porters Protective Union, was composed of mainly Chicagoans and New Yorkers, with the latter assuming leadership roles. At their first convention held in Chicago in October 1919, they assumed an aggressive stance against the Pullman Company. With later defections from their ranks induced by the Pullman Company and with their organizing methods and rituals beginning to take on the look of fraternity, this organization faded into obscurity after the war.

When the new decade of the 1920s, "the roaring twenties," opened, organizing efforts by various factions continued within the ranks of the Pullman Porters. Meanwhile, the number of black workers under the Pullman influence increased, with more young men joining the ranks of the porters and the Pullman shops at the southern tip of Chicago numbering 450 by 1920. The dominant organizations included the Pullman Porter Benevolent Association, conceived in 1920 and functioning by February 1, 1921, with 10,000 members and the Brotherhood of Sleeping Car Porters Protective Union. Chicago's Milton P. Webster belonged to the former until 1925, at which time he became convinced that another, more militant organization with a bolder approach would best serve the interests of the porters. The most ambitious continued to break away from the Pullman Company's hypnotic grip and seek success in other areas of endeavor. Lee Averett was one such person by this decade, when he pursued self-employment in the men's clothing business. His transformation was described in local, lay historian Frederick H.H. Robb's praise piece to African-American individual and group progress:

[Once in Chicago, he worked as] a porter in a store. He tried this for a while and then decided he would try and run on the road as a Pullman Porter. He did for several years, being promoted to one of the best jobs on the road. He still was not satisfied, for he thought there was something he could do for himself, and perhaps for his fellow man.

He and his wife subsequently opened a small single men's repair and pressing service at 30th and State in 1922, which blossomed through hard work into 15 such secondhand men's shops making up Lee Averett's Saving System within five years. The flagship of their operation rented space in the newly opened Michigan Avenue Garden Apartments as soon as it opened in 1929.

Necessity dictated that labor consciousness grow. Of course, hundreds upon hundreds of porters and Pullman workers remained indifferent, or in some cases, frightened, by the might of the Pullman Company. When E. Franklin Frazier (1929) wrote sarcastically that Chicago "is the headquarters of the peripatetic Knights of the Whisk-broom — the generic George of the largest independent Negro labor union in the country," he revealed the prominence of labor consciousness as part of "New Negro" thinking and motivation. This new mentality willing to challenge Pullman's house union was championed locally by Milton P. Webster, whose propensity toward leadership and independence was exhibited early in childhood. Although opposition was keen, by 1925, A. Philip Randolph's efforts to organize porters proved successful as the Brotherhood of Sleeping Car Porters and Maids was organized in the Windy City.

CHAPTER 4

The Brotherhood
Beth Tompkins-Bates

In its early work in organizing Pullman porters and maids, the Brotherhood of Sleeping Car Porters drew on the efforts of many of Chicago's social activists, such as Irene McCoy Gaines, Mary McDowell and Ida B. Wells-Barnett.

In 1925, the Brotherhood of Sleeping Car Porters (BSCP), a union recently formed in New York City, began organizing Pullman sleeping car porters and maids on Chicago's South Side. The principal target of the BSCP was the Employee Representation Plan, a union created by the Pullman Company for its porters and maids. The Brotherhood said the porters and maids needed the BSCP because it would represent their interests, not those of the Pullman Company. BSCP organizers soon discovered, however, that before they could represent the interests of porters and maids, they had to gain recognition and support from the middle-class black community on the South Side of Chicago. Not only did this elite dislike labor unions, but the majority regarded the Pullman Company as a friend of black Chicagoans. Since the black middle class controlled institutions in the black community such as the press and larger churches, their opinions mattered.

The Pullman Company started performing "good works" and pouring money into the black community on the South Side during the last decade of the nineteenth century. Florence Pullman, daughter of George Pullman, founder of the Pullman Palace Car Company, contributed a large sum of money to help found Provident Hospital in 1891. The country's first interracial hospital, Provident not only received black citizens on an equal basis with whites, but both its advisory board and medical staff were interracial, giving the black neighborhood unprecedented control over health care. Florence Pullman continued to make contributions during the hospital's periodic tough times. In 1896, George Pullman and Marshall Field purchased land adjoining Provident Hospital for a nursing school, which by World War I was training an

31

average of twenty-five nurses a year.

Quinn Chapel Photo

Above: Quinn Chapel (pictured here in 1953), where Bishop Archibald Carey of AME church began his career in Chicago. Photograph by J. Sherman Murphy. Carey strongly opposed the BSCP and forbade AME churches to invite its leaders to speak.

Pullman Company executives also provided significant financial backing for the Wabash Avenue Young Men's Christian Association (YMCA) and the Chicago Urban League. Both the Wabash Avenue YMCA, established because the downtown branch did not admit blacks, and the Urban League were important in shaping work habits of black Chicagoans as well as placing them in jobs.

Around 1900, the Reverend Archibald James Carey saved Quinn Chapel, the largest African Methodist Episcopal (AME) church in Chicago, from foreclosure, establishing his reputation as a capable financial manager. Several prominent families, including the Pullmans and the Swifts, noticed his success and promoted his rise in both political and ecclesiastical circles. The Reverend Carey, considered one of the most influential political voices on the South Side, was appointed AME

Bishop by 1920.

The Reverend Carey also expanded the multiple roles of the black church further than most ministers when he established an employment service for black workers. Carey's employment service linked the interests of black workers, discriminated against by the city's trade unions, with wealthy white families such as the Pullmans and the Swifts. When Carey announced positions with the Pullman Company from his pulpit, the company appeared to be a benevolent friend of black workers. The arrangement made sense to the black elite who thought employers had done much more for black workers than the generally racially exclusive white trade unions. Consequently, these leaders advised black workers to support management and eschew unions.

Lyn Hughes

The BSCP did not hesitate too attack African American leaders who failed to support the union This cartoon from the Messenger of January 1926 accuses a number of leaders, including Chicago's Bishop Carey, of having "sold out their race for a pottage."

34

The Reverend Carey felt so strongly that economic opportunity for black workers would result from cooperation with industrial magnates rather than solidarity between black and white workers that he forbade the congregations in his bishopric in Chicago to allow A. Philip Randolph, national leader of the BSCP, of Milton P. Webster, head of the Chicago division of the BSCP, to speak before them. Carey's comprehensive approach to ministering, with its reliance upon the Pullman Company's benevolence, helped strengthen the company's ties to the black community.

Above labor leader A. Philip Randolph, seen here in the early 1930's, headed the BSCP from its founding in 1925 until 1968. Though he never worked as a porter, he understood the difficult conditions these men faced, in contradiction to depictions of smiling porters.

While not everyone's faith in the goodwill of the Pullman Company was as strong as that of the Reverend Carey, the black middle class generally agreed with Claude Barnett, founder of the Associated Negro Press, that it would be "difficult to overestimate the economic value to the entire colored group what the business of 'Pullman Portering' has been" to the backbone of the community. The roster of defenders of the Pullman Company, the largest private employer of black workers nationally, in its struggle against the upstart union of porters and maids read like a who's who within the black community. It included Jesse Binga, head of Binga State Bank, most ministers, and Robert S. Abbott, publisher and editor of the Chicago Defender.

In his hours on duty, a porter was always on call, attending to all of the needs of passengers. Above: in this photo from a Pullman company publication, Pullman Car No.9, a porter stands by as a traveler climbs to an upper berth. Below: a Pullman porter assist women boarding a train, 1915.

When Ida B. Wells-Barnett (above,1920) failed
to find a public meeting space where the Woman'
Forum could listen to a speech by Milton P. Webster,
She held the meeting in her home at what is now
3624 South Martin Luther King Drive (below, c. 1973)

Moreover, the black middle class must have wondered why union porters and maids thought they stood a chance against the Pullman Company. When the BSCP threw down its gauntlet, it landed at the feet of a giant American corporation, an opponent with more than sufficient resources to combat union porters and maids. Finally, it was difficult to ignore the Pullman Company's success in defeating unions in the past.

Yet, despite the overwhelming odds against the BSCP effort to gain support for its labor union, the attitudes of the black middle class and elite were not as homogeneous as some scholars have argued. In December 1925, while most ministries, the press, and politicians ignored or spoke against the BSCP, the Chicago and Northern District Association of Colored Women, one of the premier women's clubs in Chicago at the time, invited A. Philip Randolph, head of the BSCP, to speak to them.

Two weeks later, the Woman's Forum, a Sunday evening civic and social discussion group at the Metropolitan Community Church, heard Randolph speak in Ida B. Wells-Barnett's home. She told Randolph that they wanted to hear his side of the story since they had not been able "to find anything in our press favorable to this movement" and had heard so much propaganda against it. Wells-Barnett had hoped to hold the meeting at the Appomattox Club, a social and fraternal club for professional and politically connected men, rather than in her home. The Appomattox Club, however, told Wells-Barnett they could not "afford to have Randolph speak" on its premises because so many of "the men who are opposing him are members here and it would embarrass them with the Pullman Company." To the twenty-five business and professional women gathered at her home Wells-Barnett said, "I can hardly conceive of Negro leaders taking such a narrow and selfish view of such vital problems affecting the race." After Randolph's remarks about the aims and purposes of the BSCP, the women endorsed the Brotherhood and asked, "What can the Woman's Forum do to help this great movement?"

Milton P. Webster, head of the Chicago division of the BSCP, wrote Wells-Barnett, seeking to expand the opening the Woman's Forum provided. He suggested that Wells-Barnett give the BSCP a copy of the membership list of the Ida B. Wells Club, a civic club formed in 1893 by Wells-Barnett, so that the BSCP could "send out publicity to the women direct." Webster also asked Wells-Barnett to encourage the women to attend BSCP meetings.

Head of BSCP'S Chicago division from its founding in 1925, Milton Webster, a former porter, played a key role in early organizing efforts. He remained a leader of the BSCP until his death in 1965.

The women, he hoped, would serve as a conduit within the black community to advertise and educate others about the Brotherhood's cause. The Ida B. Wells Club women would act as a counter to the weight of "hostility of our local newspapers against this movement."

Webster emphasized that the Brotherhood was not just a labor organization, but a social movement. "In the Brotherhood of Sleeping Car Porters the Race has staunch, progressive, militant movement, which will ever be on the alert to wield its power whenever the interests of the Race demands," he wrote Wells-Barnett. Her club members were important to the larger goal of getting the Brotherhood's message on "economic subjects of vital importance to Negro workers" out to the community, despite all attempts of the press to silence the BSCP.

To a large extent, Webster's proposal and the civic interests of members of the black club-women's movement in Chicago converged. The key issue uniting them was that of fuller citizenship rights for all African Americans, for which the BSCP employed the idiom of "manhood rights." Black women, active in the fight for the Nineteenth

Amendment, viewed the struggle for manhood rights as part of the broader efforts to claim full citizenship for all African Americans. A larger political role for black women was part of the struggle for fuller freedom for the entire black community. Fuller freedom entailed moving out from under white control and enjoying rights of first-class citizenship-achieving equality with white Americans. The work of Ida B. Wells-Barnett illustrates this point.

Ida B. Wells-Barnett began the black women's club movement in Chicago in the 1890s, in order to defend the "manhood of her race" through her anti-lynching crusade. Wells-Barnett did not neglect black women when she thought of advocating brotherly consideration; nor did she imagine only males when she and others in that ear used the term "manhood." For Wells-Barnett, women's enfranchisement was necessary to stop lynching. The vote for women would give added weight to the quest for full citizenship for both women and men. Wells-Barnett drew upon her network of club-women to work for suffrage for women, as well as other issues that would strengthen the black community, bringing African Americans more control over the direction of their lives.

Passage of the Nineteenth Amendment did not eclipse the political activism of black middle-class clubwomen. Those who had been involved in the movement for suffrage continued to focus on issues that plagued both black men and black women, a pattern that distinguished their agenda from that of their white sisters. Working with the BSCP merely broadened their agenda to include the importance of claiming economic as well as political rights. When the BSCP appealed to clubwomen to carry the BSCP message deep into the black community, these women probably envisioned a chance to be in the vanguard of a social movement designed to strengthen the overall ability of the black community to claim first-class citizenship.

The BSCP suffused its labor rhetoric, aimed at porters and maids, with the idea of manhood and manhood rights, implying self-reliance, standing tall, and moving out from under the paternalistic control of whites. In a widely-circulated poster under the banner, "Reasons Why Pullman porters and maids should join the Brotherhood of Sleeping Car Porters Now," organizer Ashley Totten wrote: "We appeal to that spark of manhood; that willingness to take the position of a man and not a coward." Within the larger community, BSCP flyers, handbills, and literature revived the nineteenth-century usage articulated by Frederick Douglass and W.E.B. DuBois, that equated manhood with full humanity and first-class citizenship.

The local black press addressed slavery, freedom, and citizenship on a regular basis. The articles, however, usually portrayed progress as a straight line flowing from slavery toward human dignity.

The emphasis that A. Philip Randolph and others of the era placed on "manhood rights" for African Americans is clear in literature promoting the BSCP, such as this application for membership from the July 1926 Messenger.

When Randolph, Webster, and other BSCP organizers discussed full-fledged "Americanism" and citizenship, they used these terms to question just what progress had been made and on whose terms. A company union denied the porters and maids the fundamental right to organize and to choose their own leaders. Similarly, black leaders in the wider community were usually chosen by white patrons. Black politicians found that the best way to contest racial exclusion was through political inclusion in what scholar Charles Branham called a "preexisting political culture," that rewarded those who learned how to adapt to machine politics.

To the porters and maids, clubwomen, and the general public, the BSCP raised the issue of the "unfinished task of emancipation," asking them to "rededicate [their] hearts and minds" to the spirit of Denmark Vesey, Nat Turner, Sojourner Truth, Harriet Tubman, and Frederick Douglass, who "shall not have died in vain." Black Americans had to assert their manhood rights to first-class citizenship and throw off what The Messenger, A. Philip Randolph's magazine, called the "grip of the old slave psychology." Claude Barnett, Bishop Carey, and Robert S. Abbott were condemned in one issue for having "a wish-bone where a backbone ought to be." With such leaders, it continued, "one can hear the clank of the slave's chain" in all they say and do. The Messenger reminded its readers that "New Negroes" had the backbone to demand full civil rights. A popular handbill harked back to nineteenth-century manhood rhetoric with a sketch of Frederick Douglass and a caption that said: "Douglass fought for the abolition of chattel slavery, and today we fight for economic freedom. The time has passed when a grown-up black man should beg a grown-up white man for anything."

To promote this outlook, the Chicago division of the BSCP began working with a committee of citizens, largely leaders from the Ida B. Wells clubs and the Chicago and Northern District Association of Colored Women. The first test of the ability of this network to overcome the opposition of Chicago newspapers and ministers came in October 1926. By the time, Irene Goins, another pioneer in women's social activism in Illinois, actively worked for the BSCP. As president of both the Chicago and Northern District Federation of Colored Women and Federated Women's Club, Goins helped expand the base of active clubwomen demanding social justice for all black Chicagoans. She influenced state politics as founder of the Women's Republican Club.

> # Pullman Porters and Sleeping Car Porters Generally, Attention!
>
> ## IF
>
> You are tired of being treated like children instead of men;
> You think you should work shorter hours;
> You think your wages should be larger;
> You are tired of doubling back;
> You are sick of Company tyranny;
> You have a backbone instead of a wishbone—
>
> ## THEN
>
> Fill out this blank and mail it immediately to A. PHILIP RANDOLPH, General Organizer, BROTHERHOOD OF SLEEPING CAR PORTERS, 2311 Seventh Avenue, New York City.
>
> Act today, don't delay.
> Spread the Good News.
> ...rowing by leaps and

Above: This advertisement urged porters to join forces with other BSCP members to improve working conditions in ways both practical and philosophical. Below: The cover of The Bulletin, *a BSCP publication, compares economic freedom with freedom from slavery.*

But Goins also had ties to the black working class. The first African American woman in the Midwest to take an active part in the labor movement, she worked for several years on the eight-hour-day bill with Agnes Nestor, president of the International Glove Workers Union. During World War I she organized the Woman's Labor Union at the stockyards, continuing her efforts to organize black women workers at the Chicago Stockyards after the war. She also served on the executive council of the Chicago Women's Trade Union League from 1917 to 1922. Clearly, Goins could carry the Brotherhood's labor message beyond middle-class club circles.

By the fall of 1926, the BSCP also gained the support of Mary McDowell. First president of the Chicago branch of the Women's Trade Union League (WTUL) and a University of Chicago settlement-house worker, she was the only white person among the Chicago citizens contesting the politics of Pullman paternalism alongside BSCP organizers in the early years. McDowell, along with Wells-Barnett and Webster, promoted the mass meeting of October 3, 1926, in the community.

Mary McDowell, co-founder of Hull-House, was one of the earliest of the BSCP's white supporters. " The Union label Bulletin" that can be seen in this undated photograph indicates her interest in union activities.

Webster and Randolph gave much thought to details such as the quality of paper used for advertising the mass meeting as well as the character of the images projected to the black community, for Webster vowed to "mobilize all of the forces in Chicago, religious, social, fraternal and otherwise," to bring out a crowd.

The fall 1926 mass meeting was a success in terms of publicity. Webster doubted that the Brotherhood could have "bought the same publicity in Chicago with the expenditure of a thousand dollars." The Brotherhood program and movement was, Webster believed, "the talk of the town." If so, it was partially the result of the efforts of McDowell and Wells-Barnett, along with the Wells Club members, broadcasting the BSCP message to the larger community.

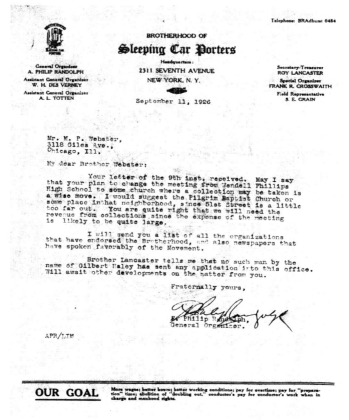

Unlike more conservative black churches, the Metropolitan community Church supported the work of the BSCP. Thee broadsides advertise mass meetings held at this church.

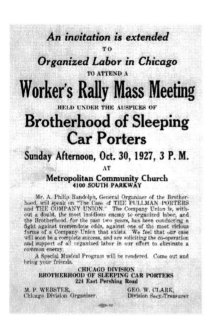

Nevertheless, the majority of representatives from the black press and pulpit-most notably the Chicago Defender-continued to speak against the BSCP, when they mentioned the Brotherhood at all. Despite this continuing lack of support, the BSCP did gain, little by little, additional recognition. Lula E. Lawson, executive secretary of the South Parkway Young Women's Christian Association (YWCA), opened up the YWCA network to the BSCP when she endorsed their goals in 1928. By the 1920s, the YWCA emphasized collective action and the importance of participation in "group work" as a means to give the individual a greater sense of self-worth and a connection with large-scale social change. The YWCA strove to revitalize the community, which it believed was fragmented through forces of modern life, such as migration and industrialization. Lula Lawson brought this perspective and experience to the BSCP. Her ability to interest individuals in the merits of a larger community vision opposed to Pullman philanthropy and patronage politics must have been valuable to the BSCP.

Dr. William D. Cook, minister of the Metropolitan Community Church, was the first minister to open his church to the Brotherhood. His support was not surprising since, as Webster told one scholar, Cook was "kind of an outlaw preacher," who once headed one of the largest and most prominent churches Bethel AME of Chicago. Cook's church had a history that stretched back to World War I of social and political leanings "not in harmony" with a majority of the AME churches in the Chicago area. Shortly after the Reverend A.J. Carey was appointed AME Bishop of Chicago in 1920, he removed Cook from Bethel forever.

Community Church of Christ and Metropolitan Community Center, dedicated to the service of humanity and the welfare of the community. Under Cook's leadership, the church, generally known as Metropolitan Community Church, sponsored activities such as educational programs and seminars on industrial relations. Cook found and rented office space for the porters and maids during the first crucial two years of the union's existence and, until his death in 1930 addressed many of the Brotherhood's meetings.

THE PULLMAN PORTERS
THE
Brotherhood OF Sleeping Car Porters
THE INDEPENDENT PULLMAN PORTERS UNION
is pleased to announce that it has

COMPLETELY DEFEATED THE STOOL PIGEON, THE WELFARE WORKER, THE PORTER INSTRUCTOR, THE LICKSPITLE POLITICIAN, THE WEAK-KNEED NEGRO BUSINESS MAN AND ALL OF DOUBLE CROSSING NEGRO NEWSPAPER EDITORS, AND IN FACT THE ENTIRE GROUP OF NEGRO RACE TRAITORS WHO WERE MOBILIZED BY SOME "MYSTERIOUS POWER" TO OBSTRUCT THE WORK OF ORGANIZING THIS

Union of, by and for Pullman Porters

The most powerful force ever lined up against a movement of this kind has not been able to retard its onward progress. After many attempts to organize a Real Union success has at last been obtained.

The REAL MANHOOD of the Pullman Porters has triumphed over the low, degraded traitorous cowardly, underhanded efforts of that unscrupulous group of Negroes who for about "THIRTY CENTS" have surrendered every principle of Manhood, Honor, Honesty and Race Loyalty in their feeble efforts to show the Pullman Porters that they are still Children and not Men.

THE BROTHERHOOD IS ON THE MAP and has started to carry out its Constuctive Program of the Organization of getting you a Living Wage, Decent Working Conditions and Manly Treatment.

Chicago Men, let's live up to the "I WILL" Spirit and finish the job by making Chicago a Ninety-Five per cent Local.

SPECIAL SERIES OF MEETINGS THIS WEEK AT UNION HEADQUARTERS, 3118 GILES AVE.

TUES. JAN. 19TH, WED. JAN. 20TH, THURS. JAN. 21ST, FRI. JAN. 22ND, SAT. JAN. 23RD, AT 8 P. M.

IMPORTANT INFORMATION WILL BE DISCLOSED AT THESE MEETINGS

Members be sure to be on hand and bring at least one new member. Office Open Day and Night

M. P. WEBSTER, Organizer.   G. A. PRICE, Act. Sec.-Treas.

Come and learn the truth about the new law to abolish the U. S. Railroad Labor Board.

The animosity of the BSCP toward African Americans who failed to support the union is expressed in this broadside from 1928, which announces the defeat of "the lickspittle politicians, the weak-kneed Negro business man and all of the double crossing Negro newspapers editors"

Dr. J.C. Austin opened up the Pilgrim Baptist Church for mass meetings of the Brotherhood soon after he came to Chicago from Pittsburgh in 1926. Known nationally as a "dynamic personality" and business leader as well as minister, Austin, as an outsider to Chicago politics, was not entangled in patronage nor paternalistic relations. He arrived with a vision of uplifting the race and building a progressive church in Chicago. Offering protection and advice to workers was just one of the church-sponsored services that Austin initiated to put uplift into practice. Pilgrim's stated mission was to reach the unreached, upon the "highway and in the hedges." Apparently, this approach to Christian ministry filled a need, for by 1930 the church had attracted more than nine thousand members, becoming one of the largest and most prosperous of the hundreds of churches on the South Side. Meanwhile, Bishop Carey continued to ban the Brotherhood from AME churches, reminding AME ministers of their responsibility to warn their membership against the evil influence of labor leaders. Also joining forces with the BSCP was Dr. Charles Wesley Burton, minister of the Lincoln Memorial Congregational Church until he began practicing law in 1926. Webster considered Burton to have a "world of experience in the various social problems that concern the Negro." When Burton took over the ministry of the Lincoln Memorial Congregational Church, he started a strong community outreach program on social issues.

At a mass meeting on October 30, 1927, the BSCP made significant gains in terms of support and recognition from the black community when more than two thousand people heard the BSCP rebuke the Chicago Defender for its editorial stance. Randolph charged that the Defender had surrendered to "gold and power." Earlier the BSCP had referred to the Defender as the Chicago "Surrender" and the "World's Greatest Weakly." Many of those who packed Cook's Metropolitan Community Church to hear the BSCP leaders lash out at the Defender were drawn to the meeting through the clubwomen's network and the distribution of more than five thousand circulars throughout the black neighborhoods on the South Side. The BSCP featured its fight against a company, union, which it pictured as a fight against whites choosing black leaders. As a result of the meeting, a large number of citizens delivered a "bushel basket of mail" to the Defender demanding an explanation for its failure to cover news of the BSCP.

Pullman Company detectives, reporting to executives about the

Brotherhood's activities, noted the increased attention the community showed toward the Brotherhood by the fall of 1927. The Defender staff also noticed: with the November 19, 1927, issue, they began supporting the Brotherhood. The change in policy was nothing if not abrupt. Roi Ottley, biographer of Robert Abbott, publisher and editor of the Defender, said Abbott changed his policy toward the union in response to both decreased circulation and charges that black editors supporting Pullman were "traitors to their race." Although the Pullman Company fired or otherwise punished the porters and maids identified with the union, sentiment within the black community was shifting towards the BSCP thanks in part to the efforts of Dr. Cook, Dr. Austin, Ida B. Wells-Barnett, Lula Lawson, and Mary McDowell. The Brotherhood held meetings several nights a week with as many as fifty to sixty porters and maids showing up. Larger "mass" meetings, aimed at the community, were held about once a month, commanding good publicity because organizers would blanket key parts of the community using their friendly networks.

In December 1927, Webster formalized the group of supportive citizens into the Citizens' Committee. He added new members at the same time. Perhaps the most important addition was Irene McCoy Gaines, leading club-woman and industrial secretary of the South Parkway YWCA. In her role as industrial secretary of the YWCA from 1920 to 1925, she advocated a labor-oriented approach to civil rights. In addition, Gaines and her husband, Harris Barrett Gaines, formerly a representative in the Illinois State Legislature and Assistant State's Attorney, had access to the social and political world of upper-class black Chicagoans. From 1924 to 1935, Irene Gaines served as president of the Illinois Federation of Republican Colored Women's Clubs, a group that she helped to organize. In January 1928, Webster appointed Gaines secretary of the Citizens' Committee.

Key members of the Lincoln Community Men's Club may have influenced the breakdown of opposition during the next couple of years among middle-class professional black men not normally familiar with the Merits of labor organizing.

George Cleveland Hall became a member of the BSCP's Citizens Committee in 1928. This photograph, c 1886, show him as a young man.

In 1928, Dr. Burton, of Lincoln Memorial Congregational Church, became chairman of the Citizens' Committee. Burton probably encouraged David W. Johnson, president of the church's Lincoln Community Men's Club, to join the committee. Johnson helped the Brotherhood by writing letters to citizens, and encouraging other members of the Men's Club to do the same.

George Cleveland Hall lent his support to the BSCP in 1928, revealing that even within the Chicago Urban League, a bastion of pro-employer sentiment, differences could be found on the issue of unionism. Hall, one of the League's founders and a well-known physician, became a member of the Citizens' Committee of the BSCP despite the fact that Pullman Company had always contributed to the Urban League. Hall hardly fit, however, the profile of a New Negro economic radical.

Considered one of the most articulate business leaders in the early part of the century, Hall in many respects appeared to be out of the Booker T. Washington camp, which believed black Americans should accept the status quo and not directly challenge second-class citizenship. Indeed, he and his wife had been personal friends of Washington. Hall promoted black business in Chicago and, in 1912, became the president of the Chicago branch of Washington's National Negro Business League, which believed capitalism was colorblind. Simultaneously, however, he was one of two active black leaders of the National Association for the Advancement of Colored People (NAACP) and participated in its committee on grievances. The contradiction implied by active membership in both a Washington and a DuBois organization at the same time one advocating an accommodating approach, the other a more direct, militant approach-did not seem to upset Hall. While he may have supported Washington out of personal loyalty or even because he subscribed to certain aspects of self-help, he did not believe in accommodating to the status of a second-class citizen. He thought that black Americans had to fight white prejudice and discrimination directly and move out from white control of black institutions, which seems to be the issue that connected Hall with the Brotherhood.

Due in part to the efforts of the Citizens' Committee, the BSCP's membership and influence grew and the Pullman company eventually recognized the union. Above: A. Philip Randolph is fourth from the left, Milton Webster third from the right

The Citizens' Committee became the official sponsor, beginning in 1928, of the Brotherhood of Sleeping Car Porters' Labor Conferences, annual meetings to educate porters and the public about labor and civil rights issues. Some members of the Citizen's Committee spoke at the conferences; others used civic and political clubs to advance the BSCP's labor point of view. Still others, such as Mary McDowell, worked with black and white labor networks and used the pages of the Federation News to discuss the BSCP approach to reform and advancement through labor organization.

By the 1930s, the BSCP, though the Citizens' Committee, influenced the protest agenda of many club members and leaders on Chicago's South Side. The Reverend Harold M. Kingsley, pastor of the Church of the Good Shepherd, described by one interviewer as "preaching to the white collar class" spoke at Brotherhood mass meetings and at its annual labor conference. His sermons emphasized the virtue and value of labor. But at the 1930 Negro Labor Conference, sponsored by the Citizens' Committee, he said the black church of the late 1920's ignored the plight of the working class just as the Russian church had before the Russian Revolution of 1917. "The Church is the one institution that gets more of the people together than any other institution," he said, but it needed to be "educated up to the economic conditions of the workers." Frederic Robb, president of the Washington Intercollegiate Club, spoke at that same labor conference an focused on the need for black workers to educate students "up to their responsibilities" and for "students to quit criticizing the worker and get in harmony with him." Finally, Robb also admonished the churches to "foster a labor psychology."

The Brotherhood's need for outreach into Chicago's black community did not disappear when the Pullman Company finally organized the BSCP as the bargaining agent for porters and maids in 1935. A loosely organized group still existed as a reserve army to counter adverse publicity put out by Pullman within key community networks. But the active years of the Citizens' Committee were between 1927 and 1933 when the BSCP needed help mobilizing support in its attack on the culture of Pullman paternalism. The Citizens' Committee raised questions about the value of a political culture that denied black Chicagoans as workers and as citizens' rights of first-class citizenship. But it also put workers' interests and unionization on the agenda of civic clubs, helping to bridge the gap between the middle and working class, and introducing labor issues into civic discourse. Finally, the work of the Chicago Citizens' Committee of the BSCP fore-shadowed alliances of the mid-to-late 1930s between groups such as the Chicago chapter of the National Negro Congress (NNC), which focused primarily on labor issues, and middle-class groups like the Chicago Council of Negro Organizations, which focused on securing civil rights for black Chicagoans. In 1939, Irene McCoy Gaines headed the Chicago Council of Negro Organizations, leading joint efforts with the left-learning NNC local to support workers' rights. Without the labor education provided to the black middle class through networks of the Citizens' Committee, alliances uniting left-wingers and more conservative groups in protests against second-class citizenship might have been harder to form

This chapter appeared as an article in the Fall 1996 issue of *Chicago History magazine*. Copyright ©1996 Chicago Historical Society. Reprinted with permission

Appendix One

Notable Alumni

The following are the names of Pullman Porters and Dining Car Waiters that we have labeled Notable Alumni, individuals who made their own mark of distinction. These are men who worked for the railroad and later moved on to other careers.

Jesse Binga, a former Pullman Porter who made his fortune in real estate. As a "blockbuster," Binga would buy one house in a white Chicago neighborhood; sell it to a black family, and scoop up the rest of the block as panicked white owners sold at bargain rates. By 1925 Binga would own his own bank on the Stroll. For now, Rich says, he helped finance Bessie's dream. Jesse Binga's pioneering ventures in banking and real estate, in the early 1900s set important precedents for subsequent economic development within the African-American community. The Binga State Bank officially opened on January 3, 1921.

Matthew Henson, a former Pullman Porter known as one of the world's greatest explorers. He was born in Baltimore, MD and is the co-discoverer of the North Pole.

James "Genial Jim" Knight, the "first mayor of Bronzeville," a former Pullman Porter turned businessman and "Policy King" — owner of the once famous, now defunct Palm Tavern, which opened in 1933. It was a place where among others you might see Langston Hughes, Joe Louis, Duke Ellington, Dizzy Gillespie, Miles Davis, and Lena Horne, just to name a few.

Malcolm Little AKA Malcolm X

Thurgood Marshall, the Supreme Court justice who worked as a train porter when he was in college and whose father was a train porter. Marshall was nominated by President John F. Kennedy for appointment to the Second Supreme Court of Appeals in 1961. The appointment was confirmed by the senate. President Lyndon B. Johnson nominated

Marshall for appointment as Solicitor General of the United States. In August of 1965, Judge Marshall took his oath. In June of 1967, President Lyndon B. Johnson nominated Judge Marshall to become an Associate Justice of the Supreme Court. This nomination was indeed an historical event; Marshall became the first African-American to serve as a Justice of the Supreme Court.

Benjamin Elijah Mays, educator, was born in 1895 in South Carolina, and graduated from Bates College in Maine in 1920. He went to the University of Chicago for his master's degree and doctorate, and while he was working on those degrees, he was ordained into the Baptist ministry. He taught at Morehouse College and at South Carolina State College. From 1934 to 1940, he served as dean of the Howard University School of Religion and then moved on to the presidency of Morehouse College, a position he distinguished for the next quarter of a century. He also served his community well, becoming the first black president of the Atlanta school board. Additionally, his contributions to the civil rights work and his leadership role in national and international orgainzations like the NAACP, as its executive director, are noteworthy.

Oscar Micheaux, the most prolific black if not most prolific independent filmmaker in American cinema. Oscar Micheaux wrote, produced, and directed 44 feature-length films between 1919 and 1948. The fifth child in a family of 13, Micheaux worked as a shoeshine boy, farm laborer, and Pullman Porter. In his early twenties, he was self-confident to the point that he invested his savings in farmland in an all-white community in faraway South Dakota. Within nine years, he had expanded his holdings to 500 acres whilst writing, publishing, and distributing his first semi-autobiographical novel, *The Conquest* (1913). He popularized it by selling it door to door to the farmers of South Dakota. In 1918, the Lincoln Film Company in Nebraska offered to film Micheaux's 1917 novel, *The Homesteader*. But when Lincoln refused to produce the film on the scale that he desired, Micheaux responded by founding his own production company and shooting the work himself.

E.D. Nixon, a Pullman Porter with a sixth-grade education and in his mid-fifties at the time of the boycott, had organized the state branch of the Brotherhood of Sleeping Car Porters in 1928 under the guidance of A. Philip Randolph. In the 1930s, Nixon organized a committee to make sure that Alabama blacks got their fair share of benefits from federal programs; in 1940, he helped organize the Montgomery Voters League; in 1944, he led a march of 750 people on the registrar's office; from 1939 to 1951, he headed the Montgomery NAACP and from 1951-53, the state conference.

Gordon Parks, internationally renowned photographer. After returning to St. Paul in 1934, Parks took a job as a Pullman Porter and a dining car waiter on the North Coast Limited. Parks became the first black photographer to work at magazines like *Life* and *Vogue*, and the first black to work for the Office of War Information and the Farm Security Administration. Parks achieved these milestones in the 1940s. Later, in the 1960s, he helped break racial barriers in Hollywood as the first black director for a major studio. He co-produced, directed, and wrote the screenplay, and composed the musical score for the film based on his 1963 novel, *The Learning Tree*. The Library of Congress later placed the film on the National Film Register. Thompson Gale
http://www.gale.com/free_resources/bhm/bio/parks_g.htm

R. Eugene Pincham, Illinois Appellate Court Judge
Retired Appellate Court Judge. Judge Pincham worked as a Dining Car Waiter in 1945 on the Santa Fe Super Chief, a streamliner that ran from Chicago to Los Angeles.

J.A. Rodgers (Joel August Rogers) was born in Negril, Jamaica in the late 1880's some report 1883. J. A. Rodgers became one of the most prolific African writers of his day producing works in journalism and history. His authorship would produce a library of works that would contribute substantial underpinnings to the accurate reporting of the history of Africans in the Diaspora. Well versed in French, German, Portuguese, and Spanish he researched in some of the world's greatest archives to record and document the African experience and contribution to civilization, although he was not formally trained. He specifically cited the works of Africans in the Arts, and wrote to dispel the unscientific theories of white supremacy — racism. J. A. Rogers worked as a Pullman Porter out of Chicago during the early 1900s, during which time he wrote the book *From "Superman" to Man*. He further worked as a journalist for the *Pittsburgh Courier*, and is noted as the sub-editor of the *Daily Negro Times* a publication produced by Marcus Mosiah Garvey.

Appendix Two

Descendants of Distinction

Throughout the ranks of black scientists, politicians, jazz artists, you'll see a disproportionate number of kids of Pullman Porters or other African-American railroad workers. Because of them we became doctors, attorneys, judges, educators, engineers, nurses, professors, politicians, business professionals, actors, TV anchors, radio and television hosts, producers, and on and on. The following are just a few.

Tom Bradley, became the first African-American elected to the Los Angeles City Council in modern times, and became the second African-American mayor of a major U.S. city.

Andre Braugher, Emmy-nominated actor.

Willie Lewis Brown, Jr., an American political figure who served over 30 years in the California State Assembly, after which he became the first African-American mayor of San Francisco.

Ron Dellums, Congressman California of CL Dellums.

Whoopi Goldberg,

Actor/comedian. Her great great-grandparents, William and Elsie Washington, were among a very small number of African-Americans who were among a very small number of African-Americans who became landowners through homesteading in the years following the Civil War. Two generations later, her grandparents were living in Harlem; her grandfather was a Pullman Porter.

Tom Joyner

Joyner, a media mogul is the grandson of "Doc" Joyner former Pullman Porter.

Archibald Motley (1891-1980), prominent artist from New Orleans, Louisiana. His parents were Archibald Motley, Sr. and Mary Huff. His family moved to Chicago, where his father worked as a Pullman Porter, and settled into a quiet neighborhood on the West Side. In his home he would listen to his father and A. Philip Randolph discuss the organization of the Pullman Porter's Union. The hard work and ambition that he witnessed as a child would carry him through his artistic career.

The Neville Brothers, world-renowned musicians and singers.

Oscar Peterson, jazz legend.

Wilma Rudolph, Olympian.

Warner Saunders, TV anchor for NBC 5 Chicago, Illinois.

Roy Wilkins, NAACP. Also co-founder with A. Philip Randolph Leadership Conference on Civil Rights.

The Chicago Connection

Jesse Binga

Binga, a former Pullman Porter who made his fortune in real estate. As a "blockbuster," Binga would buy one house in a white Chicago neighborhood; sell it to a black family, and scoop up the rest of the block as panicked white owners sold at bargain rates. By 1925 Binga would own his own bank on the Stroll. For now, Rich says, he helped finance Bessie's dream. Jesse Binga's pioneering ventures in banking and real estate in the early 1900s set important precedents for subsequent economic development within the African-American community. The Binga State Bank officially opened on January 3, 1921.

Occupying the same quarters as the private bank, Binga's professional and social stature within Black Metropolis continued to grow throughout the 1920s, and his role as an example of self-made financial success prompted him to prepare a pamphlet, "Certain Sayings of Jesse Binga," containing such homilies as:

James "Genial Jim" Knight, the "first mayor of Bronzeville," a former Pullman Porter turned businessman and "Policy King" — owner of the once famous, now defunct Palm Tavern, which opened in 1933. It was a place where among others you might see Langston Hughes, Joe Louis, Duke Ellington, Dizzy Gillespie, Miles Davis, and Lena Horne, just to name a few.

Justice R. Eugene Pincham, Retired Appellate Court Judge. Judge Pincham worked as a Dining Car Waiter in 1945 on the Santa Fe Super Chief, a streamliner that ran from Chicago to Los Angeles.

Warner Saunders

NBC Channel 5 News Chicago-TV News Anchor

My father, Gus Saunders, was born October 27,1889 in El Paso, Texas. His parents, William and Rebecca Holmes, soon returned to their home in White Castle, Louisiana where my father grew to young manhood. He hoboed to Spokane, Washington around 1915 where he worked helping to build bridges. He moved to Chicago in 1925. He married my mother, Georgia Saunders, in 1933. I was born in 1935. He went to work for the Illinois Central Railroad Company even before I was born. He worked both in the Dining Car and as a Pullman Porter for several years. I can remember that he was always getting hired and fired because of his disagreements with railroad management. During many of his down times, he waited tables at the Palmer House along with many other Porters and Waiters. His bad temper was well known to friend and foe. He ran on the City of Miami and would bring back grapefruits and oranges from Florida upon his return trips. He also worked the City of New Orleans. He was a strong supporter of the A. Philip Randolph's BSCP movement and I remember him hosting many meetings at our apartment at 432 E. 47th Street. When I was about 10 or 12 years old he opened up a cleaning shop across the street from the Illinois Central station on 12th and Michigan Ave, which served porters who had layovers in Chicago. The place also doubled as a gambling house and watering hole mainly catering to those Porters and Waiters. He died on May 17, 1962. My mother died last year at the age of 98.

Appendix Three

Who Were They
By Lyn Hughes

They were fathers, grandfathers, uncles, and brothers — men who cared enough to make the sacrifices that they made to provide for their families. They endured racism, classism, hate and bigotry, for family. They planted seeds, in a bloodline that would grow into the "I CAN spirit," a desire to want to know more, be more; they imparted in us the undeniable power of purpose, embedded in our DNA, pride in oneself and gave us the understanding that with it, the human spirit is un-crushable.

In those quiet family conversations and leading by sheer example, they imparted in us a thirst for education, and impressed upon us the knowledge that we had a right to dream and have aspirations just like anyone else. But most of all they very subtly but consistently released to us that sense of responsibility we all have to our ancestors that we must continue to strive for that better life for ourselves and for our families and in generations to come.

The Pullman Porters National Historic Registry of African-American Railroad Employees 1865-1969

Registrant ID: 58
Name: Otis Abernathy
City/State: Cincinnati, OH
Railroad: Pullman Company
Position: Pullman Porter
Years of Service: 1922-1929
Submitter's Name: Abernathy

Registrant ID: 59
Name: Walter Abrams
City/State: Chicago, IL
Railroad: Santa Fe/Burlington, Amtrak
Position: Pullman Porter
Years of Service: 40 years
Submitter' Name: Wilhelmina
Comments: My father worked for the railroad. He is now decease. He retired 1994.

Registrant ID: 67
Name: Norman E Adams
City/State: Brooklyn, NY
Railroad: Pennsylvania
Position: Pullman Porter
And a Waiter
Years of Service: 1936-1969
Submitter's Name: Mary
City/State: Brooklyn, NY
Comments: Father is 81 years old. He is glad to still be alive, and is very proud to be part of this project.

Registrant ID: 62
Name: Joseph Adams
City/State: Brooklyn, NY
Position: Pullman Porter
Submitter's Name: Patricia
City/State: Port Charlotte, FL

Registrant ID: 69
Name: Willie J. Adams
City/State: Orlando, FL

Railroad: Atlantic Coastline
Position: Station Porter
Years of Service: 20 years
1940-1960
Submitter's Name: Karen
City/State: Rochester, NY

Registrant ID: 63
Name: Leroy Adams
City/State: St. Louis, MO
Railroad: St. Louis
Position: Porter
Submitter's Name: Pamela
City/State: Saint Louis, MO

Registrant ID: 65
Name: Levi Adams
City/State: LA
Years of Service 1920's -50's
Submitter's Name: Andrea
City/State: San Francisco, CA
Comments: I don't have any details, I just remember that whenever Mr. Randolph's name was mentioned by my parents and grand parents--it was as if he was a holy being.

Registrant ID: 68
William Wadsworth Adams
City/State: AL
Railroad: B&O Railroad
Position: Sleeping Car Porter
Years : 1930's to 1956
Submitter's: Ruth & Judith
City/State: Tinton Falls, NJ
Comments: William was my father. He told us many stories about the indignities he and his colleagues had to endure, but he was always dignified and an enthusiastic supporter of the Brotherhood. It was so rewarding and inspiring to find out about

your Museum on the Web Site. William was my Grandfather. I have some very fond childhood memories of him.

Registrant ID: 66
Name: Mason Adams
City/State: Chattanooga, TN
Railroad: The Nashville, Chattanooga & St. Louis
Position: Pullman Porter
Years of Service: 3 years
Submitter's Name: Pearlena
City/State: Tuscaloosa, AL

Registrant ID: 70
Name: Frank Adams, Sr.
City/State: Chicago, IL
Position: Waiter/Cook
Years of Service: 1947
Submitter's Name: Sandra
City/State: Chicago, IL

Registrant ID: 72
Name: Lester H Addison
City/State: Baltimore, MD
Railroad: Pullman Company
Position: Pullman Porter
Submitter's Name: Addison

Registrant ID: 73
Name: Sol Addison
City/State: St. Stephen, SC
Railroad: Atlantic Coastline
Position: Railroad Workman
Years of Service: 1937-1972
Submitter's Name: Virginia
City/State: St. Stephen, SC

Registrant ID: 74
Harvey Salvadore Adkins
City/State: Chicago, AL
Railroad: Santa Fe
Position: Bar Porter

Years of Service: 1939-1965
Submitter's Name: Howard
City/State: Chicago, AL

Registrant ID: 80
Name: R. Ailes
City/State: Chicago, IL
Railroad: Pullman Rail Car Co
Position: Pullman Porter
Years of Service: 1940s
Submitter's Name: Betty
City/State: Chicago, IL

Registrant ID: 84
Name: John J. Alasgow
City/State: Hawthorne, FL
Railroad: Porter
Position: Owner
Years of Service: 10 Years
Submitter's Name: Perry

Registrant ID: 85
Name: Arthur "AA" Albert
City/State: St.Louis, MO
Railroad: Frisco
Position: Waiter-In-Charge
Years of Service: 1940's -60's
Submitter's Name: Nanette
City/State: St.Louis, MO
Comments: Worked the St. Louis to Memphis Run.

Registrant ID: 88
Name: Lovey Alexander
City/State: Harvey, IL
Railroad: Pullman Co. Chicago
Position: Pullman Porter
Submitter's Name: Janet
City/State: Indianapolis, IN

Registrant ID: 89
Name: William Alexander
City/State: Kansas City, MO
Railroad: Atchison, Topeka

And Santa Fe
Position: Pullman Porter
Years of Service: 1909 - 1921
Submitter's Name: Titus N.
City/State: Kansas City, MO
Comments: My grandfather died before I was born, so I don't know anything about his experiences.

Registrant ID: 87
Name: Clarence Alexander
City/State: Chicago, IL
Railroad: Seaboard and Southern
Position: Pullman Porter
Years of Service: 1942-46
Submitter's Name: Deborah
City/State: Omaha, NE
Comments: Worked out of Atlanta,

Registrant ID: 91
Name: Benjamin Alfonso
City/State: St. Louis, MO
Position: Porter
Years of Service: 1937-1948
Submitter's Name: Doris

Registrant ID: 92
Name: Henry Aliforle
City/State: AL
Position: Personal Attendant for Roosevelt
Years of Service: 1939-1943
Submitter's Name: Josef
City/State: AL

Registrant ID: 97
Name: John Allen
City/State: Chicago, IL
Railroad: Santa Fe
Position: Pullman Porter
Submitter's Name: Michelle

City/State: Chicago, IL

Registrant ID: 95
Name: Elmer Allen
City/State: Italy, TX
Railroad: Pullman Company
Position: Sleeping Car Porter
Years of Service: Circa unknown- 1947
Submitter's Name: Elmerine
City/State: Dallas, TX
Comments: Elmer Allen injured his left leg when he accidentally hit a baggage cart as he swung on the side of a train as it left a station in San Francisco. The injury did not heal and he was no longer able to work. The Pullman Company terminated him.

Registrant ID: 101
Name: Tom Allen
City/State: Chickasaw, OK
Years: circa1919-1920
Submitter's Name: Elmerine
City/State: Dallas, TX

Registrant ID: 99
Name: Obadiah Henry Allen
City/State: Buffalo, NY
Railroad: New York Central
Position: Waiter
Submitter's Name: Robert W.
City/State: Iona, CA

Registrant ID: 106
Name: William Leonard Allen
City/State: St. Louis, MO
Railroad: Wabash Rail Road, later merged Norfolk and Western RR
Position: Waiter -in-Charge
Years of Service: circa

1938 - 1975
Submitter's Name: Arvis V.
City/State: Lima, OH
Comments: I don't recall specific comments, positive or negative, about my father's railroad experiences. However, during his employment period, times were often oppressive and stressful. There was minimal recourse or hope for a just or fair resolution to unfair employment practices.

Registrant ID: 104
Name: William Austin Allen
Railroad: Penn. Railroad
Position: Pullman Porter
Years of Service: late 1940's 60
Submitter's Name: Dorothy
City/State: New York, NY

Registrant ID: 110
Name: Willie Allen
City/State: Oklahoma City, OK
Railroad: Rock Island
Position: Pullman Porter
Submitter's Name: Marie
City/State: Oklahoma City,
Comments: Father

Registrant ID: 103
Name: William Allen
City/State: NY
Railroad: Pennsylvania
Position: Pullman Porter
Years of Service: Circa 1947 -60
Submitter's Name: Fatimah
City/State: Phoenix, AZ
Comments: When he was with PRR, he would come home and tell us stories about Sunnyside and his travels up and down the Eastern Seaboard. We looked

forward to him walking through the door with his handsome smile after days of being away at work. Prior to working for PRR, he was a Merchant Marine. I feel the experience as a Porter enabled him to continue his life's dream of traveling. My father was a wonderful, intelligent man, who was proud to work for the Railroad. Thank you for doing this. He and all the wonderful men, who were his friends on the railroad, deserve this honor. I am proud of my father and these men and I thank you so much for honoring them.

Registrant ID: 102
Name: Walter Allen
City/State: Savannah, GA
Railroad: Hired and trained out of Atlanta, Ga.
Position: Pullman
Years of Service: 1940's
Submitter's Name: Weslynn
City/State: Stone Mountain, GA
Comments: Hired and trained out of Atlanta, GA. My father was assigned to the servicemen and seamen out of California. He said Russian seamen were good tippers.

Registrant ID: 94
Name: Earl (T.) Allen
City/State: Youngstown, OH
Railroad: Pullman Company & New York Central RR
Position: Pullman Porter
Years of Service: 1945-1964
Submitter's Name: Reginald
City/State: Youngstown, OH

Comments: My father loved his job, and I can't remember him ever missing a day of work. He talked about the hard times with his job, but he always said that it was much better after the union was established.

Registrant ID: 112
Name: Donald J. Allen Sr.
City/State: MN
Railroad: Northern Pacific and also Great Northern
Position: Porter and Porter Instructor
Years of Service: 1922-66
Submitter's Name: John R.
City/State: St. Paul, MN

Registrant ID: 113
Name: Edward Lee Allenlllin
City/State: AL
Railroad: Illinois Central
Position: Pullman Porter
Years: Before World War II
Submitter's Name: Patti
City/State: Merrit, FL
Comments: I recall his enthusiasm in meeting Eward G. Robinson while working

Registrant ID: 114
Name: Everett Allison
City/State: St. Paul, MN
Position: Porter in Charge
Submitter's Name: Richard A.
City/State: Minneapolis, MN

Registrant ID: 116
Name: James H. Allston, Jr.
City/State: Washington, DC
Railroad: Pennsylvania
Position: Porter, Cook, Chef

Years: Circa 1920-1968
Submitter (s) Vivian
City/State: Fort Washington, MD
Comments: My grandfather, started out shoveling coal into the engine in the early 1920's. His father, James Hazel Allston, Sr., was an employee and got his son a the job. They were originally from Savannah, GA.

Registrant ID: 119
Name: Robert T. Alston
City/State: Baltimore, MD
Railroad: Baltimore & Ohio/Pennsylvania R. R..
Position: Pullman Porter
Years of Service: 1933-1963
Submitter's Name: Robert
City/State: Columbia, MD
Comments: My father worked out of Mount Royal station in Baltimore Mid-on the Sleeper to NYS. Later worked the run from Baltimore Penn station to NYC Penn station. I remember traveling from B & O to I think Jersey City ,and catching ferry over to NYC.

Registrant ID: 135
Name: Grover Amica
City/State: Mount Vernon, NY
Years of Service: 1930's
Submitter's Name: Major
City/State: Savannah, GA

Registrant ID: 145
Name: Robert Ammons, Sr.
City/State: Baltimore, MD
Railroad: Baltimore & Ohio
Position: Dining Car Waiter
Years: Late '20s -'30s

Submitter's Name: Haywood
City/State: Baltimore, MD
Comments: My father worked on the railroad after completing Howard University. After leaving the railroad he spent (30) thirty plus years working for the Social Security Administration starting in Baltimore, Maryland and retiring in New York City, NY

Registrant ID: 147
Name: Jesse J. Anderson
City/State: Chicago, IL

Registrant ID: 154
Name: Tomie Anderson
City/State: CA
Railroad: Burlington and Union Pacific
Position: Dining Car Waiter
Years of Service: 1923-42
Submitter's Name: John K.
City/State: Carson, CA
Comments: As a small boy growing up on a farm, my dad and his brothers watched the trains go through the country, and could see the Porters and Waiters in their uniforms. He decided that he would like a job like that someday. After moving to Dallas from Austin and working in the Hotel industry he had a chance to give it a try, first with Burlington and others he settled with the Union Pacific. Papa as we all called my dad celebrated his 100th Birthday on October 30th he still likes to talk about his days on the road and the many places he has seen and things done all over this country, he is a real joy to listen to. He

has four sons three daughter in-law and numerous grand and great grand that enjoy his company.

Registrant ID: 156
Name: William R. Anderson
City/State: DC
Railroad: Pullman
Submitter's Name: Dawn
City/State: Concord, CA
Comments: My Great Grandfather was instrumental in helping to establish the union. He worked with A Philip Randolph during that time. As a result, my Grandfather was the first colored person to be accepted into Northeastern University.

Registrant ID: 146
Name: Clyde Anderson
Railroad: Southern Pacific
Position: Porter
Years of Service: 1898-1958
Submitter's Name: Doris
City/State: Fresno, CA

Registrant ID: 148
Name: Jessie B. Anderson
City/State: Indianapolis, IN
Position: Pullman Porter
Submitter's Name: Carolyn
City/State: Lansing, MI

Registrant ID: 149
Name: Robert L Anderson
City/State: Louisville, KY
Railroad: C&N Company
Position: Porter
Years of Service: 1947
Submitter's Name: Thelma
City/State: Louisville, KY

Registrant ID: 150
Name: Thomas Leroy Anderson
City/State: Park Forest, IL
Railroad: Santa Fe
Years of Service: Early 20's
Submitter's Name: James
City/State: Park Forest, IL
Comments: Grandfather

Registrant ID: 2819
Winston Mosby Anderson
City/State: Washington, DC
Position: Sleeping Cart porter
Years of Service: 1940 -1960
Submitter's Name: Deborah
City/State: Washington, DC
Comments: They called him
back mid-late 60's carried
soldiers to SF from Richmond VA
also Richmond
to Florida.

Registrant ID: 157
Name: C. Anderson McClaith
City/State: Fresno, CA
Railroad: Southern Pacific
Position: Porter
Years of Service: 1898-1958
Submitter's Name: David
City/State: Fresno, CA

Registrant ID: 159
Winston Mosby Anderson, Sr.
Position: Sleeping Car Porter
Service: 1940's
called back in the 1960's
Submitter's Name: Deborah
City/State: Washington, DC

Registrant ID: 163
Name: Charles James Andrews
City/State: Atlanta, GA
Railroad: Santa Fe
Years of Service: 1957-1960's

Registrant ID: 164
Name: Freddie Andrews
City/State: Glen Bernie, MD
Railroad: East Coast
(between PA and NC
Submitter's Name: Lutherina
City/State: Tacoma, WA

Registrant ID: 167
Name: William Andrews
City/State: Detroit, MI
Railroad: New York Central
Position: Pullman Porter
Years of Service: 1945-1970
Submitter's Name: Lunita
City/State: Willow Grove, PA
Comments: My uncle died in
1970. At that time he was still
employed.

Registrant ID: 169
Name: Sam Anthony
Railroad: NW Rail Road
Position: Porters
Years of Service: 1930-1940

Registrant ID: 168
Name: Sam Anthony
Railroad: N W Railroad
Position: Porter
Submitter's Name: Zella
City/State: Homewood, IL

Registrant ID: 173
Name: Webster T. Antoine Sr.
City/State: New Orleans, LA
Position: Car Attendant
Submitter's Name: Weldon .T
City/State: New Orleans, LA
Comments: Retired now

Registrant ID: 176
Name: W. T. Antoine, Sr.
City/State: New Orleans, LA

Years of Service: 1942-1968
Submitter's Name: W.
City/State: New Orleans, LA

Registrant ID: 175
Name: Mr. W. T. Antoine, Sr.
City/State: New Orleans, LA
Years of Service: 1942-1965
Submitter's Name: Mr. W
City/State: New Orleans, LA
Comments: Worked out of New Orleans.

Registrant ID: 180
Name: Elmer Ardrey
City/State: Oakland, CA
Railroad: Southern Pacific
Position: Sleeping Car Porter
Years of Service: 1944-1969
Submitter's Name: Robert
City/State: Fresno, CA
Comments: My Grandfather worked on the Railroad. He worked on the Southern Pacific from 1943-1969 when he retired.

Registrant ID: 182
Name: Stephen Argo
City/State: PA
Railroad: Reading Railroad (Philadelphia, PA.)
Position: Steward
Years of Service: 1935 - 1974
Submitter's Name: Barbara
City/State: Greensboro, NC
Comments: My father, Stephen Argo joined the Reading Railroad Company in 1935 as a waiter, and retired in 1974 as steward from the Philadelphia to New York commuter run.

Registrant ID: 184
Name: Woodrow Armstrong

City/State: AL
Railroad: I don't have the information handy at this moment, however I can get it. I do know he worked out of Chicago, Ill
Position: Pullman Porter
Submitter's Name: Catherine
City/State: Hattiesburg, MS
Comments: I know he talked of how he enjoyed working for the railroad. He didn't get a chance to finish school, but in his spare time on the train, he taught himself to read by reading a lot of books, newspapers and magazines.

Registrant ID: 183
Name: Charlie Armstrong
City/State: Bude, MS
Railroad: Illinois Central
Position: Brakeman
Years of Service: 1941-1960
Submitter's Name: Louis
City/State: Jackson, MS
Comments: Charlie Armstrong was the first African American brakeman to work for the Illinois Central Railroad in the Natchez Mississippi District. He worked at the Roundyard the maintenance facility in Natchez.

Registrant ID: 189
Name: Harry Armstrong III
City/State: Memphis, TN
Railroad: Illinois Central Gulf Rail Road
Position: Pullman Porter
Years of Service: 1968-1991
Submitter's Name: Karen
City/State: Memphis, TN

Registrant ID: 190
Name: Marion Armstrong Sr.
City/State: East Point, GA
Railroad: Southern Railway
Position: Pullman Porter
Years of Service: Early 1940's to mid 1970's
Submitter's Name: Patricia
City/State: East Point, GA
Comments: My father was stationed in Atlanta, Ga. and had regular routes to New York, Washington,D.C. and New Orleans, La. He received several service recognitions awards. M.B. Armstrong Sr. was featured in the Atlanta Journal for his service as a Pullman porter upon his passing in October of 1997 my father (born 1910) had worked for 28 yrs on the railroad until he was furloughed- as did my father's older brother (born 1894) (my uncle) and my uncle's son. They all told stories of the fight to get the union started and of all the prejudice they faced. At one point they had to start their own laundry for the black workers just so they could get their uniforms cleaned; and even so they encountered a lot of resistance. It really was a brotherhood, as they had to stick together just to survive. My father, Lee O. White Sr. and my uncle, Harold White, are now deceased. My cousin, Herbert is in his 70's.

Registrant ID: 191
Name: Fred Arnold
City/State: IL
Position: Chef

Years of Service: 1946-1978
Submitter's Name: Loretta A.
City/State: Dalton, IL

Registrant ID: 193
Name: Robyn Arrington
City/State: AL
Railroad: Line out of New York
Position: Dining Car Waiter
Years of Service: Circa1932-36
Submitter's Name: Bettye
City/State: Bloomfield Hills, MI
Comments: He partially worked his way through Meharry Medical School as a dining car waiter in the summer. He mentioned to me that he worked on a New York railroad that the NY Yankees often used. He remembered meeting Lou Gehrig and others.

Registrant ID: 194
Name: B.W. Art
City/State: Chicago, IL

Registrant ID: 195
Name: Peggy Arthur
City/State: Louisville, KY
Railroad: L&N & B&O
Position: Porter
Years of Service: 1933 & 1934
Submitter's Name: Aaron
City/State: AL
Comments: This is my grandfather and it was before I was born.

Registrant ID: 196
Name: Virginius Southall Ashe
City/State: Bronx, NY
Railroad: Erie Lackawanna
Position: Pullman Porter

Years of Service: 1929 - 1962
Submitter's Name: Eugene
City/State: Beckley, WV
Comments: Our father told us that the only TRUE time was railroad time. As kids we got very excited when our daddy came home from the ROAD. We couldn't wait to explore his black cloth work bag. Among his railroad stuff the work bag always had some goodies.

Registrant ID: 197
Name: Virginus Ashe, Sr.
City/State: NY
Railroad: All I know is he traveled from NY to Chicago
Position: Pullman Porter
Submitter's Name: Donna
City/State: Bronx, NY
Comments: I do know how important the Pullman Porter were in disseminating information throughout the African-American communities.

Registrant ID: 200
Name: Mason Ashley
City/State: AL
Position: Pullman Porter
Years of Service: 1918-1962
Submitter's Name: Grace
City/State: CA

Registrant ID: 201
Chester Arthur Ashworth
City/State: Akron, OH
Railroad: L and N
Position: Pullman Porter
Years of Service: 1920 -1923
Submitter's Name: Doris
City/State: Akron, OH

Comments: Ran from Louisiana to New York

Registrant ID: 203
Name: Joseph James Atkinson
City/State: Washington, DC
Railroad: Atlantic Coast Line East and West Coast Champion
Position: Waiter
Years of Service: 1945-1960
Submitter's Name: Bevelyn
City/State: Capitol Heights, MD

Registrant ID: 204
Name: Gladstone Atwell
Position: Waiter
Years: Late 30's - 40's
Submitter's Name: Joan
City/State: Brooklyn, NY

Registrant ID: 181
Name: Elmer Audrey, Sr.
City/State: AL
Railroad: Southern Pacific
Position: Chair Car Porter
Years of Service: 27
Submitter's Name: Erie
City/State: Highland Village, TX

Registrant ID: 220
Name: Maple Austin
City/State: AL
Railroad: Southern Pacific
Position: Porter
Years of Service: 1955-1980
Submitter's Name: Cheryl
City/State: Chandler, AZ
Comments: Mr. Austin was my uncle. He and my aunt have both passed. Mr. Austin passed in 1997. I am not exactly sure when he started working for the railroad but I was a little girl. He retired when I was an adult.

Registrant ID: 217
Name: Henry O. Austin
City/State: Chicago, IL
Railroad: Santa Fe and Amtrak
(as a security guard)
Position: Pullman Porter
Years of Service: 1930-1980
Submitter's Name: Jan
City/State: Chicago, IL

Registrant ID: 223
Name: Warren Avant
City/State: Jacksonville, FL
Position: Pullman Porter
Years of Service: 1947-1970
Submitter's Name: Phyllis
City/State: Detroit, MI

Registrant ID: 221
Name: Harvey Avant
City/State: Omaha, NE
Railroad: Union Pacific
Position: Pullman Porter
Years of Service: 47 years
Submitter's Name: Jacqueline
City/State: Omaha, NE

Registrant ID: 230
Name: C.B. Bailey
Position: Pullman Porter
Years of Service: Over 25
Comments: B.S.C.P Union .

Registrant ID: 245
Name: S.J. Bailey
Position: Pullman Porter
Years of Service: Over 25
Comments: Member of B.S.C.P
union

Registrant ID: 236
Name: Clinton Bailey
City/State: Belleville, MI
Position: Pullman Porter

Submitter's Name: Karen
City/State: Detroit, MI
Comments: I think his run was
Detroit Chicago. He would be
gone for a week at a time. And he
retired form service I would think
in the early 1970's

Registrant ID: 246
Name: William Bailey
City/State: Roseville, CA
Railroad: Southern Pacific
Years of Service: 1954-1958
Submitter's Name: Bethany
City/State: East Hartford, CT
Comments: This was my
grandfather who is now
deceased. I'm not sure of any
other information at this time.
Deceased

Registrant ID: 249
Name: William Bailey
City/State: Kansas City, KS
Railroad: Kansas City Southern
Position: Porter
Years of Service: 1938-69
Submitter's Name: Erma
City/State: Kansas City, KS
Comments: I think my father
really enjoyed his work there.
When we were small he would
always bring us books that were
left on the train. Even tell us
stories. But I think best of all we
would get a railroad pass and go
to Texas every summer for
vacations.

Registrant ID: 238
Name: Edward Bailey
City/State: Kansas City, KS
Railroad: Kansas City Southern

Position: Train Porter
Years of Service: 1904 - 1934
Submitter's Erma, Louise
City/State: Kansas City, KS
Comments: He was my grandfather. I barely remember him I was 5 yrs old when he passed.

Registrant ID: 250
Name: William Bailey
City/State: Kansas City, KS
Railroad: Kansas City Southern
Position: Porter
Years of Service: 1938-1969
Submitter's Name: Rose
City/State: Kansas City, MO

Registrant ID: 242
Name: Harry Bailey
City/State: Chicago, IL
Railroad: Santa Fe
Position: Dining Car Waiter
Years of Service: 1922 - 58
Submitter's Name: Lois
City/State: Union City, CA
Comments: My grandfather and his brother, Walter Bailey, worked for the Sante Fe Railroad for over 36 years. I was told that they worked longer than than any other Dining Car waiter. As a child, I remember stories from my grandfather about serving famous movie stars.

Registrant ID: 251
Name: Walter L. Bailey Sr.
City/State: Memphis, TN
Railroad: Illinois Centra and Amtrak
Position: Mail handler and Pullman porter
Years of Service: 1955-1980

Submitter's Name: D'Army
City/State: Memphis, TN
Comments: Bailey was a Porter for Illinois Central Gulf Railroad and Amtrak for some 25 years, working aboard the City of New Orleans passenger train, which serves cities between New Orleans and Chicago. He frequently attended national checkers conventions.

Registrant ID: 254
Name: Prophet I. Bailey, Sr.
City/State: Washington, DC
Railroad: NY to Miami Line
Position: Pullman Porter
Years of Service: 1925-1950
Submitter's Name: George C.
City/State: Washington, DC

Registrant ID: 256
Name: Joseph Bain
City/State: Jamaica, NY
Position: Waiter
Years of Service: 1948-1969
Submitter's Name: Willie
City/State: Greensboro, NC

Registrant ID: 255
Name: Joseph Bain
City/State: Jamaica, NY

Railroad: NY Central
Position: Waiter
Years of Service: 1932-1959
Submitter's Name: Jean
City/State: Jamaica, NY
Comments: In 2003 at he is 103 years and still with us.

Registrant ID: 260
Name: Paul Baker
City/State: NC

Railroad: Atlantic Coast Line
Position: Track Worker
Years of Service: 5 Years
Submitter's Name: Cynthia
City/State: Bronx, NY

Registrant ID: 258
Name: John "J.C." Baker
City/State: Laurel, MS
Position: Pullman Porter
Years of Service: Unk start date
–through 1928
Submitter's Name: Melverta
City/State: Buffalo, NY

Registrant ID: 261
Name: James Edward Baldwin
Railroad: Union Pacific
Position: Porter
Years of Service: 49 Years
Submitter's Name: Deborah

Registrant ID: 264
Name: Franklin (Frank) Ball
City/State: Chicago, IL
Position: Pullman Porter
Years of Service: 1930-50s
Submitter's Name: Marjorie
City/State: Detroit, MI
Comments: Mr. Ball lived in
Chicago on South Park Way. He
did runs from Chicago to Los
Angeles and from Chicago to
Florida. He was born August
1913 and died in Chicago in
November 1967. He was my
uncle's (younger brother of my
father), and was also known as
Sonny.

Registrant ID: 263
Name: Clemen Franklin Ball
City/State: Chicago, IL

Railroad: Pullman Company
Position: Pullman Porter
Years of Service: 1946 - 1967
Submitter's Name: Alfred
City/State: Somerset, NJ

Registrant ID: 268
Name: Robert Ballard
City/State: Detroit, MI
Railroad: Pullman Company
Position: Porter
Years of Service: 1948-1968
Submitter's Name: Constante

Registrant ID: 266
Name: Ralph Ballard
City/State: Atlanta, GA
Position: Cook
Years of Service: 20 plus
Submitter's Name: DeBorah
City/State: Los Angeles, CA
Comments: My grandfather is
deceased, however as a child I
always heard about what he did
to provide for his family. His son
Ralph Ballard Jr. is still alive.

Registrant ID: 265
Name: Calvin D. Ballard
City/State: Bowie, MD
Position: Dining Car Waiter
Years of Service: 1945-1946
Submitter's Name: Anna M.
City/State: Washington, DC

Registrant ID: 269
Name: William Baltimore Jr.
City/State: Elizabeth, NJ
Railroad: Conrail
Position: Trainmen
Years of Service: 30
Submitter's Name: Shron
City/State: Montclair, NJ

Comments: My dad died before his retirement eligibility.

Registrant ID: 273
Name: Sandy Alexnader Banks
City/State: Philadelphia, AL
Railroad: New York
Position: Porter/ Conductor
Years of Service: Retired when Pullman Company closed
Submitter's Name: Geraldine
City/State: Philadelphia, AL
Comments: My father Sandy Alexander Banks started with the railroad at the age of 18 years. His father Sandy E.T. Banks was a Redcap. When I was a child my father went from Pennsylvania station in New York to California. He would be gone for about two weeks.

Registrant ID: 272
Name: Fred Banks
City/State: KS
Railroad: Pullman Company
Position: Porter
Submitter's Name: Beverly
City/State: Wichita, KS
Comments: Fred was born in La Porte, Indiana 1880

Registrant ID: 274
Name: Arnold Bankston, Sr.
City/State: AL
Railroad: Union Pacific
Position: Porter
Years of Service: Early 1900's
Submitter's Name: Adrienne
City/State: Ontario, CA
Comments: My father passed away 14 years ago so I haven't gotten any info about

grandfather. All I knew is that he was a wonderful man.

Registrant ID: 275
Name: E.M. Barbee
Position: Pullman Porter
Years of Service: 25 Plus
Comments: He was an active union member

Registrant ID: 276
Name: Charles Barber
City/State: College Park, GA
Railroad: Pennsylvania RR
Position: Parlor Car Attendant
Years of Service: 26
Submitter's Name: Charles
City/State: New Orleans, LA
Comments: My Father, Charles H. Barber, was a Parlor Car Attendant and a Club Car attendant for Pennsylvania Rail Road for about 20 years. His run was from Boston to Miami and from N.Y. to Washington D.C. The last 6 years of service was with Amtrak when they took over.

Registrant ID: 277
Name: Vaughn Barber, Sr.
City/State: Chicago, IL
Railroad: Chicago to California
Position: Dining Car Porter
Submitter's Name: Vaughn
City/State: Chicago, IL

Registrant ID: 278
Name: John Barnabus
Position: Clerk
Submitter's Name: Edwina
City/State: Brooklyn,

Registrant ID: 280
Name: Cherry Leon Barnes
City/State: San Francisco, CA
Railroad: Southern Pacific
Position: Red Cap
Years of Service: 1924 -1962
Submitter's Name: Joana
City/State: AL

Registrant ID: 282
AbbLeon Leon Barnes, Sr.
Position: Pullman Porter
Years of Service: 1940-1974
Submitter's Name: Elvira

Registrant ID: 287
Name: Ms. Barnett
City/State: Oakland, CA
Railroad: South Carolina RR
Years of Service: 1969

Registrant ID: 286
Name: Herman Barnett
City/State: Chicago, IL
Railroad: Illinois Central
Position: Pullman Porter
Submitter's Name: Lezah M.
City/State: Hammond, IN
Comments: Herman Roosevelt Barnett worked for the Illinois Central Railroad during the depression years. Born in 1909, in 1930 he was 21. It has been said by many relatives and extended family members that without my father and other Pullman porters, many would not have had much to eat during that time. His job was the most money to be made during the depression by African-American males. Being a Pullman Porter financed his education and went on to receive a Masters degree

from George Williams College in 1953. He joined the Alpha fraternity during the 1940's and was extremely active in union, housing, labor and civil rights organizations of this period.

Registrant ID: 284
Name: Edward Barnett
City/State: AL
Position: Pullman Porter
Years of Service: 1945?--1959
Submitter's Name: Yvonne
City/State: New York City, NY
Comments: My father lived in Chicago, Illinois. He was on a line that went West. He was often in ST. Paul Minneapolis. He went to Mexico at least one time.

Registrant ID: 289
Name: James Barr
City/State: Prairie Du Chien, WI
Position: Porter
Years of Service: 1880's per the 1880 census.
Submitter's Name: Vega
City/State: San Francisco, CA
Comments: My family was searching the internet and found in the 1880 census my great grandfather and his wife and children. Among them my grandfather, was listed as "Sleeping Car Porter" and since he was black, I thought he would have worked for Pullman.

Registrant ID: 290
Name: Commodore Barrett
City/State: Jamaica, NY
Position: Waiter
Years of Service: 6 Years

Registrant ID: 294
Name: Woody Walter Barrett
Railroad: Illinois Central
Position: Fireman
Years of Service: 1930-1970
Submitter's Name: Billie Jean
City/State: Los Angeles, CA

Registrant ID: 292
Name: Moses Barrett
City/State: Ridgeway, SC
Railroad: Pennsylvania RR
And Amtrak RR
Position: Car Cleaner/Yardman
Years of Service: 35
Submitter's Name: Carol
City/State: New York, NY
Comments: Moses Barrett began
working for Pennsylvania RR in
the Compton-Laclede RR yards
in St. Louis, Mo. Around 1966
he was transferred to the N.Y.
City RR Yards. He began
working as a Yardman and Car
Cleaner. He retired 1976.

Registrant ID: 296
Name: Claude Barrow
Submitter's Name: Rev.Willie
City/State: Chicago, IL
Comments: Wife

Registrant ID: 297
Name: Chester " Bob" Bassett
City/State: Peoria, IL
Railroad: Rock Island Railroad
Position: Track Department
Maintenance of way
Years of Service: 1940's
Submitter's Name: Rose
City/State: Peoria, IL

Registrant ID: 300
Name: Josh Bates

City/State: AL
Railroad: El Paso
Years of Service: 1977's
Submitter's Name: Lawrence
City/State: AL

Registrant ID: 301
Name: Lee Bates
City/State: Washington, DC
Railroad: Pennsylvania
Position: Porter
Years of Service: 1930s
Submitter's Name: Willene
City/State: Arlington, VA

Registrant ID: 299
Name: Elmo Bates
City/State: Washington, DC
Railroad: Pennsylvania
Position: Bartender and waiter
Years of Service: 1930s
Submitter's Name: Willene
City/State: Arlington, VA

Registrant ID: 304
Name: Livingston Batteast
City/State: AL
Railroad: I believe it was the
Southern Pacific -Train Name:
City of San Francisco)
Position: Pullman Porter
Years of Service: 1930-1965
Submitter's Name: Angela
City/State: Chicago, IL

Registrant ID: 305
Name: Leo Bausley
City/State: Marshall, TX
Railroad: Missouri Pacific and
Amtrak
Position: Dining Car Waiter
Years of Service: 30 Plus
Submitter's Name: Janice
City/State: Fort worth, TX

Comments: When he worked for Missouri Pacific he was stationed in St Louis Missouri. He had the Little Rock to St. Louis route

Registrant ID: 306
Name: Claude Baxter
City/State: Philadelphia, PA
Position: Pullman Porter
Years of Service: 1930's
Submitter's Name: Vivian A.
City/State: Hephzibah, GA
Comments: I remember seeing pictures of my uncle with his Pullman Porter hat. He was very proud to be working for the railroad. I tell my sons all the time that my uncle was a Pullman Porter. I am glad they are being recognized.

Registrant ID: 307
Name: Milton Bayard Sr.
City/State: Blufield, WV
Position: Porter
Years of Service: 1870
Submitter's: Vera Maxine
City/State: Columbus, OH

Registrant ID: 308
Name: Arthur G. Sr. Baylor
City/State: Philadelphia, PA
Railroad: Pennsylvania RR
Position: Sleeping Car Porter
Years of Service: 1922-1952
Submitter's Arthur G. & Alicia
City/State: Philadelphia, PA
Comments: Arthur was my father who for many years was a Sleeping Car Porter on the New York City to Miami, FL run. He left the family home in Germantown, Philadelphia,

Pennsylvania on Monday mornings and returned on Thursday evenings of the same week. He also made several special trips to Yellowstone Park serving as the Sleeping Car Porter for special groups. I also remember my father serving as the Sleeping Car Porter for Princeton University Male Glee Club as it toured the country in the late twenties or early thirties. Pullman Porters stayed at his house in Philadelphia because of segregation. However, my father did not join the Sleeping Car Porter's Union for personal reasons although he was asked to join many times. My father retired about 1952 after 30 years service as a Pullman Sleeping Car Porter. He died in 1967 at 80 years old.

Registrant ID: 309
Name: King Richard Bayne
City/State: Los Angeles, CA

Registrant ID: 310
Name: Lester Bazel
Position: Porter
Years of Service: Circa WWII - 1960
Submitter's Name: Agustin
City/State: Chicago, IL
Registrant ID: 312
Name: Guy Demarcus Beale
Position: Pullman Porter
Years of Service: 1937-1960
Submitter's Name: John D.
City/State: Philadelphia, PA

Registrant ID: 314
Name: John D. Beale Jr.

City/State: Philadelphia., PA
Railroad: Pennsylvania Railroad
Position: Pullman Porter
Years of Service: 1937-1960
Submitter's Name: Guy
Demarcus
City/State: AL

Registrant ID: 315
Name: Howard Beamer
City/State: Cleveland, OH
Registrant ID: 316
Name: Edgar Randoph Beanum
City/State: New York, NY
Railroad: Pullman Company
Position: Pullman Porter
Years of Service: Circa-1908
Submitter's Name: Beanum

Registrant ID: 317
Name: Tom Beardy
City/State: AL
Railroad: Pullman/Chicago
Position: Clean the trains
Years of Service: 1942
Submitter's Name: Luella
City/State: Las Vegas, NV
Comments: My mother also
worked on this railroad as well.
Her name Is Mary Maniece-
Meardy but she spells her
married name Merdy.

Registrant ID: 319
Name: Preston Beasley
Railroad: Santa Fe
Submitter's Name: Harriet
City/State: Chicago, IL

Registrant ID: 318
Name: Joseph Beasley
City/State: Chicago, IL
Railroad: Illinois Central
Submitter's Name: Harriet

City/State: Chicago, IL

Registrant ID: 4291
Soyer William Beatley
City/State: Browns Mills, NJ
Railroad: U.S Canada Route
Years of Service: 1920
Submitter's Name: Claurene B
City/State: Brownsmills, NJ

Registrant ID: 321
Name: Adam H. Beatty
City/State: New York, NY
Railroad: Penn Central
Position: Pullman Porter
Years of Service 30 years.
Submitte(s): Letitia
City/State: High Point, NC

Registrant ID: 323
Name: Prentice Jr. Beaty
City/State: Winslow, AZ
Submitter's Name: Donnie
City/State: Altadena, CA

Registrant ID: 324
Name: Howard Beckett
City/State: Baltimore, MD
Railroad: B&O railroad
Position: Cook
Submitter's Name: Steven
City/State: Levittown, PA

Registrant ID: 325
William McKinley Beckton
City/State: Philadelphia, PA
Railroad: Reading Railroad
Position: Foreman, Trackman
Years of Service: 1949- 1999
Submitter's: Monica, Jamilah
City/State: Philadelphia, PA
Comments: My father was a very
strong individual with a great big

arms, and shoulder muscles. He sometimes brought home the pick and the hammer he used to hammer the nails in the track with. Of course, they replaced that system with a machine. He faced discrimination as well.

Registrant ID: 326
Name: John Samuel Beecham
City/State: Philadelphia, AL
Position: Porter
Years of Service: 1909 - 1920
Submitter's Name: Barry
City/State: Philadelphia, PA
Comments: My Grandfather was also a Pullman Porter. He died in 1963, I was 13 years old when he died. He told me stories of his experience as a soldier, With WWI and Black Jack Pershing.

Registrant ID: 329
Name: Gillmore Belcher
City/State: NY
Position: Porter
Years of Service: 1945-1970
Submitter's Name: Anthony
City/State: NY

Registrant ID: 333
Name: DeMilt Bell
City/State: Kansas City, MO
Position: Pullman Porter
Years: Retired in the 1960's
Submitter's Name: Joann

Registrant ID: 339
Name: Nedra Bell
City/State: Dublin, CA
Railroad: Southern Pacific
Position: Porter
Submitter's: Wayne Simon
City/State: CT

Registrant ID: 330
Name: Charles Monroe Bell
City/State: Albany, CA
Railroad: California-Between Oakland and Chicago
Years of Service: 50's-60's
Submitter's Name: Gloria
City/State: Alvany, CA
Comments: Father in law

Registrant ID: 342
Name: Spencer Bell
City/State: AL
Railroad: Zephyr
Position: Porter
Years of Service: 1940's-60's
Submitter's Name: Craig
City/State: Brooklyn, NY
Comments: My father worked for years as a Porter and a Dinning Car Waiter on a number of other trains (Penn, NY Central) In addition, my step father, Richard Rouse, worked waiter, as a Dining Car Steward.

Registrant ID: 340
Name: Q Bell
City/State: Buffalo, NY
Position: Nurse
Years of Service: 1969-2002
Submitter's Name: Sara
City/State: Buffalo, NY

Registrant ID: 344
Name: Spencer B. Bell
City/State: Chicago, IL
Railroad: Great Northern, Santa Fe, NY Central,
Position: Pullman Porter
Years of Service: 1937-1974
Submitter's Name: Julia P.
City/State: Chicago, IL

Comments: My father, Spencer B. Bell, was a proud, hard-working man who instilled in his children a very positive work ethic. We graduated from college and reached high levels of achievement in our chosen fields. More importantly, my dad taught us how to negotiate through life's adversities and to meet each day in a positive manner. I contracted polio at five years of age and my parents were told I would never walk. My dad refused to accept that prognosis and found a specialist that was willing to perform experimental surgery on me. My dad's tenacity made it possible for me to walk and lead a normal life. Upon retiring I was one of the highest ranked Black women in my corporation. The Brotherhood of Sleeping Car Porters gave my dad life choices that poor Black men seldom got, and he, in return, provided opportunities to his children."

Registrant ID: 335
Name: Earl Cranston Bell
City/State: IL
Position: Waiter-Porter
Years of Service: 1930's-50's
Submitter's Name: Lucille
City/State: Chicago, IL

Registrant ID: 336
Name: Gold Bell
City/State: AL
Railroad: Union Pacific
Position: Pullman Porter
Years of Service: 1920s-1940s
Submitter's Name: Jacqueline

City/State: Dallas, TX
Comments: I don't know much. My uncles Gold, Dos and Norman (my grandfather's brothers) worked on the line between Texas and Los Angeles where they eventually settled.

Registrant ID: 337
Name: Julius Nathaniel Bell
Railroad: Southern Railroad
Position: Porter
Submitter's Name: Barbara
City/State: Nashville, TN

Registrant ID: 338
Name: Julius Nathaniel Bell
City/State: Nashville, TN
Railroad: Southern Railroad
Position: Porter
Submitter's Name: Barbara
City/State: Nashville, TN
Comments: Her father, she remembers a secret meeting with Mr. Randolph with her father.

Registrant ID: 345
Name: Joe Belser
City/State: AL

Railroad: Louisville & Nashville
Position: Machinist
Years of Service: 1920-1960
Submitter's Name: Carolyn
City/State: Detroit, MI
Comments: Joe was my maternal grandfather. He worked for the Louisville/Nashville Railroad, Union Station, Montgomery, Alabama, starting in 1920 as a "Red Cap". He was a good worker and liked so much that he was given a job as a

machinist. He retired from the L & N Railroad.

Registrant ID: 346
Name: Russell J. Benjamin
City/State: New York, NY
Railroad: New York Central
Position: Pullman Porter
Submitter's Name: LaVerne
City/State: Hempstead, NY
Comments: Mr. Benjamin was my grandfather. One of his runs, was to Chicago. He was also a graduate of Dillard University in Louisianna. He died in 1986 at the age of 88.

Registrant ID: 348
Name: Arthur Benner
City/State: Minneapolis, MN
Railroad: GN
Position: Porter
Comments: It was one of the best job a student could have.

Registrant ID: 353
Name: Adell Bennett
City/State: West Point, MS
Railroad: Pullman Co. headquarters Memphis, TN
Position: Pullman Porter
Years of Service: 1940's until
Submitter's Name: Charles D.
City/State: West Point, MS
Comments: He traveled with the soldiers during world War II and President Harry S. Truman was the president. He lived away from home with his headquarters being in Memphis, TN. We have postcards he sent from the majority of the states that he traveled to.

Registrant ID: 355
Name: Andy "Frog" Bennett
City/State: Lewisburg, TN
Railroad: Hummingbird, Dixie
Position: dining car waiter
Years of Service: Before 1945
Submitter's Name: Zonna
City/State: Lewisburg, TN

Registrant ID: 361
Name: Charles Richard Bennett
Position: Porter
Years of Service: 1901-1935
Submitter's Name: Phyllis
City/State: Kendall Prk., NJ

Registrant ID: 362
Name: Julius Kelsey Bennett
City/State: Philadelphia, AL
Railroad: Pullman Company, Pennsylvania RR
Position: Busboy, cook
Years of Service: 1945-1961
Submitter's Name: Stephanie
City/State: Cape May, NJ
Comments: Worked his way up from Bus boy to Cook on railroad line Philadelphia to Miami FL.

Julius K. Bennett 4th from the -L

Registrant ID: 363
Name: George William Bentley
City/State: Brownsmills, NY
Years of Service: 1920's
Submitter's Name: Clarence B.

Registrant ID: 365
Name: James Bentley Smith
City/State: Nashville, TN
Railroad: Pullman Company
Position: Porter
Years of Service: 1936-1970
Submitter's Name: Colhert S.

Registrant ID: 366
Name: L Benton
City/State: Abilene, TX
Position: Pullman Porter
Submitter's Name: D A. C
City/State: Abolene, TX

Registrant ID: 367
Name: Levi Jesse Jr. Benton
City/State: Harlington, TX

Position: Brakeman and Conductor
Years of Service: 1935-75
Submitter's Name: Kenneth J.
City/State: Harlington, TX

Registrant ID: 369
Name: Joseph Berchana
Position: Porter
Years of Service: 1905
Submitter's Name: Edwina M.
City/State: Brooklyn, NY

Registrant ID: 371
Name: Claude Berger, Sr.
City/State: Washington, DC
Railroad: C&O
Position: Dinning Car Waiter
Years of Service: 1936-1949
Submitter's Name: Vera E
City/State: Washington, DC
Comments: Father in-law he worked for 13 years.

Registrant ID: 373
Name: Earnest Henry Bernard
City/State: Oakland, CA
Position: Dining Car Waiter
Years of Service: 1944-19
Submitter's Name: Mrs. Evelyn
City/State: Oakland, CA
Comments: Widow

Registrant ID: 375
Name: Johnny Bernstein
City/State: Mobile, AL
Position: Track layer
Years of Service: 1930's-40's
Submitter's Name: Audra
City/State: Chicago, IL
Comments: Submitted by his sister Octavia C. and his grandniece Audra

Registrant ID: 374
Name: Theodore Berrien
City/State: AL
Railroad: Southern Railroad
Position: Pullman Porter
Service: Circa l940's to 1969
Submitter's Name: Corliss
City/State: College Park, Ga, AL
Comments: My grandfather was chosen to accompany President Roosevelt's remains from Washington to his home in Georgia. He spoke of how kind Mrs. Roosevelt was in thanking him for his services during the trip.

Registrant ID: 377
Name: Horace Sr. Berry
Railroad: Pennsylvania
Position: Pullman Car porter
Submitter's Name: Ronal W Sr.
Comments: My Father, worked on the railroad for 44 years.

Registrant ID: 378
Name: Ronnie Berry
Railroad: Penn Railroad
Position: Sleeping Car Porter
Years of Service: 44 Years

Registrant ID: 383
Name: Clarence M. Sr. Berry
City/State: Evanston, IL
Railroad: Amtrak
Position: Pullman Porter
Years of Service: 1937-1968
City/State: AL

Registrant ID: 376
Name: Clarence C. Berry
City/State: Chicago, IL
Railroad: Basedout of Chicago, IL
Position: Pullman Porter

Years: Circa: 1933-1970
Submitter's Name: Sandra G.
City/State Shaker Heights, OH
Comments: My Uncle Clarence, who is deceased, was one of those black men who had a college education in the '30s, but could not find a comparable position to his education level because of racial discrimination. He found the travel of a Pullman Porter exciting and educational, and stayed with the Company for 35 years, retiring in the early 1970's.

Registrant ID: 382
Name: Zachariah Berry
City/State: Washington, DC
Railroad: Pullman Company
Position: Porter-Attendant
Years of Service: 1924-1963
Submitter's Name: Evelyn
City/State: Washington, DC
Comments: I am providing this information on behalf of myself and my children. My husband began his services for the Pullman Company as a porter and retired in the position of Attendant after more than 30 years of service. He was active in the formation of the union.

Registrant ID: 386
Name: Hershel Best, Sr.
City/State: No. Babylon, NY
Position: Passenger Conductor
Years of Service: 1955-1992

Registrant ID: 387
Name: Robert Cullie Bethea
Position: Pullman Porter
Years of Service: 39 Years

Submitter's Name: Maggie
City/State: Danville, IL

Registrant ID: 388
Emerson Alonzo Jr. Bettis
Railroad: L&M RR
Position: Sleeping Car Porter
Years of Service: 1932-1940
Submitter's Name: Alice Bettis
City/State: Prospect, KY
Comments: Worked for 8yrs out of Louisville, KY Deceased

Registrant ID: 389
Emerson Alonzo Bettis, Jr.
Railroad: L & M
Position: Sleeping Car Porter
Years of Service: 1932-1940
Submitter's Name: Alice
City/State: Prospect, KY

Registrant ID: 391
Name: Leon Beverly Sr.
Railroad: The Missouri Pacific
Position: Pullman Porter
Service: Late 1920's- 1950's
Submitter's Name: Danice
City/State: Las Vegas, NV
Comments: Leon Rupert Beverly Sr. is my uncle. Information provided by my mother. His run was from San Antonio, Texas to St. Louis, Mo. Occasionally the train would run to Laredo, TX. He was a WWI veteran and is buried at Fort Sam Houston in San Antonio, TX.

Registrant ID: 392
Name: Isaac Cook Bey
City/State: Chicago, IL
Submitter's Name: Sabrina Lee
City/State: Chicago, IL
Comments: Great Grandfather

Registrant ID: 393
Benjamin Franklin Bezzell
City/State: Milwaukee, WI
Position: Clerk
Years of Service: 1969-1971

Registrant ID: 395
Name: Morris Biggers
City/State: Dennison, TX
Position: Pullman Porter
Years of Service: 1926
Submitter's Name: Morris
City/State: Washington, DC
Comments: My Great Grandfather was Mathew Biggers and his son Morris Biggers were both railroad men. Pullman Porters.

Registrant ID: 396
Name: James E. Biggs, Jr.
City/State: Boston, MA
Position: Porter
Years of Service: 1930's - 1950's
Submitter's Name: Maria
City/State: Indianapolis, IN

Registrant ID: 397
Name: George Bigsby
Position: Cook
Years of Service: 1920-1940
Submitter's Name: Diane
City/State: Athens, GA

Registrant ID: 398
Name: Andrew Eldrige Bishop
City/State: Lisle, IL
Railroad: Santa Fe
Position: Dining Car Waiter
Submitter's Name: Joseph
City/State: Lisle, IL
Comments: He was my father

Registrant ID: 402
Name: Henry Blackburn
City/State: Chicago, IL
Position: Porter
Years of Service: 1942-1953
Submitter's Name: Joyce
City/State: Chicago, IL

Registrant ID: 401
Name: Elias Blackburn
City/State: Cincinnati, OH
Railroad: Chesapeake and Ohio
Position: Porter
Years of Service: 1925-
Submitter's Name: Luvenia
City/State: Cleveland, OH
Comments: Mr. Blackburn had
encountered a lot of prejudice
during his term of employment.
He resigned from his job after
World War II started.

Registrant ID: 403
Name: Albert B. Blackman
City/State: Chicago, IL
Position: Head Burret Porter
Years of Service: 30 Years
Submitter's Name: Venetia C.
City/State: Great Lakes, IL

Registrant ID: 404
Name: Henry Blackmon
City/State: Sedalia, NC
Railroad: Southern Railroad
Years of Service: 1943-1970
Submitter's Name: Henry
City/State: Sedalia, NC
Comments: Worked for 27 years

Registrant ID: 405
Name: Amos Blackwell
Railroad: Chesapeake & Ohio
Position: Sleeping Car Porter
Years of Service: 1930s-1950s

Submitter's Name: Edda
Comments: Father's friend and
not sure about the info

Registrant ID: 406
Name: Lovett Blackwell
City/State: OH
Railroad: NY Central "El
Capatain,
Cincinnati to Chicago to LA
Position: Dining Car Waiter
Years of Service: Early
1940's-60's
Submitter's Name: Laurence
City/State: Alameda, CA

Registrant ID: 407
Name: Edward Norman Blair
City/State: Edenton, NC
Railroad: Norfolk & Western
Position: Pullman Porter
Years of Service: 1935-1951
Submitter's Name: E. Lorraine
City/State: DC
Comments: Mr. Blair was Miss
Cherry's uncle.

Registrant ID: 408
Name: Henry Blair
City/State: AL
Railroad: B/E
Out of St. Louis, MO
Position: Pullman Porter
Submitter's Name: Edward
City/State: San Diego, CA
Comments: My father left his
family of 12 children in 1953 and
went to Chicago. He started to
work on the railroad shortly after
that. He would come home to St.
Louis, MO on some weekends
and bring us food and money for
my mother.

Registrant ID: 410
Name: Robert Blair
City/State: Baltimore, MD

Registrant ID: 412
Name: Robert Blake
City/State: Augusta, GA
Railroad: Southern Railway-ACL
Position: Porter
Years of Service: 1900-1907
Submitter's Name: Maranda
City/State: Columbia, SC
Comments: This information was given to me by my mother who was born in 1912. She did not know the name of the Railroad that he worked on. Just that it ran between Charleston, SC and Augusta, Georgia.

Registrant ID: 415
Name: Theodore W. Blakeney
City/State: Fort Washington, MD
Railroad: Pullman; Pennsylvania; Seaboard; Santa Fe ; Long Island
Position: Pullman Porter, Cook, waiter, and Bartender
Years of Service: 1942-1978
Submitter's Name: Gardenia
City/State: Fort Washington, MD
Comments: My father was very active in the Brotherhood of Sleeping Car Porters Union. He attended meetings at the DC local regularly.

Registrant ID: 3719
Name: Charles Smith Blame
City/State: Detroit, Michigan
Position: Sleeping Car Porter
Years of Service: 1920

Submitter's Name: Smith

Registrant ID: 416
Name: Jerry T. Blanchard
City/State: Cleveland, OH
Position: Porter
Years of Service: 1920-1935
Submitter's Name: Raquel A.
City/State: Euclid, OH
Comments: Grand-daughter

Registrant ID: 417
Name: Aaron Bland
City/State: OH

Registrant ID: 419
Name: Ellotions Blanks
City/State: Philadelphia, PA
Position: Porter
Submitter's Name: Don
City/State: Philadelphia, PA

Registrant ID: 420
Name: Henry Blanks
City/State: MO
Railroad: The Pullman Co Trains out of St. Louis
Position: Pullman Porter
Years of Service: 1941-1969
Submitter's Name: Cynthia
City/State: Saint Louis, MO
Comments: My father is now deceased, however I have fond memories of him talking about the CC camps, during the war. Transporting the soldiers

Registrant ID: 421
Name: Howard Blassengale
City/State: Horst M Boyd, NJ
Railroad: NY Pullman/Amtrak
Position: Sleeping Car Porter
Years of Service: 1934-1969
Submitter's Name: Ruth A

City/State: Horst M Boyd, NJ

Registrant ID: 1582
Name: Richard T Hardy-Blount
City/State: LA, CA
Position: Porter
Submitter's Name: Mr. Albert
City/State: AL

Registrant ID: 423
Name: Ervin James Blue, Sr.
City/State: CA
Railroad: Southern Pacific
Position: Pullman Porter
Years of Service: Circa
1935 - 1941
Submitter's Name: Janet
City/State: Oakland, CA
Comments: My grandfather
worked a line that went from
Louisiana to California. It also
went through Chicago. My
grandfather had the
nickname of 'Big Blue' because of
his size (6'8")and 'Blue' his last
name. Eventually as a result of
his exposure during his run to
California, my grandfather
moved his family from Louisiana
to California--where we took root
and continued to reside.

Registrant ID: 424
Name: Howard Hobart Bluff
Position: Pullman Porter
Years of Service: 1922-1956
Submitter's Name: Birdie
City/State: Chicago, IL

Registrant ID: 425
Name: Charles L. Bocage
City/State: New Orleans, LA
Submitter's Name: Charlotte
City/State: Los Angeles, CA

Registrant ID: 426
Name: George Bolden
City/State: IL
Position: Pullman Porter
Submitter's Name: Deborah
City/State: Chicago, IL
Comments: This gentleman was
a neighbor of ours when we lived
on the 72nd block of Indiana
from 1969 to the present. He has
since moved and we have lost
contact with him but my Mom
and I remember him as a
railroad man.

Registrant ID: 428
Name: Clifton Bolds
City/State: Chicago, IL
Railroad: Penn Central
Position: Pullman Porter
Years of Service: 1920 -1970
Submitter's Name: Kersey
City/State: Chicago, IL

Registrant ID: 429
Name: Robert Bomer L
City/State: Central City,
Railroad: Pullman Company
Position: Brakeman
Years of Service: 1968-1993

Registrant ID: 430
Name: Frank Bone
City/State: Nashville, TN
Railroad: Louisville & Nashville
Position: Pullman Porter
Years of Service: 32 years,
Circa 1926-1958
Submitter's Name: Stephanie
City/State: Newport News, VA
Comments: Information given
above was my father's home
address while he was employed

with the railroad. He died in 1974.

Registrant ID: 431
Name: Booker T. Bonner
Position: Pullman Porter
Years of Service: Over 25
Comments: B.S.C.P Union member. Member

Registrant ID: 432
Name: Norman Bonner, Sr.
City/State: Far Rockaway, NY
Position: Porter
Submitter's Name: Valerie
City/State: Far Rockaway, NY
Comments: Ruth Bonner, Wife Of Porter Norman Bonner Jr. Austin TX Lawyer.

Registrant ID: 433
Name: Eugene E Bonser
City/State: Indianapolis, IN
Position: Porter
Years of Service: 1942-1984
Submitter's Name: Emery D
City/State: Chicago, IL

Registrant ID: 438
Name: Randle Robert Booker
City/State: MS
Railroad: Circa Illinois Central.
Position: Brake-man
Years of Service: Circa 1900
Submitter's Name: Eddaq
City/State: St. Louis , MO
Comments: This is one of my grandmother's uncles. He was born in Yalobusha County in 1870, had an accident where his pelvis or lower abdomen was crushed in the late 1890s. He then went on to become one of the founding elders of the Church of God in Christ.

Registrant ID: 441
Name: Walter E. Boone
City/State: Montclair, NJ
Position: Dining Car Waiter

Registrant ID: 439
Name: Charles W. Boone
Position: Pullman Porter
Years of Service: 25 Years
Comments: He was active with the BSCP Union

Registrant ID: 440
Name: Edom Henry Boone
City/State: St. Louis, MO
Railroad: Missouri Pacific
Position: Pullman Porter
Years of Service: 1942-1945
Submitter's Name: Leonard
City/State: St. Louis , MO
Comments: My father speaks proudly and fondly of the years he spent as a Pullman Porter during WWII.

Registrant ID: 442
Name: Sammy Lee Boose
City/State: AR
Railroad: Cottonbell
Position: Turn-engine
Years of Service: 7 or 8 years
Submitter's Name: Mildred
City/State: Southfield, MI
Comments: He was my aunt's husband who died 4 or 5 years ago. According to my aunt her husband's job was to turn the engine around. I am not sure of what position you would call this, but he worked there for 7 or 8 years.

Registrant ID: 443
Name: John R. Borum, Sr.
City/State: College Park, GA
Railroad: L&N Railroad
Position: Coach Attendant
Years of Service: 1944-1969
Comments: Too numerous to mention. Long hours, low pay!!!!!

Registrant ID: 444
Name: Robert Bosley
City/State: Kansas City, MO
Railroad: Rock Island Railroad
Position: Dining Car Waiter
Submitter's Name: Melanie
City/State: St. Louis , MO
Comments: Robert Bosley was my great-grand uncle. He was born in 1886. Started working for the railroad about 1939. He retired in 1961 after 22 years of service. I was told that he worked as a Dining Car Waiter on a private railroad car.

Registrant ID: 445
Name: John Bossieux
City/State: Chicago, IL
Railroad: New York Central
Position: Dinning Car Water
Years: Circa 1930'-51
Submitter's Name: Joan
City/State: University Park, IL
Comments: His assignment was out of the Root Street Office on the near South Side of Chicago. Traveled to New York City, there for 3 days, and returned to Chicago for 3 days. He became ill in the early 50's and retired early. His full name was John Eugene Bossie.

Registrant ID: 448
John Stanhope Ray Bourne
City/State: Boston, MA
Railroad: Boston,MA-- RR DEPOT
Position: Red Cap
Years of Service: 1912-1916
Submitter's Name: Charles
City/State: Berkeley, CA
Comments: John Stanhope Ray Bourne (born in 1873 in Barbados, W.I.; died 1958 in Boston, MA) was my grandfather he held a job at the train depot as a redcap while putting himself through law school (Northeastern) He received his LLB and higher Law degrees. John was the first black lawyer to have a law office in downtown Boston in 1926. One of his first cases was the "Sleeping Car Porter's Case" with Randolph and Dellums. (A. Philip Randolph was a friend of the family based on John Bourne's involvement on that case.) John's involvement was a direct result of his familiarity with and commitment to the Sleeping Car Porters' struggle for unionization that John participated in, and wrote about (in the "CRISIS" Magazine) during his years at the RR depot.

Registrant ID: 1510
Name: Charles Bowden
City/State: MO
Railroad: Pennsylvania
Position: Porter and a Dining Car Waiter
Years of Service: World War II
Submitter's Name: Shirley

City/State: St. Louis , MO
Comments: My father died on July 31, 1983. He spoke often and fondly about his time working on the railroad. I learned that his railroad job) enabled him to be the first person in his family to complete college. He also had the op-portunity to travel to places that he had only heard of.

Registrant ID: 451
Name: Arthur Bowen
City/State: Columbus, OH
Railroad: Pennsylvania
Position: Porter in Dining Road
Submitter's Name: Shirley
City/State: Columbus, OH
Comments: Worked for 20 years

Registrant ID: 452
Name: Turnerfry Bowens
City/State: St. Louis, MO
Railroad: Missouri Pacific
Position: Waiter
Years of Service: Approx 30
Submitter's Name: Elmo
City/State: Wentzville, MO
Comments: Turnerfry Bowens was my Uncle. Thanks Elmo Johnson

Registrant ID: 453
Name: Frank Bowers
City/State: Chicago, IL
Position: Diesel Mechanic
Years of Service: 1940-1960
Submitter's Name: Angela C.
City/State: Chicago, IL

Registrant ID: 454
Name: Roland Bowers

City/State: Jacksonville, FL
Railroad: East Coast Railroad
Position: Pullman Porter, and a Conductor
Years of Service: 1926-1968
Submitter's Name: Bonnie J.
City/State: Hyde Park, MA
Comments: *Mr. Bowers was the first African-American Conductor, promoted to the position on the Silver Star line.*

Registrant ID: 455
Name: Martin Bowles
City/State: Chicago, IL
Railroad: Santa Fe Railroad
Position: Cook
Years of Service: 1946-1975

Registrant ID: 457
Name: James Bowman
City/State: Robbins, IL
Railroad: Pullman Company
Position: Porter
Submitter's Name: Beverly
City/State: Calumet City, IL

Registrant ID: 459
Name: Earl W. Bowman, Sr.
City/State: Minneapolis, MN
Position: Pullman Porter
Years of Service: 1922-1958
Submitter's Name: Harriet
City/State: Minneapolis, MN

Registrant ID: 461
Name: Emery D. Bowser
City/State: Indianapolis, IN
Position: Pullman Porter
Years of Service: 1942-1969
Registrant ID: 460
Name: Emery D. Bowser
City/State: Chicago, IL
Position: Porter

Years of Service: 1942-1984
Submitter's Name: Eugene E.
City/State: Chicago, IL

Registrant ID: 462
Name: Clifford Lee Boyd
Position: Pullman Porter
Years of Service: Over 25 Years
Comments: He was a member of
the union

Registrant ID: 464
Name: Rufus "Jerry" Boyd
City/State: Lansing, IL
Railroad: Union Pacific
Position: Waiter
Years of Service: One
Comments: I was very fortunate
to meet many elderly African
American Males with degrees in
higher learning. Unfortunately,
proper compensation was not
available to them, in the fields of
study where they were
educationally prepared to work.

Registrant ID: 463
Name: Raymond Boyd
City/State: Denver, CO
Railroad: Union Pacific
Position: Chef Cook
Years of Service: 46 yrs
Submitter's Name: Jan
City/State: Denver, CO

Registrant ID: 467
Name: Ernest Boykin Sr.
City/State South Ozone Park, NY
Railroad: unknown
Position: Pullman Car Porter
Submitter's Name: James
City/State: Hempstead, NY

Registrant ID: 469
Name: Bennie Bozeman

City/State: Chicago, IL

Registrant ID: 471
Name: James A. Bradfield
City/State: Memphis, TN
Position: Pullman Porter
Years of Service: 1940-1947
Submitter's Name: Ernest
City/State: Apache Junction, AZ
Comments: My Mother wasn't
too happy about staying home
and taking care of the 7 children
by herself, she wanted him to
find work that would keep him at
home more.

Registrant ID: 472
Name: Eugene Breed Bradford
City/State: AL
Railroad: New York Central
Position: Waiter
Years of Service: 1945
Submitter's Name: Yvonne
City/State: Chicago,, IL

Registrant ID: 477
Name: Hughie Bradley
City/State: Detroit, MI
Position: Porter
Years of Service: 1920's
Submitter's Name: Theresa B
City/State: AL

Registrant ID: 480
Name: Robert J. Bradley
City/State: CA
Railroad: Oakland, California
to Portland, OR route
Position: Pullman Porter
Years of Service: 1920s-1940s
Submitter's Name: Matthew
City/State: NC
Comments: My grandfather
Robert J. Bradley, was mainly a
porter on the Oakland to

Portland route in the 1920s-1940s. He was based in Oakland, and also did some Texas routes occasionally.

Registrant ID: 479
Name: Johnson Bradley
City/State: Chicago, and Tupelo Mississippi
Railroad: Illinois Central
Position: Pastry Chef
Years of Service: 1920-1930
Submitter's Name: Velmon
City/State: Evanston, IL
Comments: All of the information that I gave you is based on oral history from my dad. He is now deceased, but as a little girl I remember his stories about his travels and how he was treated. I never forgot and wanted to honor him in this way.

Registrant ID: 473
Name: Edward James Bradley
City/State: St. Louis, MO
Railroad: Pullman Company
Position: Sleeping Car Porter
Years of Service: 1933 to 1954
Submitter's: Charles William
City/State: Oak Bluffs, MA
Comments: He was the 26th Vice President of the BSCP You will find pictures of him and information in a book titled "A Long Hard Journey" , by Patricia and Fredrick McKissack. Copyright in 1989

Registrant ID: 476
Name: Godfrey Bradley
City/State: Oakland, CA
Railroad: Pacific Railroad
Position: Pullman Porter

Years of Service: 1950-1965
Submitter's Name: Alfred
City/State: Oakland, CA

Registrant ID: 478
Name: John Sill Bradley
City/State: Detroit, MI
Position: Sleeping Car Porter
Years of Service: 1920's
Submitter's Name: Theresa B
City/State: Southfield, MI

Registrant ID: 481
Name: Jesse J. Bradley, Sr.
City/State: Grandview, MD
Railroad: Louisiana/Arkansas L&A
Position: Dinning Car Porter
Years of Service: 1925-1984
Submitter's Name: Jesse J
City/State: Grandview, MD
Comments: Father, worked with Randolph during forming of the Union.

Registrant ID: 482
Name: Samuel J. Bradley, Sr.
City/State: Los Angeles, CA
Railroad: Southern Pacific
Position: Dining Car Waiter
Years of Service: 1937-1957
Submitter's Name: Kathryn
City/State: LA, CA

Registrant ID: 485
Name: Neat Bradshaw
Position: Porter
Years of Service: 1918-1937
Submitter's Name: Angela
City/State: Chicago, IL
Comments: This gentleman was my first cousin three times removed; tuberculosis ended his career as a Pullman Porter. He lived on Chicago's Southside at 47th and State Street, where he

lived with and supported his
mother.

Registrant ID: 483
Name: Charles Preston
Bradshaw
City/State: AL
Railroad: Union Pacific
Position: Porter
Years of Service: After 1906
Submitter's Name: Ann Marie
City/State: Evanston, IL
Comments: This was my
grandfather.

Registrant ID: 486
Name: Thomas G. Bradshaw
City/State: Oakland, CA
Railroad: Pennsylvania Railroad
Position: Dining Car Waiter
Service: Circa 1945 to 1956
Submitter's Name: Carol L.
City/State: Oakland, CA

Registrant ID: 487
Name: Troy Brailey
City/State: Baltimore, MD
Railroad: B & O
Position: Pullman Porter
Submitter's Name: Alice
City/State: Baltimore, MD
Comments: My father worked
very closely with A. Philip
Randolph and B.F. Mc Laurin in
the organization of the
Brotherhood of Sleeping Car
Porters and the March on
Washington. He was one the
youngest presidents of a local.

Registrant ID: 488
Name: Samuel Brandon
City/State: New York, NY
Railroad: New York/Pullman Co.

Position: Cook
Years of Service: 1942-1943
Submitter's Name: Clarice A.
City/State: New York, NY
Comments: My father started
working for the railroad when he
was discharged from the Army.
He worked as a cook. He also
loaded linen on the railroad cars.

Registrant ID: 489
Name: Lewis A. Brandon, Jr.
City/State: Asheville, NC
Railroad: Southern
Position: Pullman Porter
Years of Service: 1940's-60's
Submitter's Name: Lewis A.
City/State: Greensboro, NC
Comments: My father worked
during WWII and was furloughed
at the end of the war. He
returned to work in 1957 and
remained until Southern move
its Asheville, NC operations to
Washington, DC.

Registrant ID: 490
Name: Herbert Branker
City/State: New York City, NY
Railroad: Atlantic Coastline
Position: Sleeping Car Porter
Years of Service: 40's to 60's
Submitter's Name: Camille
City/State: Bronx, NY
Comments: I remember my
father saying the name of the
train was the Champion. His run
was to Florida.
My father died in 1979.

Registrant ID: 491
Name: Gilbert L. Brannon
Position: Pullman Porter
Years of Service: 1938-1954

Submitter's Name: Maxine L.
City/State: Dallas, TX

Registrant ID: 494
Name: Gerald O. Brashears, Sr.
City/State: Denver, CO
Railroad: Union Pacific
Position: Porter/Waiter
Years of Service: 1942-1953
Submitter's Name: Gerald O.
City/State: Denver, CO

Registrant ID: 496
Name: Ezra Bratcher
City/State: Little Rock, AR
Railroad: Missouri/Pacific
Position: Dining Car Waiter
Years of Service: 1940s-51
Submitter's Name: Raye Jean
City/State: West Hyattsville,MD.
Comments: My uncle "ran on
the road", based out of St. Louis.
He would come home to Little
Rock for his "layovers" and then
go back to St. Louis for his runs.
I met many of his friends who
"ran on the road", they are Travis
Uttly (St. Louis) and Willie Long

Registrant ID: 497
Name: Paul Brazil
Position: Pullman Porter
Years of Service: 1935-1965
Submitter's Name: Betty
City/State: Kansas City, MO

Registrant ID: 498
Name: Ebbie Brazile
City/State: Metairie, LA
Position: Pullman Porter
Years: 42 Years, 11mos.
Submitter's Name: Tara Ann
City/State: Marietta, GA

Registrant ID: 499
Name: Kato "Uncle" Breckenudge
City/State: Chicago, IL
Submitter's Name: Annie
City/State: Chicago, IL

Registrant ID: 500
Name: Warner Brent
City/State: Los Angeles, CA
Railroad: Pullman Company
Position: Pullman Porter
Years of Service: 1942-1975

Registrant ID: 501
Name: James A. Brent, Sr.
City/State: Staunton, VA
Railroad: C & O
Position: Porter
Years of Service: Circa
1935 - 1948
Submitter's: Patsye
City/State: Middletown, PA
Comments: We were a large
family (10 children). The train
tracks ran behind our house.
Daddy would be on the train for
a number of days...and then he'd
get a couple of days off. During
the days when he wasn't
scheduled to stop, Momma hung
a green light out.

Registrant ID: 504
Name: W.H. Brewer
Position: Pullman Porter
Years of Service: Over 25 Y
Comments: He was a member of
the union

Registrant ID: 505
Name: James Brewer, Sr.
City/State: Chicago, IL
Railroad: Pullman-Standard
Position: Porter, Electrician

Years of Service: 20 years
Submitter's Name: Carol
City/State: Chicago, IL
Comments: Worked as a porter during World War II hauling troops. Later became an electrician at the Calumet Shops and at Pullman Standard on 111th Street in Chicago.

Registrant ID: 506
Name: Rich Brewington II
City/State: Quincy, FL
Railroad: Seaboard Railroad/Seaboard Coastline
Position: Signal Gang cook
Years of Service: 30 Years
Submitter's Name: Eunice
City/State: FT. Walton Beach, FL
Comments: My father, rich Brewington, is deceased. He related many stories about his work and experiences with the railroad. For that time period, I guess you could say his experiences were that of the Porters. However, he was also isolated with the signal crew for the railroad.

Registrant ID: 507
Name: Marvin Curtis Bridgeforth
City/State: Chicago, IL
Railroad: Santa Fe
Position: Waiter
Years of Service: 1937-1946
Submitter's Name: Wanda

Registrant ID: 508
Name: James A. Bridges
City/State: Mattapan, MA
Railroad: Pullman Company through 1968, then Penn Central, then Amtrak
Position: Pullman Porter

Years of Service: 37 years
Comments: As a young man, I saw the movie, "Emperor Jones" where Paul Robeson played a Pullman Porter. I was impressed by the amount of tips he collected in the movie and decided that I'd like to be a Pullman Porter. I applied for the job and was hired, because

Registrant ID: 509
Name: Richard Briggs
City/State: Richmond, VA
Railroad: B & O and RF&P
Position: Porter
Service: Circa 1910 to 1948
Submitter's Name: LaVerne
City/State: Randallstown, MD
Comments: I am the granddaughter of Richard Hunter Briggs. He passed away about 1951.

Registrant ID: 511
Name: Jasper Bright
City/State: Chicago, IL
Railroad: New York Central - Pennsylvania RR
Position: Cook Waiter
Years of Service: 47 Years
Submitter's Name: Doreen
City/State: Detroit, MI
Comments: My father did not serve in the military service during World War II, he instead worked on the railroad transporting military personnel. He died at age 85 and continued to love trains. The last gift I gave him was a wristwatch which made the sound of a train.

Registrant ID: 512
Name: Reginald Bright
Railroad: Santa Fe Railroad and Northern Pacific Railroad Carmen and Car Inspector
Years of Service: 1929- 1969
Submitter's Name: Beverly
City/State: Mountlake Terrace, Washington
Comments: He became an apprentice with Santa Fe RR in Topeka, KS from 12-02-1929 thru 04-16-34 ..Laborer with Santa Fe from 07-19-27 to 05-- 29. 12-02-29 he was Freight Carman to 04-16-34 when he graduated to Carman & worked until 11-30-1937...

Registrant ID: 514
Name: Asbury Britt
City/State: Richmond, VA
Railroad: Atlantic Coast Line
Position: Porter
Years of Service: 1932 to 1956
Submitter's Name: W Ashley
City/State: Alexandria, VA

Registrant ID: 515
Name: Ernest Herman Britt Jr.
City/State: Omaha, NE
Railroad: Union Pacific
Position: Dining Car Waiter
Years of Service: Circa 1940-1960
Submitter's Name: Arminta L.
City/State: Irmo,, SC
Comments: He would tell my sister and brothers and, I how much he enjoyed working and traveling on the road, that is what he called the railroad, he talked about how pretty the country side was as they traveled from Omaha to Chicago, and from Omaha though Denver, Co

Registrant ID: 516
Name: Samuel Broadbelt
City/State: Bronx, NY
Railroad: Pennsylvania
Position: Waiter
Years of Service: Uncertain of start date but he retired in 1969
Submitter's Name: Beverlyn
City/State: Ardsley, NY
Comments: Samuel Broadbelt is deceased.

Registrant ID: 519
Name: Donald Broadnick
City/State: Amityville, NY
Railroad: Pennsylvania/Amtrak
Position: Pullman Porter
Years of Service: 1942-1963

Registrant ID: 520
Name: Clarence Brockington
City/State: NY
Railroad: Pennsylvania
Position: Pullman
Years of Service: 1930-1950
Submitter's Name: Clarence
City/State: Bloomfield, NJ
Comments: My grandfather would always tell my mother that he walked from New York to Ohio

Registrant ID: 521
Name: Dick Brodges
City/State: Peoria, IL
Railroad: Rock Island Railroad
Position: Track Department Maintenance of way
Years of Service: 1947
Submitter's Name: Rose
City/State: Peoria, IL

Registrant ID: 522
Name: Earl S. Brody
City/State: AL

Railroad: New York Central/ Pullman Company
Position: Attendant - Bar car
Years of Service: 25
Submitter's Name: Joyce
City/State: Chicago, IL
Comments: Mr. Brody was my father he is now deceased.

Registrant ID: 527
Name: John Bronner
City/State: Riverdale, GA
Position: Porter
Years of Service: 1947-1971
Submitter's Name: Gayle
City/State: Riverdale, GA

Registrant ID: 528
Name: James Anderson Brookins
Position: Porter
Years of Service: 35 years
Submitter's Name: Marguerite
City/State: Louisville, KY

Registrant ID: 529
Name: Elmo Brooks
City/State: Dallas, TX
Railroad: Pullman Company
Position: Pullman Porter
Years of Service: 25yrs
Submitter's Name: McMillan

Registrant ID: 531
Name: John H. Brooks
Position: Sleeping Car Porter
Submitter's Name: Edwina
City/State: Brooklyn, NY

Registrant ID: 532
Name: John H. Brooks
Position: Sleeping Car Porter
Years of Service: 1905
Submitter's Name: Edwina M.

City/State: Brooklyn, NY

Registrant ID: 534
Name: Will Brooks
City/State: MS
Railroad: L & M Railroad
Position: Sleeping Car Porter
Years of Service: 1920- 1955
Submitter's Name: Robert
City/State: Colorado Springs, CO
Comments: I was told about my father's uncle working on the railroad from my father (R.J. Holmes) who is in his 80s and is presently living in Miami Florida.

Registrant ID: 533
Name: Ponrel Brooks
City/State: Madison, WI
Railroad: Chicago Line
Position: Pullman Porter
Submitter's Name: Joan
City/State: Madison, WI

Registrant ID: 536
Name: Joseph Broussard
City/State: Buffalo, NY
Railroad: New York Central
Position: Waiter- in-Charge
Years of Service: 1927-1969
Submitter's Name: Geraldine
City/State: Euclid, OH
Comments: My father was hired in 1927 as a Dining Car Waiter. He retired from the New York Central Railroad after 42 years of service. He was eventually promotrd in 1937.

Registrant ID: 539
Name: Brenda J.M. Brown
City/State: St Louis, MO
Position: Shop Stewart
Years of Service: 1922-Ret
Submitter's Name: Ezra E.

City/State: St. Louis , MO

Registrant ID: 541
Name: Charles Brown
City/State: Knoxville, Tennessee
Railroad: Pullman Company
Position: Porter
Years of Service: 1930-1940
Submitter's Name: Bussell Gist

Registrant ID: 542
Name: Cleo Brown
City/State: GA
Railroad: The Pullman Co.
Position: Pullman Porter
Years : Circa 1940's-50's
Submitter's Name: Thomas
City/State: Stone Mountain, GA
Comments: We are very excited about this project.

Registrant ID: 543
Name: Dan Brown
Submitter's Name: Marguerite
City/State: Louisville, KY

Registrant ID: 544
Name: Edward L. Brown
City/State: Elberton, VA
Railroad: The Pullman Co.pany
Position: Sleeping Car Porter
Submitter's Name: Samuel
City/State: Bronx, NY

Registrant ID: 545
Name: Edward Lee Brown
City/State: Elberton, VA
Railroad The Pullman Co.
Position: Porter
Service: Early to -mid 1940's
Submitter's: Samuel and Nathan
City/State: Bronx, NY

Comments: Don't really know more. This submission is a resubmission of one given yesterday with some of the facts incorrect.

Registrant ID: 546
Name: Emanuel Brown
City/State: Chicago, IL
Railroad: Santa Fe Railroad and Amtrak Railroad.
Position: Pullman Porter
Years of Service: Circa 1946-1975.
Submitter's Name: Lena
City/State: Chicago, IL
Comments: My father met a couple of celebrities. One was Dorothy Kilgallon. She was a regular on a game show entitled "What's My Line." He was a hardworking family man who struggled to support a wife and five children. He was more than fit for the job.

Registrant ID: 547
Name: Esker H. Brown
City/State: Los Angeles, CA
Railroad: Pennsylvania RR
Position: Waiter
Years of Service: 1940's
Submitter's Name: Fannie L.
City/State: Dayton, OH

Registrant ID: 590
Name: George Oliver Brown, Sr.
City/State: Baltimore, MD
Railroad: B&O Railroad
Position: Porter (Red Cap)
Years of Service: 44 years 1927-1971
Submitter's Name: Muriel
City/State: Randallstown, MD

Comments: He was a dedicated employee who never was late for work in 44 years. He always reminded us that "A train waits for no-one." He loved his job, and often took his kids and grandkids to the station with him. He made all of us become big tippers.

Registrant ID: 549
Name: H. A. Brown
City/State: Chicago, IL
Railroad: Pullman Co.
Position: Cook
Submitter's Name: H. A.

Registrant ID: 551
Name: Irwin Brown
City/State: Roxbury, MA
Position: Pullman Porter
Years of Service: 1943-1957
Submitter's Name: Irwin
City/State: Roxbury, MA
Comments: Was a Pullman Porter for 14.5 years and worked a total of 38 years.

Registrant ID: 557
Name: James Brown
City/State: Orangeburg, SC
Railroad: Pullman Company

Registrant ID: 555
Name: James Brown
City/State: PA
Railroad: Pennsylvania
Position: Waiter
Years of Service:42 Years
Submitter's Name: Ivy
City/State: Pittsburgh, PA
Comments: My Grandfather was a dedicated hard working Man. Forty-Two Years he worked

faithfully. My Mother ,is his daughter He was a Waiter and a terrific cook he descended from Georgia. He worked from 1920-1962.

Registrant ID: 558
Name: Jamie Earl Brown
City/State: Philadelphia, PA
Position: Sleeping Car Porter
Years of Service: 1942-1944
Submitter's Name: James Earl

Registrant ID: 588
Name: James Brown Sr.
City/State: Pittsburgh, AL
Railroad: Pennsylvania
Position: Waiter
Years of Service: 42 years
Submitter's Name: James
City/State: San Francisco, CA

Registrant ID: 589
James Howard Brown, Jr.
City/State: St. Louis, MO
Position: Pullman Porter
Submitter's Name: Madeline
City/State: Huntsville, AL
Comments: I am one of the granddaughters of James Howard Brown, Jr. He died at the young age of 44 in September 1945, ten years before my birth. I was told he was very proud of his position as Pullman Porter and made a good living supporting his family.

Registrant ID: 559
Name: Jessie Brown
City/State: Hampton, VA
Railroad: Chesapeake & Ohio (C&O), Newport News, VA
Position: Track man

Years of Service: 1943-1984
Comments: Before I retired, I was promoted to foreman.

Registrant ID: 561
Name: John S. Brown
City/State: Englewood, NJ
Railroad: New York Central
Position: Pullman Porter
Years of Service: Early 1940s
Submitter's Name: Arnold E.
City/State: Englewood, NJ
Comments: My Grandfather worked the New York Central line from New York City to Chicago. He died in 1946 a resident of Englewood, NJ

Registrant ID: 562
Name: Johnie Brown
City/State: Chicago, IL
Railroad: Illinois Central
Position: Waiter and Porter
Years of Service: 1946-1983
Submitter's Name: Karen
City/State: Chicago, IL
Comments: My father stated it was hard and tedious work.

Registrant ID: 563
Name: Johnnie Brown
City/State: Fort Worth, TX
Railroad: Fort Worth-Denver
Position: Pullman Porter
Years of Service: 1927 - 1941
Submitter's Name: Cynthia
City/State: Bowie, MD
Comments: My grandfather, who is now deceased, was a Pullman porter for the FW & D Railroad for close to 20 years. In fact, he died on the train while on duty in 1941. Like all of the Pullman porters, my grandfather

was a proud, hard-working man who suffered many injustices.

Registrant ID: 564
Name: Johnny Archer Brown
Railroad: Rock Island
Years of Service: 40-60
Submitter's Name: Mary Ellen
Comments: 21years

Registrant ID: 565
Name: Johnny Mack Brown
City/State: Jackson, MS
Railroad: Santa Fe/IC and NY Central
Position: Pullman Porter
Years of Service: 1945-1968
Submitter's Name: Gregory M.
City/State: Jackson, MN
Comments: Hired before 1969 worked for 23years

Registrant ID: 560
Name: John Brown
City/State: AL
Railroad: B & O Railroad
Position: Pullman Porter
Years of Service: Unknown – start dat date to 1948
Submitter's Name: Theresa
City/State: Upper Marlboro, MD
Comments: I saw the story in the 2/2002 issue of Ebony. While flipping through the pages, I came across this story. Remembering that my great grandfather was a Pullman Porter, I was immediately interested."PAPA" as I called him worked many years as a Pullman Porter.

Registrant ID: 566
Name: Joseph Brown

City/State: MA
Position: Porter
Submitter's Name: William I.
City/State: Whitsett, NC
Comments: He was my uncle, his run was from Massachusetts, to Jones Colorado to North Carolina

Registrant ID: 569
Name: Lawrence Brown
City/State: Fredericksburg, VA
Railroad: RF & P
Position: Dinning Car Porter
Years of Service: 1942-1958
Submitter's Name: Sandra L
City/State: Frelenchsbwry, VA
Comments: Great uncle from Richmond VA

Registrant ID: 571
Name: M. McKinley Brown
City/State: Memphis, TN
Submitter's Name: Lavera
City/State: Shaker Heights, OH

Registrant ID: 572
Name: Mac Brown
City/State: Hapeville, GA
Position: Maintenance
Submitter's Name: Theresa
City/State: Smyrna, GA
Comments: I cannot remember the railroad. This was way back. The above is my grandfather and he is now deceased. He was born in 1929. He told me about his work. He also help to build railroad tracks from Georgia through other cities and states.

Registrant ID: 571
Name: M. McKinley Brown
City/State: Memphis, TN

Submitter's Name: Lavera
City/State: Shaker Heights, OH

Registrant ID: 572
Name: Mac Brown
City/State: Hapeville, GA
Position: Maintenance
Submitter's Name: Theresa
City/State: Smyrna, GA
Comments: I cannot remember the railroad. This was way back. The above is my grandfather and he is now deceased. He was born in 1929. He told me about his work. He also help to build railroad tracks from Georgia through other cities and states.

Registrant ID: 573
Norris Washington Brown
City/State: Los Angeles, CA
Railroad: Southern Pacific RR
Position: Chef
Years of Service: 1920-1964
Submitter's Name: Ranza G.
City/State: Los Angeles, CA
Comments: Additional Descendant Mattie Garr

Registrant ID: 574
Name: Paul   E. X. Brown
City/State: Atlanta, GA
Railroad: Pullman Co.
(Chicago West)
Position: Porter-in-charge
Service: 1937 thru Spring of 1942

Registrant ID: 576
Name: Robert Sr. Brown
City/State: TX
Position: Porter
Years of Service: 1940-1945
Submitter's: Margaret, Jewel

City/State: Dallas, TX

Registrant ID: 575
Name: Robert E. L. Brown
City/State: Hollis, NY
Position: Porter in Charge
Years of Service: 1943-1963
Submitter's Name: Mr. Rodney
City/State: Flushing, NY

Registrant ID: 577
Name: Roland Brown
City/State: Roxbury, MA
Railroad: Pullman Rail Car Co.
Years of Service: 1943-1961
Submitter's Name: Ronald
City/State: Roxbury, MA
Comments: A. Philip Randolph was his president.

Registrant ID: 578
Name: Thomas T. Brown
City/State: St. Clair Shores, MI
Railroad: Michigan Central Depot   (Detroit)
Position: Sleeping Car Porter
Years of Service: 35
Submitter's Name: Thomas T.
City/State: Detroit, MI

Registrant ID: 582
Name: William Brown
City/State: Williamsport, PA
Railroad: Southern Pacific And Penn Central. RR
Position: Pullman Porter
Years of Service: From Age of Nine to 1963
Submitter's Name: Willie
City/State: Jersey City, NJ

Registrant ID: 3517
Name: William Seaye Brown
City/State: St. Petersburg, FL

Railroad: Seaboard Railway & NY New Hanen Harlford Line
Submitter's Diana & Elise
City/State: Miami, FL
Comments: Diana Ststed: My grandfather, Willie worked for Seaboard. He worked for them for many years. I remember walking with my aunts through the rail yard at night and my grandfather would be cleaning the cars. I was such a little girl, but I remember it as if it were yesterday. 'Elise Writes: He was my grandfather.

Registrant ID: 581
Name: Wilford Brown
City/State: White Plains, NY
Railroad: Penn R.R. N.Y.
Position: Pullman Porter
Years of Service: 1944-1946
Submitter's Name: Janet
City/State: Mount Vernon, NY
Comments: I am his daughter

Registrant ID: 583
Name: William C. Brown
City/State: Los Angeles, CA
Railroad: Union Pacific
Position: Dining Car Waiter
Years of Service: 1953-1954
Comments: I was a university student working on the Dining Car "extra board" for Union

Registrant ID: 584
Name: William S. Brown
Railroad: NY New Haven
Submitter's Name: Elise

Registrant ID: 585
Name: William U. Brown
City/State: Chicago, IL

Registrant ID: 586
Name: Willie C. Brown
City/State: Council, NC
Position: Sleepers
Years of Service: Circa 1949
Submitter's Name: Janice
City/State: New York, NY

Registrant ID: 592
Name: Edward Browne
City/State: Dayton, OH
Position: Sleeping Car Porter
Years of Service: 1930's
Submitter's Name: Cecile M.
City/State: Dayton, OH

Registrant ID: 591
Name: Albert Browne
Railroad: Union Pacific
Position: Pullman Porter
Years of Service: 1947 to 1950's
Submitter's Name: Leora
City/State: Los Angeles, CA

Registrant ID: 594
Name: Andrew Brown-Robinson
City/State: Clinton, SC
Railroad: New Haven Railroad
Position: Porter
Submitter's Name: Arlene

Registrant ID: 595
Name: Edward Bruce
City/State: MN
Railroad: Soo line,
Chicago/northwestern,
Burlington
Position: Waiter
Years of Service: 1940's
Submitter's Name: Myrna
City/State: Jamaica, NY
Comments: As I remember, my
father served on the above lines

working to and from Altoona,
Chicago, and Seattle.

Registrant ID: 598
Name: John Brunson
City/State: AL
Railroad: Illinois
Central/Amtrak
Position: Pullman Porter
Years of Service: 1939-1978
Submitter's Name: Sandra
City/State: San Diego, CA

Registrant ID: 604
Name: Terrance Bryan
Position: Sleeping Car Porter
Years of Service: 1920's-30's
City/State: Bronx,

Registrant ID: 599
Name: Terrance Bryan
City/State: New York, NY
Position: Sleeping Car Porter
Years of Service: 1920's-30's
City/State: Bronx, NY

Registrant ID: 605
Name: Arthur Bryant
City/State: ST. Louis, MO
Position: Sleeping Car Porter
Years of Service: 25 Years
Submitter's Name: Ron
City/State: Detroit, MI
Comments: My grandfather
worked out of St. Louis,
Missouri.

Registrant ID: 606
Name: Arthur L Bryant
City/State: Detroit, MI
Position: Porter
Years of Service: 1940-1960
Submitter's Name: Susan M
City/State: Detroit, MI

Registrant ID: 609
Name: James J. Bryant
City/State: Marilyn Dr., CA
Railroad: Santa Fe and the San Francisco Chief
Position: Pullman Porter
Years of Service: 1928-67
Submitter's Name: Jackie
City/State: Granada Hills, CA
Comments: My father worked on all major railroads and I have many pictures, news articles and memorabilia. I have pictures of Mr. Randolph, Mr. Dellums and Mr. Webster on the West Coast. My mother was active and was an officer in the Women's Auxiliary.

Registrant ID: 607
Name: Charles Bryant
City/State: Chicago, IL
Railroad: Santa Fe
Position: Porter, and Inspector
Years of Service: 1947 - 1974
Submitter's Name: Carol
City/State: Hattiesburg, MS
Comments: Started working as a Pullman Porter right after WWII, with a college degree from Alcorn College in Ms. Transferred to the Santa Fe. Promoted and continued with the 20th Central running to California, serving many of the movie stars.

Registrant ID: 612
Name: Legette Allen Sr. Bryant
City/State: TX
Railroad: T & P Railroad
Position: Waiter
Years of Service: 1926-1968
Submitter's Name: Marietta
City/State: Houston, TX

Registrant ID: 608
Name: Charles Bryant
City/State: Kansas City, MO
Railroad: Kansas City Southern
Position: Waiter
Years of Service: 42 years
Submitter's Name: Kinkesha
City/State: Kansas City, MO
Comments: Had a lot of interaction between the passengers and the staff. I enjoyed talking with the passengers.

Registrant ID: 608
Name: Frank A. Bryant
City/State: Philadelphia, PA
Years of Service: 1924-1968
Submitter's: Barbara Elaine
City/State: Philadelphia, PA
Comments: Daughter

Registrant ID: 611
Name: Joseph Dennis Bryant
City/State: Warren, OH
Railroad: New York Central
Position: Sleeping Car Porter/Pullman Porter
Years of Service: 1944-63
Submitter's Name: Barbara J.
City/State: Shaker Heights, OH
Comments: Joe Dennis my father is deceased. He died in Dec. 1963 I do have two pictures of my father taken in uniform with a group of Boy Scouts. He enjoyed his job as I remember, and of course my sister and I enjoyed the special attention we received.

Registrant ID: 614
Name: William A. Bryson
City/State: AL

Position: Porter
Submitter's Name: Grayola
City/State: Chicago, IL

Registrant ID: 615
Name: O.C. Buckner
City/State: IL
Railroad: Worked out of Chicago
Position: Porter
Years of Service: 1941 or 1942
Submitter's Name: Yvonne
City/State: Chicago, IL
Comments: Father

Registrant ID: 616
Name: William A Underwood
Sr Buffkin
City/State: Omaha, NE
Railroad: Union Pacific
Position: Waiter, Porter, Conductor
Years of Service: 20yrs
Submitter's Name: Keith
City/State: Omaha, NE
Comments: He was my Godfather

Registrant ID: 617
Name: William A. Bufkin, Sr.
City/State: Omaha, NE
Railroad: Union Pacific
Position: Waiter, Barber and Conductor
Years of Service: 20 Years
Submitter's Name: Keith

Registrant ID: 618
Name: Bennie Buggs
City/State: TN
Submitter's Name: Kaye
City/State: Detroit, MI
Comments: I don't have specific information. He has is daughter Clara Buggs Shepherd who lives

in Chattanooga Tennessee. His picture and uniform is currently displayed in the Afro American Museum in Chattanooga.

Registrant ID: 619
Name: Chester Buice
City/State: Chicago, IL
Railroad: Pullman Rail Car Co.
Position: Pullman Porter
Years of Service: 1942-1950's
Submitter(s): Gwen
City/State: IL
Comments: He had a strong work ethic and believed that you always gave a good day's work and service to the public (Davis and Peggees Family)

Chester Buice

Registrant ID: 622
Name: Bennie L. Bullock
City/State: Boston, MA
Railroad: The Pullman Co., then Penn Central
Position: Pullman Porter
Years of Service: 1940's-70's
Submitter's Name: Audrey
City/State: Boston, MA
Comments: Bennie was my husband

Registrant ID: 623
Name: Ivory Bullucks
City/State: Cincinnati, OH

Registrant ID: 624
Name: Carl Bunn
City/State: Los Angeles, CA
Railroad: Missouri Pacific, Santa Fe, Union Pacific, AMTRAK
Position: Waiter, Steward, Chief, District Supervisor, Mangr of LAX
Years of Service: 1944 - 1993
Comments: Working for the railroad you experienced low pay and prejudice. When I retired it was still the same. 49 years with the railroad.

Registrant ID: 625
Name: Ernest Ambrose Bunn
City/State: Chicago, IL
Railroad: Chicago North District
Position: Pullman Porter
Years of Service: 1887 to Sept.1933
Submitter's: Donald, Yvonne
City/State: Sacramento, CA
Comments: Decendants State: Our Grandfather and grat grandfather was a Pullman Porter assigned to Chicago North District. My Grandfather and his wife Edna L Bunn lived at 420

East 46th Street, Chicago IL. After he died in 1934 my grandmother continued to rent rooms to Pullman Porters who would stay over.

Registrant ID: 627
Name: Wardlow Bunyon
City/State: Cincinnati, OH
Railroad: Penn Railroad
Position: Pullman Porter
Years of Service: 06-1926-61
Submitter's: Sara Rubena
City/State: Hempstead, NY
Comments: I still have his Pullman Company identification card from 05/17/43 also his membership dues book, official receipt up until 1961, description of rates for accommodations from 1957 uniforms hats, report of cash fare

Registrant ID: 628
Name: Joseph Bura
Railroad: N W Railroad
Position: Porter
Submitter's Name: Zella
City/State: Homewood, IL

Registrant ID: 629
Name: Joseph Buran
Railroad: NW Rail Road
Position: Porters
Years of Service: 1930-1940

Registrant ID: 631
Name: Clarence Burgin
City/State: Chicago, IL
Railroad: Pennsylvania
Position: Pullman Porter
Years of Service: 1924-1960
Submitter's Name: Carl

City/State: Chicago, IL
Comments: Descendants were the first blacks to work in the signal division in Chicago's Union Station

Registrant ID: 633
Name: Lonnie Burkertt
City/State: Louisville, KY
Railroad: L&N RR
Position: Master Chef,
Years of Service: 1920-1961
Submitter's Name: Robinson

Registrant ID: 634
Name: Lonnie Burkett
City/State: Louisville, KY
Position: Master Chef
Years of Service: 1930-1970
Submitter's Name: Mary F
City/State: Louisville, KY

Registrant ID: 635
Name: Wesley Burley
City/State: Bronx, NY
Railroad: Grand Central
Years of Service: 1940-1966
Submitter's Name: Beverly
City/State: Bronx, NY
Comments: Worked for the railroad for 26 years.

Registrant ID: 636
Name: Ms. Burneet
City/State: Oakland, CA
Submitter's Name: Ms.
City/State: Oakland, CA

Registrant ID: 637
Name: Sidney Burnett
City/State: AL
Railroad: Union Pacific
Position: Pullman Porter
Years of Service: 40's to 70's

Submitter's Name: Paul
City/State: Omaha, NE
Comments: My father was a Pullman porter for Union Pacific Railroad. He held that position with great pride and distinction. He accepted every aspect of the job - realizing that the opportunity Union Pacific afforded him always outweighed the indignities that ignorant people hurled at him.

Registrant ID: 638
Name: Mrs. Ala Dys Burns
City/State: Milwaukee, WI
Position: Pullman Porter
Years of Service: 1940-1965
Submitter's Name: David
City/State: AL

Registrant ID: 639
Name: Robert Burns
City/State: Houston., TX
Railroad: Southern Pacific
Position: Sleeping Car Porter and also a Red Cap
Years of Service: 1922 to 1967
Submitter's Name: Mary Violet
City/State: Seattle, WA
Comments: My father, Robert Lee Burns, was a railroad employee from 1922, when he was 18, until 1967, when he retired at 63. His usual route was Houston to Chicago, Illinois. He joined the Brotherhood as a young man and believed firmly in the vision of A. Philip Randolph.

Registrant ID: 642
Name: Thomas Burrell
City/State: Pittsburgh, PA
Railroad: Pullman Company

Pennsylvania RR
Position: Pullman Attendant
Years of Service: 1910-1952
Submitter's Name: Harold
City/State: Pittsburgh, PA
Comments: His longest run was between Pittsburgh and Detroit for 13 years.

Registrant ID: 643
Name: Thomas L. Burrell
Railroad: Pennsylvania
Position: Sleeping Car Porter
Years of Service: 1910-1952
Submitter's Name: J. Harold
City/State: Pittsburgh, PA
Comments: Sometime soon, I hope to visit the museum, which, I think, provides a long overdue tribute to the Brotherhood of Sleeping Car Porters.

Registrant ID: 644
Name: Morris Burroughs
City/State: Chicago, IL
Railroad: Chicago and Alton
Position: Porter and waiter
Years of Service: 1887-1903
Submitter's Name: Tony
City/State: Chicago, IL

Registrant ID: 644
Name: Eddie Burton
City/State: McComb, MS
Railroad: Illinois Central
Position: Pullman Porter
Years of Service:
Circa 1940-1978
Submitter's Name: Deborah
City/State: Baton Rouge, LA
Comments: My father, Eddie S. Burton lived in Chicago and worked the Chicago to New Orleans route, Chicago to

California, New York, Washington D. C. while in Chicago he lived at the Harmonia Dalton hotel as did many other railroad workers during that time.

Registrant ID: 645
Name: James Clifton Burton
City/State: St Louis, MO
Railroad: Union Pacific
Position: Pullman Porter
Years of Service: 1869-1963
Submitter's Name: Fred
City/State: Detroit, MI
Comments: He Made History for Blacks, Only Black Inspector for Railroads. Father who worked for 4 years, he was the first Black inspector for PP he also trained other porters. He was the only black Pullman Porter inspector.

Registrant ID: 647
Name: Arthur T. Burton, Sr.
City/State: Phoenix, IL
Railroad: Santa Fe and others
Position: Pullman Porter and porter-in-charge **1930-1968**
Submitter's Name:
Evelyn, Charles & Art.
City/State: Chesterfield MO and Phoenix, IL
Comments: Charles Writes: His service laid the ground work for my being awarded a Pullman Foundation Scholarship to attend college and to fulfill a life long dream of my father who valued education so much. He was 21 years old when he completed his 8th grade studies in Arkansas. Art writes: My father worked for the Pullman

Company during the heyday of the railroads. On many occasions my father would chuffer Mr. Webster to union meetings in Chicago. My father worked the followings trains: SantaFe, the Scout, the Grand Canyon, the Chief the Navajo, The Super Chief, Union Pacific, the Portland, The city of Los Angeles

Registrant ID: 649
Name: Samuel Bushnell
City/State: Seattle, WA
Railroad: Great Northern
Position: Waiter, Cook
Years of Service: 1940-76
Submitter's Name: Holly
City/State: Kirkland, WA
Comments: My Grandfather is deceased. He retired from Great Northern and seemed to be quite content with his employment and pension.

Registrant ID: 654
Name: Stephen Butler
Railroad: Pennsylvania
Position: Porter
Years of Service: 1930's
Submitter's Name: Stephen
City/State: Richmond, IN
Comments: Dad always spoke about "running on the railroad" and kept his Pullman brush (shaped something like a boat or banana). His brother, Nelson Butler, was also a Pullman Porter.

Registrant ID: 651
Name: Andrew Butler
City/State: IL

Railroad: New York Central
Position: Cook, Waiter
Years of Service: 1945-1949
Submitter's Name: Janet
City/State: Las Vegas, NV

Registrant ID: 650
Name: Andrew H. Butler
City/State: AL
Position: Pullman Porter
Submitter: Grace
City/State: Cleveland, OH
Comments: DOB 4-22-02 Worked New Orleans and Cincainati.

Andrew H. Butler (Center)

Registrant ID: 652
Name: Houston Butler
City/State: NC
Railroad: Pullman Co.

Trains out of North Carolina where he lived.
Position: Porter or Conductor
Years of Service: 1910-1950
Submitter's Name: Dietrich
City/State: Murfreesboro, TN
Comments: My great-great uncle (Houston or John Houston Butler) and his wife had to ride in separate car when traveling to Mississippi to visit his family. He looked white and my great-great aunt didn't.

Registrant ID: 653
Name: Nelson C Butler
City/State: Brooklyn, NY
Railroad: Pennsylvania R.R.
Position: Pullman Porter
Years: Circa 1943-1945
Submitter's Name: Harold W
City/State: Westbury, NY
Comments: My father passed on in 1964. I don't remember very much. I was about six years old during the time he worked for the R.R. I do know that we used to ride to N.C. for free on the R.R. as far as the Penn. R.R. went, which I think was to Washington, D.C.

Registrant ID: 655
Name: Walter Butler Jr.
City/State: AL
Railroad: Pennsylvania
Position: Pullman Porter
Years of Service: (1942-1961)
Submitter's Name: Walter
City/State: Bronx, NY
Comments: My late father was a Pullman Porter for the Pennsylvania Railroad from age 18 to age 37, after which he left

the railroad and became a NYC Police Officer. I believe he ran on the Broadway Limited from New York to Chicago.

Registrant ID: 657
Name: Milton Sr. Byard
City/State: Blue Field, WV
Position: Pullman Porter
Years of Service: 1870
Submitter's: Vela Maxine
City/State: Columbus, OH

Registrant ID: 659
Name: Allen Caldwell
City/State: Danville, KY
Railroad: L&N and Humming Bird
Position: Pullman Porter and a Dining Car Waiter
Years of Service: 1945 - 1950
Submitter's Name: Dr. Betty S.
City/State: Frankfort, KY
Comments: Allen, my father, known as "Bo-bie" or "Yellow" served as a Porter and a Waiter. During the summers, I traveled with him from Louisville to Miami, Omaha to Oakland. The experiences learned from passengers and my fathers colleagues are credited with my level of professionalism.

Registrant ID: 660
Name: Edward Calhoon
City/State: Detroit, MICH
Railroad: Pullman Company
Position: Faght Hander
Years of Service: 1946-1950
Submitter's Name: Hopkins
Registrant ID: 661
Name: Clifton Calhoun
City/State: MI

Registrant ID: 664
Name: Alfred Calloway
City/State: OH
Railroad: Baltimore & Ohio
Position: Dining Car Waiter
Years of Service: Until 1960
Submitter's Name: Denise
City/State: Altadena, CA
Comments: Mr. Calloway was based out of Cincinnati, Ohio. He died in 1987.

Registrant ID: 663
Name: Alfred Jeep Calloway
City/State: Los Angeles, CA
Railroad: B & O
Position: Dining Car Waiter
Years of Service: 1949-1959
Submitter's Name: Omani

Registrant ID: 668
Alirauder Calvin Johnson
City/State: Miami, FL
Position: Sleeping Car Porter
Years of Service: 1950-1981
Submitter's Name: Cara S
City/State: Miami, FL
Comments: Husband

Registrant ID: 671
Name: Jerome Campbell
City/State: Boston, MA
Position: Chef
Years of Service: 1941-1947
Submitter's Name: N.
City/State: Boston, MA

Registrant ID: 669
Name: Charles k. Campbell
City/State: AL
Railroad: New York Central
Position: Waiter
(dinning & club car)
Years of Service: 1915-1963

Submitter's Name: Charles h.
City/State: Buffalo, NY
Comments: Charles K. is my grandfather born in 1896 Richmond, Virginia who I believe started working after high school for the railroad. drafted in WW1 and resumed after the war.

Registrant ID: 673
Name: Malcolm Campbell
Railroad: Pullman Union (414)
Years of Service: 1946-1958
Submitter's Name: Lucille
City/State: Charleston, VA

Registrant ID: 670
Name: Clifford Campbell
City/State: TX
Railroad: Santa Fe
Position: Trucker
Years of Service: 1939-1969
Submitter's Name: Lynn
City/State: Dallas, TX
Comments: My late father was very, very proud of his work and the work of his fellow employees during World War II. They kept troops, equipment and important materials moving. Our family lived in Temple, Texas which was the main railroad portal that moved people.

Registrant ID: 674
Name: William Campbell
Railroad: Southern Pacific
Position: Cook & Porter
Submitter's Name: Deborah
City/State: Sparton Burg, SC
Comments: Great-grandfather

Registrant ID: 675
Name: Louis Grady Cannon

City/State: Woodrow, SC
Railroad: Baltimore
Submitter's Name: Sandra

Registrant ID: 679
Name: David Caple
City/State: Memphis, TN
Position: Pullman Porter
Years of Service: 1940-1965
Submitter's Name: Gladys
City/State: Milwaukee, WI

Registrant ID: 681
Name: Alfred E CargeL
City/State: New York, NY
Railroad: Pennsylvania RR
Position: Baggage Department
Years of Service: 1930's-50's
Submitter's Name: Dolores C.
City/State: New York, NY
Comments: Grandfather.
Passed away in the late 50's

Registrant ID: 682
Name: Elisha "Red" Carlton
City/State: Mulberry, FL
Railroad: Seabolt
Years of Service: 1946-1974
Submitter's Name: Richard
City/State: Mulberry, FL
Comments: Jackson

Registrant ID: 683
Name: Hubert Carmichael
City/State: Boston, MA
Position: Pullman Porter
Years of Service: 1930's
Submitter's Name: Began
City/State: Cincinnati, OH
Comments: Hubert Carmichael
worked on a line out of Atlanta,
then moved to Boston in 1938.
He was retired by the early
1960's.

Registrant ID: 684
Name: Linson Joseph
Carmouche
Position: Waiter
Years of Service: 1930-1943
Submitter's Name: Linton J.
City/State: Chicago, IL

Registrant ID: 685
Name: David Carolina
City/State: CO
Position: Porter
Years of Service: 1924-1959
Submitter's Name: Sandra
City/State: Aurora, CO

Registrant ID: 688
Name: Hampton Carr
City/State: New York, NY
Railroad: New York to Montreal
Position: Pullman Porter
Years of Service: 1945-1955
Submitter('s): Harold Lee
And Larry
City/State: New York, NY
Comments: I don't know a lot
about my father's work. Here's
what I do know: he worked on a
line that ran from New York to
Montreal. I know this because
he always brought home
Canadian bacon. He met my
mother on the railroad where she
worked, I believe as a maid.

Registrant ID: 692
Name: Frank Carroll
Railroad: Norfolk & Western -
Southern – Lackawanna
Position: Dining car Waiter -
porter personal valet to
Company Owner **Years of
Service:** Circa 1870 - 1960
Submitter's Name: Elizabeth

City/State: Newark, NJ
Comments: My father worked on the railroad with his father as a child in Tazewell Va. As a WWI Vet returning from Europe in 1921 he began working on the Railroad out of Roanoke Va. area. Later family moved to Newark NJ my dads last RR job was with the Lackawanna.

Registrant ID: 690
Name: Leander Carroll
Railroad: Norfolk & Western - Southern - Lackawanna
Position: Dining Car Waiter - porter personal valet to the railroad company Owner
Years of Service: Circa 1870 - 1960
Submitter's Name: Elizabeth
City/State: Newark, NJ
Comments: My Granddad

Registrant ID: 695
Name: Cleveland Carson
City/State: St. Louis, MO
Railroad: Pullman Company out of Philadelphia
Position: Sleeping Car Porter
Years of Service: 1945-1960
Submitter's Name: Clarice
City/State: St. Louis , MO

Registrant ID: 696
Name: Andrew Lyle Carter
City/State: Pittsburgh, PA
Railroad: Penn Railroad
Position: Pullman Porter
Years of Service: 10 Years
Submitter's Name: Geraldine

Registrant ID: 701
Name: Major Wade Carter

City/State: Bronx, NY
Railroad: NY Central
Position: Porter
Years of Service: Over 20
Submitter's Name: Colleen
City/State: Bronx, NY
Comments: Great Uncle

Registrant ID: 698
Name: Charles M. Carter
City/State: Charlottesville, VA
Railroad: Chesapeake and Ohio
Position: Waiter
Years of Service: 1949-1977
Submitter's Name: Lucian J.
City/State: Charlottesville, VA

Registrant ID: 704
Name: Walter Carter
City/State: MI
Position: Porter
Submitter's Name: Neighbor
City/State: Grand Rapids, MI

Registrant ID: 700
Name: Fred Carter
City/State: TX
Position: Porter
Submitter's Name: Nae
City/State: Houston, TX

Registrant ID: 702
Name: Moses Prophet Carter
City/State: Washington, DC
Railroad: Seaboard Railroad NY/Newhaven/Hartford
Position: Pullman Porter and A Dining Car Waiter
Years of Service: Circa 1922-32
Submitter's Name: Joyce
City/State: Suitland, MD
Comments: My grandfather worked for the railroad for 10 years. According to my father he

was very proud of the work he did on the Railroad.

Registrant ID: 699
Name: Cornel Lee Carter
City/State: DC
Railroad: Seaboard RR
Position: Chef
Years of Service: 1946-1972
City/State: Washington, DC
Comments: His run was New York to Miami and other parts of Florida. We lived in Washington, DC My Dad died in 1974. My grandfather was an active member of the Brotherhood of Sleeping Car Porters. He was Secretary of the local chapter and attended many national conventions

Registrant ID: 705
Name: James Carthen
City/State: Memphis, TN
Railroad: Frisco Railroad (Popular Street Depot)
Position: Pullman Porter
Years: Late 1880-1916
Submitter's Name: Ida Mae
City/State: East St. Louis, IL
Comments: Started off working as a Laborer, laying tracks. While working as a laborer my grandfather received a serious leg injury. The railroad then gave him a lifetime job as a Pullman Porter. Unfortunately his leg had to be amputated and he developed gangrene

Registrant ID: 707
Name: Albert Case
City/State: AL
Position: Pullman Porter

Submitter's Name: John
City/State: Suffolk, VA
Comments: I don't know much about my Uncle accept that he was a porter for most of his adult life.

Registrant ID: 709
Name: B.C. Cash, Sr.
Position: Pullman Porter
Years of Service: 1936-1957
Submitter's Name: Edwin B.
City/State: Dallas, TX

Registrant ID: 710
Cornelius Luis Cassimere
City/State: Berkeley, CA
Railroad: Southern Pacific
Position: Pullman Porter
Years of Service: 1920 to 1958
Worked for 38yrs
Submitter's Name: Gerald
City/State: Modesto, CA

Registrant ID: 712
Name: Sergill L. Cave, Sr.
City/State: Vestal, NY
Position: Pullman Porter
Years of Service: 1918-1939
Submitter's Name: Allan C.
City/State: Vestal, NY

Registrant ID: 713
Name: Walter Cavitt
City/State: AL
Railroad: Illinois Central
Position: Breakman
Years of Service: 1920's-50's
Submitter's Name: Sybil
City/State: Louisville, KY
Comments: Walter Cavitt was married to Lucille Vick Cavitt and had two step-children, one

of which was Harvey O. Vick, Sr.
who later went on to work for the
IC Railroad as well.

Registrant ID: 714
Name: Lewis Chambers
City/State: Okmulgee, OK
Railroad: Not certain
Position: Pullman Porter
Submitter's Name: Shana
City/State: Denver, CO
Comments: I am thinking it
must have been during the
20's,30's or 40's. Jackie H.
Chambers, was My father

Registrant ID: 715
Bessie Chandler (nee) Jones
City/State: Brooklyn, NY
Railroad: Palm Beach, Florida
Position: Maid
Years of Service: Circa 5 years
Submitter's Name: Yvette
City/State: Jersey City, NJ
Comments: My mother's
employment was during the
1920's. She met and married
James S. Jones, who was a
Pullman porter for the railroad
for 45 years.

Registrant ID: 716
Name: John T. Chany
City/State: MI
Years of Service: 41 years
Submitter's Name: Marcellus
City/State: Flint, MI
Comments: Grandson

Registrant ID: 718
Name: Iris Fabiola Chapa
City/State: Colorado
San Diego, California
Railroad: Pullman Company

Registrant ID: 722
Name: Jesse Chapman
Railroad: Union Pacific
Position: Porter
Years of Service: Circa 1958
Submitter's Name: Debra
City/State: Chicago, IL
Comments: Disabled- 1958 (due
to accident on train

Registrant ID: 719
Name: Charles Henry Chapman
City/State: Philadelphia, PA
Railroad: Penn
Position: Pullman Porter
Years of Service: 1900-1920
Submitter's Name: Deborah
City/State: Torrance, CA
Comments: Charles H.
Chapman was born in 1859 in
Barbados, BWI. He was
naturalized in Charleston, S.C.
1860. He married Rachel
Moffet in 1874 and had 7
children. He was a Seaman and
later moved to Philadelphia and
began working for the Pullman
Company.

Registrant ID: 5001
Name: Cornelius Charles
City/State: Chicago, IL
Railroad: Great Northern
Position: Porter
Years of Service: 30 + Years
Submitter's Name: Clifton
City/State: Chicago, IL

Registrant ID: 723
Name: Clarence Albert Charles
Position: Porter
Years of Service: 1920's-40's.
Submitter's: Elizabeth,
Marie and Charles

City/State: Chicago, IL
Comments: My father and A. Philip Randolph lectured every Sunday in Washington Park in Chicago to organize and unionize the Brotherhood of Sleeping Car Porters. Mr. Randolph ate dinner at our home on countless numbers of Sundays after the rallies...I will be 77 years

Registrant ID: 725
Name: Charles Charlton
City/State: Chicago, IL
Railroad: Pullman Company
Position: Busboy attendant; Club Car attendant; and Porter
Years of Service: Jan. 1943-56
Submitter's Name: Linda
City/State: Chicago, IL
Comments: The person that I am registering is my father, Charles Charlton. He is currently 91 years of age and often shared the sometimes-humiliating experiences of working on the railroad. Conversely, he was very proud to be an employee of the Pullman Company

Registrant ID: 726
Name: Joe Chatham
City/State: TX
Railroad: Southern Pacific
Position: Pullman Porter
Years of Service: 1940's
Submitter's Name: Milton R.
City/State: Beaumont, TX
Comments: Father, Joe Chatham, now deceased. He worked out of San Antonio, and was from Centerville, TX

Registrant ID: 727
Name: Herbert Cheatom
Position: Pullman Porter
Years of Service: 1915-1917
Submitter's Name: Jackie
City/State: Omaha, NE

Registrant ID: 729
Name: Curtis L. Cherry
City/State: Philadelphia, PA
Railroad: Pennsylvania
Position: Pullman Porter
Years of Service: 1930's- 1960's
Submitter's Name: Aisha
City/State: Atlanta, GA
Comments: My father loved working for the railroad because he loved to travel. Being able to travel was an educational event all on in itself. There was always a since of excitement when he was able to go on the road. He was able to travel all over the United States.

Registrant ID: 731
Name: Alex Chess
City/State: Chicago, IL
Railroad: Pullman Railcar Co
Position: Pullman Porter
Years of Service: 1950-1960
Submitter's Name: Jan
City/State: Largo, MD
Comments: My great uncle, Alex, was a very boisterous and outgoing man. He was a disc jockey on the radio as well. Very social and outgoing he enjoyed his comradeship with other porters and liked traveling a lot. Raised in Mississippi.

Registrant ID: 733
Name: Alfred J. Chestnut

City/State: Knoxville, TN
Position: Fireman
Years of Service: 1904-1969
Submitter's Name: Marian P.
City/State: Knoxville, TN

Registrant ID: 732
Name: Alfred E. Chestnut
Position: Fireman
Years of Service: 1904-1961
Submitter's Name: James A.
City/State: Knoxville, TN

Registrant ID: 734
Name: James Carl Chevas
City/State: Chicago, IL
Railroad: New York Central
Position: Pullman Porter
Years of Service: 30 Years
Submitter's : Minnie & Edith
City/State:Chicago &
Galesburg, IL

Registrant ID: 735
Name: William Childress
City/State: Pittsburgh, PA
Railroad: Pittsburgh, PA
Position: Porter
Service: 1940 to 1953
Submitter's Name: Beverly
City/State: Detroit, MI
Comments: I am filling this out
for my mother, Beverly Troup.
William Childress was my
grandfather.

Registrant ID: 736
Name: Arthur Childs
City/State: New York, NY
Railroad: Grand Central
Position: Pullman Porter
Years of Service: circa 1941
Submitter's Name: Gwendolyn
City/State: NY

Comments: My dad was working
as a porter before I was born in
1944. I remember him having
pockets filled with change.
Sometimes he and my Mom
would be laughing and counting
when his change exceeded his
pay check. My dad took up
shinning shoes on his run to
increase

Registrant ID: 737
Name: Randolph Childs
City/State: FL
Position: Track Layer
Years of Service: 1900's
Submitter's Name: Peggy Inez
City/State: Indianola, IA

Registrant ID: 738
Name: James Marvin Chisholm
City/State: San Diego, CA
Position: Dining Car waiter
Years of Service: 1935-1960
Submitter's Name: Stephanie
City/State: San Diego, CA

Registrant ID: 740
Name: Earl Christian
City/State: St. Louis, MO
Railroad: Union Pacific
Position: Pullman Porter
Years of Service: 1924-1942
Submitter's : Kennette Nicole
City/State: Chicago, IL
Comments: He worked out of
Mississippi and eventually
moved to St. Louis, Missouri.

Registrant ID: 742
Name: Cecil Christwell
City/State: AL

Union Pacific and Southern Pacific
Position: Waiter/claims clerk
Years of Service: 1952-1981
Submitter's Name: Debra R
City/State: lansing, IL
Comments: Hired in Kansas City Kansas, transferred to Ogden, Utah ran from Ogden to LA. then from Kansas city to New Orleans. returned to Kansas city where he worked in the office as a claims clerk My father is now deceased, but I would like him to be mentioned.

Registrant ID: 743
Name: Charles Allen Church
Railroad: Illinois Central
Submitter's Name: Harriet
City/State: Chicago, IL

Registrant ID: 745
Name: Noble J. Church Sr.
City/State: Chicago, IL
Railroad: Santa Fe
Position: Dining Car, Bartender
Years of Service: 1940's-63
Submitter's Name: Harriet
City/State: Chicago, IL
Comments: I am 67 years old. When I was born in 1934 my father (was working on the railroad. He was instrumental in seeing that all the men in the family got railroad jobs...I heard many funny stories growing up.

Registrant ID: 746
Name: H.C. Clardy
Position: Pullman Porter
Years of Service: Over 25
Comments: He was a member of the B.S.C.P union local.

Registrant ID: 748
Name: Carl Winfield Clark
City/State: Washington, DC
Railroad: Norfolk
Position: Porter
Submitter's Name: Mary
Comments: President of Norfolk BSCP local

Registrant ID: 750
Name: George Clark
City/State: Philadelphia, PA
Railroad: Pennsylvania RR
Position: Pullman Porter
Years of Service: 1926-1958
Submitter's Name: Theda
City/State: Chestnut Ridge, NY
Comments: My uncle was very proud of his prestigious position at the time. He would give me $1.00 (a large sum then) each time he came back from a trip.

Registrant ID: 760
Name: Tobias Clark
Railroad: NY Central
Years of Service: 1921-1962
Submitter's Name: Fran Cena
City/State: Jamaica, NY

Registrant ID: 756
Name: Sandy Clark
City/State: Chicago, IL
Route: Washington, D.C - Chicago, IL.
Position: Chef
Years of Service: 1930's
Submitter's Name: Marva
City/State: Los Angeles, CA

Registrant ID: 752
Name: James, Sr. Clark
City/State: Michigan City, IN

Railroad: Chicago South Shore & South Bend Railroad
Position: Porter; ticket agent; accounting clerk
Years: Approx 1960-87
Submitter's Name: Debra
City/State: Minneapolis, MN
Comments: My father was one of the very first African Americans hired to work for the South Shore Railroad, and he helped many other African Americans to get hired at the railroad, especially women. He was a dedicated and dependable employee and worked very hard

Registrant ID: 749
Name: Elliott Clark
City/State: New York, NY
Position: Dining Car Waiter/Cook
Years of Service: 1933-1950's
Submitter's Name: James C.
City/State: Rochester, NY

Registrant ID: 754
Employees Name Ray Clark
City/State: Ennis, TX
Position: Turned trains around at the end of the line
Years: Retired in 1954
Submitter's: Virginia Margo
City/State: Sacramento, CA

Registrant ID: 758
Name: Thomas James Clark
City/State: St. Louis, MO
Railroad: Pullman Company
Position: Porter, Truck Driver
Submitter's Name: Estelle
City/State: St. Louis , MO

Comments: My father had more than 40 years of railroad experience.

Registrant ID: 753
Name: Joseph G. Clark
City/State: Jacksonville, FL
Railroad: Seaboard
Position: Pullman Porter
Years of Service: 1935 to 1980
Submitter's: Willie and Lawana
City/State: Tallahassee, FL
Comments: My grandfather worked on the rail road for over 40 plus years. He traveled a lot and was usually gone.

Registrant ID: 747
Name: Carl W. Clark
City/State: Norfolk, VA
Years of Service: 1940's
Submitter's Name: Melvin
City/State: Washington, DC

Registrant ID: 762
Name: Allan Clarke
City/State: Bronx, New York,
Railroad: New York Central
Position: Dining Car Waiter
Years of Service: 1940s & 50s
Submitter's Name: Beverly
City/State: Brooklyn, NY
Comments: My father is now deceased. I know that my father, traveled between New York & Cleveland, New York and Chicago, New York & Detroit and New York & Buffalo. My brothers and I once traveled with him on his Buffalo run.

Registrant ID: 763
Name: Walter Clarke
City/State: St. Albans, NY

Position: Chef
Submitter's Name: Jean
City/State: Queens Village, NY

Registrant ID: 764
Lucas Chauncey Clarkston
City/State: Chicago, IL
Railroad: Milwaukee/St. Paul
(and other runs)
Position: Pullman Porter
Years of Service: 1927 to 1967
Submitter's: Muriel & Elaine
City/State: Chicago, IL
Comments: Lucas Clarkston my
father worked very closely with
the Brotherhood of Sleeping Car
Porters. He Knew Milton P.
Webster (the president of the
Chicago local of the Brotherhood
of Sleeping Car Porters.

Registrant ID: 765
Name: Cleudes Clarlton
City/State: Chicago, IL
Position: Porter
Submitter's Name: Linda
City/State: Chicago, IL

Registrant ID: 766
Name: Jimmie or Jimmy
Clayborn, Claborne or Claiborne
City/State: MS
Railroad: Southern Railroad
Years of Service: circa 1930's
Submitter's Name: Carolyn
City/State: Los Angeles, CA
Comments: Many spellings for
his last name. After his death in
1951 my mother and family
members received monthly
benefits from the railroad. We
lived in Columbus, Miss until
Jan. 1956 then moved to Los
Angeles, CA.

Registrant ID: 768
Name: Richard Clemons
City/State: Riverdale, NY
Railroad: Rock Island
Position: Pullman Porter
Years of Service: 30 Years
Submitter's: Adolph & Gary
City/State: Atlanta, GA
Comments: I believe my father
worked for the Rock Island
railroad for twenty-five (25) years
and retired account disability
about 1957 or 1958. I do not
know the exact dates.

Registrant ID: 770
William Aka "Bill" Clemons
City/State: IL
Railroad: What is now called the
"city of new Orleans" route
Position: Pullman Porter
Years: Circa 1945-59
Submitter's Name: Yvette
City/State: Chicago, IL
Comments: This is my great
uncle. My knowledge is limited.
My interest was sparked while
watching a cable show which
highlighted Oscar Webb. He was
a Pullman salesman and
happens to be the grandfather of
a good friend.

Registrant ID: 771
Name: Ronald H Cleveland
City/State: Cleveland, OH
Railroad: Pullman Company
Position: Switchman
Years of Service: 69-71

Registrant ID: 772
Name: Kaiser Cleveland Brooks
City/State: Detroit, MI
Years: Late 1800's early 1900's

Submitter's Name: Lori E
City/State: Detroit, MI

Registrant ID: 773
Name: Herman Clifton
City/State: Chicago, IL
Railroad: Santa Fe and Amtrak
Position: Dinning Car Waiter
Years of Service: 1943 to 1983
Submitter's: Barbara Ann
City/State: Calumet City, IL
Comments: He died August 27, 2003 at the age 0f 81.

Registrant ID: 775
Name: Oque Clinkscales
City/State: Manning, SC
Railroad: Unsure. Worked in Washington, D.C.
Position: Porter
Submitter's Name: Rita
City/State: Manning, SC

Registrant ID: 774
Name: Jessie Lee Clinkscales
City/State: AL
Railroad: Pennsylvania
Position: Trackman
Years of Service: 1946 - 1979
Submitter(s): Rodnie , Lynn
City/State: Philadelphia, PA
Comments: My grandfather started working for the railroad in South Carolina (he was from Due West, South Carolina). He joined the war effort and served in W.W.II from 1943 - 1945. He went back to his job with the railroad after his return from military duty.

Registrant ID: 777
Name: Fred G. Clough
City/State: Omaha, NE

Railroad: Union Pacific RR
Submitter's Name: Dorothy L.
City/State: Omaha, NE
Comments: Deceased 1983

Registrant ID: 778
Name: Frank James Clowers
City/State: Atlanta, GA
Railroad: Southern Railway
Position: Elevator Operator
Years of Service: 35 plus years
Submitter's: Kathy Elaine
City/State: Blue Island, IL
Comments: Mr. Clowers was my Grandfather. He worked as an elevator operator in the Southern Railways Corporate Office in Atlanta, GA, 99 Spring St., in the 1930's until 1961 or 1962.

Registrant ID: 779
Name: Hayward Jr. Cochran
City/State: Toccoa, GA
City/State: GA

Registrant ID: 782
Woodrow (Woody) Cochran
City/State: Denver, CO
Railroad: Union Pacific
Position: Dining Car Waiter
Submitter's Name: Larry
City/State: Denver, CO
Comments: My deceased father worked and enjoyed 19 years as an employee of the Union Pacific Railroad.

Registrant ID: 780
Name: Samuel J. Cochran
Railroad: Chattanooga, TN
Position: Porter
Years of Service: 1951-1954
Submitter's Name: Kimberly
City/State: Detroit, MI

Comments: He always said the work was hard and laborious. He described the racial discrimation that he experienced. There was no respect for the Porter's he knew that was not the type of treatment that he wanted to endure. The job motivated him to move his family

Registrant ID: 784
Name: William T. Codrington
City/State: Montreal, Canada
Position: Pullman Porter
Years of Service: 1920-1957
Submitter's Name: Myrtle
City/State: Laurelton, NY

Registrant ID: 785
Name: Morris Benny Cody SR.
City/State: AL
Railroad: Started with Northern Pacific and transferred to Union Pacific
Position: Started as a Cook and then as a Pullman Porter
Years of Service: 20 Plus years
Submitter's Name: Corrine
City/State: Pocatello, ID

Registrant ID: 787
Name: Charles L. Cole
City/State: Chicago, IL
Railroad: The Pullman Co.
Position: Pullman Porter
Years of Service: 1943 to1969
Comments: I found out about this project through my daughter Geraldine wh lives in Chicago. Despite the challenges, It was the most enjoyable job I could rvrt have. I visited every state in the United States. I really loved the job.

Registrant ID: 792
Name: M. Coleman
City/State: Washington, DC
Position: Nurse
Years of Service: 1959-2000

Registrant ID: 802
Name: Singleton W Coleman
City/State: Danville, KY
Position: Mil Carrier
Years of Service: 1917-1955
Submitter's Name: Singleton

Registrant ID: 798
Name: Samuel Coleman
City/State: Las Vegas, NV
Railroad: Burlington CBQ RR
Position: Dining Car Waiter
Years of Service: 25
Comments: Took part in organizing the Brotherhood of Sleeping Car Porters to represent the Dining Car Employees of the CBQ Railroad.
(Late 50's or early 60's).
Chicago, IL Still a part of the Canel Street Club, Chicago, IL - The club members are all retired railroad men.

Registrant ID: 799
Name: Shead Coleman
City/State: Chicago, IL
Railroad: Burlington Railroad, Illinois Central
Position: Pullman Porter
Years of Service: 1940-1976
Submitter's Name: Sharyn
City/State: Alpharetta, GA
Comments: Daddy loved his job as a Pullman Porter. He would

always say that when I was born he was out of town but felt every labor pain Mom had while having me. When he retired, I still believe that was his darkest moment, because he could no longer do the job he loved.

Registrant ID: 796
Name: Robert Coleman
City/State: PA
Railroad: Reading Company
Position: Dining car Waiter
Years of Service: 1925-1940
Submitter's Name: Lemuel
City/State: Berlin, MD
Comments: Robert Ernest Coleman, was a Dining Car Waiter for fifteen years. He was killed on April 4, 1940 in Allentown, PA. when he and a cook, Allen Evans crossed the tracks intending to go to a lodging home, a tender of a locomotive struck them from the rear.

Registrant ID: 804
Name: Ulysses Coleman
City/State: Flossmoor, IL
Railroad: Illinois Central
Years of Service: 1925-1937
Submitter's Name: Mildred
City/State: Flossmoore, IL
Comments: Father

Registrant ID: 797
Name: Robert   (Bob) Coleman
City/State: Indianapolis, IN
Position: Sleeping Car Porter
Submitter's Name: Pamela
City/State: Indianapolis, IN
Comments: I don't know much that is why I am looking for him.

His wife's name was Fannie Coleman. Both of them came from West Virginia, but ended up in Indianapolis, Indiana. He had 3 children Elizebeth, Archie, & Albert. Elizabeth died in West Virginia.

Registrant ID: 788
Daniel Marshall Coleman
City/State: Knoxville, TN
Railroad: Southern
Position: Dining Car Waiter
Years of Service: 1930's - 40's
Submitter's Name: Betty
City/State: Knoxville, TN
Comments: My father Daniel Marshall Coleman was a Dining Car Porter in the 1930s and 40s. He worked on the Tennessean that ran from Knoxville to Washington, DC and the Carolina Special that ran from Knoxville to Asheville, NC to Asheville, North Carolina.

Registrant ID: 790
Name: George D. Coleman
Position: Train Driver
Years of Service: 1800-1900
Submitter's Name: Alameda
City/State: Oakland, CA

Registrant ID: 789
Name: Edward W Coleman
City/State: Richmond, VA
Railroad: Pullman Co-R&P
Position: Sleeping Car Porter
Submitter's Name: Edward W
City/State: Richmond, VA
Comments: Retired in 1944 late 50's-60's worked out of Richmond District, Baltimore, Jacksonville

Registrant ID: 793
Name: Prince Coleman
City/State: AL
Railroad: Union Pacific (last)
Position: Porter
Years of Service: 1927-52
Submitter's Name: Cheryl
City/State: Vancouver, WA
Comments: I don't know a lot because he was my great-grandfather, and I was a little girl when he talked about his travels as a Porter on the train. But I know he knew Mr. Randolph personally and he was a good union man and a leader in Denver, Colorado.
He died in 1963.

Registrant ID: 805
Name: Walter Collier
Railroad: I think it was the Union Pacific Railroad
Position: Porter
Years of Service: 1930's-60's
Submitter's Name: Frank
City/State: Florissant, MO

Registrant ID: 813
Name: J.E. Collins
Railroad: El Paso
Years of Service: 1977's
Submitter's Name: Lawrence Lars

Registrant ID: 806
Name: Dempsey Collins
City/State: Gary, IN
Position: Pullman Porter
Years of Service: 1940's
Submitter's: Ida, Lorraine and Linda
City/State: Minneapolis, MS
Comments: Uncle

Registrant ID: 814
Name: John Colston
City/State: Washington, DC
Railroad: The Pullman Co.
Position: Pullman Attendant/Club Car Waiter
Years of Service: 10
Submitter's Name: Gwendolyn
City/State: Washington, DC
Comments: John Little Colston is my grandfather. He is my paternal parent. He has one child that lives in the Washington Metropolitan Area. He has three grand daughters and two great grandchildren. He also has two sisters that live in North Carolina, a brother.

Registrant ID: 3520
Name: Golden Selas
City/State: Kalamazoo, MI
Position: Sleeping Car Porter
Years of Service: 1938-1969
Submitter's Name: Marcella
City/State: Chicago, IL

Registrant ID: 816
Name: Charles S. Compton
City/State: St. Paul
Railroad: PullmanLine # 808/Hartpass
Position: Pullman Porter
Years of Service: 1923-1960
Submitter's: Faheem , Akbar, Aaliyah
City/State: Chicago, IL
Comments: He was our grandfather. His route was from Billings to Spokane Washington

Registrant ID: 817
Name: Charles Conn
Position: Pullman Porter

Years of Service: 1922-1942
Submitter's Name: Bernard J.
City/State: Chicago, IL

Registrant ID: 818
Name: Douglas Conner
City/State: Pueblo, CO
Railroad: Santa Fe R. R.
Position: Chair Car attendant
Years of Service: 1961-1971
Comments: I belonged to the sleeping car porters labor union from1961 to1971.

Registrant ID: 819
Name: Fred Conners Griffith
City/State: Dorchester, MA
Years of Service: 1936-1956
Submitter's Name: Arthur
City/State: Dorchester, MA

Registrant ID: 825
Name: John H. Contee
City/State: Baltimore, MD
Railroad: Baltimore and Ohio
Position: Personal Cook to the President, B&O
Years of Service: 1920-1947
Submitter's Name: Thelma C.
City/State: Baltimore, MD
Comments: Since my father was the personal cook to the president of B&O, we enjoyed the privilege of having passes and never having to pay fares when traveling. When I was a little girl, my mother, sister and I went on a private tour of the president's personal car.

Registrant ID: 837
Name: Robert Cook
City/State: Chicago, IL
Railroad: Great Northern

Position: Pullman Porter
Years of Service: 25 years
Submitter's: Robert Jr. and Yolanda
City/State: Chicago, IL
Comments: Our father regular ran was to Portland, Oregon.

Registrant ID: 829
Name: Frank Cook
City/State: Cincinnati, OH
Position: Pullman Porter
Years of Service: 1945-1953
Submitter's Name: Phillip
City/State: Cincinnati, OH

Registrant ID: 827
Name: Cleveland Cook
City/State: Winston Salem, NC
Railroad: No sure I have insurance paper from the united states railroad retirement board 844 rush street Chicago Ill. Illinois dated nov 8th 1945 a reply refering to R.R.B No.A-251951he was my grandfather on my mother
Position: Pullman Porter
Submitter's Name: Shirley
City/State: Rosedale, NY
Comments: My mother and aunt his surviving sister says he was a Pullman Porter many years until he died. I never saw a picture of him. I would like to honor him by including him in this historic national registry.

Registrant ID: 834
Name: Isaac I. Cook
City/State: IA
Railroad: Burlington, Iowa
Position: Dining Car Waiter
Years: Circa 1925-1940

Submitter's Name: Sandra G.
City/State: Shaker Heights, OH
Comments: I never knew my Uncle I saac Isaiah Cook, however, in interviewing other family members for genealogical history, especially my Uncle Robert Craighead (who was a Pullman Porter),

Registrant ID: 831
Name: Haywood Cook
City/State: AL
Position: Porter
Submitter's Name: Carlotta
City/State: Wichita, KS

Registrant ID: 838
Name: Charles Cooke
City/State: Roxbury, MA
Railroad: Boston & Maine – Boston New Haven
Position: Pullman Porter
Years of Service: 1907 - 1952
Submitter's Name: Myrtle
City/State: Plymouth, MA
Comments: My father worked on the railroad for 45 years, until he was seventy years old. He was a wonderful husband to my mother and they raised 8 successful children.

Registrant ID: 851
Name: William Peter Cooper
City/State: Coco, FL
Railroad: Chesapeake & Ohio
Position: Pullman Porter
Years of Service: 1948-1950's
Submitter's Name: Dr. Essie

Registrant ID: 845
Name: Darwin M Cooper
Railroad: Pullman Company

Position: Sleeping Car Porter
Years of Service: 1930's
Submitter's Name: Cooper

Registrant ID: 842
Name: Charles Cooper
City/State: Chicago, IL
Railroad: Burlington Northern
Position: Sleeping Car Porter
Years of Service: 1928-1975
Submitter's: Charles & Gerard.
City/State: Chicago, IL
Comments: My Dad worked with A. Phillip Randolph to help desegregate the housing at 1400 S. Canal Street also "known as" Crooks Terminal.

Registrant ID: 848
Name: Luther H. Cooper
City/State: Fairless Hills, PA
Railroad: Seaboard Railroad
Position: Dining Car Waiter
Service: Circa 1942 to 1944
Submitter's Name: Gregory
City/State: Fairless Hills, PA
Comments: Luther H. Cooper worked for Seaboard Railroad during war as a Dining Car Waiter, he say's that his experience was a good one he felt that people treated him very well. Luther H. Cooper just turn Eighty One and his birthday is February 4, 1921.

Registrant ID: 841
Arthur George Sr. Cooper
City/State: New Orleans, LA
Railroad: Louisville & Nashville
Position: Pullman Porter
Years of Service: 1919-1967
Submitter's Name: Audrey
City/State: New Orleans, LA

Comments: He ran from New Orleans to Chicago and St. Louis but most of his trips were from New Orleans to New York. He was also called George.

Registrant ID: 850
Name: William Cooper
City/State: Pittsburgh, PA
Submitter's Name: Dolores D.
City/State: Pittsburgh, PA

Registrant ID: 844
Name: Charles Cooper
City/State: Memphis, TN
Position: Pullman Porter
Years of Service: 1919-
To July 1, 1956
Submitter's Name: Hiji Cooper
City/State: Riverdale, NY
Comments: Mr. Charles Cooper worked with A. Philip Randolph to organize the Brotherhood of Sleeping Car Porters in Memphis, TN. Once the union was formed, he served as Secretary and Treasurer for fifteen years.

Registrant ID: 852
Name: Robert Cooper, Sr.
City/State: DC
Railroad: Atlantic Coast Line
Position: Pullman Porter
Years of Service: 1925-1956
Submitter's Name: Waltine
City/State: Mitchellville, MD
Comments: My father supported a wife and Nine children on his salary alone. My parents depended heavily on the tips that my father received. My father would be gone 3-4 days at a time, and would prepare his cars at Union Station in Wash., D.C.

Registrant ID: 853
William Harvard Copeland
City/State: Denver, CO
Railroad: So Pacific
Position: Pullman Porter
Service: Circa1913 to early 60's
Submitter's Name: Shirley
City/State: Inglewood, CA
Comments: Mr. Copeland was my. He passed away in 1963. The family has his watch that was given to him when he retired.

Registrant ID: 854
Name: Willie Coppage
City/State: Jackson, MI
Railroad: Pullman Company
Position: Porter
Years of Service: 1940-1950

Registrant ID: 855
Name: Thomas Corbett
City/State: Washington, DC
Railroad: B & W
Years of Service: 29Years
Submitter's Name: Trevino
City/State: Richmond, VA

Registrant ID: 856
Name: Thomas Sunny Corbin
City/State: Columbus, SC
Railroad: Southern Railroad
Fired Up Trains &Cleaned Engines
Years of Service: 18 Years
Submitter's Name: Carry
City/State: Columbus, SC

Registrant ID: 859
Name: Hartwell Cornelius
City/State: NY
Railroad: Sunnyside Yard
Submitter's Name: Gloria

City/State: Aurora, IL
Comments: I am his daughter

Registrant ID: 863
Name: Dalton Cosby
City/State: Owensboro, KY
Railroad: L&N
Position: Cook
Years of Service: 1915 -
Submitter's Name: Jesse
City/State: Springfield, OH

Registrant ID: 865
Name: Jim Cosmond
City/State: East St. Louis, MO
Railroad: Fresco Railroad
Years of Service: 1880's-1916
Submitter's Name: Ida

Registrant ID: 866
Name: Jim Cosmond
City/State: East ST. Louis, MO
Railroad: Freseu Railroad
Years of Service: 1880-1916
Submitter's Name: lda Mae
City/State: East St. Louis, MO
Comments: My grandfather

Registrant ID: 867
Name: William H. Costen
City/State: Bloomfield, CT
Railroad: Union Pacific
Position: Chair Car Attendant
Years of Service: 1965 - 1969
Comments: I worked summers
and Christmas as a college
student. Enjoyed the Experience.
I worked runs on the Union
Pacific Railroad from Omaha, NE
to (1)Pocatello,ID (2)Ogden,UT
(3)Denver,CO (4)Cheyenne,WY.

Registrant ID: 871
Name: William Theodore Costen

City/State: Atlanta, GA
Railroad: Union Pacific
Position: Porter
Years of Service: Late 1800s-
1900s
Submitter's Name: James H.
City/State: Atlanta, GA

Registrant ID: 870
Name: William J. Costen
City/State: Omaha, NE
Railroad: Union Pacific
Position: Pullman Porter
Submitter's Name: William H.
City/State: Bloomfield, CT

Registrant ID: 873
Name: Tommy Coston
City/State: Wallace, NC
Railroad: Silver Meteor NY,
Rout was FL, to CA
Position: Pullman Porter
Years of Service: 1946-1969
Submitter's Name: Helen
City/State: Wallace, NC
Comments: Also EL Capital from
Chicago to California.

Registrant ID: 875
Name: Fletcher Sr. Cottrell
City/State: Tacoma, WA
Railroad: Union Pacific
Position: Porter/Steward
Years of Service: 1938-44
Submitter's Name: Fletcher Jr.
City/State: Tacoma, WA
Comments: My Dad died Two
years ago. The railroad brought
him and his brother to Ogden,
Utah.

Registrant ID: 879
Name: Willie Allen Counts
Position: Pullman Porter

Years of Service: Over 25
Comments: He was also a member of the union.

Registrant ID: 876
Name: Fred McCoy Counts
City/State: Haverstraw, NY
Railroad: New York Central
Position: Pullman Porter
Years of Service: 10to 20 years
Submitter's Name: Shirlee E
City/State: Philadelphia, PA
Comments: I was a child when my father worked on the railroad, but now I'm an adult and very interested in the article in the Ebony magazine article about the A. Philip Randolph Pullman Porter Museum and the original SHOWTIME move 10K Black Men Named George.

Registrant ID: 882
Name: John H. Courtney
City/State: AL
Position: Sleeping Car Porter
Submitter's Name: John H.
City/State: AL

Registrant ID: 886
Name: Leroy Cowan
City/State: Compton, CA
Railroad: Headquarters was in Omaha, Nebraska /relocated to California.
Position: Car Waiter
Submitter's Name: Brenda
City/State: Midwest City, OK
Leroy was my mother's brother

Registrant ID: 887
Name: Otis Byron Cowan
City/State: Boley, OK
Railroad: Union Pacific

Position: Pullman Porter
And Dining Car Waiter
Years of Service: 1935-1945
Submitter's: Leonard S.
City/State: New Orleans, LA
Comments: I am his son.
Deceased

Registrant ID: 889
Name: Curtis Cox
City/State: Dayton, OH
Position: Laborer
Years of Service: 1948-1950

Registrant ID: 892
Name: Samuel Cox
City/State: Pittsburgh, PA
Railroad: Pennsylvania
Position: Pullman Porter
Years of Service: 1918 - 1945
Submitter's Name: Debra
City/State: Harrisburg, PA
Comments: He was deceased before I was born, but I wrote to the Railroad Retirement Board, and received a copy of his application.

Registrant ID: 890
Name: Frank Cox
City/State: Oklahoma City, OK
Railroad: Pullman Company
Position: Pullman Porter
Years of Service: 1929 - 1960
Submitter's Name: Frank
City/State: Oklahoma City, OK
Comments: Frank Cox, my father, received many commendations regarding his service and dedication to his customers. Notably, he received a letter from Marvin Miller ("Michael Anthony"), the star of the TV program, "the

Millionaire". He was a member of the B.S.C.P union

Registrant ID: 888
Name: Cleveland Cox
City/State: Peoria, IL
Railroad: Rock Island Railroad
Position: Track Department Maintenance of way
Years of Service: 1950's --
Submitter's Name: Rose
City/State: Peoria, IL

Registrant ID: 893
Name: Prince Craddock
City/State: Santa Monica, CA
Railroad: Southern Pacific
Position: Porter
Years of Service: Circa 1900 - 1906
Submitter's Name: Debra
City/State: Santa Monica, CA
Comments: This was my grandfather and I just remember him talking about being a Porter on the train. He was from Atlanta, GA and in 1906 he moved to California. My mother believes that he worked for Southern Pacific.

Registrant ID: 894
Name: George Richard Craig
City/State: Cincinnati, OH
Railroad: C&O
Position: Dining Car Waiter
Years of Service: 1930-1970
Submitter's Name: Marlene
City/State: OH
Comments: Daughter of a Dining Car Waiter

Registrant ID: 896
Name: Gordon Craig
City/State: Baltimore, MD
Railroad: Seaboard Coastline

and Amtrak
Position: Dining Car Waiter
Years of Service: 32 Years
Submitter's Name: Linda
City/State: Baltimore, MD
Comments: Although my father is deceased, he was active in a group which is headquartered in Washington D.C, and they called themselves the associa-tion of retired railroad men.

Registrant ID: 895
George Washington Craig
City/State: KY
Position: Porter
Years of Service: 1915--1945
Submitter's Name: Darlene
City/State: Westport, KY

Registrant ID: 898
Name: Charles Cranshaw
City/State: Chicago, IL
Railroad: Milwaukee Railroad
Position: Porter-Waiter
Years of Service: 1920-1930's
Submitter's Name: Mary
City/State: Cleveland, OH
Comments: Charles Cranshaw was my father. He met and married my mother in Tacoma Washington in 1921,while he worked for the railroad.

Registrant ID: 899
Name: Charles Virty Cranshaw
City/State: Tacoma, WA
Railroad: Milwaukee
Position: Sleeping Car Porter
Submitter's Name: Charlotte
City/State: Tacoma, WA
Comments: My father passed in 1965. He worked on the Milwaukee line that ran from

Chicago to Spokane and Tacoma Washington. He waited tables and attended guest in the Sleeping Cars - and whatever else he was requested to do. I still have a pin from the Brotherhood

Registrant ID: 903
Name: Kenneth C Crawford
City/State: Anderson, IN
Railroad: Pullman Company
Position: Pullman Porter
Years of Service: 1943-1945
Submitter's Name: Crawford

Registrant ID: 905
Name: Mose Crawford
City/State: Augusta, GA
Railroad: Atlantic Coast Line and Georgia Railroad
Position: Red Cap Porter
Years of Service: 1925 to 1972
Comments: I am retired. I worked for the railroad for 47 years. I was born September 10,1904. I live in Augusta Georgia. I am 97 years old and still drive my truck. . I am the father of 18 children.

Registrant ID: 904
Name: Malvern L. Crawford
City/State: MI
Railroad: Santa Fe
Position: Porter
Years of Service: 1943-1972
Submitter's Name: Alan O
City/State: MI

Registrant ID: 902
Name: Kenneth C Crawford
City/State: Anderson, IL
Railroad: Pullman Co.

Out of Indianapolis
Position: Sleeping Car Porter
Years of Service: 1943-1945
Submitter's Name: Kenneth C
City/State: Andersn, IL

Registrant ID: 909
Name: Squire Crawford
City/State: AL
Railroad: Louisville & Nashville
Submitter's Name: Dorris
City/State: Grandview, MO

Registrant ID: 908
Name: Overton W. Crawford
City/State: Elworth, Maine
Railroad: Pullman Rail Car Co
Position: Pullman Porter
Years of Service: 1936-39
Submitter's Name: Ellen
City/State: North Redding, MA
Comments: Oveton W. was my grandfather.

Registrant ID: 907
Name: Overton V. Crawford
City/State: Elworth, Maine
Railroad: Pullman Rail Car Co.
Position: Pullman Porter
Years of Service: 1900-1930's
Submitter's Name: Ellen
City/State: North Redding, MA
Comments: My father later went to medical school

Registrant ID: 911
Name: Joyce Crawford Reese
City/State: EL, Harbor
Railroad: Pullman Company
Position: Torbert

Registrant ID: 912
Name: Henry B.J. Creditt
City/State: SC

Position: Porter
Submitter's: Rev Barbara
City/State: Florence, SC

Registrant ID: 914
Name: Kenneth Crenshaw
City/State: IL
Railroad: Santa Fe
Position: Dining Car Waiter
Years of Service: 1941 - 1962
Submitter's Name: Claudette
City/State: Chicago Heights, IL
Comments: My dad was the number one dining car waiter on the El Captain, the Chief and the Super Chief (Chicago to Los Angeles). I remember some of his stories from his trips away. My dad's wages were low, in his last years he was only making about $4,000.00 annually.

Registrant ID: 915
Name: Seth Crenshaw
City/State: TN
Submitter's Name: Kaye
City/State: Detroit, MI
Comments: I dont have specific information but he has two daughters Renee Crenshaw of Murphysboro TN and Teri Crenshaw of Oakland CA.

Registrant ID: 916
Name: Thomas A. Crenshaw
City/State: St. Louis, MO
Position: Founded Pullman Porter Benefit Assn
Years of Service: Retired 1932
Submitter's Name: Margot
City/State: Peoria, AZ

Registrant ID: 918
Name: Coy (David) Crews

City/State: AL
Railroad: Washington, D.C.
Years of Service: 1940's- 60's
Submitter's Name: Gale
City/State: Durham, NC
Comments: I do remember that he worked for the railroad for many years in Washington, D.C.

Registrant ID: 919
Name: Arnett Crider
City/State: IL
Railroad: Illinois Central
Position: Dining Car Waiter
Years of Service: 31
Submitter's Name: Shirley
City/State: South Holland, IL
Comments: Arnett resided in Chicago while working for the Illinois Central Railroad. Known as "Smilin' Jack", he was a "Waiter-In-Charge. During his 31 years of service, he "ran" on the City of New Orleans and his final years on the Green Diamond.

Registrant ID: 920
Name: Lourinza Crier
City/State: New Orleans, LA
Railroad: Pullman Co.
Position: Pullman Porter,
Years of Service: 1941 to 1968
Submitter's Name: Ron
City/State: Houston, TX
Comments: President of New Orleans Brotherhood of S. C. Porters 1960s

Registrant ID: 921
Robert Cleveland Crittenden
City/State: CA
Position: Porter
Years of Service: 1919-1956

Submitter's Name: Daphne
City/State: Fontana, CA
Registrant ID: 924
Name: George Washington Crittendon
Position: Porter
Years: Circa 1930'-1960's
Submitter's: George
City/State: Bronx, NY
Comments: My grandfather worked for 33 years as a Pullman Porter and he received a gold watch when he retired. We have a letter from Mr. H E. Worley, Superintendent of the Pullman Company that came from Pennsylvania Terminal May 8, l962.

Registrant ID: 928
Name: William Crockett
Position: Porter
Submitter's Name: Edwina
City/State: Bronx, NY

Registrant ID: 926
Joseph Benjamin Crockett
City/State: Lancaster, SC
Railroad: Southern Railroad
Submitter's Name: Carrie
City/State: Colorado Springs, Colorado
Comments: I don't know too much about my grandfather. I know they lived in Lancaster, South Carolina, and later moved to Rock Hill, South Carolina. He and several men were killed in a tornado named Hugo, in 1926. His wife's name was Freddie Crockett.

Registrant ID: 930
Name: William Cromwell

City/State: Seattle, WA
Position: Dining Car Waiter
Years of Service: 1943-1970
Submitter's Name: Muriel C.
City/State: Seattle, WA

Registrant ID: 932
Name: Walter Croom
City/State: Pittsburgh, PA
Railroad: Baltimore and Ohio
Position: Dining Car Waiter/Steward
Years of Service: 1916 - 1948
Submitter's Name: Taru
City/State: Pittsburgh, PA

Registrant ID: 933
Name: Joseph B. Cropper
City/State: Chicago, IL
Railroad: Southern Pacific
Position: Pullman Porter
Years of Service: 1931-1965
Submitter's Name: Theresa
City/State: Chicago, IL
Comments: His trains ran out of the Polk Street Station and during most of his years with the railroad, he worked on the Chief and Super chief trains. He always brought magazines home. Magazines we could not afford, but those books and my father sparked my interest in reading. To this day I am still a reader. My dad is now deceased.

Registrant ID: 935
Name: William E. O. Cross
City/State: AL
Position: Porter
Years of Service: 1928-1929
Submitter's Name: Shirley
City/State: Chicago, IL

Registrant ID: 934
Name: Maurice Cross
City/State: Cleveland, OH
Years of Service: 1960's-1980's
Submitter's Name: Jacenta
City/State: Cleveland, OH
Comments: Niece

Registrant ID: 938
Name: Elgie Crow
City/State: Amarillo, TX
Railroad: Santa Fe
Position: Chair Car Attendant,
Porter, and Conductor
Comments: I experienced much
Racism and Unfair Labor
Practices during my 30 plus
years with the Santa Fe
Railroads in Amarillo, Texas.
After a National Class Action
LawSuit, I was promoted to a
Conductor position.

Registrant ID: 936
Name: Charles Howard Crow
City/State: Taylor, MI
Railroad: Evansville, IN
Position: Waiter
Years of Service: 1945-1955
Submitter's Name: Deborah

Registrant ID: 940
Name: Lucien Eugene Cruce
City/State: IL
Position: Clerk in Charge
Years of Service: 1928-1960
Submitter's Name: Kenneth L.
City/State: Chicago, IL

Registrant ID: 941
Name: Johnie E. Crumbley
City/State: Jacksonville, FL
Position: Laborer and
Station Porter

Years of Service: 1943 1976
Submitter's Name: Alberta C.
City/State: Jacksonville, FL

Registrant ID: 942
Name: Jesse L. Crutcher
City/State: Chicago, IL
Railroad: Chicago &
Ogden Railroad
Position: Dining Car Waiter

Registrant ID: 943
Name: Jesse L. Crutecher
City/State: Chicago, IL
Railroad: Chg & Ogden Rail
Road -Dinning Chef Waiter
Position: Dinning Car Waiter
Submitter's Name: Jesse L.
City/State: Chicago, IL
Comments: Also Chicago & NW
Dining Car Waiter. Burlington
Northern-Dining car waiter-
Waiter in Change-Steward
until Amtrak took over.

Registrant ID: 944
Name: Clyde Cullens
City/State: Atlanta, GA
Railroad: Pullman Company
With various railroads
Position: Pullman Porter
Years of Service: 1940 to 1959
Submitter's Name: Ricardo
City/State: Memphis, TN
Comments: At the time of this
submission, he is 91 years old
and is still living. I believe he
may be one of the oldest living
Pullman Porters. I am his son,
Ricardo Cullens.

Registrant ID: 945
Name: Isaiah Culpreath
Railroad: Union Pacific

Position: Porter
Years of Service: 1949-1953
Submitter's Name: Deborah
Comments: My uncle retired in 1971 My father retired 1963

Registrant ID: 946
Name: Mitchell Cumberbatch
Railroad: NY Central
Years of Service: 1921-1962
Submitter's Name: Fran Cena
City/State: Jamaica, NY

Registrant ID: 951
Name: Wiley Cunningham
City/State: AL
Railroad: Union Railway Company, **Position:** Trucker, caller, loader, scaler, sealer and
Years of Service: 1939-1946
Submitter's Name: Pamela
City/State: Highland Park, MI
Comments: Worked out of Memphis, Tennessee. Wiley Cunningham died in 1948.

Registrant ID: 948
Name: Myles Cunningham
City/State: Jersey City, NJ
Railroad: Erie-Lackawanna
Position: Pullman Porter
Years: Circa 1918 - 1960
Submitter's Name: Myles
City/State: Jersey City, NJ
Comments: This was my grandfather. He told me he worked the New York - Chicago run during his career. He passed away in 1971.

Registrant ID: 950
Name: Wilbur Cunningham
City/State: New York, NY
Railroad: New York Central

Position: Pullman Porter
Years of Service: Circa 1930's-60's
Submitter's Name: Barbara
City/State: Queens Village, NY
Comments: I'm not sure of the years my father worked as a Pullman Porter but I'm hoping that he'll be recognized and that his name will find a place in the national registry and your museum. Thank you.

Registrant ID: 955
Name: Thomas Curry
City/State: Chicago,, IL
Railroad: Rock Island
Position: Pullman Porter
Years of Service: 1924-1959
Submitter's Name: Audrey
City/State: Hinsdale, IL
Comments: My father was a great man who loved and enjoyed his job. He loved his family and took good care of us. He died in 1965. His son David Curry was also a Porter. My father traveled from Chicago to California, and New York and also to Colorado Springs.

Registrant ID: 954
Name: Rufus F. Curry
City/State: Newark, NJ
Railroad: Pennsylvania RR
Position: Pullman Porter
Years of Service: 1947 to 1951
Submitter's Name: R. Frank
City/State: Maplewood, NJ
Comments: When I was just a little kid my dad worked for the railroad, I really only remember a little from that time. He used to work a run between the New

York-New Jersey area going to
Chicago, Illinois.

Registrant ID: 952
Name: Elzie Either Curry
City/State: MD
Railroad: Baltimore & Ohio
Position: Instructor of Porters,
Train Attendant,
Years of Service: 1924-1966
Submitter's Name: Marc A.
City/State: Owings Mills, MD
Comments: He was an original
Charter Member of the
Brotherhood of Sleeping Car
Porters. I currently have an
original publication entitled
"Baltimore & Ohio Magazine"
dated September 1947 with a
article about my grandfather
(Elzie Either Curry). Mr. Curry,
at that time was a instructor of
the porters for the new porters.

Registrant ID: 956
Name: George E. Cutchins
City/State: Columbus, OH
Position: Porter
Submitter's Name: George E.
City/State: Charleston, SC

Registrant ID: 959
Name: Lonzo Cuts
Submitter's Name: Slania
City/State: St. Louis , MO
Position: Porter
Comments: Lonzo was my

Registrant ID: 961
Name: Puther Cuts
City/State: St. Louis, MT
Position: Porters
Submitter's Name: Slania
City/State: St. Louis, MT

Comments: He was my brother

Registrant ID: 963
Name: Lonzo Cutz
Position: Porter
Submitter's Name: Gloria

Registrant ID: 964
Name: Rahert Cutz
City/State: St. Louis, MO
Position: Porter
Submitter's Name: Gloria

Registrant ID: 965
Name: John Cuyjet
City/State: PA
Position: Summer employee
while in college
Years of Service: Circa1937-40
Submitter's Name: Michael
City/State: Louisville, KY
Comments: My father
occasionally told the story
about working one or more
summers while he was in college
as a Pullman Porter, traveling
from Philadelphia westward.

Registrant ID: 966
Name: Johnnie Cyrus
City/State: AL
Railroad: Pennsylvania RR
Position: Pullman Porter
Years of Service: Over 20
Submitter's Name: Anette
City/State: Laurelton, NY
Comments: My grandfather was
born in 1900. His name was
Johnnie C. Cyrus. He lived in
Brooklyn, NY. He worked for the
Pennsylvania Railroad for over
20 years as a Pullman Porter.

Registrant ID: 967
Name: John Carter Dabney
Submitter's Name: Minnie
Brown & Herman Wesley
City/State: Richmond,
Comments: My grandmother's
uncle, Mr. Dabney, served 40
years on the R F&P. He was tall,
dark, and good looking, with a
beautiful smile, and played the
piano.

Registrant ID: 969
Name: Earl Dailey
City/State: South Euclid, OH
Railroad: New York Central-
Chicago & North Western
Position: Cook & Waiter
Years of Service: 1947-1951
Comments: A great help in
obtaining finances to further my
education. Work was mostly
during summer months and an
occasional Christmas Holiday
work.

Registrant ID: 974
Name: Lawrence E. Dandridge
City/State: Battle Creek, MI
Position: Porter
Years of Service: 1942-1945
Submitter's Name: J. Walter
City/State: Battle Creek, MI

Registrant ID: 975
Name: John Daniel
City/State: Chicago, IL
Railroad: Northwestern
Position: Pullman Porter
Years of Service: 1938 - 1961
Submitter's Name: Barbara
City/State: Chicago, IL
Comments: My father, John
Arthur Daniel, Jr., did not and

would answer to the name of
"George". He worked the route
from Chicago to Los Angeles
during WWII and after the war,
he was on the Chicago to
Portland route. He always
brought home plenty of silver
dollars

Registrant ID: 977
Name: John Arthur Daniel
City/State: IL
Years of Service: 1936-1963
Submitter's Name: Barbara J
City/State: Chicago, IL

Registrant ID: 976
Name: John Daniel
City/State: Chicago, IL
Railroad: Union & Pacific
Position: Sleeping Car Porter
Years of Service: 1935-1968
Submitter's Name: Dolores
City/State: Chicago, IL
Comments: My father went out
on a run with the railroad during
World War II. The railroad
dropped many men over to fight
in the war.

Registrant ID: 978
Name: Ernest Daniels
City/State: Jamaica
(Long Island), NY
Railroad: The Pullman Co.
Position: Pullman Porter
Years of Service: 1921- 966
Submitter's Name: Shirlene
City/State: Chicago, IL
Comments: Mr. Ernest Daniels
was my Grandfather. I do not
know exactly what railroad line
he worked on. I just know that
he worked at the Penn Station in

New York. My Grandfather fought very hard for the porters to have a union. He was one of the first African Americans to become apart of the union. Striking to become a union member was very costly for my Grandfather. It cost him his marriage to my grandmother

Registrant ID: 980
Name: Luther Louis Daniels
City/State: Atlanta, GA
Railroad: Chicago -LA
Years of Service: 1928-1960
Submitter's Name: Dorothy
City/State: Atlanta, GA
and seeing his two sons grow up. He almost lost the home he was buying in Long Island. He told me that back in the 20's and 30's working conditions were very bad for African Americans. African Americans were not permitted to organize into unions. They worked with little benefits. They did not have pensions, vacation time,or sick pay. They were expected to work overtime without pay. My Grandfather said that for the sake of the children he will continue to strike until the black porters had a union.

Registrant ID: 982
Name: William Walter Dansey
City/State: Alsip, IL
Railroad: Burlington Railroad
Years of Service: 44 Years
Submitter's Name: Kimberly
City/State: Alsip, IL

Comments: My Great Grandfather. worked for the railroad for 44 years

Registrant ID: 983
Name: Earl Stubblefiel Darody
City/State: Chicago, IL
Railroad: NY Central
Years of Service: 25 Years
Submitter's Name: Madonna
City/State: Chicago, IL

Registrant ID: 984
Name: Sam Darrett
City/State: Houston, TX
Position: Brakeman
Submitter's Name: Jessica
City/State: New York, NY

Registrant ID: 985
Name: Fred Daugherty
City/State: NY
Position: Porter
Years of Service: 3 years
Submitter's Name: Marcus
City/State: Bronx, NY

Registrant ID: 986
Name: John Wesley Davenport
City/State: Laurel, MD
Position: Pullman Porter
Submitter's Name: Delcina
City/State: Laurel, MD

Registrant ID: 987
Name: Elliot Davidson, Sr.
City/State: NY
Position: Waiter/Porter

Registrant ID: 989
Name: John Arthur Davie
City/State: Chicago, IL
Years of Service: 1936-1963
Submitter's Name: Barbara J.

Registrant ID: 992
Name: George Davies
City/State: Greenville, NC
Railroad: Pullman Company
Position: Pullman Porter
Years of Service: 1940-1948

Registrant ID: 1012
Name: Joe Davis
City/State: Pittsburgh, PA
Railroad: Penn Railroad
Position: Conductor
Submitter's Name: Andrew J.

Registrant ID: 1031
Name: P.C. Davis
Position: Pullman Porter
Years of Service: Over 25
Comments: Union member

Registrant ID: 1032
Name: Riley Marcilous Davis
Railroad: Baltimore and Ohio
Position: Pullman Porter
Years of Service: 43 Years
Submitter's Name: Riley

Registrant ID: 1019
Name: John D. Davis
City/State: Duncanville, TX
Railroad: Santa Fe
Position: Pullman Porter
Years of Service: 1927-1965

Registrant ID: 1023
Name: Lawrence W. Davis
City/State: Washington, DC,
Railroad: C&O, B&O
Position: Pullman Porter
Years of Service: 1925-1969
Comments: I worked 48 years
for the railroad. I started in
1925 and worked for Pullman as
a Sleeping Car Porter until 1969.

I then worked as a Sleeping Car
Porter for C&O B&O from 1969
to 1973. I ran out of
Washington, DC.

Registrant ID: 995
Name: Aubrey Davis
City/State: Duncanville, TX
Railroad: Santa Fe
Position: Pullman Porter
Years of Service: 1922-1964

Registrant ID: 999
Name: Authur Davis
City/State: Chicago, IL
Submitter's Name: Beverly D.
City/State: AL

Registrant ID: 1006
Name: Floyd Davis
City/State: AL
Railroad: Chicago Northwestern
Position: Pullman Porter
Years of Service: 1910-1967
Submitter's Name: Everett S.
City/State: Baton Rouge, LA
Comments: My father traveled
from Chicago to LA

Registrant ID: 1011
Name: Homas Davis
City/State: Bronx, NY
Position: Pullman Porter
Years of Service: 1943-1951
Submitter's Name: Daisy
City/State: Bronx, NY

Registrant ID: 1020
Name: John Perry Davis
City/State: Bainbridge, GA
Railroad: Central Georgia
Position: Pullman
Years of Service: circa 1935 -60

Submitter's Name: Enis, Castine, Janice Wichta, KS
City/State: Brooklyn, NY
Comments: My father is still alive at age 108 years old. He retired from the railroad. I have never heard any stories but as a child I remember asking him about it but all he would say is that "That was bad times" and he would not say anymore.

Registrant ID: 1016
Name: John Davis
City/State: High Point, NC
Position: Dining Car Waiter
Years of Service: 1917-1936
Submitter's Name: Gwyn
City/State: Charlotte, NC
Comments: My great uncle died in 1936. From his obituary, I found that he worked on trains # 37 & 38 and waiting on President Coolidge on the Coolidge Special.

Registrant ID: 999
Name: Carl Davis
City/State: Chicago, IL
Railroad: Burlington
Position: Waiter
Submitter's Name: Carl
City/State: Chicago, IL

Registrant ID: 1005
Name: Floyd Davis
City/State: Chicago, IL
Railroad: Chicago North Western
Position: Pullman Porter
Submitter's Name: Everett
City/State: Chicago, IL

Registrant ID: 1010
Name: Herman Albert Davis

City/State: Cincinnati, OH
Position: Pullman Porter
Years of Service: 1930-1962
Submitter's Name: Hermena
City/State: Cincinnati, OH

Registrant ID: 1037
Name: William E. Davis
City/State: Gretna, VA
Railroad: Southern Railroad
Position: Laborer, Chef
Submitter's Name: Valerie
City/State: College Park, GA
Comments: William E. Davis was my grandfather (My father's father). I have been told by other relatives that he started as a laborer on the train and worked his way up to Chef. He would leave on Sunday and return home on Fridays.

Registrant ID: 1035
Name: Van Davis
City/State: Corbett, OR
Railroad: Southern Pacific
Position: Cook
Years of Service: 26
Submitter's Name: Vincent
City/State: Corbett, OR
Comments: He was fired because of an accident after 23 years, He was rehired after some years, and after a court case.

Registrant ID: 1027
Name: Michele E. Davis
City/State: Detroit, MI
Position: Clerk
Submitter's Name: Lisa
City/State: Detroit, MI

Registrant ID: 1024
Name: Leslie Davis

City/State: Niles, MI
Railroad: New York Central
Position: Dining Car Waiter
Years of Service circa 1943 -55
Submitter's Name: Lestine
City/State: Detroit, MI

Registrant ID: 1036
Name: William Davis
City/State: Washington, DC
Submitter's Name: John H.
City/State: Greensboro, NC

Registrant ID: 1018
Name: John Davis
City/State: Dallas, TX
Railroad: Santa Fe
Position: Pullman Porter
Years of Service: 1927-1965
Submitter's Name: Tracy
City/State: Houston, TX
Comments: He was my great
uncle. He was a union member.
He and his brother (my
Grandfather Aubrey L. Davis
both worked on the Santa Fe.

Registrant ID: 1013
Name: Joseph Davis
City/State: Parsons, KS
Railroad: Pullman company
Position: Pullman Porter and
Brakeman
Years of Service: 25 years
Submitter's Name: Deborah
City/State: Kansas City, KS
Comments: His run was
Missouri-Kansas-Texas. My
father was a Pullman Porter he
also performed brakeman duties
when warranted yet was never
compensated for that.

Registrant ID: 1025
Name: Mattie Davis
City/State: Little Rock, AR
Railroad: Missouri Pacific
Position: Pullman Porter
Years of Service: 1941-49
Submitter's Name: Curtis
City/State: Little Rock, AL
Comments: He was with Civil
Defense until the war was over.
He injured his back on the
railroad, but continued to work
several more years wearing a
brace for the rest of his life. He
stayed with the troops once they
embarked the train until they
disembarked.

Registrant ID: 1003
Name: Clyde D Davis
City/State: Los Angeles, CA
Railroad: Southern Pacific
Position: Pullman Porter
Years of Service: 1944-1955
Submitter's Name: Glenda
City/State: Los Angeles, CA
Comments: My father

Registrant ID: 998
Name: Augustus Davis
City/State: Macon, GA
Railroad: Central of Georgia
Position: Pullman Porter
Years of Service: circa 1928-52
Submitter's Name: Willie
City/State: Macon, GA
Comments: Augustus 'Gus'
Davis was born in Monroe
County, Georgia. He was first
hired on as a Pullman porter
however later in his career he
switched to working as a
brakeman.

Registrant ID: 1029
Name: Moses Davis
City/State: Memphis, TN
Railroad: Illinois Central
Position: Mail Loader
Years of Service: Retired
Submitter's Name: Mozetta
City/State: Memphis, TN

Registrant ID: 1033
Name: Robert Davis
City/State: Chicago, IL
Position: Porter
Submitter's Name: Julia
City/State: Milwaukee, WI
Comments: He was my
grandfather. When I was a little
girl, I went with my father to
meet him at Chicago's Union
Station.

Registrant ID: 1007
Name: Glasco Davis
City/State: New York, NY
Position: Pullman Porter
Submitter's Name: Diane
City/State: New York, NY
Comments: Unfortunately, I
don't have much information
since I was a little girl at the
time. My mom, aunts and uncle
are all deceased now.

Registrant ID: 1028
Name: Milo R P Davis
City/State: Ocala, FL
Railroad: NY Central
Position: Porter/Waiter
Years of Service: 29 1/2 Years
Submitter's Name: Loretta
City/State: Ocala, FL

Registrant ID: 1026
Name: McKinley Davis
City/State: Richmond, VA
Railroad: C&O.
Position: Pullman Porter and
Acting Conductor
Years of Service: Circa 40's or
50's to the early 70's
Submitter's Name: Ann
City/State: Richmond,VA
Comments: He also had a run
between NY And Florida
Sometimes he worked on the
dining car and as a conductor,
but did not receive the pay. He
worked during the time that
soldiers used the train and was
given foreign coins, which he had
in a collection until I took them
to school to share for show and
tell.

Registrant ID: 1008
Name: Harry Jr. Davis
City/State: Riverdale, GA
Railroad: Atlantic Coastline RR
Position: Carr
Years of Service: late 50's-60's
Submitter's Name: Ancel
City/State: Riverdale, GA
Comments: Brother

Registrant ID: 1001
Name: Clifford Davis
City/State: Cincinnati, OH
Position: Pullman Porter
Submitter's Name: Judith
City/State: Romulus, MI

Registrant ID: 1000
Name: Charlie Davis
City/State: Ennis, TX
Position: He turned trains
around at the end of the line

Years of Service:1930's- 50's
Retired in 1954
Submitter's: Virginia and Margo
City/State: Sacramento, CA
Comments: Charlie Davis is my
Mother's father.

Registrant ID: 1021
Name: Lawrence Davis
City/State: Washington, DC
Position: Porter
Years of Service: 50+ Years
Submitter's Name: Urseline
City/State: Temple Hills, MD

Registrant ID: 1034
Name: Royal Edward Davis
City/State: MN
Railroad: Northern Pacific
Position: Waiter - Steward
Years of Service: 1918- - 1953
Submitter's Name: Sharman
City/State: Wayzata, MN
Comments: I believe he was the
first African American Steward
for Northern Pacific Railroad,
Minneapolis to Seattle route. His
name is mentioned in the book,
Dining Car Line to the Pacific by
William A. McKenzie. Have in
my possession several letters of
commendation

Registrant ID: 1039
Name: Wallace Davis, Jr.
City/State: IL
Position: Porter
Years of Service: 1925 -- 1975
Submitter's Name: Charles
City/State: Phoenix, AZ
Comments: My uncle, Wallace
Davis Jr., was from South
Carolina. He moved to the
Chicago area with his father

Wallace Davis senior, and his
mother Mary Davis and younger
sister Mattie. He found
employment as a Porter in
Chicago.

Registrant ID: 1040
Name: Edward Davis, Sr.
City/State: New Orleans, LA
Railroad: Southern Railroad
Position: Pullman Porter
Years of Service: 37 years
Comments: My working years
were most enjoyable, I met may
people during my years of travel

Registrant ID: 1041
Name: William Davis, Sr.
Position: Sleeping Car Porter
Submitter's Name: Lois
City/State: Syracuse, NY

Registrant ID: 1042
Name: Elliot Davisdson
City/State: NY
Railroad: NY-Chicago
Position: Waiter Porter
Submitter's Name: Elliot Jr.
City/State: NY
Comments: Father

Registrant ID: 1044
Name: Arthur Dawson
City/State: Jersey City, NJ
Railroad: New York Central
Position: Pullman Porter
Years of Service: Circa 1900-35
Submitter's : Rosalind Serena
City/State: Laurelton, and
Queens, NY

Registrant ID: 1045
Name: Robert Dawson
City/State: AL

Railroad: Chicago Northwestern
Position: Pullman Porter
Submitter's Carlton
City/State: Lynwood, IL and
Marilyn **City/State:** Chicago, IL

Registrant ID: 1043
Name: Arthur Dawson
City/State: NJ
Position: Pullman Porter
Years of Service: Early 1900's
Submitter's Name: Annamarie
City/State: Newark, NJ
Comments: Meeting stars on the
train. About the good people and
the big tippers. Kate Smith was
mentioned as a favorite by
Grandpa or his son-in law also a
Pullman Porter about her
pleasant personality.

Registrant ID: 1048
Name: Georgia Ira Dean
City/State: IL
Railroad: Pullman-Amtrak
Position: Sleeping Car Porter
Years of Service: 1933 -1974
Submitter's Name: Arleavie
City/State: Chicago, IL
Comments: Snowstorm of 1966
my husband called his job and
asked if he should report for
work. The reply was if you want
your job you better come in. with
no transportation he walked.

Registrant ID: 1049
Name: Joseph Dean
City/State: Chicago, IL
Railroad: Illinois Central
Position: Porter
Years of Service: 1917-1949
Submitter's Name: Ray
City/State: Chicago, IL

Registrant ID: 1047
Name: Dallis Dean
City/State: Cincinnati, OH
Position: Steward
Years of Service: 1946-1982
Submitter's Name: Virgila
City/State: Cincinnati, OH
Comments: Daughter

Registrant ID: 1050
Name: Vincent A. Dean
City/State: Cincinnati, OH
Position: Pullman Porter
Years of Service: 1900-1915
Submitter's Name: LaVenia
City/State: Cincinnati, OH

Registrant ID: 1051
Name: William A Debram
City/State: Belmar, NJ
Position: Pullman porter (NY)
Years of Service: circa
1918-1940's
Submitter's Name: Maryorie
City/State: Belmar, NJ
Comments: Worked for 25 years
his route was from New York to
Boston

Registrant ID: 1052
Name: Michael A. Decatur IL
City/State: Jacksonville, FL
Railroad: Atlantic Coastline
Position: Head Waiter
Years of Service: 1941-1981
Submitter's Name: Michael A.
City/State: Savannah, GA
Comments: My Father died in
1998

Registrant ID: 1053
Name: Addie B Deckard
City/State: Canton, OH
Railroad: Pullman Company

Position: Car Cleaner
Years of Service: 1937
Submitter's Name: Howard

Registrant ID: 1056
Name: William Dein
Position: Pullman Porter
Years of Service: 10yrs
Submitter's Name: Williams

Registrant ID: 1057
Name: G.W. Delce
Position: Pullman Porter
Years of Service: Over 25 Years
Comments: He was a union member

Registrant ID: 1058
Name: Wade Denley
City/State: AL
Submitter's Name: Josephine
City/State: Bronx, NY
Comments: My "grandfather" worked as a Pullman Porter. He was a college graduate from South Carolina who also went to medical school for a couple of years. I remember as a young girl being raised in NYC and that he would go to work every day with a briefcase.

Registrant ID: 1059
Name: Alvin Dennis
City/State: AL
Railroad: Santa fee
City/State: AL

Registrant ID: 1060
Name: George Dennis
City/State: Cincinnati, OH
Position: Porter
Years of Service: 1945-1971
Submitter's Name: Elisa M.

City/State: Cincinnati, OH

Registrant ID: 1061
Name: Robert Dent
City/State: Roxbury, MA
Railroad: Boston-Maine RR
Position: Pullman Porter
Years of Service: 1919-1960
41 years
Submitter's Name: Renee
City/State: Laurelton, NY
Comments: Daughter

Registrant ID: 1062
Name: George Ira Deon
City/State: Chicago, IL
Position: Pullman Porter
Years of Service: 36-38 Years
Submitter's Name: Connie
City/State: Chicago, IL

Registrant ID: 1068
Name: James Dickerson
City/State: CO
Railroad: Union Pacific
Position: Pullman Porter
Dining Car Chef
Years of Service: 24 years
Submitter's Name: Pauline
City/State: Austin, TX

Registrant ID: 1065
Name: Earle Dickerson
City/State: NY
Railroad: Pennsylvania RR
Pullman Car Division
Position: Car Cleaner
Years of Service: circa 1949
Submitter's Name: Mary
City/State: Bronx, NY

Registrant ID: 1066
Name: George Dickerson
City/State: Atlantic City, NJ

Submitter's Name: Joi
City/State: Los Angeles, CA
Comments: My grandfather was a Pullman Porter and I'm sure he never minded being called "George" since his real name is George. He is in his 90's and still living today. His father was also a Pullman Porter named George Dickerson.

Registrant ID: 1067
Name: Jacob F. Dickerson
City/State: Pittsburgh, PA
Railroad: The Pullman Co.
Position: Porter
Years of Service: 1912-48
Submitter's Name: Joan P.
City/State: Pittsburgh, PA
Comments: Randolph came to dinner one time when my father was a boy. They had to clean the house from top to bottom, even the chandeliers, and everything had to sparkle. They had a roast chicken for dinner. It was probably about the YMCA on Center Ave, which was

Registrant ID: 1071
Name: Thurmon Dickson
Railroad: Union Pacific
Position: Dining Car Porter
Submitter's Name: Khalil
City/State: Los Angeles, CA
Comments: My grandfather took pride in being a Pullman Porter. I was also proud as a youngster to see him coming home after being out on a long trip. He would often bring us back souvenirs from the places he had been.

Registrant ID: 1070
Name: Thurmon Dickson
City/State: CA
Railroad: Pullman Company
Position: Pullman Porter
Years of Service: 1942 to 1975
Submitter's Name: Elaine
City/State: Los Angeles, CA

Registrant ID: 1069
Name: Joseph Dickson
City/State: New York City, NY
Railroad: Lehigh-Valley RR
Position: First Cook
Submitter's Name: Connie
City/State: Sparkill, NY
Comments: He received a Certificate of Attendance on July 3, 1945 for completing a special course in food sanitation given at New York City by the U.S. Public Health Service. He signed a Visitor's Card for the PULLMAN PORTER'S ATHLETE AND SOCIAL CLUB, INC.

Registrant ID: 1074
Name: Johnnie Diggs
City/State: AL
Submitter's Name: Veronica
City/State: Hercules, CA
Comments: My father is deceased, but told us the stories of when he worked on the railroad after WWII. I think he worked on the Santa Fe, from Mississippi to California, where he eventually came to live. The timing was during the early forties.

Registrant ID: 1075
Name: Walter Diggs
City/State: NY

Railroad: Pennsylvania
Position: Pullman porter
Years of Service: Unknown at this time but he was a porter long enough to retire with a pension.
Submitter's Name: Geraldine
City/State: Philadelphia, PA
Comments: Walter T. Diggs was my grandfather and he was a Pullman Porter. It has always been my understanding that he traveled all over the United States. He an excellent historian.

Registrant ID: 1076
Name: Arthur Dinkins Sr.
City/State: Mount Vernon, NY
Railroad: Pullman Co. **Position:** Pullman Porter/Safetyman
Years of Service: 1943-1947
Comments: Greatest experience I had in my life

Registrant ID: 1077
Name: William Dison
City/State: Denver, CO
Railroad: Union Pacific
Position: Pullman Porter
Years of Service: 1940*1958
Submitter's Name: Janice
City/State: Los Angeles, CA

Registrant ID: 1079
Name: Walter Divers
City/State: St. Louis, MO
Position: Pullman Porter
Years of Service: 1940-1966
Submitter's Name: Robert
City/State: St. Louis , MO

Registrant ID: 1080
Name: James Dixon
City/State: Chicago, IL

Railroad: Santa Fe
Position: Pullman Porter
Years of Service: Not Sure but before and during the 60's
Submitter's Name: Beverly
City/State: Chicago, IL
Comments: I remember that my grandfather was a Pullman Porter and that he wore a white suit and a cap. I have an old picture of him in his uniform. I do not know the dates that he worked.

Registrant ID: 1082
Name: William Dixon
City/State: Chicago, IL
Position: Pullman Porter
Years of Service: 1900's
Submitter's Name: B
City/State: Chicago, IL

Registrant ID: 1085
Name: Jonathan Dixon, Sr.
City/State: Waycross, GA
Railroad: Atlantic Coastline/Seaboard Coastline
Position: Pullman Porter
Years of Service: 23 Years
Comments: It was a way to support my family and I enjoyed meeting people while providing a service to the public.

Registrant ID: 1084
Name: Benjamin Dixon, Sr.
City/State: Asheville, NC
Railroad: Southern Railway
Position: Pullman Porter
Years of Service: 1925 - 1964
Submitter's Name: Maben
City/State: Arlington, VA
Comments: He was President of Asheville Local of the

Brotherhood of Sleeping Car Portersin NC. A. Philip Randolph visited the Asheville Pullman Porters local, he was the guest speaker at the Association in the early 1940s, and dined at the home of Benjamin Dixon at 153 Burton Street, West Asheville, N.C.

Registrant ID: 1087
Sherman H. Dobbins, Sr.
City/State: Chicago, IL
Submitter's Name: Delayna
City/State: Hazelcrest, IL

Registrant ID: 1089
Name: Paul Dobine
City/State: Hemet, CA
Railroad: All major railroads traveling throughout the US and Canada
Position: Pullman Porter
Years of Service: Circa 1938-52
Submitter's Name: Gwen
City/State: Hemet, CA
Comments: My dad has told us so many stories throughout all my life about this experience of 'running on the road'. It was always a 'journey into a time past' that was 'romantic' and historic. I say romantic because my father loved the opportunity to visit other cities.

Registrant ID: 1091
Name: Sherman H. DoBouis
City/State: Chicago, IL

Registrant ID: 1092
Name: Claude Dodson
City/State: Ossining, NY

Railroad: Grand Central Terminal, NYC
Position: Dining Car Waiter
Years of Service: 1941
Submitter's Name: Omar
City/State: Spring Valley, NY

Registrant ID: 1093
Name: Benjamin Doleman
City/State: Washington, DC
Position: Waiter-Porter
Years of Service: 1900-1940
Submitter's Name: Mary
City/State: Bronx, NY

Registrant ID: 1095
Name: Emmanuel Donaldson
City/State: New Orleans, LA
Submitter's Name: Marceline
City/State: Cambridge, MA
Comments: I don't have much. I just discovered he was a Pullman Porter. Not sure of his dates, but he lived somewhere between 1900-45.

Registrant ID: 1098
Name: Axem Donnetley
City/State: Jamaica, NY
Position: Sleeping Car Porter
Submitter's Name: Harriet
City/State: Jamaica, NY
Comments: Worked until his death in 1944 his Father He knew Mr. Randolph

Registrant ID: 1099
Name: Leroy J. Dorn, Sr.
City/State: St, Louis, MT
Railroad: Penn. Central, Amtrak
Position: Pullman Porter
Years of Service: Retired 1969
Submitter's Name: Valerie
City/State: St. Louis , MT

Registrant ID: 1101
Name: John Larvell Dorsey
Railroad: Baltimore & Ohio
Position: Dining Car Waiter
Years of Service: 20 Years
Submitter's Name: Luvenia G.
City/State: Bay Shore, NY

Registrant ID: 1103
Name: Thomas Dorsey
City/State: Cleveland, OH
Railroad: Nickel Plate Railroad
Position: Dining Car Waiter
Years of Service: 1958 to 1963
Submitter's Name: Wendy
City/State: San Diego, CA

Registrant ID: 1104
Name: Virgil Dorsey
City/State: AL
Railroad: Santa Fe
Position: Chair Aar Attendant
Years of Service: 1954 - 1959
Submitter's Name: Ruthann
City/State: Colorado Springs,
Comments: Virgil was my father.

Registrant ID: 1105
Name: William Dorsey
City/State: KS
Railroad: ATSF
Position: Section Laborer and
Crossing Flagman
Years of Service: Sept. 1927 -
Dec. 1936 and Sept.1949 -
Dec.1959
Submitter's Name: Ruthann
City/State: Colorado Springs, CO
Comments: My grandfather is
now deceased. I have no further
information

Registrant ID: 1107
Name: Curtis Dotson
City/State: Denver, CO

Railroad: Denver & Rio Grande
Position: Pullman Porter and
Dining Car Waiter
Years of Service: 1945 - 1981
Submitter's Name: Dr. Curtis
City/State: Denver, CO
Comments: My father took
much pride in his work. He
prepared his uniform with a
crisp white shirt, freshly cut
hair, and highly shined shoes for
each run. His work took him
from Denver to Chicago, then
Chicago back to Denver and on
to Oakland and back home. He
was out six days and in six days.
He most of all enjoyed the
comradeship of his fellow porters
as well as the interaction with
the passengers. He retired in
1981 after 36 years on the road.

Registrant ID: 1106
Name: Claude Dotson
City/State: Spring Valley, NY
Railroad: Grand Central NY
Submitter's Name: Claude
City/State: Spring Valley, NY

Registrant ID: 1113
Name: Horace Douglas
City/State: Columbus, OH
Comments: Horace was my
grandfather.

Registrant ID: 1118
Name: Jerome Douglas
City/State: Hempstead, NY
Railroad: New York Railroad
Position: Pullman
Submitter's Name: Tonya
City/State: Charlotte, NC
Comments: This is my
grandfather that worked with the

railroad most of his life. I am not sure about the name of the railroad. It may have been the Long Island Railroad. He worked as a Pullman Porter.

Registrant ID: 1117
Name: Howard C. Douglas
Railroad: Kansas City
Years of Service: 40's-50's
Submitter's Name: Genive
City/State: Chicago, IL
Comments: My uncle

Registrant ID: 1111
Name: Donald Robert Douglas
City/State: Chicago, IL
Railroad: Pennsylvania
Years of Service: 39-45
Submitter's Name: Genive
City/State: Chicago, IL
Comments: He was my brother

Registrant ID: 1120
Name: C.R. Douglass
Position: Pullman Porter
Years of Service: Over 25
Comments: He was active in the union

Registrant ID: 1122
Name: Charlie Douglass
City/State: Kansas City, KS
Position: Sleeping Car Porter
Submitter's Name: Kelly
City/State: Federal Way, WA

Registrant ID: 1123
Wellington Maceo Dowdell, Sr.
City/State: Jacksonville, FL
Railroad: Atlantic Coastline
Position: Pullman Porter

Years of Service: 35 years
Submitter's Name: Irene
City/State: Jacksonville, FL

Registrant ID: 1124
Name: Hayward Doyle, Sr.
City/State: Denver, CO
Railroad: Pullman Company
Position: Sleeping Car Porter
Years: Circa. 1926-69
Submitter's Name: Hayward
City/State: Denver, CO
Comments: He was President Of the Denver Branch of Pullman Porters.

Registrant ID: 1126
Name: Louis Drake
Railroad: Pullman Co.
Chicago from Cleveland
Position: Sleeping Car Porter
Years of Service: 1930's
Submitter's: Barbara Ann
Comments: My Father

Registrant ID: 1125
Name: James Drake
City/State: AL
Railroad: Washington, DC
Position: Porter
Years of Service: 35 yrs.
Submitter's Name: Yolanda
City/State: Washington, DC
Comments: My Grandfather is currently deceased. He worked on the railroad from 1935-1970.

Registrant ID: 1127
Name: Carlton Draper
Position: Cook
Submitter's Name: Harriet
City/State: Chicago, IL
Registrant ID: 1128
Name: Lawrence E. Drew

City/State: Washington, DC
Position: Pullman Porter
Years of Service: 1919 to 1957
Submitter's Name: Benjamin
City/State: Fort Washington,
DC

Registrant ID: 1129
Name: Thomas Drish
City/State: Champaign, IL
Railroad: City of New Orleans
Position: Porter
Years of Service: 10 years
City/State: AL

Registrant ID: 1130
Name: Jasper Driver
City/State: Oakland, CA
Railroad: Union Pacific & the
Pullman Company
Position: Pullman Porter
Years of Service: 1936 - 1958
Submitter's Name: James
City/State: Sierra Vista, AZ
Comments: Held position as
Pullman Inspector from (1942 –
1946 Was on the World's Fair
Exhibition Team at Treasure
Island, California in 1937

Registrant ID: 1131
Name: Albert Duckett
City/State: Detroit, MI
Railroad: Originally- New York
Central Later it became Penn-
Central Railroad
Position: Machinist- Then
Machinist Supervisor
Years of Service: 1945-1985
Submitter's Name: Saundra
City/State: Detroit, MI
Comments: I only remember
that he went to school for several
years while working at the

railroad. He trained to become a
machinist. As a child he often
took me to visit, what he called
the round house. He later
became a supervisor.
Retired 1985.

Registrant ID: 1133
Name: Whitfield Dudley
City/State: Jamaica, NY
Position: Pullman Porter
Years of Service: 1943-1945
Submitter's Name: Carol
City/State: Chesapeake, VA
Comments: My father did not
serve in the military service
during World War II, he instead
worked on the railroad
transporting military personnel.
He died at age 85 and continued
to love trains. The last gift I gave
him was a wristwatch which
made the sound of a trains.

Registrant ID: 1135
Name: Marlene D Duffel
City/State: Kansas City, MO
Railroad: Santa Fe Railroad
Position: Chair Car Attendant
Years of Service: 1950 - 1964
Submitter's Name: Orlando
City/State: Kansas City, MO

Registrant ID: 1136
Name: Nathaniel Dunagan
City/State: IL
Railroad: Burlington
Position: Dining Car Waiter
Years of Service: 1939-1972
Submitter's Name: Eleanor
City/State: Gilbert, AZ
Comments: My father, Nathaniel
Dunagan, worked on the
Burlington RR for many years.

He ran from Chicago to Minneapolis and later to Denver. He belonged to a club made up of railroad men living in Chicago. It was called "The Canal Club".

Registrant ID: 1140
Name: Alphonso Duncan
City/State: Ocala, FL
Railroad: Atlantic Coastline
Position: Chair Car attendant, Secretary of A Philip Randolph Pullman Porter Chapter
Years of Service: 1942-1982
Submitter's Name: Patricia
City/State: Ft Lauderdale, FL
Comments: The family has heard some incredible stories of the traveling experiences, and we believe is absolutely behind the growth of my stepfather into the wonderful man he became.

Registrant ID: 1143
Name: Tilman Leroy Duncan
City/State: Naples, NY
Position: Porter
Years of Service: 1932-1945
Submitter's Name: Randolph
City/State: Ionia, MI

Registrant ID: 1144
Name: Ollie Lee Duncan, Sr.
City/State: Baltimore, MD
Railroad: Penn Railroad
Position: Cook
Years of Service: 1940's
Submitter's Name: Janet F.

Registrant ID: 1145
Name: Napeleon B. Duncan/White/Johnson
City/State: Chicago, IL
Position: Pullman Porter

Years of Service: Late 1920's
Submitter's Name: Bebe
City/State: Chicago, IL

Registrant ID: 1146
Name: Henry Dunlap Sr.
City/State: Chicago, IL
Railroad: Milwaukee Road
Position: Dining Car Waiter
Years of Service: 1931-1963
Submitter's Name: David
City/State: Chicago, IL
Comments: He was my father. I have other relatives who were railroad employees. James Duncan Dunlap Dining Car Waiter Roy Clanton Law Chef, Sam Robert Singley Railway Clerk.

Registrant ID: 1150
Name: John Lee Dunn
City/State: Park Forest, IL
Railroad: Santa Fe – Illinois Central
Position: Pullman Porter
Years of Service: 1930's-1970
Submitter's Name: Deborah

Registrant ID: 1151
Name: Thomas Elry Dunn
City/State: Washington, DC
Railroad: B & O Railroad; running on the National Limit from NY to St. Louis, and the Capital Limit from New York to Chicago and Wildcat Cars.
Position: Chef
Years of Service: 1945 - 1946
Submitter's Name: Mary R.
City/State: Alexandria, VA
Comments: My father is now 75 and he will be 76 years old in two months. I remember him

mentioning that he worked on the train as a cook. Many times, it would be weeks before he would leave the train to explore the city life.

Registrant ID: 1148
Name: James Dunn
City/State: AL
Railroad: Pullman Co.
Chicago was his home base
Position: Porter
Years of Service: 1950's
Submitter's Name: Byron
City/State: Dallas, TX

Registrant ID: 1152
Name: Guy Dunn Sr.
City/State: Athens, GA
Railroad: Southern Railroad
Years of Service: 1935-1940's
Submitter's Name: Sylvia
City/State: Highland Park, MI
Comments: I am registering for my grandfather who was disabled while working on the railroad in the 1930's or early 40's. I am not sure what his job title was, but I think he worked as a labor on the "rail roads" and possible a porter.

Registrant ID: 1153
Name: William Dunnigan
City/State: Chattanooga, TN
Railroad: Southern Railroad
Position: Porter
Years of Service: 30 plus years
Submitter's Name: Iris
City/State: Antioch, TN
Comments: Train Station is now the Chattanooga Choo Choo. Came from Meridian Mississippi

as one of the first black train Porters.

Registrant ID: 1154
Name: William Dunston
City/State: Richmond, VA
Railroad: Seaboard Coastline
Position: Pullman Porter
Years e: Circa 1950 - 1975
Submitter's Name: Marilyn
City/State: Glen Allen, VA

Registrant ID: 1155
Name: William F. Durham
City/State: NC
Position: Pullman Porter
Years of Service: 1920-1950
Submitter's Name: Jean
City/State: Burke, VA

Registrant ID: 1156
Name: David Durrette
City/State: Cleveland, OH
Submitter's Name: Carol
City/State: Wexford, PA
Comments: This man was my great-uncle. He was from West Newton, PA originally. I know that he lived in Cleveland and had a wife but no children. He died in 1953.

Registrant ID: 1158
Name: Alexander Duson
City/State: Newton Ctr., ME
Railroad: Oakland
Submitter's Name: M.
City/State: Newton Ctr., ME

Registrant ID: 1160
Name: Walter H Eady
City/State: Summerville, SC
Railroad: Carolina Special
Position: Pullman Porter

Years of Service: 1919-1945
Submitter's Name: Young

Registrant ID: 1162
Name: Jamie Earl Brown
City/State: Philadelphia, PA
Position: Sleeping Car Porter
Years of Service: 1942-1944
Submitter's Name: James
City/State: Philadelphia, PA
Comments: Father

Registrant ID: 1166
Name: DeWitt Earle
City/State: AL
Railroad: Southern Railroad
Position: Dining car waiter
Years of Service: Retired after
15 - 20 years.
Submitter's Name: Gloria
City/State: Houston, TX
Comments: My Uncle Dewitt
was a Dining Car Waiter with the
Southern Railroad he worked on
the railroad prior to the 2nd
world war and was retired on
disability. His run was from
Washington DC to Nashville TN

Registrant ID: 1170
Name: Spurgeion D Earle
City/State: Washington D.C.,
Railroad: Southern Pacific
Position: Dining car waiter
Years of Service: 1919-1950
Submitter's: Jennie and Gloria
City/State: Washington DC and
Houston, DC & 'TX
Comments: Jennie B Write:
Regular run from Washington
D.C. to Atlanta, Ga.on trains
numbers 17&18;Helped to
organize dining car waiters union

in the D.C. area and was elected
as its first president. Was
selected as the first waiter to
man the first club car on the
Southern line. Gloria Write: My
uncle Spurgeon worked on the
Southern Railway as a Dining
Car Waiter. As I remember he
also worked on the Private Car of
the President of the Southern
Railroad. He was very Active in
the union and held a position
with the Union.

Registrant ID: 1167
Name: Dewitt T Earle
Railroad: Southern Pacific
Position: Cook
Submitter's Name: Jennie B
City/State: Washington,
Comments: Uncle

Registrant ID: 1172
Name: Lawrence Early
City/State: Washington, DC,
Railroad: He worked out of
Washington, DC
Position: Cook
Years of Service: Retired in the
late 1940's or early 1950's
Submitter's Name: Daryl
City/State: Washington, DC
Comments: Lawrence Early's
brother, John Early also retired
from the railroad. He was either
a Pullman Porter or Dining Car
Waiter.   Both are from
Washington, DC are both retired
from the railroad. My great
grandfather, Lawrence and A.
Philip Randolph were friend

Registrant ID: 1174
Name: Jordon "Boot" Easley

City/State: Montgomery, TX
Submitter's Name: Courtney
City/State: Beaumont, TX
Comments: Years of employment are unknown. He and his brothers Judge and Stanley Easley were actually part of the construction of the railroads.

Registrant ID: 1176
Name: Stanley "Stant" Easley
City/State: Montgomery, TX
Submitter's Name: Patricia
City/State: Montgomery, TX

Registrant ID: 1178
Name: J.A. Eatman
Position: Pullman Porter
Years of Service: 25
Comments: He was also a BSCP Union member

Registrant ID: 1179
Name: Lausie M. Edge
City/State: Chicago, IL
Railroad: Pullman Co.
Position: Pullman Porter
Worked out of Chicago
Years of Service:
Started in 1920 , but not sure of retirement date
Submitter's Name: Mildred
City/State: Atlanta, GA
Comments: I do remember that he did worked in Chicago. After his death they did give him his last train ride home to Atlanta. My husband is deceased now so some of the information you may need I can try to get from his brother in Richmond, VA. THANK YOU!

Registrant ID: 1180
Name: Joseph Edinburg, Sr.
City/State: New Orleans, LA.,
Railroad: Sunset Limited
Position: Sleeping Car Porter
Years of Service: Began 1939
Submitter's Name: Octavia
City/State: New Orleans, LA
Comments: My grandfather loved his job, He was proud of his profession and remained active with his local organization of Sleeping Car Porters in New Orleans until his death.

Registrant ID: 1181
Name: John Edmonds
City/State: South Point, OH
Position: Porter
Submitter's Name: Gary
City/State: Gahanna, OH
Comments: Porter of the year met with President Eisenhower at the White House.

Registrant ID: 1182
Name: James Edward
Years of Service: 1940- 1960's
Submitter's Name: Deborah

Registrant ID: 1183
Name: Milton Edward
City/State: Chicago, IL
Position: Porter
Years of Service: 1942-1965
Submitter's Name: Sandra
City/State: Chicago, IL
Comments: Daughter

Registrant ID: 1191
Name: Herman Edwards
City/State: Henderson, NV
Railroad: NYC/Pennsylvania
Position: Waiter

Years of Service: 1944-1947
Comments: I was never called George we had name tags.

Registrant ID: 1190
Name: Eugene Jr. Edwards
City/State: Euclid, OH
Railroad: Pen. RR
Position: Pantry Man, Dinning Car

Registrant ID: 1189
Name: Don W. II Edwards
City/State: AL
Railroad: Wabash Pacific
Position: Porter
Years of Service: 1942-1960
Submitter's Name: Blerin
City/State: AL

Registrant ID: 1186
Name: Blakely Edwards
City/State: Crossett, AR
Position: Porter
Years of Service: Until 1960s
Submitter's Name: Windy
City/State: MD
Comments: I named my son after my Uncle Blakely. I remember him as a figure standing on the back platform of a train waving to us with a white handkerchief as he passed through town. We would wave back.

Registrant ID: 1187
Name: Dewitt Edwards
City/State: Bronx, NY
Railroad: N.Y Central
Position: Waiter
Years of Service: 1941-1965
Submitter's Name: Dewitt
City/State: Bronx, NY

Registrant ID: 1192
Name: John Edwards
City/State: Chicago, IL
Position: Porter
Submitter's Name: Anita M.
City/State: Gary, IN

Registrant ID: 1193
Name: Othean Edwards
City/State: CA
Railroad: Santa Fe/El Capitan
Position: Cook
Years of Service: 1940-1975
Submitter's Name: Jean
City/State: La Mesa, CA

Registrant ID: 1194
Name: William Henry Edwards
City/State: St. Louis, MO
Railroad: Pullman Company - attached to all railroads
Position: Sleeping Car Porter
Years: 20 years –1943-1963
Submitter's Name: Inez L.
City/State: St. Louis , MO
Comments: On one particular run, he was asked to do various duties by a passenger on the car he was assigned, but the gentleman instead of using his proper name of William the man insisted on calling him Rastus. He replied, Sir. Rastus did ot come today, but may I help you.

Registrant ID: 1188
Name: Don W. Edwards
Railroad: Wabash Pacific
Position: Porter
Years of Service: 1942-1960
Submitter's Name: Gloria Jean
City/State: St. Louis , MO

Registrant ID: 1195
Name: William Henry Edwards
City/State: St. Louis, MO
Submitter's Name: Regina
City/State: St. Louis, MT
Comments: William was my father

Registrant ID: 1196
William Edwards Flowers
City/State: Dicson, TN
Railroad: Pullman Company
Position: Pullman Porter
Years of Service: Circa 1942
Submitter's Name: Robertson

Registrant ID: 1201
Name: Moses Elam Jr..
City/State: Chicago, IL
Railroad: Santa Fe and the Pullman Company
Position: Pullman Porter
Years of Service: 1927-1961
Submitter's Name: Michelle
City/State: Chicago, IL

Registrant ID: 1200
Name: Moses Elam Sr.
City/State: Chicago, IL
Railroad: Santa Fe
Position: Pullman Porter
Submitter's: Jeanette & Lula
City/State: Chicago, IL
Comments: Moses Elam Sr. enjoyed working on the Santa Fe railroads very much and was proue of his job

Moses Elam Sr.

Registrant ID: 1206
Name: Estelle Elbert
City/State: Willingboro, NJ
Railroad: Pennsylvania RR
Position: Coach Cleaner
Years of Service: 20
Submitter's Name: Corrine
City/State: Willingboro, NJ
Comments: She worked as a coach cleaner from 1942, which was when the railroad hired women and African Americans to clean the coaches because the war made white men scarce. She worked until 1962 when she retired. For most of those years she worked and lived in Jersey.

Registrant ID: 1208
Name: David Elfe
City/State: St. Augustine, FL
Railroad: Pennsylvania RR
Position: Pullman Porter
Years of Service: 31 Plus yrs
Submitter's Name: Beatrice
City/State: Augustine, FL

Registrant ID: 1209
Name: Ornestus Elgin
City/State: Denver, CO
Position: Pullman Porter
Submitter's Name: Peggy
City/State: Denver, CO
Comments: My Father ran on the railroad all of my life. I think he retired in 1968 at that time our address was 3515 Harrison St-Denver, Colorado.

158

Registrant ID: 1210
Name: Joseph Ellies
City/State: Denver, CO
Railroad: Santa Fe
Position: Pullman Porter
Years of Service: Uncertain
Submitter's Name: Milodie E
City/State: Denver, CO
Comments: Father, Worked across the country.

Registrant ID: 1211
Name: Paul Watts Elligan
City/State: Denver, CO
Railroad: Union Pacific Railroad
Position: Dinning Car Waiter
Years of Service: 1940-1970
Submitter's Name: Michaella
City/State: Aurora, CO
Comments: My father, Paul,(now deceased) started working summers as a college student. His father, Lemuel Elligan, a physician, had himself worked on the Railroad in Atlanta, Georgia. My father moved to Chicago, Illinois and was ultimately transferred to Denver Colorado.

Registrant ID: 1213
Name: Gerald Elliot Sleigh
City/State: New York, NY
Railroad: Penn. Railroad
Position: Waiter
Years of Service: 1942-1970
Submitter's Name: Denise
City/State: New York, NY
Comments: Was closely associated with A Philip Randolph.

Registrant ID: 1218
Name: Harry Ellis
City/State: IL
Railroad: Illinois Central
Position: Pullman Porter
Submitter's Name: Charisse
City/State: Chicago, IL

Registrant ID: 1217
Name: Essic Albertis Ellis
City/State: Cincinnati, AL
Position: Pullman Porter
Submitter's Name: Brian
City/State: Cincinnati, OH
Comments: I don't really remember much other than seeing the pictures of my Grandfather.   I just wanted to make sure his name was listed.

Registrant ID: 1215
Name: Charles Ellis
City/State: Kirkwood, MO
Position: Pullman Porter
Submitter's Name: jenny
City/State: Cincinnati, OH

Registrant ID: 1223
Name: Joseph Ellis
Railroad: Pullman Co.
And the Santa Fe
Position: Porter
Submitter's Name: Melodie E.
City/State: Denver, CO

Registrant ID: 1224
Name: Solon Ellis
City/State: Minneapolis, MN
Railroad: Great Northern
Position: Dining Car Waiter
Years of Service: 25 years
Submitter's: Thomas & Wanda
City/State: Minneapolis & Memphis, MN & TN

Comments: My Father was a Dining Car waiter on the Empire Builder. His run was from St. Paul to Seattle, Washington. Even though I was a young boy I can remember the anticipation of going to the railroad station to meet my father upon his return.. I enjoyed the travel.

Registrant ID: 1222
Name: John Ellis
City/State: Montgomery, WV
Railroad: C & O
Position: Porter
Years of Service: 1950-60s'
Submitter's Name: Carmen
City/State: Reston, VA

Registrant ID: 1214
Name: Benjamin F. Ellis
City/State: Chicago, IL
Railroad: Chicago & Northwestern
Position: Sleeping Car Porter
Years of Service: 1903-1943
Submitter's Name: Barbara
City/State: South Holland, IL

Registrant ID: 1227
Name: William Ellison
Railroad: NY Central
Years of Service: 1921-1962
Submitter's Name: Fran Cerra
City/State: Jamaica, NY

Registrant ID: 1229
Name: Bob Ellyson
City/State: Cincinnati, OH
Submitter's Name: Barb
Comments: Lost both legs while working on railroad. They were finally replaced with cork legs p. 194 "Cincinnati Colored Citizens" by William Dabney

Registrant ID: 1230
Name: James Elmore
City/State: AL
Position: Fireman
Years of Service: 1919-1966
Submitter's Name: Daisy
City/State: Montclair, NJ

Registrant ID: 1231
Name: Thomas J Emery
City/State: Chicago, IL
Years of Service: Uncertain
Submitter's Name: Elizabeth
City/State: Chicago, IL

Registrant ID: 1232
Name: Thomas J Emery
City/State: Chicago, IL
Position: Waiter
Years of Service: 1891-1929
Submitter's Name: Harriett
City/State: Chicago, IL
Comments: My father

Registrant ID: 1233
Name: James Enoch
City/State: Toledo, OH
Railroad: B & O.
Position: Sleeping Car Porter and Car Steward
Years of Service: 1933 - 1950's
Submitter's Name: Tammy
City/State: Toledo, OH
Comments: We have all of his uniforms and hats and I think his membership/union card. I wondered where my father learn to dress so impeccably. The movie '10,000 MEN NAMED

GEORGE' explained it. Thanks for the history lesson.

Registrant ID: 1235
Name: Samuel Entzminger
City/State: AL
Railroad: Pennsylvania
Position: Pullman Car Porter
Years of Service: 1932 - 1968
Submitter's Name: Monica
City/State: Jamaica, NY

Registrant ID: 1237
Name: James Arthur Epps
City/State: Asheville, NC
Position: Pullman Porter
Years of Service: Circa 1920's to the early 1960's.
Submitter's Name: Harold
City/State: Fort Wayne, IN
Comments: Lived in Asheville, North Carolina

Registrant ID: 1239
Name: Bordtu T. Eres
City/State: Brownsville, TX
Position: Porter
Years of Service: 1947-1976

Registrant ID: 1242
Name: Alva Ervin
City/State: AL
Position: Porter
Years of Service: 1943-1959
Submitter's Name: Nattalie M.
City/State: Dallas, TX
Comments: He was my Grandfather

Registrant ID: 1243
Name: Robert Ervin Jr.
City/State: Baltimore, MD
Railroad: Patapsco and Back River

Position: Motor Vehicle Operator
Years of Service: 1946 to 1974
Submitter's Name: Terra
City/State: Baltimore, MD
Comments: According to my grandfather if there was an accident on the train tracks he was the person to divert oncoming trains to other tracks so they did not run into the accident. He also said that he had to help clean up the debris from the tracks. He retire

Registrant ID: 1244
Name: Robert Ervin Sr.
City/State: AL
Railroad: Patapsco and the Back River Railroad
Position: Railroad Trackman
Years of Service: 1920 to 1965
Submitter's Name: Terra
City/State: Baltimore, MD
Comments: I received the above information from his son Robert Ervin Jr.

Registrant ID: 1245
Name: Jesse Essex
City/State: Kansas, MT
Railroad: Amtrak
Position: Chair Car attendant
Years of Service: 1960's -70's
Submitter's Name: Mark
City/State: Emporia, KS

Registrant ID: 1251
Name: Albert Evans
City/State: AL
Years of Service: Uncertain
Submitter's Name: Annie
City/State: AL

Registrant ID: 1258
Name: Henry Evans
City/State: Jersey City, NJ
Railroad: A New York City to Chicago line **Position:** cook
City/State: Austin, TX

Registrant ID: 1265
Name: Morgan Evans
City/State: Chicago, IL
Railroad: Great Northern Railroad Burlington Route
Position: Pullman Porter
Years of Service: Jun 1927 to Sept 1968 (41yrs)
Submitter's Name: Carol
City/State: Chicago, IL
Comments: My father spoke often of the many famous people that traveled on the Pullman Coaches.   His two favorites were autographs from Mrs. Eleanor Roosevelt and the Chicago Opera and Ballet Cast during the 1935 Spring Tour.

Registrant ID: 1254
Name: Elson Evans
City/State: AL
Position: Porter
Submitter's Name: Debra
City/State: Chicago, IL
Comments: My grandfather Elson Evans worked on the railroad. great uncle Orville Slaughter. His regular run was from Washington D.C. to Atlanta, GA. on trains numbers 17and 18. He helped to organize the dining car waiters union in the D.C. area and was elected as

Registrant ID: 1253
Name: Clifton Evans

City/State: Chicago, IL
Position: Cook, Dining Car Waiter, Pullman Porter
Years of Service: circa 1929-61
Submitter's Name: Rose L.
City/State: Miami, FL
Comments: I don't recall which railroad my grandfather worked for, but I do recall that he was on a southern route out of Chicago, IL. Whenever he was on the road, he always went south. Those times that I was with him (during the summer), were some of the best.

Registrant ID: 1267
Name: Paul Bennett Evans
City/State: Oklahoma City, OK
Position: Porter and Waiter
Years of Service: 1940's
Submitter's Name: Lamona
City/State: Oak City, OK

Registrant ID: 1260
Name: Lewis Evans
City/State: AL
Railroad: Chicago to Oakland
Position: Pullman Porter
Years of Service: 40's and 60's
Submitter's Name: Carol
City/State: Oakland, CA
Comments: I know very little. He died in the 60's

Registrant ID: 1256
Name: Ezra E. Evans
City/State: St. Louis, MO
Position: Head Porter/Shop Stewart
Years of Service: 1922 until Retirement
Submitter's: Brenda and J.M.
City/State: St. Louis , MO

Registrant ID: 1268
Name: Frizell Evenston Jones
City/State: Charlottesville, VA
Railroad: C&O In VA
Position: Dining Car Waiter
Years of Service: 1946-1947
Submitter's Name: Debbie
City/State: Charlotteville, VA

Registrant ID: 1269
Name: Albert Ewing
City/State: AL
Submitter's Name: Cathy
City/State: Dolton, IL

Registrant ID: 1270
Name: Raymond T. Ewing
City/State: Kansas City, MO
Position: Pullman Porter
Years of Service: 1918-1965
Submitter's: Glenda Faye
City/State: Toledo, OH

Registrant ID: 1271
Name: Fred   D. Fair
City/State: DC
Railroad: Pullman Company
Position: Personal porter to President Franklin Delano. And also Roosevelt – President Harry S, Truman
Years of Service: 1940 to 1969
Submitter's Name: Fredrita
City/State: Clinton,, MD
Comments: My grandfather (Fred D. Fair) served as the personal Dining Car Waiter to Pres. F. D. Roosevelt and President Harry S.
Truman. My grandfather passed away March 13, 1999 at the age of 101 years old. He was also in the film for the documentary on HBO.

Registrant ID: 1273
Name: James D. Fairley
City/State: Greensboro, NC
Railroad: Pullman Company, New York Central
Position: Sleeping Car Porter
Years of Service: 45 years
Comments: I became a Porter for the Pullman Company out of Grand Central Station in New York City on March 30, 1923. When I began working, the Pullman Company, used stool pigeon porters as well as two newspapers to prevent the organization of the Union initially.

Registrant ID: 1272
Name: James D. Fairley
City/State: Greensboro, NC
Railroad: New York - Chicago
Position: Pullman Porter
Years of Service: 44 years
Submitter's Name: Valerie
City/State: Greensboro, NC
Comments: My Uncle who turned 98 years old on Tuesday, with a excellent memory. He worked as a Pullman Porter for 44 years, he was part to the original group who worked with A Phillip Randolph to help unionized the Pullman Porters.

Registrant ID: 1275
Name: Ural L. Farris
City/State: Denison, TX
Railroad: MKT Lines & Frisco
Position: Train Porter operating crew
Years of Service: 1938 - 1958

Comments: Rewarding, hard, detailed work that allowed me to provide for my family.

Registrant ID: 1276
Name: George Handy Fassett
City/State: Philadelphia, PA
Railroad: Pennsylvania RR
Position: Porter
Submitter's Name: Phyllis
City/State: Philadelphia, PA
Comments: He retired sometime in the 1930's and married my grandmother in 1934 (Sydney Jane Lane Earle Hutchinson). He had a vest watch which was a retirement present. He was not a blood relative but I thought of him as Pop

Registrant ID: 1278
Name: Clarence W. Faucette
City/State: Little Rock, AR
Position: Pullman Porter
Submitter's Name: Merilon C.
City/State: Little Rock, AR

Registrant ID: 1279
Name: Frank Faulkner Sr.
City/State: Chicago, IL
Railroad: Rock Island and the Union Pacific
Position: Sleeping Car Porter
Years of Service: 1927-1965
Submitter's Name: Sharon
City/State: Country Club Hills, IL
Comments: My grandfather told me that he hated it when the whites as he stated would call him boy. He said however many times he would make more in tips than what he was paid. My

grandfather died in August of 1972.

Registrant ID: 1282
Name: John Faust
Submitter's Name: Lee B
Comments: Friend

Registrant ID: 1280
Name: James Faust
City/State: AL
Submitter's Name: Lee B
City/State: AL
Comments: Friend

Registrant ID: 1283
Name: William Fentress
City/State: Chicago, IL
Position: Waiter
Years of Service: 35 Years
Submitter's Name: Bennie
City/State: Chicago, IL

Registrant ID: 1286
Name: Thomas Fields
City/State: New York, NY
Railroad: B & O, Lacawanna, and Penn Central
Position: Pullman Porter
Years of Service: 1926-1971
Submitter's Name: Barbara
City/State: Brooklyn, NY
Comments: My father was an original charter member of the Brotherhood of Sleeping Car Porters Formed in the mid 1930's.

Registrant ID: 1287
Name: William Fields
City/State: Clemson, SC
Railroad: NY Central
Position: Porter
Years of Service: 1800s-1900s

Submitter's Name: Arlene
City/State: Clemson, SC
Comments: 1878-1978

Registrant ID: 1285
Name: Simon Fields
City/State: Dorchester, MA
Railroad: New Haven Railroad
Position: Pullman Porter
Years of Service: 1940's 1959
Submitter's Name: Lynnette
City/State: Dorchester, MA
Comments: My father, known as S.P., worked the New Haven Railroad Line, coming up from Atlanta, GA with several friends including Fred Griffeth, known as Rochester, and others. Some of the trains he worked on were the Night Owl, the Lakeside and the Merchants' LTD

Registrant ID: 1288
Name: Roland Finger
City/State: New York, NY
Position: Pullman Porter
Submitter's Name: Louis G.
City/State: Orlando, FL
Comments: I knew my great uncle Roland worked for the railroad for many years and retired from the railroad. I was very young, but I knew my uncle carried himself with dignity and he overcame injustice, prejudice and held his head up high always.

Registrant ID: 1289
Name: Charles (Coley) Finley
City/State: New York, NY
Railroad: New York Central
Position: Dining Car Waiter
Years of Service: 1942-58

Submitter's Name: Charles N.
City/State: Teaneck, NJ
Comments: My father was a waiter who worked on the 20th Century Limited run between NYC & Chicago. He frequently mentioned the LaSalle Street Station at the end of the run in Chicago.

Registrant ID: 1292
Name: Charles Finney
City/State: St. Paul, MN
Railroad: Great Northern
Position: Porter, Steward
Years of Service: 30 plus years
Submitter's Name: Lettie
City/State: St Paul, MN

Registrant ID: 1293
Name: Isadore Fisher
City/State: Bronx, NY
Position: Sleeping Car Porter
Submitter's Name: Sandra
City/State: Bronx, NY
Comments: Father

Registrant ID: 1295
Name: David Pierce Fitts
City/State: NY
Railroad: Pennsylvania
Position: Red Cap and a Pullman Porter
Years of Service: 37 years
Submitter's: Frederick and Douglas
City/State: Tucson, AZ
Comments: My Grandfather started in West Virginia as a coal miner then changed over to a railroad track worker. Not sure what year but eventually he became a "Red Cap" as they were known then and worked in

Pennsylvania Station, New York City as it was called.

Registrant ID: 1298
Name: Thomas D. Fitzgerald
Position: Porter
Years of Service: 1945
Submitter's Name: Cleveland
City/State: Birmingham, AL

Registrant ID: 1297
Blaine McKinley Fitzgerald
City/State: Birmingham, AL
Railroad: L & N , IC
Position: Pullman Porter
Years of Service: 1920-1946
Submitter(s): Cleveland and Hazel
City/State: Inglewood CA and Birmingham, AL
Comments: Blaine McKinley Fitzgerald and his brother Thomas Fitzgerald, two country boys born in Courtland, Alabama, were Pullman porters out of Birmingham, Alabama for more than a quarter of a century. Blaine's major route was from Birmingham to New York. He also He also worked the Rose Bowl trips to California when Alabama was a major contingent. Interesting to note that when A. Philip Randolph met with Pullman Porters in Birmingham, it was at Blaine Fitzgerald's home at 117 Avenue 'D' in Titusville or the Masonic Temple. In fact, it was under the leadership of. A. Philip Randolph at one of these meetings at Blaine's home, that the Brotherhood of Sleeping Car Porters for that region was born.

Blaine raised a family of six children who all attended black colleges. They all became teachers, lawyers, and engineers."

Registrant ID: 1301
Name: N.J. Fleming
Position: Pullman Porter
Years of Service: Over 25
Comments: He was active with the union

Registrant ID: 1300
Name: Frank Fleming
City/State: Los Angeles, CA
Railroad: Union Pacific Railway
Position: Pullman Porter
Years of Service: 1919 - 1932
Submitter's Name: Rosa Lee
City/State: Los Angeles, CA
Comments: Frank Fleming. Born February 8,1887 and died July 27, 1932.

Registrant ID: 1302
Name: William Vernell Flowers
City/State: Chicago, IL
Railroad: Burlington/Amtrak
Position: Pullman Porter/Conductor
Years of Service: 1936-1972
Submitter's Name: Silvia

Registrant ID: 1303
Name: William V Flowers, Sr.
City/State: Chicago, IL
Railroad: Pullman Co
Position: Pullman Porter, BO Commissary Supervisor
Years of Service: 1937-77
Submitter's Name: William V
City/State: Chicago, IL

Registrant ID: 1305
Name: George Isaac Ford
City/State: Louisville, KY
Railroad: Southern Railroad and
K & I Railroad
Position: Pullman Porter
Years of Service: 1952 – 1974

Registrant ID: 1309
Name: William Ford
City/State: Dallas, TX
Railroad: Southern Pacific
Position: Pullman Porter
Years of Service: 35 years
Submitter's Name: Ron
City/State: Dallas, TX

Registrant ID: 1306
Name: James (Jim) Ford
City/State: Miami, FL
Railroad: Florida and East Coast
Position: Pullman Porter
Years of Service: 1925 - 1959
Submitter's Name: Patricia
City/State: Fort Washington, MD
Comments: My grandfather is
now deceased. He began
working on the freight train prior
to joining the Florida East Coast
Railroad. He used to allow my
mother to take the journey with
him between Miami and
Jacksonville, Florida.

Registrant ID: 1308
Name: Thaddeus McCune Ford
City/State: Washington, DC
Position: Sleeping Car Porter
Years: 1930's-1940's
Submitter's Name: Reginald F.
City/State: Washington, DC
Comments: I was a teenager
when he died around 1947. I do
know he enjoyed his work and

the living it provided for his
family. In those days he and his
family lived in the Langston
Terrace apartments in N. E.
Washington which were at the
time top class apartments for
Black people.

Registrant ID: 1307
Name: Osie Ford
City/State: Worcester, MA
Union Station Worcester MA
Position: Redcap
Submitter's Name: Frances
City/State: Worcester, MA

Registrant ID: 1310
Name: Raymond Fordham
City/State: FL
Position: Pullman Porter
Years of Service: 1930's-50's
Submitter's Name: Carla
City/State: Eustin, Florida
Comments: Cousin

Registrant ID: 1311
Name: Edward L. Forest
City/State: Federal Way, WA
Railroad: Northern Pacific
and Amtrak
Position: Sleeping Car Porter
Years of Service: 1960's -70's
Comments: I am second
generation railroad my father
who is now deceased hired out
for The Pullman Company June
6, 1946 and retired in 1987 his
name Foy Lee Robinson.

Registrant ID: 1313
Name: George Foskey
City/State: Roxbury, MA
Railroad: Pullman Co.out of
North Station

Position: Pullman Porter
Years of Service: 1940's-50's
Submitter's Name: James
City/State: Boston, MA

Registrant ID: 1318
Name: Levan Foster
City/State: Chicago, IL
Railroad: Pullman District &
Dearborn Station
Position: Sleeping Car Porter
Years of Service: 6 Years
Submitter's Name: Levan
City/State: Chicago, IL
Comments: Worked for 6 years

Registrant ID: 1317
Name: Jesse Foster
City/State: Detroit, MI
Railroad: Michigan Central
Position: Pullman Porter
Years: Circa 1910-1937
Submitter's Name: Martin
City/State: Los Angeles, CA

Registrant ID: 1316
Name: Henry Foster
City/State: IL
Position: Porter
Years of Service: Began working
at turn of century
Submitter's Name: Darryl
City/State: Naperville, IL
Comments: Henry Foster was
my great grandfather. He
purchased property in different
locations throughout the country
as he traveled through the
different states as a Porter. He
was a very enterprising and
intelligent man.

Registrant ID: 1315
Name: Daniel Foster
City/State: Chicago, IL
Railroad: Santa Fe
Position: Pullman Porter
Submitter's Name: Darlene
City/State: Spring Valley, CA

Registrant ID: 1314
Name: Allen Foster
City/State: St. Charles, MD
Railroad: Northern Pacific
Position: Cook
Submitter's Name: W Anita
City/State: St. Charles, MD

Registrant ID: 1325
Name: Robert Augustus Fowler
City/State: Cincinnati, OH
Submitter's: Barb Rousey
Comments: Listed in
"Cincinnati's Colored Citizens"
pages 252 as founder of Colored
Railway Employees Beneficial
Assoc of America

Registrant ID: 1323
Name: Haywood Fowler
City/State: Chicago, IL
Position: Porter, worked for 6
years.   Dates not included
Years of Service: 1930-1940's
Submitter's Name: Velma
City/State: Chicago, IL

Registrant ID: 1327
Name: Leander Fox-West
City/State: Los Angeles, CA
Railroad: Texas Chief
Position: Waiter
Years of Service: 1863-1969
Submitter's Name: Caroline
City/State: Los Angeles, CA

Registrant ID: 1328
Name: Emanuel Foxworth
City/State: AL
Railroad: Missouri Pacific
Position: Pullman Porter
Years: Late 1920's - 30's
Submitter's Name: Emanuel
City/State: Summit, MS
Comments: I know that he traveled from Chicago to New Orleans. He went to the Missouri Pacific hospital when he was sick with the TB. from which ailment he died in 1939.

Registrant ID: 1329
Name: James France
City/State: AL
Railroad: Illinois Central
Position: Porter
Years: Circa 1940's- 60's
Submitter's Name: Phyllis
City/State: Randallstown, MD
Comments: My father's name was James Abe France (4/23/1898 - 5/4/72). He worked for the Illinois Central railroad until approximately 1964. I am not sure of when he was hired but it was prior to the 1950s. He probably was hired out of Chicago, IL.

Registrant ID: 1330
Name: Clarence Frank
City/State: AL
Railroad: Sunset Limited
Position: Porter
Years of Service: 1915-1951
Submitter's Name: Olga Frank
City/State: New Orleans, LA

Registrant ID: 1331
Name: John Franklin
City/State: Berkeley, CA
Position: Pullman Porter
Comments: I am the granddaughter of Mr. John Franklin. My grandfather died when my mother was 14 yrs. old. He worked out of Oakland, CA. he worked at least 18 years. I believe he started working on a Detroit, Michigan line.

Registrant ID: 1332
Name: Clifford Franklin Davis
City/State: Cincinnati, OH
Railroad: Pennsylvania and New York Central
Position: Sleeping Car Porter
Years of Service: 1920-1950
Submitter's Name: Clara O
City/State: Cincinnati, OH
Comments: Father, he had 7 siblings who belonged to Brotherhood of Sleeping Car Porters union formed by Randolph

Registrant ID: 1336
Name: William Frazier
City/State: Indianapolis, IN
Years of Service: 1953-1959
Submitter's Name: Pamela
City/State: Indianapolis, IN

Registrant ID: 1334
Name: Oscar B Frazier
City/State: AL
Railroad: Pennsylvania
Position: Waiter
Years of Service: 1926 - 1965
Submitter's Name: James E
City/State: Staten island, NY

Registrant ID: 1337
Name: Alivie Frebble
Years of Service: 1968
Submitter's Name: Constrare
City/State: White,

Registrant ID: 1338
Name: Nobbie Frederick
City/State: Detroit, MI
Position: Secretary, typed and received shorthand
Years of Service: circa 1945 - 47
Submitter's Name: Pauline
City/State: Detroit, MI
Comments: Our father always told us with pride how he typed letters and took shorthand from the business people who boarded the train and needed his services. He also worked as a Porter. I still have the typewriter he used on the train during his years of service

Registrant ID: 1339
Name: Nathaniel Fredrerick
City/State: Jacksonville, FL
Position: Pullman Porter-
Years of Service: 20-30 Years
Submitter's Name: Doris
City/State: Chicago, IL

Registrant ID: 1344
Name: Robert Lee Freeman
City/State: Atlanta, GA
Railroad: Southern
Position: Dining Car Waiter
Years: 1938-retirement
Submitter's Name: Eleanor
City/State: Detroit, MI
Comments: Can't really give experiences. I do have a brochure where he was photographed doing his job, and I cherish the light that he gave

me (porter's signaling light) that he acquired after his retirement.

Registrant ID: 1341
Name: Frank Freeman
City/State: New York, NY
Submitter's Name: Cleyardis
City/State: Evanston, IL

Registrant ID: 1342
Name: James Freeman
City/State: Atlanta, GA
Railroad: Southern Railroad
Position: Pullman
Years of Service: 40 years
Submitter's Name: Dwight
City/State: Tuskegee, AL
Comments: My granddad worked a train which run from Atlanta to New York.

Registrant ID: 1343
Name: John Mack Freeman
City/State: PA
Position: Steward
Years of Service: 1907-1954
Submitter's Name: Maxine F.
City/State: Woodlyn, PA

Registrant ID: 1345
Name: Jesse Freeman
City/State: Kansas City, KS
Position: Porter
Years of Service: Circa 1942 47
Submitter's Name: Mauris
City/State: Port Orchard, WA
Comments: He said he worked a lot of trains that carried the troop during WWII.

Registrant ID: 1346
Name: Vincent Frember
City/State: Brooklyn, NY
Registrant ID: 1347

Name: William T Frye
Railroad: Pullman Company
Position: Pullman Porter
Years of Service: 1935-1948
Submitter's Name: Frye Johnson

Registrant ID: 1348
Name: Hurley Fuggett
City/State: AR
Railroad: Southern Pacific
Position: Pullman
Years of Service: 1924-58
Submitter's Name: Robert
City/State: Colorado Springs, CO
Comments: I was told of my Grandfathers experiences working on the railroad from my uncle (James Fuggett) in Augusta, Ga. He is proud of the fact that he was born on the railroad between the state lines of Arkansas an Missouri.

Registrant ID: 1351
Name: Fowell (Fred) Fulbright
City/State: MN
Railroad: Northern Pacific and Burlington Northern
Position: Pullman Porter
Years of Service: 1937 - 1971
Submitter's Name: Marlys
City/State: Hugo, MN

Registrant ID: 1353
Name: Albert B. Fulton
City/State: Pittsburgh, PA
Railroad: The Pullman Company, Pennsylvania Station
Position: Pullman Porter
Years of Service: 45 years
Comments: Albert B. Fulton is deceased, however, I thought it would be a great tribute to my

stepfather to have his name included in this registry.

Registrant ID: 1354
Name: Isaac Fultz
City/State: VA
Railroad: Pennsylvania Norfolk and Western
Position: Porter and Dining Car Waiter
Submitter's Name: John
City/State: Fort Washington, MD

Registrant ID: 1355
Name: Oliver Elbridge Furt
Railroad: Pennsylvania and New York Central
Years of Service: 1919-1923
Submitter's Name: Walter W
Comments: Worked with A. Phillip Randolph during formation of union.

Registrant ID: 1357
Name: Jimmy Mason Gaddis
City/State: Chicago, IL
Submitter's Name: Ruth
City/State: Chicago, IL

Registrant ID: 1358
Name: Alexander Gaines
City/State: AL
Railroad: Southern Cresent & Amtrak
Position: Sleeping Car Porter
Years of Service: 1942 1980
Submitter's Name: Alexes
City/State: Baltimore, MD
Comments: He was been featured in the Asheville Citizen Times about his job as a Pullman Porter. He was also featured in the movie "Eleanor and Franklin: The White House Years", he played the role of a Pullman

Porter. He also received
numerous awards such as
Southern

Registrant ID: 1359
Benjamin Franklin Gaines
City/State: Evanston, IL
Position: Club car. Attendant
Years of Service: 1945-1962
Submitter's: Benjamin
City/State: Evanston, IL

Registrant ID: 1360
Name: William C. Gaines
City/State: Buffalo, NY
Railroad: B&O
Position: Dining Car Waiter
Years of Service: 15 years
Submitter's Name: Faye L.
City/State: Silver Spring, MD
Comments: I can remember as a
child, my father traveling from
Baltimore to Pittsburgh.
We lived in Chicago in the early
1940's. We later move to Buffalo
N.Y. and he continue to work.

Registrant ID: 1362
Name: William Gainey
City/State: AL
Position: Pullman Porter
Years of Service: 1940's-50's
Submitter's Name: Stanley
City/State: Horseheads, NY
Comments: William Gainey is
my father. He passed away in
August 1972 and is buried in
New York. I recall him telling us
about his travels to the south
and Midwest to Chicago area.

Registrant ID: 1363
Name: (Jasper) LeRoy Gainor
Position: Pullman Porter

Years of Service: 1930s-1940s
Submitter's: Margaret Gainor
City/State: Berkeley, CA

Registrant ID: 1364
Name: Herschel Gaither
City/State: Minneapolis, MN
Burlington Northern, Amtrak
Position: Brakeman
Years of Service: 1950s-80s
Submitter's Name: Chanelle
City/State: Smyrna, GA
Comments: I am not sure what
my fathers' job on the railroad
was , but I know that worked on
the railroad

Registrant ID: 1365
Name: John Galloway
City/State: AL
Railroad: Milwaukee Road
Position: Dining car bus boy,
And waiter, inspector
Years of Service: 42 years
Submitter's Name: Joan
City/State: Detroit, MI
Comments: My father (deceased)
started in the dining car as a bus
boy in 1927. He eventually
became a waiter and worked in
that position for many years. I
don't remember when he was
promoted, but he became the
first black dining car inspector
for the Milwaukee Road.

Registrant ID: 1367
Name: Bobby Gamble R
City/State: Richmond, VA
Railroad: Pullman Company
Position: Pullman Porter
Years of Service: 1963-1968

Registrant ID: 1368
Name: William J. Gamble, Sr.
City/State: Atlanta, GA
Railroad: Montgomery
Position: Porter
Years of Service: 1930-1950's
Submitter's Name: William J.
City/State: Atlanta, GA

Registrant ID: 1369
Name: Johnny W. Gambrell
City/State: Atlanta, GA
Position: Pullman Porter
Years of Service: Circa 1940's-50's
Submitter's: Johnnie and Marie
City/State: Philadelphia, AL
Comments: I know he had the New Orleans to New York run. After his death we received his pension for the five of us of 99.00 a month per child. My mom's name was Mamie Lee Gambrell.

Registrant ID: 1373
Name: Robert Lee Gandy
City/State: IL
Railroad: New York Central, Northwestern, Burlington
Position: Dining Car Waiter, waiter-in-charge; Pullman porter
Years of Service: 1938-1969
Submitter's Name: Brenda
City/State: South Holland, IL

Registrant ID: 1374
Name: Chester Gant, Sr.
City/State: Port St. Joe, FL
Railroad: Apalachicola & Northern
Position: Pullman Porter
Years: circa 1917 - 1970
Submitter's Name: Elitha
City/State: Attapulgus, GA
Comments: Papa Chest was a Pullman porter for this railroad

until passenger trains were discontinued. He then worked as a Breakman.

Registrant ID: 1378
Name: Ted Gardner
City/State: Chicago, IL

Registrant ID: 1376
Name: Dempsey Gardner
City/State: AL
Railroad: El Paso
Years of Service: 1977's
Submitter(s) Name: Lawrence
City/State: AL

Registrant ID: 1375
Name: Danish Gardner
City/State: New York, NY
Railroad: New York Central between NYC and Buffalo
Position: Porter
Years of Service: Pre-world War II
Submitter's Name: William
City/State: New York, NY
Comments: There's not much I can tell you. He trained to be a teacher. I have his college graduation picture) and was not proud about having been a Porter. Thus he never spoke much about it and I was too young to realize how important having that job was.

Leroy Gardner

Registrant ID: 1377
Name: Leroy Gardner
City/State: Amityville, NY
Railroad: Eastern Seaboard (Pennsylvania) Railroad aka Amtrak
Position: Pullman Porter
Years of Service: 42 years
Submitter's Name: Kenya
City/State: Bayshore, NY
Comments: Leroy Gardner worked the railroad route that took him from New York to Florida and during his time he met many celebrities, among them Bob Hope. He also received numerous awards for his service throughout the years he was employed.

Registrant ID: 1379
Name: Abraham Garnett
Position: Cook
Years of Service: 1935-1962
Submitter's Name: Brenda
City/State: Waldorf, MD

Registrant ID: 1380
Name: Leroy Garrett
City/State: Chicago, IN
Railroad: Santa Fe
Position: Pullman Porter
Years of Service: 1935 to 1960
Submitter's Name: Leon
City/State: Chicago, IL
Comments: My grandfather loved working for the railroad until he retired

Registrant ID: 1381
Name: Marian T. Garrett
City/State: Nutley, NJ
Railroad: He worked on the New York to Miami Florida line.
Position: Pullman Porter
Years of Service: Circa 1925-63
Submitter's Name: Sauda
City/State: Oakland, CA
Comments: I have my dad's Pullman Porter hat. He kept it immaculate. It remains in perfect condition.

Registrant ID: 1382
Nearious Gilchrist Garrett
City/State: Atlanta, GA
Railroad: Southern & Crescent
Position: Pullman Porter
Years of Service: 1941-1973
Submitter's Name: Virginia
City/State: Tempe, AZ

Registrant ID: 1385
Name: Leon H. Garriest

City/State: Bronx, NY
Railroad: Pennsylvania
Position: Pullman Porter
Years of Service:
Circa 1929-1933
Submitter's Name: Gwen
City/State: Philadelphia, PA
Comments: My father worked
for short time as a Pullman
porter out of NY where he lived
with my mother and brother. My
brother was born in NY in 1930.
They re-located to Philadelphia.
during the depression after the
crash of 1929,when my father
was "laid off"

Registrant ID: 1386
Name: Isaac Garrison
Position: Pullman Porter
Years of Service: Over 25
Comments: He was also a
member of the union

Registrant ID: 1388
Name: Salis Thomas Garrison
City/State: SC
Position: Porter
Submitter's Name: Marcell D.
City/State: Philadelphia, PA

Registrant ID: 1387
Name: Lester Garrison
City/State: St. Louis, MO
Railroad: Pennsylvania
Position: Pullman Porter/Dining
Car Waiter
Years of Service: 1947-1968
Submitter's Name: Kimberly
City/State: St. Louis , MO

Registrant ID: 1391
Name: Central Lee Gaston
City/State: Chicago, IL

Railroad: Pullman Company and
the Rock Island
Position: Pullman Porter
Years: Late 1940's -60's
Submitter's Name: Esther J.
City/State: Country Club Hills, IL

Registrant ID: 1390
Name: Albert Anderson Gaston
City/State: Gulfport, MS
Submitter's: Annie Malnette
City/State: Picayune, MS
Comments: Son

Registrant ID: 1392
Name: Otis Gates Jr.
City/State: Wellesley, MA
Railroad: New Haven R. R.
Position: Sleeping Car Porter
Years of Service: 1942- 1975

Registrant ID: 1393
Name: Ralph Gatewood
City/State: IL
Railroad: Pennsylvania
Position: Pullman Porter
Years of Service: 1920s
Submitter's Name: Audrey
City/State: Lansing, MI
Comments: Grew-up in Boston
(Dorchester), MA. I believe he
began working for the
Pennsylvania while still in
Boston, but he eventually wound
up in Chicago where he settled
for good. Even though he no
longer worked for the railroad he
never outgrew his love of trains.

Registrant ID: 1395
Name: Reginald Gay
City/State: Chicago, IL
Railroad: New York Central,
And B & O
Position: Pullman Porter

Years: Approx 30 years.
Submitter's Name: Nettie
City/State: Chicago, IL
Comments: Reginald M. Gay
was my grandfather. Upon the
death of my Mom in '57, he
raised myself and 2 brothers. He
traveled from Chicago to Boston.
Met many celebrities. Pres.
Eisenhower asked him to take
care of his son on one trip.
Talked about hauling soldiers.

Registrant ID: 1396
Name: Arnold , W Gee
City/State: Indianapolis, IN
Position: Porter
Comments: My uncle to and
from Portland Oregon.

Registrant ID: 5006
Employee Name: Leonard Geno
Railroad: Pennsylvania
Position: Dining Car Waiter
Years of Service: Circa
1930's-50's
Submitter's Name: Yvonne
City/State: Chicago, IL
Comments: He was my father

Registrant ID: 2618
Name: Francisco Medel George
Railroad: Pullman Company
Position: Trackman
Years of Service: 1948-1960
Submitter's Name: Medel M

Registrant ID: 1398
Name: Menphila Gert
City/State: Meniruilee, IN
Railroad: BUTO
Position: DCW
Years of Service: 1967-2002
Submitter's Name: Menphila

City/State: Meniruilee, IN

Registrant ID: 5010
Name: Herbert Gettridge Jr
Position: Pullman Porter
Railroad: The Pullman Co.
Submitter's Name: Tira
City/State: Brooklyn, NY

Registrant ID: 1399
Name: Clarence Geyen
City/State: WA
Railroad: Northern Pacific
Position: Pullman Porter
Years of Service: Before 1945
Submitter's Name: Sandre
City/State: Lynnwood, WA
Comments: My dad died in
1972. He was a Pullman Porter
on the Northern Pacific that ran
from Galveston Texas to Seattle,
Washington. He met my mother
in 1945 and they were married.
He then settled in Seattle,
Washington and opened one of
the first black owned businesses.

Registrant ID: 1402
Name: Lymon S. Gibbs
City/State: Columbus, SC

Registrant ID: 1403
Name: William C. Gibbs, JR
City/State: AL

Registrant ID: 1404
Name: William C. Gibbs, Sr.
City/State: Chicago, IL
Railroad: Pullman Company
Position: Pullman Porter
Years of Service: 1924 - 1934
Comments: My father worked
for the Pullman Company during
his years as a student at

Meharry Dental School. He graduated in 1926, but continued to work for the company until 1934. He began his practice of Dentistry in 1940. He died May 21, 1985

Registrant ID: 1406
Name: Walter F. Gibson
Submitter's Name: Sharon G.
City/State: Chicago, IL
Comments: My father, Walter F. Gibson, had 9 children, most of whom have remained in the Chicago area.

Registrant ID: 1409
Name: William Gibson
City/State: New York, NY
Position: Waiter/Porter
Years of Service: 1920-1960
Submitter's Name: John Q.
City/State: Harrisburg, PA

Registrant ID: 1405
Name: Lee Gibson
City/State: Los Angeles, CA
Submitter's Name: Gloria
City/State: Los Angeles, CA

Registrant ID: 1414
Name: William Gideon
City/State: KS
Railroad: All
Position: Pullman Porter
Years of Service: 25 plus years
Submitter's Name: Delois
City/State: Kansas City, KS
Comments: He was a Pullman Porter with Mr. Willard Shelton, Mr. Gillespie & Mr. Wilson. He worked out of the Union Station in Kansas City ., MO. We met actresses Tallulah Bankhead and

Shirley Boothe while he worked as a Porter on the trains.

Registrant ID: 1412
Name: Andrew Gideon
City/State: KS
Railroad: All
Position: Fireman
Years of Service: 1901 - 45
Submitter's Name: Delois
City/State: Kansas City, KS

Registrant ID: 1415
Name: Freddie Gilbert
City/State: AL
Position: Porter
Years of Service: 1929
Submitter's Name: Barbara
City/State: New Orleans, LA

Registrant ID: 1416
Name: Glasgow Gilbert
City/State: New York, NY
Railroad: New York Central
Position: Waiter
Years of Service: 15 years
Submitter's Name: Adjoah
City/State: Queens Village, NY

Registrant ID: 1417
Name: Arthur Gilchrist
City/State: AL
Railroad: Frisco
Position: Engine Cleaner
Years of Service: 1935-1956
Submitter's Name: Patrice
City/State: Carson, CA
Comments: Please disregard previous information concerning my grandfather's employment with the railroad as previous stated it was from memories and not from factual information obtained from my mother. His

daugher in-law and my father
(his son). Thank you again for
this registry.

Registrant ID: 1419
Name: Riley Gilchrist, Sr.
City/State: M, MN
Position: Dining Car Porter
Submitter's Name: Edda
City/State: Detroit, MI
Comments: Uncle he lived in
Minnesota

Registrant ID: 1420
Name: Richard Giles
City/State: VA
Position: Coal Tender

Registrant ID: 1421
Name: John Gilford
City/State: KS
Position: Sleeping Car Porter
Submitter Rev Dr. Lucius
City/State: Wichita, KS
Comments: Died at 90 years old.

Registrant ID: 1422
Name: Sherman N. Gillard
City/State: Chicago, IL
Railroad: Northwestern Railroad
Pullman Co.
Position: Pullman Porter
Years of Service: Laid off in the
early to mid 60's Retired n1970
Submitter's: Ruthchurn H.
City/State: Chicago, IL
Comments: My father Sherman
Nathaniel Gillard never got over
not being able to work or run on
the road as he would say. He
started working on the road at a
very young age. His brother-in-
law helped him secure a position

by putting his age up by some
years.

Registrant ID: 1423
Name: Roy Gillespie Sr.
City/State: Detroit, MI
Position: Sleeping Car Porter
Submitter's Name: Eleanor G.
City/State: Detroit, MI

Registrant ID: 1425
Edward Cleveland Gilliam Jr.
City/State: East Orange, NJ
Railroad: Penn Central Railroad
Position: Brakeman
Years of Service: 1968 & 1969
Submitter's Name: Donna
City/State: East Orange, NJ
Comments: Youngest employee
hired at that time.

Registrant ID: 1427
Name: Vicent Gilliarp
City/State: Chas, SC
Railroad: Pullman Company

Registrant ID: 1428
Name: Leopold Gilliean
City/State: IL
Submitter's Name: Sandra
City/State: Flossmoor, IL
Comments: He retired from
service sometime in the 50's due
to a heart attack and my
grandmother did receive his
social security benefits.

Registrant ID: 1429
Name: Thomas Gilling
City/State: Washington, DC
Railroad: Atlantic Coast Line
Position: Waiter
Years of Service: 1925-1949
Submitter's Name: Roda

City/State: Washington, DC
Registrant ID: 1430
Name: James Mitchell Gilmore
Position: Pullman Porter
Submitter's Name: Wilford C
City/State: Chicago, IL

Registrant ID: 1431
Name: Atwell Gladstone
Position: Waiter
Years of Service: Late1930's -40's
Submitter's Name: Joan Atwell
City/State: Brooklyn , NY

Registrant ID: 1432
Name: Alvin Russell Glasper
City/State: Oklahoma City, OK
Railroad: Burlington Northern
Position: Dining Carter
Comments: My grandfather is deceased but this is to register him in the Museum archives. Thank you.

Registrant ID: 1435
Name: Millie Glass
City/State: Los Angeles, CA
Position: Car Cleaner
Years of Service: 20 plus years
Submitter's Name: Debra
City/State: Los Angeles, CA
Comments: Both grandparents worked for the railroad.

Registrant ID: 5011
Name: Roosevelt Glass
City/State: Los Angeles, CA
Position: Car Cleaner
Years of Service: 20 plus years
Submitter's Name: Debra
City/State: Los Angeles, CA
Comments: They spoke many times of transporting different celebrities. They even had the pajamas of Lucy and Desi Arnaz!

Registrant ID: 1438
Name: Walter Sr. Glen
City/State: Chicago, IL
Position: Sleeping Car Porter
Years of Service: 1940's-1950's
Submitter's Name: Michelle
City/State: Chicago, IL
Comments: Walter was my father

Registrant ID: 1439
Name: Benjamin Glison
Railroad: The Atlantic Coast Line
Position: Sleeping Car Porter
Years of Service: 1935 to 1947
Submitter's Name: Fred
City/State: Raleigh, NC
Comments: He was also a graduate of North Carolina A&T

Registrant ID: 1440
Name: Benjamin Glisson
City/State: Brooklyn, NY
Position: Waiter
Years of Service: circa late 1930's
Submitter's Name: Evelyn
City/State: Nashville, TN

Registrant ID: 1442
Name: Thomas Glover
City/State: Bronx, NY
Railroad: Grand Central Station, New York
Position: Red Cap Captain
Years of Service: 56 years
Submitter's Name: Mario
City/State: Newark, ID
Comments: Initially started his career on the railroad as a Pullman at the age of 18. He retired from the railroad in 1970.

Registrant ID: 1441
Name: Ruth Adams Glover
City/State: Tinton Falls, NJ
Railroad: Baltimore and Ohio
Position: Pullman Porter
Submitter's Name: William W.
City/State: Red Bank, NJ
Comments: My father's name
was William Wadsworth Adams.
I am 88 Years old so he was with
the railroad during the early
1940s and 50s. We lived in Red
Bank New Jersey.

Registrant ID: 1443
Name: James Gnatt
City/State: Chicago, IL
Position: Porter
Years of Service: 1937-1960
Submitter's; Louis McFerrin
City/State: Philadelphia, PA

Registrant ID: 1445
Name: David L. Goodlow, Jr.
City/State: St. Paul, MN
Railroad: Northern Pacific
Position: Waiter
Years of Service:
1956 thru 1967
Submitter's Name: Erick
City/State: St. Paul, MN

Registrant ID: 1447
Name: Edward Goodrum
Railroad: Amtrak
Position: Waiter
Years of Service: 40
Submitter's Name: Kenneth
City/State: Chicago, IL

Registrant ID: 1448
Name: Lewis Pratt Goodson
City/State: Terrell, TX
Railroad: Texas & Pacific

Position: Section Foreman
Submitter's Name: Marion L.
City/State: Cerritos, CA

Registrant ID: 1449
Name: Clifton Goodwin
City/State: McColl, SC
Railroad: Seaboard Coastline
and Amtrak
Position: Section and
Crankhank
Years of Service: 30

Registrant ID: 1454
Name: Roy Goodwin
City/State: Ogden, UT
Railroad: Union Pacific
Position: Red Cap
Years of Service: 1922-1968
Submitter's Name: Roietta
City/State: Citrus Heights, CA
Comments: My father worked
for 46 years for the railroad as a
Red Cap. He would often tell us
stories of the famous people who
were riding the train--musicians
and athletes. He sometimes got
their autographs. His wife is still
living.

Registrant ID: 1455
Name: Sherman Goodwin
City/State: AL
Railroad: Southern Pacific-
California
Position: Porter
Years of Service: 8 years
Submitter's Name: Gloria
City/State: Rialto, CA
Comments: I remember my
father being gone from home for
long periods of time, he missed
my brothers birth. He related
stories of how he was treated by

other races and his treatment by the railroad management. His stories included relationships he developed with many passengers.

Registrant ID: 1452
Name: Hampton Goodwin
City/State: Bronx, NY
Railroad: Atlantic Coast Line
Position: Cook and Waiter
Years of Service: 1941-43
Submitter's Name: George
City/State: Teaneck, NJ
Comments: Deceased. He was my father. I was to young at that time, but my mother told me that it was very difficult doing that time. His run was from Florida to New York and he was laid off twice during 1941-1943.

Registrant ID: 1453
Richard Marshall Goodwin
Position: Pullman Porter
Years of Service: 1908-1952
Submitter's Name: Norma E.
City/State: Wappingeus Falls, NY

Registrant ID: 1457
Name: Emory Gordon
City/State: MS
Position: Porter
Years of Service: 50 years
Submitter's Name: Celia
City/State: Summit, MS
Comments: His run was from Chicago to California. My Father was glad to have a job and the protection of the "Brotherhood of Sleeping Car Porters." I remember hearing him talk to my Mother about the racism that he had to endure from white passengers and employees, because he could not find adequate work.

Registrant ID: 1460
Name: Frank Goseer
City/State: Albany, GA. 31705,
Railroad: Atlantic Coastline/City of Miami Run.
Position: Porter
Submitter's: Kenneth & Erin
City/State: Albany, GA

Registrant ID: 1461
Name: William Gough
Railroad: Pullman Company
Position: Civil Engineer
Years of Service: Apprx 1917-20
Submitter's Name: Bette
City/State: Oak Park, IL

Registrant ID: 1462
Name: Eloise Grace
Railroad: Pullman Company
Position: Maid
City/State: Pittsburgh, PA

Registrant ID: 1463
Name: Louis Grady Cannon
City/State: Woodrow, SC
Railroad: Baltimore MD
Submitter's Name: Sandra
City/State: Woodrow, SC

Registrant ID: 1467
Name: Jim Graham
City/State: Chicago, IL
Position: Pullman Porter
Years of Service: 1920's
Submitter's Name: Pamela
City/State: C.C. Hills, IL
Registrant ID: 1465
Name: Dennis Graham
City/State: Pittsburgh, PA

Railroad: Pennsylvania
Position: Red Cap
Submitter's Name: Doris
City/State: Fayetteville, NC

Registrant ID: 1466
Name: Emma Graham
City/State: Philadelphia, PA
Railroad: Union pacific
Position: Labore/Maid
Years of Service: 1924-1956
Submitter's Name: Cecilia
City/State: Philadelphia, PA
Comments: Grandmother

Registrant ID: 1468
Name: John Graham
City/State: Bremen, GA
Submitter's Name: Wilhelmina
City/State: Pittsburgh, PA
Comments: John D Graham was my great grandfather born Feb. 11, 1864 and died Apr. 16, 1961. His wife my great-grandmother was named Augusta. My grandmother Sedalia Graham Nolan was one Of 3 of his children. My grandmother was born in Sept. 1900 and died in 1991.

Registrant ID: 1471
Name: James H. Granberry
Railroad: Chicago & North Western/ City of San Francisco
Position: Pullman Porter
Years of Service: 44 years
Submitter's Name: Albert
City/State: Chicago, IL

Registrant ID: 1472
Name: Leslie Grannum
City/State: Chicago, IL
Railroad: Pullman

Position: Waiter
Years of Service: 2 or 3
Submitter's Name: William
City/State: Chicago, IL
Comments: Also My Uncle Claude Grannum & William Wilson were Porter's for the Pullman Company around 1942-1945

Registrant ID: 1474
Name: Roy Lewis Grant
City/State: Chicago, IL
Position: Porter
Years of Service: 1940-1969
Submitter's Name: McNair
City/State: Chicago, IL

Registrant ID: 1475
Name: Willie Grant
City/State: Meridian, MS
Railroad: Empire Builder, North Coast Limited
Years of Service: circa 1946-55
Submitter's Name: Barbara
City/State: Gardena, CA
Comments: He made lots of tips and he learned how to cook fine dishes by watching the chefs prepare meals. He made the best home made egg nog I have ever tasted.

Registrant ID: 1473
Name: Joe Grant
City/State: Columbus, GA
Position: Porter
Years of Service: 1940 - 1950's
Submitter's Name: Shirley
City/State: Greenwood, SC
Comments: Having grown up in Michigan with my parents, my mothers uncle Joe Grant

would come to visit, and he would bring his sister, my grandmother Pearl Grant Watt with him to visit, they would talk about the people he met and the things he did.

Registrant ID: 1479
Name: Leon Graves
City/State: Cincinnati, OH
Railroad: Norfolk & Western/Southern
Position: Laborer
Years of Service: 7/9/46-9/83
Submitter's Name: Sarah
City/State: Cincinnati, OH

Registrant ID: 1478
Name: Joe Graves
City/State: Cincinnati, OH
Railroad: Norfolk & Western/Southern
Position: Laborer/Asst. Foreman
Service: 1/13/48-10/31/88
Submitter's Name: Sarah
City/State: Cincinnati, OH

Registrant ID: 1480
Name: Oscar Graves
City/State: Denver, CO
Railroad: Union Pacific
Position: Dining Car Waiter
Submitter's Name: David
City/State: Honolulu, HI

Registrant ID: 1476
Name: James Graves
City/State: IL
Railroad: New York Central
Position: Cook
Submitter's Name: Carlton
City/State: Lynwood, IL

Registrant ID: 1483
Name: Alonzo Gray
City/State: Philadelphia, PA

Registrant ID: 1485
Name: Ed Gray
City/State: TX
Position: Pullman Porter
Submitter's Name: Gerald
City/State: Rialto, CA

Registrant ID: 1487
Name: Milton Gray
City/State: TX
Position: Dining Car Waiter
Submitter's Name: Gregory
City/State: San Francisco, CA

Registrant ID: 1484
Name: Dexter Gray
Position: Cook
Years of Service: Circa 1931-1960
Submitter's Name: Virginia
City/State: Tempe, AZ

Registrant ID: 1486
Name: John Gray
City/State: AL
Railroad: Worked out of Chicago
Submitter's Name: Evelyn
City/State: Tucson, AZ
Comments: He was my uncle. I had the opportunity to see "10,000 Black Men Named George". Great movie. What a struggle we've all gone through.

Registrant ID: 1489
Name: Martin Luther Gray Sr.
City/State: Memphis, TN
Railroad: IL Central
Position: Sleeping Car Porter, Dining Car Waiter

Years of Service: 1939 - 1950
Submitter's Name: Martin
City/State: Bogalusa, LA
Comments: My dad would always tell us a story about his last trip. We could not wait until he got home, because we knew he had a new story to tell us.

Registrant ID: 1508
Name: Mr. Green
City/State: Rochester, NY
Years of Service: Circa 1936-1940
Submitter's Name: Patricia

Registrant ID: 1500
Name: Harold Green
City/State: Denver, CO
Railroad: Union Pacific
Position: Waiter
Years of Service: 1940's

Registrant ID: 1491
Name: Apella Green
City/State: Chicago, IL
Railroad: Pullman Rail Car Company
Position: Maid
Years of Service: 45yrs 1905-1950
Submitter's Name: Alberta
City/State: Chicago, IL

Registrant ID: 1506
Name: John Edward Green
City/State: Chicago, IL
Railroad: Santa Fe Railroad
Years of Service: 1946-1956
Submitter's Name: Sharon
City/State: Chicago, IL
Comments: Fatal train accident in Santa Fe derailment, in Mexico 1956

Registrant ID: 1495
Name: Arthur W. Green
City/State: Elgin, IL
Railroad: Pullman Rail Car Company
Position: Pullman Porter
Years of Service: 1911 to 1951
Submitter's: Arthur W.and Alberta
City/State: Elgin, IL

Registrant ID: 1490
Name: Alexander Green
City/State: Florence, SC
Railroad: Atlantic Coastline
Position: Porter
Years of Service: Approx. 1915-1955 (40 years of service)
Submitter's Name: Cynthia
City/State: Florence, SC
Comments: My grandfather was told by railroad officials that the only reason he was not a conductor was because he was a Negro. He was quiet spoken and always a gentleman.

Registrant ID: 1507
Name: Joseph Green
City/State: Denver, CO
Railroad: Union Pacific
Position: Waiter and waiter/instructor
Years of Service: 1924 - 1964
Submitter's Name: Deborah
City/State: Ft Lupton, CO
Comments: Joseph D Green was my grandfather. He is now deceased. He worked for Union Pacific until the day he died. He was the first black Waiter-Instructor with Union Pacific Railroad. UP did have a film of him.

184

Registrant ID: 1494
Name: Arthur Green
City/State: Greenbelt, MD
Railroad: Chesapeake and Ohio
Position: Porter
Submitter's Name: Thomas
City/State: Greenbelt, MD
Comments: I do not have very much in the way of documentation. I have a railway identification card for my grandfather and I speak with my grandmother often about his experience on the railroad. She is an elderly woman and the story changes often.

Registrant ID: 1499
Name: George Alexander Green
City/State: Chicago, IL
Railroad: B & O Railroad
Position: Waiter
Years of Service: 1920-60
Submitter's: Joyce Green
City/State: Hazel Crest, IL
Comments: My father George A. Green started working as a waiter when he was 16 years old. He came to Chicago from Monroe,La. to seek employment and was hired by the B & O R.R. He worked as a waiter traveling to Washington D.C. on the Capitol Limited for 40 years.

Registrant ID: 1493
Name: Archille Green
City/State: Lakewood, CA
Railroad: Southern Pacific out of New Orleans
Position: Pullman Porter
Submitter's Name: Constance
City/State: Lakewood, CA

Comments: He was working as a Pullman Porter long before they had a union. He was not treated very kindly most of the time. Most of the white people referred to him a "boy." He enjoyed traveling and meeting people.

Registrant ID: 1197
Name: Carl Edward Green
City/State: Shreveport, LA
Position: Sleeping Car Porter
Years of Service: 1945-1950
Submitter's Name: Linda
City/State: Shrieveport, LA
Comments: Grandfather

Registrant ID: 1497
Name: Charles Fletcher Green
City/State: San Antonio, TX
Railroad: Southern Pacific Missouri Pacific
Position: Pullman Porter
Years of Service: Unknown start date woorkd 1960
Submitter's Name: Charles A.
City/State: Los Angeles, CA
Comments: He (my father) had a run from San Antonio to Washington D. C. for a while and another from San Antonio to New York. He would be gone away from home 5 days and at home with me and my mother for 6 days. He had the job for at least 20 years, maybe longer.

Registrant ID: 724
Name: Wade Green
City/State: Omaha, NE
Railroad: Pacific & Union
Position: Porter
Years of Service: 30 plus

Submitter's Name: Roy F
City/State: Norwood, MA
Comments: Don't recall too many details. Mostly I remember my parents and relatives discussing how often grandfather was always away working on the railroad because of the war (WWII).

Registrant ID: 1503
Name: Herman "Tricky" Green
Railroad: B & O/P & E Railroads
Years of Service: late 1920's-30's
Submitter's Name: Betty Jean
City/State: Pittsburgh, PA

Registrant ID: 1496
Name: Carl Edward Green
Position: Porter
Years of Service: 1945-1950's
Submitter's Name: Linda
City/State: Shreveport, LA

Registrant ID: 1498
Name: Eugene Green
City/State: AL
Railroad: Illinois Central
Position: Porter
Years of Service: 1952-1954
Submitter's Name: Jean
City/State: Utica, MS
Comments: My father worked for Illinois Central for a short time as a Porter.

Registrant ID: 1514
Name: Ezekiel "Zeke" Green Sr.
City/State: Memphis, TN
Railroad: L & N (Louisville & Nashville)-Cincinnati
Position: Pullman Porter
Years of Service: Approx 27
Submitter's Louise B. & Zeke
City/State: Memphis, TN

Comments: He hauled soldiers during WWII and met many celebrates

Registrant ID: 1515
Name: James Greene
City/State: Cleveland, OH
Years of Service: 1941-1968
Submitter's: Edward & Debra
City/State: Passellville, TN

Registrant ID: 1517
Name: Flemon Greer
City/State: Cincinnati, OH
Railroad: Louisville Nashville
Position: Porter
Submitter's Name: Richard
City/State: Plainfield, NJ
Comments: My grandfather; his brothers, John Robert and Nathaniel were also Porters.

Registrant ID: 1521
Name: James B Greese
City/State: Marion, IND
Railroad: Pullman Company
Position: Walkerd the gates
Years of Service: 1950-1980
Submitter's Name: Greese Walker

Registrant ID: 1522
Name: Harry Grever
City/State: Minneapolis, MN
Railroad: Great Northern RR
Position: Porter and, Waiter
Years of Service: 40 years
Submitter's Name: Helen
City/State: Mesquite, TX
Comments: This is my grandfather. Never knew him, just heard stories from my father who also worked for the railroad.

186

Registrant ID: 1523
Name: Addison Grevious
City/State: New York, NY
Position: Sleeping Car Porter
Years: Mid1920's-50's
Submitter's Name: Joseph
City/State: Rockville Centre, NY

Registrant ID: 1525
Name: Fred Conners Griffeth
City/State: MA
Railroad: New Haven R.R.
Position: Pullman Porter
Years of Service: 1940's-60's
Submitter's Name: Arthur
City/State: Dorchester, MA
Comments: He worked on the merchant Limited and the Lakeside to Chicago. His Nick-Name was Rochester.

Registrant ID: 1527
Name: Jesse Griffin
City/State: Markham, IL
Railroad: Penn Central
Position: Mechanic, **Years of Service:** 42 years
Submitter's Name: Cheryl
City/State: Dolton, IL
Comments: he was my father

Registrant ID: 1528
Name: William Griffin
City/State: New York, NY
Railroad: Boston to New York and many other places
Position: Waiter, and a Dining Car Porter
Years of Service: 1930's-50's
Submitter's Name: Ellen
City/State: Jamaica, NY

Registrant ID: 1529
Name: Joseph Griffin Sr.

City/State: Hamlet, ND
Railroad: Seaboard
Position: Brakeman and Porter:
Years of Service: 50 years
Submitter's Name: P. Elizabeth
City/State: Providence, RI
Comments: My grandfather, Joseph H. Griffin, Sr. was a brakeman. He retired in the 1960's after 50 years of service. They sent his retirement watch to his house because the retirement affairs were not integrated. He had two sons both were porters. One, my father, Joseph Jr. and Ernest T. I don't know their years of service. My grandfather is dead, but my father and uncle are still alive.

Registrant ID: 1530
Name: Wirt Griffin, Sr.
City/State: Chicago, IL
Railroad: Santa Fe
Position: Porter
Years of Service: 1920's-1930's
Submitter's Name: James
City/State: Park Forest, IL
Comments: I was a little boy when my great uncle who is now deceased would talk about working on the railroad.

Registrant ID: 1531
Name: Will Griggs
City/State: Atlanta, GA
Position: Pullman Porter
Submitter's Name: Leta
City/State: Buffalo, NY

Registrant ID: 1532
Name: Charles Grigsby
City/State: MN

Railroad: Soo Line
Position: Pullman Porter
Years of Service: 1940-1960's
Submitter's Name: Cheryl
City/State: Minneapolis, MN
Comments: I am pleased to be able to acknowledge my relatives on this registry. Two and two grandfathers. Thank you for the opportunity.

Registrant ID: 1533
Name: Walker Boone Groadus
Railroad: Kentucky
Position: Pullman Porter
Submitter's Name: Gertrude

Registrant ID: 1537
Name: Robert Grundy
City/State: Louisville, KY
Railroad: Louisville and Nashville
Position: Pullman Porter
Years of Service: 1940's
Submitter's Name: Joyce
City/State: Brooklyn, NY

Registrant ID: 1535
Name: James Grundy
City/State: AL
Position: Pullman Porter
Years : Circa 1920 - 1930.
Submitter: Jacqueline
City/State: Chicago, IL
Comments: James Grundy (deceased, 1957) was my grandfather.

Registrant ID: 1536
Name: Robert Grundy
City/State: Louisville, KY
Railroad: Operating Union Station, Louisville, Ky.
Position: Pullman Porter

Submitter's Name: Joann
City/State: Tampa, FL
Comments: Robert E. Grundy was my father, I know at that time that was a very upstanding job for a black man. He took great pride in his job, and shared lots of stories with his family.

Registrant ID: 1538
Name: Robert E Gundy
City/State: Louisville, KY
Railroad: L & M
Position: Porter
Years of Service: 1940's- 50's
Submitter's Name: Phyllis
City/State: Louisville, KY

Registrant ID: 1540
Name: Mr. Leslie Gurley
City/State: Flint, MI
Railroad: Departed from Pittsburgh Pennsylvania
Position: Porter
Years of Service: 1947-1949
Submitter's Name: Julia
City/State: Redford, MI
Comments: I remember hearing stories as a little girl about how much my Grandfather enjoyed working as a Porter. He talked about traveling and meeting people in New York, Chicago etc. My Grandfather has since passed away in 1973

Registrant ID: 1541
Name: Verna B Habersham
City/State: Samtur, SC
Railroad: North Carolina
Position: Pullman Porter
Years of Service: 1940
Submitter's Name: Levine

Registrant ID: 1543
Name: Ira D. Hackett
City/State: Ashland, VA
Position: Porter
Years of Service: 1926's 1940's
Submitter's Name: Carolyn
City/State: Washington, DC
Comments: My grandfather worked on the rail line that ran from Richmond, VA thru Washington and up the East coast. I am not sure of the which railroad it was. My grandfather died in 1957.

Registrant ID: 1544
Name: Skeeter Haddon
City/State: Decatur, IL
Position: Porter
Submitter's Name: Shawn
City/State: Sacramento, CA
Comments: Worked as a Porter during 1914 through 1920.

Registrant ID: 1545
Name: Virgil Hadley
City/State: Minneapolis, MN
Railroad: Great Northern, Burlington-Northern, Amtrak
Position: Chief Cook
Years of Service: 42+
Submitter's Name: F. E.
City/State: Minneapolis, MN

Registrant ID: 1547
Name: Wilma Haines
City/State: Gary, IN
Railroad: Pullman Co.
Position: Car Cleaner
Years: Early 1920's- 50's
Submitter's Name: Denise
City/State: Gary, IN
Comments: My grandmother worked at the Pullman railroad

station located in Chicago, IL @ 12TH Roosevelt. My mother recalled when she was a child how important the presence of the Black Porter was, when she, along with her sisters, traveled by train to visit relatives.

Registrant ID: 1548
Name: Charles L. Hairston
City/State: New Rochelle, NY
Railroad: Baltimore & Ohio
Position: Trackman (Gandy Dancer)
Service: July 1942 -April 1943
Comments: It was hard physically taxing work and at times under extreme weather conditions, but the friendship among the workers was great.

Registrant ID: 1549
Name: Andrew Jack Halbert
City/State: Denver, CO
Railroad: Rio Grand R&R
Position: Cook & Pullman Porter
Submitter's: Burdette
City/State: Denver, CO

Registrant ID: 1550
Name: Percy Hall
City/State: Omaha, NE
Railroad: Union Pacific ; but worked out of Omaha, NE
Position: Dining Car Waiter
Years of Service: 1939 - 1957
Submitter's Name: Brian
City/State: Chicago, IL
Comments: Percy Hall was my maternal Grandfather, and he appeared in many photographs which promoted the railroad contemporaneously with the time he worked for Union Pacific. He

was known personally by many celebrities of his day who frequently traveled via railroad

Registrant ID: 1551
Name: Perry A Hall
City/State: Chicago, IL
Position: Porter
Years of Service: 1923-1930
Submitter's Name: Emily
City/State: Detroit, MI

Registrant ID: 1555
Name: Wesley Hall
City/State: Jersey City, NJ
Railroad: Erie Lackawanna
Position: Pullman Porter
Years of Service: 1928 - 1969
Submitter's Name: La Vivian
City/State: Old Bridge, NJ

Registrant ID: 1553
Name: Robert Hall
City/State: Pittsfield, MA
Railroad: Grand Central Terminal NY Central District
Position: In charge of club cars
Years of Service: 1926-1965
Submitter's Name: Helene
City/State: Piscataway, NJ

Registrant ID: 1556
Name: Cullen Ham
Position: Pullman Porter
Years: 1930's -1960's
Submitter's Name: Helen
City/State: Orangeburg, SC
Comments: This was my first Grand Uncle.

Registrant ID: 1557
Name: Joseph Hamelton Sr.
City/State: Decatur, GA
Railroad: Pennsylvania RR

Position: Sleeping Car Porter
Years of Service: 40's-50's
Submitter's Name: Carol
City/State: Decatur, GA
Comments: Grandfather

Registrant ID: 1558
Name: David Hamer
City/State: Columbia, MD
Railroad: Atlantic Coast Line Railroad Co./Pullman Company
Position: Dining Car Waiter
Years of Service: Employee card issued for 12/28/4 thru 6/5/43
Submitter's Name: Revolon
City/State: Columbia, MD
Comments: He had to sleep in the bathroom at night. The white passengers had threatened to throw him off the train because they wanted service when he was off duty. His supervisor overheard the conversation and told them to leave him alone.

Registrant ID: 1559
Name: David L. Hamer, Sr.
City/State: Columbia, MD
Position: Pullman Porter
Years of Service: 1932 - 1947
Submitter's Name: David L.
City/State: Henderson, NV
Comments: My Dad often told stories about his travels out west on railroad. As far as we know he was based either in Detroit or Washington, DC. My father often related stories about the callous manner with which was treated and also being called "George"

Registrant ID: 1560
Andrew Joseph Sr. Hamilton

Railroad: Pullman Co
Position: Sleeping Car Porter
Years of Service: Retired 1969
Submitter's Name: Cordelia
City/State: Chicago, IL
Comments: Worked for 34
Born Dec 1 1910 in New Orleans
Passed in 1979 in Arizona

Registrant ID: 1561
Nathaniel William Hamilton
City/State: ST. Louis, MO
Railroad: Missouri Pacific
Position: Waiter-in-Charge
Years of Service: 1935 - 1965
Submitter's Name: Jacqulin
City/State: Chicago, IL

Registrant ID: 1562
Name: Andrew Joseph Hamilton Sr.
City/State: Sioux City, IA
Railroad: Burlington Northern
Submitter's: Andrew
City/State: Sioux City, IA
Comments: He was my father.
He was born in 1910

Registrant ID: 1564
Name: Joe Hamm
City/State: Houston, TX
Railroad: Southern Pacific
Position: Railroad Yardsman
Years of Service: 33
Submitter's Name: Deborah
City/State: Houston, TX
Comments: He worked at night
because of the horrible heat in
the day time. He worked on the
railroad only to be laid off
because of illness.

Registrant ID: 1565
Name: Charles Hammock
City/State: Columbus, OH
Railroad: Pennsylvania RR

Position: Porter/Waiter
Years of Service: 20's-40's
Submitter's Name: Mary A
City/State: Columbus, OH
Comments: Columbus to St
Louis

Registrant ID: 1566
Name: James J, Jr Hammon
City/State: Jacksonville, FL
Railroad: Pullman Company
Position: Pullman Porter
Years of Service: 1941-1977

Registrant ID: 1567
Name: Richard D. Hammond
City/State: Toccoa, GA
Position: Porter
Years of Service:
1940's to 1960's
Submitter's Name: Marlo
City/State: North Olmsted, OH
Comments: My Grandmother,
Mrs. Mary Martin is his Sister.

Registrant ID: 1568
Elmer Johnson Hammonds Sr.
City/State: Louisville, KY
Railroad: L&N Railroad
Position: Pullman Porter
Submitter's: Elmer Lucille
City/State: Louisville, KY
Comments: I had photographs
of my father with A. Philip
Randolph when he was
organizing the Pullman Porters of
the L & N. I never understood
why my father disliked Pullman
company officials until I read
about the porters legacy a
magazine article.

Registrant ID: 1569
Name: Charles Hampton
City/State: Cincinnati, OH
Submitter's: Berney & Thomas
City/State: Cincinnati, OH

Registrant ID: 1570
Name: Granville Hampton, Jr.
City/State: Memphis, TN
Railroad: Northern Pacific
Railway The Pullman Company
Position: Pullman Porter
Submitter's Name: Lois
City/State: Memphis, TN

Registrant ID: 1571
Name: Allan Alonzo Hancock
City/State: MO
Railroad: Union Pacific from
Chicago -Omaha to California
Position: Sleeping Car Porter
Years of Service: 1945-47
Submitter's Name: Thelma
City/State: Laurel, MD
Comments: I don't really
remember much about daddy on
the railroad. I just remember
going down to Union Station in
Omaha, Nebraska to meet him
when he came home.

Registrant ID: 1574
Name: Talbot Hankerson
City/State: Augusta, GA
Railroad: New York, New Haven,
Hartford
Position: Dining Car Waiter
Years of Service: Circa1915 -29
Submitter's Name: Virginia
City/State: Richmond, VA

Registrant ID: 1575
Name: Arthur Hansbro
City/State: Louisville, KY

Railroad: Louisville and
Nashville
Position: Pullman Porter
Years of Service: 1950-1960
Submitter's Name: John
City/State: Bowling Green, KY

Registrant ID: 1576
Name: Thomas Hardeman
City/State: MO
Railroad: Wabash
Position: Dining Car Waiter-
Parlor Car Attendant
Submitter's Name: Thomasina
City/State: St. Louis , MO

Registrant ID: 1577
Name: James Harden
City/State: Oakland, CA
Railroad: Southern Pacific
Position: Waiter
Submitter's Name: Oliver
City/State: AL

Registrant ID: 1581
Name: J.A. Hardy
Position: Pullman Porter
Years of Service: Over 25
Comments: He was also member
of the union.

Registrant ID: 1579
Name: Hugh Hardy
City/State: OH
Railroad: L&N (Louisville and
Nashville), Cincinnati, Ohio
Position: Pullman Porter
Years of Service: 1930 - 1936
Submitter's Name: H. Hugh
City/State: Hudson, OH

Registrant ID: 1583
Name: Fred Harmon
Years of Service: 1950's

Submitter's Name: Tanya
City/State: Chicago, IL

Registrant ID: 1585
Fredrick (Douglass) Harmon
Railroad: Union Pacific
Position: Pullman Porter
Years of Service: 1948 - 50's
Submitter's Name: Lenora
City/State: Los Angeles, CA

Registrant ID: 1586
Name: Charles Harold Crow
City/State: Jaytor, MN
Railroad: Evansville , IN
Position: Waiter
Years of Service: 1945-1955
Submitter's Name: Deborah
City/State: Jaytor, MN

Registrant ID: 1593
Name: John Harper
City/State: Jonesville, LA
Railroad: Illinois Central
Position: Brakeman
Years of Service: 1964-1974
Comments: I loved working on the railroad and would go back right now if I could. My right leg was amputated after being run over by a box car.

Registrant ID: 1591
Name: Harry Harper
City/State: Indianapolis, IN
Railroad: Union Station of Indianapolis
Position: Chief of Redcaps
Years of Service: 1911-1966
Submitter's Name: Jared
City/State: Anderson, IN
Comments: My grandfather worked at Union Station in Indianapolis, IN. for 55 years.

He used to tell us his salary was $1.00 per year and he had to live off tips from customers. At the time of his retirement he had worked for the Station longer than any other employee.

Registrant ID: 1587
Name: Dave Harper
City/State: Chicago, IL
Railroad: Pennsylvania
Position: Pullman Porter
Submitter's Name: Eric
City/State: Chicago, IL
Comments: My grandfather, died on July 4, 1998. I remember his telling us all about working on the Railroad as a Porter. Upon his death, and earching the basement, I began to notice small items which were related to the railroad.

Registrant ID: 1592
Name: James Harper
City/State: NY
Railroad: Canadian Pacific
Position: Pullman Porter
Years of Service: 1949 - 1960
Submitter's Name: Eleanor
City/State: Mount Vernon, NY
Comments: My father has been deceased since Nov. 1977. I am not sure of the exact year that he started working for Canadian Pacific. I belie it was after World War II since he was a soldier in the Canadian Army.

Registrant ID: 1594
Name: Newton Harper
City/State: Philadelphia, PA
Railroad: Pennsylvania RR
Position: Pullman Porter

Years: Approx 35 years
Submitter's Name: Debbi
City/State: Philadelphia, PA
Comments: My father was there during the inception of the Brotherhood of Sleeping Car Porters. He knew A. Philip Randolph; and my older sister said that my father would come home and talk about the plan to unionize the Pullman Porters. 'My father would bring home fruit in big bags, sometimes oranges, grapefruit," Chinese apples", mangoes and sometimes fruit we had never seen before. He would tell us about the people he met and the places he had been.

Registrant ID: 1588
Name: Frank Peter Harper
City/State: PA
Railroad: Penn Central Station
Position: Pullman Porter
Years of Service: 1917-1960
Submitter's Name: Olivia
City/State: Pittsburgh, PA
Comments: Frank Peter Harper was my Grandfather and our family received a congratulations proclamation from the National Railroad Passenger Corp. Amtrak honoring our relative for his service with the Pullman Company and the Brotherhood of Sleeping Car Porters. This

Registrant ID: 1596
Name: Sherman H. Harper
Position: Pullman Porter
Submitter's Name: Virgule
City/State: St. Paul, MN

Registrant ID: 1597
Name: Henry Harrat
City/State: Columbus, OH
Railroad: Pennsylvania RR
Position: Lineman
Years of Service: 1934-1959
Submitter's Name: Brown

Registrant ID: 1598
Name: Ralph Harrell
City/State: Chicago, IL
Railroad: Pullman
Position: Waiter
Years of Service: 10 Plus years
Submitter's Name: Vivian
City/State: Ellicott City, MD

Registrant ID: 1599
Name: Willie L. Harriford
City/State: Cola City, CA
Railroad: Union Pacific and Southern
Position: Dining Car waiter
Years of Service: 1937 to 1941
Submitter's Name: Willie L. Jr.
City/State: Columbia, SC
Comments: My father moved to Colorado from Kansas City, to work on the Union Pacific railroad. He was laid off and found work on the Southern Railroad running from New York to Florida. My mother and I lived in Denver while he was working out of New York.

Registrant ID: 1601
Name: Albert Harris
City/State: Cambridge, MA
Position: Baggage Man
Submitter's Name: Anita T.
City/State: Boston, MA
Comments: Worked 20 years

Registrant ID: 1602
Name: Arthur Bruce Harris
City/State: Detroit, MI
Railroad: Cincinnati Union Terminal
Position: Sleeping Car Porter
Years of Service: Retired 1955
Submitter's Name: Judith
City/State: Detroit, MI
Comments: Grandfather born 1885 -1971

Registrant ID: 1633
Name: Aubrey Harris, Jr.
Railroad: Missouri Pacific
Position: Porter and Brakesman
Years of Service: 1948 to 1968
Submitter's Name: Whitney
City/State: Canton, MO
Comments: Aubrey was my father. He was married to Ida Carmon. He began working on the RR in 1948 and remained with them until March 1968.

Registrant ID: 1604
Name: Blair Harris
City/State: Columbia, MD
Railroad: Pullman Company
Position: Porter
Years of Service: 1935-1950
Submitter's Name: Jackman

Registrant ID: 1603
Name: Bessie Harris
Railroad: Pullman Porter Railroad
Position: Cleaning Woman
Submitter's Name: Chef

Registrant ID: 1605
Name: Charles Harris
City/State: Roxbury, MA

Railroad: Boston & Maine, New Haven Central
Position: Steward, Chef
Submitter's Name: Charles
City/State: Roxbury, MA
Comments: I was told that he was the first African American Steward.

Registrant ID: 1606
Name: Curtis Harris
City/State: McGehee, AR
Railroad: Missouri Pacific
Position: Porter
Years of Service: 30 or more
Submitter's Name: Rehear
City/State: Duncanville, TX
Comments: As a child, I remember him providing us with passage to Chicago most summers to stay with other relatives. His daughter Terez still lives in Arkansas.

Registrant ID: 1608
Name: David Earl Harris
City/State: Gary, IN
Years of Service: 1941-1945
Submitter's Name: Yvonne
City/State: Gary, IN

Registrant ID: 1607
Name: David Harris
City/State: Yellow Springs, OH
Railroad: Canadian Pacific
Position: Porter-In Charge, Sleeping Car Porter
Years of Service: 1920/1946
Submitter's Name: William
City/State: Xenia, OH
Comments: My dad myself, and my brother all worked for the Canadian Pacific, as a Porter,

and as a Sleeping car conductor, they called it Running in charge.

Registrant ID: 1610
Name: Earl Harris
City/State: AL
Railroad: Chicago
Position: Pullman Porter (also union "shop steward")
Years of Service: 1930 to 1966
Submitter's Name: Rose M.
City/State: Alexandria, VA
Comments: My dad was proud of his position as Pullman Porter. He was fastidious about keeping all part of his uniform cleaned and pressed, shoes shined, and cap brushed with shining braid. He shined shoes for people who purchased berths on the train.

Registrant ID: 1611
Name: Fred Harris
City/State: North Carolina, NC
Railroad: Southern
Position: Sleeping Car Porter
Years of Service: Early 1900's
Submitter's Name: Annie
City/State: Chesapeake, VA

Registrant ID: 1612
Name: George Harris
City/State: Dorchester, MA
Railroad: Boston Station
Position: Porter
Years of Service: 1890-1920
Submitter's Name: Sheryl
City/State: Dorchester, MA
Comments: My uncle

Registrant ID: 1613
Name: Gid Harris
City/State: Kansas City, KS
Railroad: Rock Island

Position: Laborer (swept switches)
Years of Service: 1950-63
Submitter's: Freddie Mae
City/State: Tonawanda, NY
Comments: My father went to Kansas City, Kansas from Montgomery County Mississippi in 1944. He found work at the Sunflower plant until he was injured. After his recovery he was hired as a laborer by the Rock Island Railroad (around 1949 or 1950) where he worked

Registrant ID: 1614
Name: Hernan Harris
City/State: Baltimore, MD
Railroad: Pullman Company
Position: Trackman
Years of Service: 1946-1981

Registrant ID: 1634
Name: James Melvin Harris, Sr.
City/State: TN
Railroad: Southern Railway
Position: Cook
Submitter's Name: Willie Mae
City/State: Chattanooga, TN
Comments: As a child my grandfather often spoke of the days when he worked as a cook for the railroad system. I believe that he travel from Chattanooga, Tennessee and throughout Georgia.

Registrant ID: 1615
Name: Jacob Harris
City/State: New York, NY
Railroad: Rule Washington Terminal
Position: Dining Car Waiter
Submitter's Name: Robert

City/State: Fort Wayne, IN

Registrant ID: 1617
Name: Julien Harris
City/State: Pensacola, FL
Railroad: Dixie Hummingbird
Position: Waiter
Years of Service: 1930's-1959

Registrant ID: 1618
Name: Leonard Louis Sr. Harris
City/State: Chicago, IL
Railroad: Pullman Rail Car Co.
Position: Pullman Porter
Years of Service: 1940's-1960's
Submitter's Name: Leonard Jr.
City/State: Chicago, IL
Comments: He was my father

Registrant ID: 1621
Name: Miles Harris
City/State: Bangor, MI
Railroad: California Zephyr
Position: Pullman Porter
Years of Service: Probably from about 1938 to about 1960.
Submitter's Name: Betty Jean
City/State: Chicago, IL
Comments: Memories of my father and his friends who were Pullman Porters and their wives were so very positive. They were proud men. They had great pride related to their work and were supportive of one another. I have often tried to figure out why employees in organizations and companies today do not seem to be as supportive to one another. As I have pondered this question, I have come to believe they came together in such support for one another due to their work in their union and their union

leader, A. Phillip Randolph. My father always had positive comments to make about his work, those he worked with and people he served. My dad as well as the other men who were Porters had personalities that were warm. They knew how to meet people. He met many wonderful people during the years of serving for the railroad. He instilled in my sister and myself many positive values related to work, being a good citizen, and to work for a good education. As an educator in an institution of higher learning I do hope I too can serve my students and the institution I work for as well as my dad and these men have served the public as they did on their jobs.

Registrant ID: 1622
Name: Mose Harris
City/State: Jacksonville, FL
Railroad: Seaboard Coastline
Position: Pullman Porter
Submitter's Name: Pamela
City/State: Jacksonville, FL

Registrant ID: 1624
Name: Phillip Harris
City/State: South Boston, VA
Railroad: Ohio Railroad
Years of Service: 1927 to Approximately 1940's Or 1950's
Submitter's Name: Halle Jean
City/State: Saluda, VA
Comments: This information I received from my Mother (Willie Mary Corr Holmes) who is Phillip Harris's granddaughter. Her

mother was Phillip Harris's daughter, Hallie.

Registrant ID:
Name: Randolph Harris
City/State Chicago, IL
Railroad: The Pullman Co.
Years of Service: 1920's
Submitter: Robert
City/State: Bloomfield, CT

Registrant ID: 1625
Name: Randall Harris
City/State: Corsicana, TX
Railroad: Southern Pacific
Position: Pullman Porter
Submitter's Name: Willie
City/State: Houston, TX

Registrant ID: 1628
Name: Sam Harris
City/State: Opelika, Alabama,
Position: Pullman Porter
Submitter's Name: Nancy
City/State: New Orleans, LA

Registrant ID: 1629
Name: Stephanie Harris
City/State: Indianapolis, IN
Submitter's Name: Rodney
City/State: Indianapolis, IN

Registrant ID: 1632
Name: Willie Harris
City/State: Chicago, IL
Position: Pullman Porter
Submitter's Name: Barbara
City/State: Dolton, IL

Registrant ID: 1635
Name: Daniel Webster Harrison
Position: Pullman Porter
Years of Service: 1929-1937
Submitter's Name: Betty B.

City/State: Oakland, CA

Registrant ID: 1637
Name: Robert E Harrison
City/State: Winston Salem, NC
Railroad: New York
Position: DCW
Years of Service: 1944-1945
Submitter's Name: Robert E
City/State: Winston Salem, NC

Registrant ID: 1638
Name: Harvey Hart
City/State: Omaha, NE
Railroad: Union Pacific
Position: Porter
Years of Service: 43yrs
Submitter's Name: Jacqueline
City/State: Omaha, NE

Registrant ID: 1626
Name: Randolph Harris
Railroad: Chicago Zephyr
Position: Cook and Porter
Years of Service: 1930-1934
Submitter's Name: Robert
City/State: Bloomfield, CT
Comments: The only information that I have about my father is that he worked for the Railroad in the early 1920's

Registrant ID: 1640
Name: Thomas Hart Weston
City/State: Florissant, MD
Railroad: Pacific
Position: Sleeping Car Porter
Years of Service: 30yrs
Submitter's Name: Rosemary
City/State: Florssart, MD
Comments: Father, Starter when they first started passed in 1967 went to St Louis -LA

Registrant ID: 1642
Name: Alvin J. Hartman
City/State: Elk Grove, CA
Position: Waiter
Years of Service: 1935-1945
Submitter's Name: Patricia H.
City/State: Elk Grove, CA

Registrant ID: 1654
Name: Arnette H. Harvey
City/State: Jacksonville, NC
Position: Porter
Submitter's Name: Ellen

Registrant ID: 1655
Name: Sidney Harvey
City/State: St. Louis, MO
Railroad: Union Pacific
Position: Pullman Porter
Years of Service: 1950's
Submitter's Name: Brenda
City/State: St. Charles, MO
Comments: Sidney Harvey is deceased. I'm his daughter. I'm only sure that he worked as a Pullman Porter in the 1950's. I will look for information that might tell me just when.

Registrant ID: 1656
Name: George E. Harvey Sr.
City/State: AL
Railroad: M. K. & T. and Union Pacific
Position: Porter
Years of Service: 1945-1982
Submitter's Name: Joseph L.
City/State: Boise, ID
Comments: He finally became a conductor with Union Pacific out of Denver, CO. before he retired in 1982.

Registrant ID: 1657
Name: Frederick Haskins
City/State: NC
Years of Service: 1920's -1930's
Submitter's Name: Martha E.
City/State: Wilmingham, NC

Registrant ID: 1661
Robert Lee Paul Hawkins
City/State: Cincinnati, OH
Railroad: Pullman Company
Position: Porter
Years of Service: 1929-1936
Comments: I was hired by the Pullman Company and traveled all railroads all over USA.

Registrant ID: 1660
Name: Jerome Hawkins
City/State: Howell, NJ

Registrant ID: 1659
Name: Benjamin Hawkins
City/State: Chicago, IL
Railroad: New York Central
Position: Fireman/Fire Knocker
Years of Service: Start date unknown died in 1946
Submitter's Name: Robbie
City/State: Poulsbo, WA
Comments: Benjamin Franklin Hawkins was my father. A few years prior to his death I believe he received a 20 year award for never being late or absent.

Registrant ID: 1664
Name: William Hawkins
City/State: Cleveland, OH
Railroad: New York Central - 20th Century Ltd & Mercury
Position: Dining Car Waiter
Submitter's Name: Anton
City/State: Snellville, GA

Registrant ID: 1667
Name: Theodore R Hayes
City/State: Cleveland, OH
Railroad: Pullman Company
Position: Pullman Porter
Years of Service: 1927-1951
Submitter's Name: Hayes Allen

Registrant ID: 1668
Name: Luther Melvin Hayes
City/State: Chicago, IL
Railroad: Union Pacific
Position: Pullman Porter
Years of Service: 1939-1952
Submitter's Name: Robert E.
City/State: Elgin, IL
Comments: He was on the
Chicago to Los Angeles run.

Registrant ID: 1669
Name: Elmer E. Hayes, Sr.
City/State: Cleveland Heights
Ohio
Position: Equipment Operator
Years of Service: 1940-1968
Submitter's Name: Allan
City/State: Cleveland Hts., OH

Registrant ID: 1674
Name: Joseph Haynes
City/State: AL
Railroad: L and N Railroad
Position: Pullman & Mail –
handler
Years of Service: 1920-40
Submitter's Name: Lucindy
City/State: Columbus, OH
Comments: My grandfather
work as a Pullman porter for 4
years. After that he would get
mail from the post office and
push it to the train and load the
train with mail. Deceased

Registrant ID: 1672
Name: Fred Haynes
City/State: NY
Position: Porter
Submitter's Name: Gail R.
City/State: New York, NY
Comments: I only heard my
grandfather and father talking
among themselves when I was a
small child.

Registrant ID: 1677
Name: Joseph Haynes
City/State: NE
Railroad: Union Pacific
Position: Sleeping Car Porter
Years of Service: Early 1940's
Submitter's Name: Mrs. J.
City/State: Oakland, CA
Comments: My father "ran on
the road" from Omaha to
Oakland

Registrant ID: 1673
Name: John Henry Haynes
City/State: Los Angeles
(formerly Chicago), CA
Railroad: Illinois Central
Position: Sleeping Car Porter
Years: Circa early 1900's-1952
Submitter's Name: Dr. Jane H
City/State: Silver Spring, MD
Comments: Considered a very
prestigious job to work on the
railroad at that time. His boss,
lived in Macomb MS. and
persuaded Grandpa to move to
Chicago and work on the
railroad. Previously Grandpa had
worked as a lineman, laying the
lines for the telephone poles.

Registrant ID: 1670
Name: Archie Haynes
City/State: AL
Railroad: L and N Railroad
Position: Pullman Porter and Mail Handler
Years of Service: 1920-40
Submitter's Name: Lucindy
City/State: Whitehall, OH

Registrant ID: 1679
Name: Alvin Haynes, Sr.
City/State: New Orleans, LA
Submitter's Name: Doris
City/State: South Bend, IN
Comments: William Marshall, Jr. (cross-reference), my great-uncle Alvin Haynes, Sr.

Registrant ID: 1680
Name: Lee C. Haywood
Position: Pullman Porter
Years of Service: Over 25
Comments: He was also a member B.S.C.P union.

Registrant ID: 1682
Name: Ebony Head
City/State: Cleveland, OH

Registrant ID: 1683
Name: Lawrence J.M. Heard
City/State: AL
Railroad: Pullman Company
Position: Pullman Porter
Years of Service: 36
Submitter's Name: William
City/State: AL

Registrant ID: 1684
Name: Oscar Hearn
City/State: Chicago, IL
Position: Pullman Porter
Years of Service: 1941- to

Submitter's Name: Napoleon
City/State: Jonesville, SC
Comments: My dad was a college graduate who found that this was the best work option open to black men at that time.

Registrant ID: 1685
Name: Andrew Helm
City/State: Kansas City, MO
Position: Dining Car Waiter
Years of Service: 1929-1973
Submitter's Name: Stephanie
City/State: Jamaica, NY

Registrant ID: 1686
Name: Fay L. Henderson
City/State: Oakland, CA
Railroad: Southern Pacific
Position: Pullman Porter
Years of Service: 1940-1960
Comments: It was a wonderful opportunity to travel, meet people and see the United States. The work was hard and demeaning, but it provided needed money for my family. It was not much opportunity for advancement. However, I was thankful to have a job.

Registrant ID: 1689
Name: Louis B Henderson
City/State: Norwalk, CA
Railroad: California Zephyr
Years of Service: 1940-1970
Submitter's Name: Carol
City/State: Norwalk, CA
Comments: Worked for 30 years

Registrant ID: 1687
Name: John Henderson
City/State: Durant, MS
Railroad: Illinois Central

Position: Car Cleaner
Years of Service: 1910
Submitter's Name: Tyrone
City/State: Robbins, IL
Comments: John Henderson is brother to my great - grandmother Cordilia Henderson-Haymore. John move his wife and 6 children to Chicago, IL in 1923. His son Charles H. Henderson was a Porter on the "City Miami" and another son John H. Jr. was a waiter on the "CITY".

Registrant ID: 1695
Name: Henry Henderson, Jr.
City/State: Greenwood, SC
Railroad: Seaboard Coast Line
Position: Pullman Porter
Years of Service: 45 years Retired in 1979
Submitter's Name: Mary H.
City/State: Irmo, SC
Comments: Mr. Henry Henderson is deceased. He traveled to Monroe, North Carolina, South Carolina & Georgia.

Registrant ID: 1698
Name: Lenneal Henderson, Sr.
City/State: San Francisco, CA
Railroad: Southern Pacific
Position: Pullman Porter
Years of Service: 1945-1952
Comments: Overall, my experience was uneventful. Since I liked to travel, I enjoyed my work. I happen to be a very fair skinned, straight-haired African American man so I believe I did not receive the amount of discrimination that my darker skinned counterparts.

Registrant ID: 1696
Name: Henry D. Henderson, Sr.
City/State: W. Corina, CA
Railroad: Illinois Central
Years of Service: 1944-1946
Submitter's Name: Shirley
City/State: W. Corina, CA

Registrant ID: 1699
Clarence Janies Hendricks
City/State: Toledo, OH
Position: Porter
Submitter's Name: Maurine
City/State: Toledo, OH
Comments: Wife of a Porter

Registrant ID: 1700
Name: John Henry
Railroad: Detroit-Fl-NY
Position: Porter
Years of Service: 1937-1948
Submitter's Name: Doris

Registrant ID: 1701
Name: John Matt Henry
City/State: Gurdon, AR
Railroad: Missouri Pacific
Position: Railroad Worker
Years of Service: 1920-1962
Submitter's Name: Pan
City/State: Oakland, CA

Registrant ID: 1702
Name: Woody Henry
City/State: AL
Railroad: Missouri Pacific
Position: Railroad Worker
Years of Service: 1917-1962
Submitter's Name: Pam
City/State: Oakland, CA

Registrant ID: 1704
Name: Wilfred Herbert
City/State: New Orleans, LA
Railroad: Southern Pacific
Sunset Limited
Position: Pullman Porter
Years of Service: 30 years
Submitter's Name: Nancy
City/State: Lancaster, CA
Comments: His trip run-was
New Orleans to Los Angeles. He
retired in 1952.

Registrant ID: 1705
Name: Walter Herd
Railroad: Pullman Company
Position: Pullman Porter
Years of Service: 1944-53
Comments: This is my father.
He worked for the Pullman

Registrant ID: 1707
Name: LeRoy Herman
City/State: Chicago, IL
Railroad: Pennsylvania RR
Position: Chef
Years of Service: 1920-1940
Submitter's Name: Pamela
City/State: Gwynn Oak, MD
Comments: My mother
(Antoinette Herman Jackson),
told me that my Uncle LeRoy
started as a cook on the
Pennsylvania and worked up to
the position of a chef. His
nickname was "Mighty Fine".

Registrant ID: 1708
Name: Leonard Herrod
City/State: Oklahoma City, OK
Railroad: Rock Island
Position: Porter
Years of Service:1940's-70's
Submitter's Name: Howard

City/State: Spencer, OK
Comments: Uncle Leonard, from
all indicators was one of the
most dynamic porters on the job.
I get a real thrill listening to him
call off the towns the train that
would pass through. He still has
his uniform cleaned and pressed
as though he has to go out at

Registrant ID: 1709
Name: Emmett Hester
City/State: Gary, IN
Position: Pullman Porter
Years of Service: 1940's
Submitter's Name: Ida Lorraine
and Linda
City/State: Minneapolis, MS
Comments: Uncle

Registrant ID: 1710
Name: Edmond Hewlett
City/State: AL
Railroad: Southern Pacific
Position: Dining Car Waiter
Years of Service: 1930-1945
Submitter's Name: Monique
City/State: Fairburn, GA

Registrant ID: 1711
Name: James Heyliger
City/State: Jamaica, NY
Railroad: New York Central
Position: Chef
Years of Service: 1943-1976
Submitter's Name: James
City/State: Jamaica, NY
Comments: James J. Heyliger
was awarded twice as Chef of the
year.

Registrant ID: 1713
Name: Eli Sherman Hickman
City/State: AL
Railroad: Great Northern and Northern Pacific
Position: Baggage Man
Years of Service: 1941-1968
Submitter's Name: Cynthia
City/State: Minneapolis, MN

Registrant ID: 1715
Thomas C. Hickman, M.D.
City/State: AL
Railroad: Northern Pacific
Position: Dining Car Waiter
Years of Service: 1949-1954
Submitter's Name: Cynthia
City/State: Minneapolis, MN

Registrant ID: 1716
Name: Albert Hicks
City/State: AL
Position: Porter
Years of Service: Late 20'-30's
Submitter's Name: Deborah
City/State: Chicago, IL
Comments: I believe my grandfather worked a route that was Chicago to New York or Memphis to New York.

Registrant ID: 1718
Name: Earlage B Hicks
City/State: Chicago, IL
Railroad: Santa Fe Railroad
Position: Pullman Porter
Years of Service: 1923-1968
Submitter's Name: Howard
City/State: Chicago, IL
Comments: My grandfather worked two routes- Chicago to California, and Chicago to Florida. My grandfather was a early union member.

Registrant ID: 1722
Name: Milton Hicks
City/State: Chicago, IL
Position: Pullman Porter
Submitter's Name: Sally
City/State: Chicago, IL
Comments: Worked out of Chicago

Registrant ID: 1727
Name: William Hicks
City/State: Chicago, IL
Railroad: Illinois Central
Position: Porter
Years of Service: 1950 - 1959
Submitter's Name: Theresa
City/State: Country CLub Hills, Illinois

Registrant ID: 1720
Name: Harry Hicks
Submitter's Name: Roberta
City/State: Landover, MD

Registrant ID: 1729
Leonard Russell Higginbotham
City/State: New York, NY
Railroad: Pullman Company
Position: Pullman Porter
Years of Service: 1920s- 930s
Submitter's Name: Elizabeth
City/State: Wilmington, DE
Comments: My father was born in 1909 and I was born in 1948. He was a bartender and waiter in NYC when I was born, but had worked on the railroad earlier in this life. He worked mostly out of Chicago at that time. When my siblings and I were young, we would talk.

Registrant ID: 1730
Name: Sherman Higgins

City/State: Omaha, NE
Railroad: Union Pacific
Position: Porter/waiter
Years of Service: 50 Years
Submitter's Name: Adrienne
City/State: Omaha, NE

Registrant ID: 1731
William Randolph Highbaugh
City/State: IN
Railroad: Southern Pacific, Amtrak
Position: Pullman Porter
Years of Service: 1925 - 1960
Submitter's Name: Theresa
City/State: Oak Park, CA
Comments: Main travel between Indianapolis, IN and New York.

Registrant ID: 1733
Name: Andrew Jackson Hilbert
City/State: Denver, CO
Railroad: Rio Grande
Years of Service: 1900's
Submitter's Name: Lee

Registrant ID: 1735
Name: Dock Hill
City/State: East ST Louis, IL
Railroad: Cottonbelt Railroad
Position: Cook
Years of Service: 15 YEARS
Comments: My dad (dock hill) died November 29 1976.

Registrant ID: 1739
Name: Tom Henry Hill
Position: Laborer
Years of Service: Late 1930's To Mid 1950's
Submitter's Name: Virginia
City/State: Bremerten,

Registrant ID: 1736
Name: Henry Hill
City/State: Chicago, IL
Position: Yardman
Submitter's Name: Bennett
City/State: Evanston, IL
Comments: Began working for the railroad in Decatur, Alabama during the early part of the century. Fatally injured in yard accident in Chicago in 1945 or 1946.

Registrant ID: 1738
Name: Moses Hill
City/State: NY
Position: Porter
Submitter's Name: Jane
City/State: Southgate Street, NY

Registrant ID: 1734
Name: Abner Hill
City/State: Spokane, WA
Railroad: Great Northern Milwaukee
Position: Porter
Years of Service: 1920- 1932
Submitter's Name: Jerrelene
City/State: Spokane, WA
Comments: My Father worked as a Porter on either of these Railroad Lines, out of Spokane, Washington. He was a resident of Spokane.

Registrant ID: 1737
Name: Leroy Hill
City/State: Callahan, FL
Railroad: Coastline
Position: Laborer
Years of Service: 1924-1958
Submitter's Name: D.
City/State: St. Marys, GA

Comments: Lee Roy Hill was my grandfather, he worked as a laborer for the railroad.

Registrant ID: 1741
Name: Horace Hill Sr.
City/State: Chicago, IL
Railroad: Santa Fe
Position: Pullman Porter
Years of Service: 1927-1929
Submitter's Name: Wilbert
City/State: South Holland, IL

Registrant ID: 1742
Name: Oscar Hill Jr.
City/State: Muncie, IN
Submitter's Name: Tyrhonda
City/State: Indianapolis, IN
Comments: My uncle in now deceased. Do not have further info, I was a young child.

Registrant ID: 1743
Name: Walter Hill Jr..
City/State: Jenkintown, PA
Railroad: Union Pacific (Challenger)
Position: Waiter
Years of Service: Summers 1939-40
Submitter's Name: LOIS
City/State: Jenkintown, PA
Comments: My father was a dining car waiter on the Union Pacific Challenger train during the summers of 1939 and 1940 while attending the University of Omaha part time. He went into the military in May 1941. His run covered Omaha to Laramie and Salt Lake City.

Registrant ID: 1745
Name: Otho Earl Hilliard

City/State: San Antonio, TX
Railroad: Extra Board and Missouri Kansas Texas (MKT or Katy)
Position: Porter and Porter-In-Charge
Years of Service: 1936-1955
Submitter's Name: Robert L.
City/State: San Antonio, TX
Comments: Born August 2, 1904 died May 13,1970. Worked un Seattle Washington 1936-1940.Worked in San Antonio, Texas 1940-1955- disability retirement(heart attack) worked Extra Board and the Missouri Kansas Texas Railroad. He was always a member of Brotherhood.

Registrant ID: 1746
Name: Dcaleve Hill-Menton
Submitter's Name: Dcaleve
City/State: College Park, GA

Registrant ID: 1749
Name: L R Nelson Hilton
City/State: Hammoth, NC
Railroad: Seaboard Coastline
Years of Service: 1941-1978

Registrant ID: 1748
Ferdinand DeLarge Hilton
City/State: New York, NY
Position: Porter
Years of Service: 1945-1955
Submitter's Name: Caroline
City/State: Yonkers, NY

Registrant ID: 1747
Name: Capers Preston Hilton
City/State: New York, NY
Position: Porter
Years of Service: 1916-1946

Submitter's Name: Caroline
City/State: Yonkers, NY

Registrant ID: 1750
Name: Porter Hilton Jr.
City/State: AL
Railroad: Seaboard Air Line
Atlantic Coast Line
Position: Porter
Years of Service: 1945-52
Submitter's Name: Stanley
City/State: Worcester, MA
Comments: I'm not sure as to
the years or which railine but
both he and his brother Fred
worked for the railroad. They
worked for opposite lines. My
father died in 1982.

Registrant ID: 1751
Name: Roman L Hindamar
City/State: Daron, OH
Railroad: Pullman Company
Position: Porter
Years of Service: 1943-1945
Submitter's Name: Hindamar

Registrant ID: 1756
Name: William G. Hines
City/State: CA
Railroad: Southern Pacific
Chicago to California
Position: Dining Car Waiter
Years of Service: 1942-1948
Submitter's: Beverly and
Rosalyn
City/State: Kensington, CA
Comments: Many thanks

Registrant ID: 1753
Name: William Hines
City/State: CA
Railroad: Southern Pacific
Position: Dining Car Porter

Years of Service: 1938-1946
Submitter's Name: Beverly
City/State: Kensington, CA

Registrant ID: 1758
Name: George Hines, Sr.
City/State: Chicago, IL
Railroad: Santa Fe Railroad
Years of Service: 30's,40' - 50's
Submitter's Name: George
City/State: Chicago, IL

Registrant ID: 1759
Name: Sheldon Hinton
City/State: Durham and
Raleigh, North Carolina
Position: Pullman Porter
Submitter's Name: Margaret
City/State: Kennesaw, GA
Comments: I have already
registered my great grandfather
Alexander Hinton, Sr. and I am
now registering my uncle
Sheldon Hinston). Unfortunately
I don't know what their former
addresses or, when they worked
the railroad.

Registrant ID: 1760
Name: Alexander Hinton, Sr.
City/State: Durham and
Raleigh, NC
Position: Pullman Porter
Years of Service: Approx 1880's
& the late 1890's
Submitter's Name: Margaret
City/State: Kennesaw, GA
Comments: This information
comes from my mother who is 86
years old. Her grandfather was a
Pullman porter and so was her
great uncle. She is not certain of
the exact period of time but gave
and estimate.

Registrant ID: 1761
Name: James R. Hivv
City/State: AL
Position: Diesel Mechanic
Years of Service: 1922-1969
Submitter's Name: Sandra
City/State: Chicago, IL

Registrant ID: 1762
Name: William Hoard
City/State: McDonough, GA
Railroad: Pennsylvania
Railroad/Seaboard/Atlantic
Coastline
Position: Pullman Porter
Years of Service: 35 plus
1942 until 1972
Submitter's Name: Stephanie
City/State: Albany, GA
Comments: My grandfather was
a Pullman Porter on the
Pennsylvania railroad. He was
also a member of the
Brotherhood of Sleeping Car
Porters. While I was growing up
my grandfather would tell us
stories of his most recent trips.
He traveled all over the United
States

Registrant ID: 1764
Name: Garland Hobson
City/State: AL
Railroad: Southern Railroad
Position: Pullman Porter
Years of Service: 1920-1970
Submitter's: Cheryl A. Sona A.
City/State: Huntsville, AL
Comments: Great Niece & Niece

Registrant ID: 1765
Name: Dawson Hodges
City/State: Chicago, IL
Railroad: Santa Fe

Position: Pullman Porter
Years of Service: 1926 - 1968
Submitter's Name: Bernadette
City/State: Chicago, IL
Comments: Mr. Hodges was
featured in a 2001 PBS film
produced for Chicago's Channel
11 regarding life as a Pullman
Porter. He was 99 years old at
the time of the interview and very
candid.

Registrant ID: 1766
Name: Alfred A. Hoggard Jr.
City/State: New York, NY
Railroad: Norfolk Line & New
York Pennsylvania
Position: Pullman Porter
Years of Service: 1949-69
Submitter's Name: Beverly
City/State: Neptune, NJ

Registrant ID: 1767
Name: Jonnie Hohnson
City/State: Chicago, IL
Position: Porter
Years of Service: 1948-1965
Submitter's Name: Betty
City/State: Clevland, IL

Registrant ID: 1769
Name: Leslie Holden
City/State: Natchitoches, LA
Railroad: Texarkana
Position: Pullman Porter
Years of Service: 1920-1924
Submitter's Name: L. Renee'
City/State: Natchitoches, LA
Comments: I have a picture of
my grandfather in his uniform in
front of his home on Texas Street
in Natchitoches, Louisiana. As
the story goes when the train
would come rumbling down the

tracks it passed directly in front of the house where my mother,grandmother were standing.

Registrant ID: 1768
Name: Isomer Holden
City/State: New York, NY
Railroad: Hamlet North Carolina, Seaboard Coastline
Position: Waiter Porter
Years of Service: 1938-1952
Submitter's Name: Charles
City/State: New York, NY
Comments: My grandfather, uncle, and mother-in-law also worked for the railroad

Registrant ID: 1770
Name: Gus Holderness
City/State: AL
Railroad: Illinois Central
Position: Dining Car Waiter
Years of Service: 1941-1971
Submitter's Name: Debra
City/State: Denver, CO
Comments: Dad hired on with the Illinois Central Railroad sometime late in 1941 or early 1942. My mom, who is 85 and Daddy would be 89, she could not remember the exact dates.

Registrant ID: 1776
Name: John C. Holland
City/State: Lincoln, NE
Railroad: Burlington
Position: Dining Car Steward
Years of Service: 30
Submitter's Name: Dora L.
City/State: Denver, CO
Comments: Mr. Holland is not a relative but a good friend. He was the first Black Dining Car

steward for Burlington Railroads. At the time of this submission, is still with us.

Registrant ID: 1775
Name: John Holland
City/State: Lincoln, NE
Position: Pullman Porter
Submitter's Name: Mary
City/State: Hampton, VA
Comments: My uncle at the time of this submission is 85 years old with a very sharp mind

Registrant ID: 1777
Name: Walter Holland
City/State: Mayberry, WV
Railroad: Norfolk & Western
Position: Rail Maintainer
Years of Service: 1943-1968
Submitter's Name: Emma
City/State: Rio Rancho, NM
Comments: It was the only job that my husband ever had or wanted. He started working on the railroad when he was 16 years old. He then went into the military, he served in the (Korean War). After returning from the war, he went back to working on the railroad until

Registrant ID: 1771
Name: Arthur Chester Holland
City/State: Rio Grande, NJ
Railroad: Pullman Rail Car Co
Position: Chef Cook
Years of Service: 1927-1941
Submitter's Name: Georgia
City/State: Williamsburg, VA
Comments: Arthur Chester Holland was a fine and, distinguished husband, father and dedicated worker on the

railroad in the Pullman car service.. He held a second job in the U.S. Postal Service in order to be a sound provider for his family.

Registrant ID: 1778
Name: Charles Holland, Sr.
City/State: Cincinnati, OH
Railroad: B & O
Position: Chef Cook
Years of Service: 18 yrs.
Submitter's Name: Gwen
City/State: Cincinnati, OH
Comments: Meeting different people around the U.S.and knowing the different types of food they eat, and the different type of food one could cook.

Registrant ID: 1779
Edward Thadeus Hollingsworth
City/State: Keyser, WV
Railroad: (B&O) Boiler Roundhouse
Service: 1923-63
Submitter's Name: Jean
City/State: Detroit, MI

Registrant ID: 1780
Franklin Horace Hollingsworth
City/State: AL
Railroad: Union Pacific
Position: Dining Car Waiter
Years of Service: 1956-1968
Submitter's Name: Kimberly
City/State: Norwalk, CA
Comments: My father was a very proud man who enjoyed working and traveling throughout this country on the Railroad. However, the mistreatment of my father for being a Black man was

too much to bare some days and he became bitter.

Registrant ID: 1783
Name: Arthur Hollins
City/State: Elk Grove, CA
Position: Pullman Porter
Years of Service: 1905-1954
Submitter's Name: Beverly
City/State: Elkgrove, CA
Comments: Grandfather, Muskogee Ok line #74401
Comments: L.A. to Chicago

Registrant ID: 1784
Name: Overton Hollins
City/State: LA
Railroad: Southern-Pacific
Position: Pullman Porter
Years of Service: 1935-69
Submitter(s): Philip and Olga
City/State: New Orleans, LA

Registrant ID: 1785
Name: Perry Hollins
City/State: Fort Worth, TX
Position: Brakeman
Years of Service: 1910-1960
Submitter's Name: Majorie
City/State: Fort Worth, TX

Registrant ID: 1788
Name: Walter B. Hollis
City/State: Washington, DC
Railroad: B&O and Coast Seaboard
Position: Cook
Years of Service: 1948-1960
Submitter's Name: Kenneth
City/State: Placerville, CA
Comments: He worked primarily for the B & O out of Washington DC. In the winters he made the run to Florida on the Coast

Seaboard. He lived with lots of others cook and waiters. Most of the time he worked on the east coast.

Registrant ID: 1789
Name: Jason Holloway
City/State: Blue Island, IL
Railroad: Pullman Company
Position: Field
Years of Service: 1963-1969

Registrant ID: 1792
Name: Charles T. Holloway
Position: Pullman Porter
Years of Service: Approx. 40
Submitter's Name: Lillie
City/State: Florence, AL

Registrant ID: 1791
Name: Charles Holloway
City/State: St. Louis, MO
Position: Pullman Porter
Years of Service: 1923-1936
Submitter's Name: Leona
City/State: Los Angeles, CA
Comments: He was my uncle

Registrant ID: 861
Herbert Cornelius Holloway
City/State: New York, NY
Railroad: Southern Railroad
Position: Sleeping-Car Porter and Conductor
Years of Service: 1941- 1972
Submitter's Name: Bernadette
Comments: My father attended Johnson C Smith University. He taught school in North Carolina before going to New York to work on the railroad. I remember him working on the Silver Meter. He often talked about his travels.

Registrant ID: 1793
Name: Pink Holloway
City/State: Chicago, IL
Position: Porter
Submitter's Name: Elvin
City/State: Omaha, IL
Comments: Pink Holloway is my maternal grandfather. He has been deceased since 1956.

Registrant ID: 1795
Name: Eddie Holloway Jr.
City/State: Victoria, VA
Railroad: Baltimore and Ohio
Years of Service: During WWII
Submitter's Name: Myron
City/State: Baltimore, MD
Comments: Eddie laid track and ran equipment for Patapsco and Back river railroad in Sparrows Point from 1950's- late 1960's.

Registrant ID: 1796
Name: William Holly Pinson
City/State: East Elmhurst, NY
Position: Waiter
Years of Service: 1942 to
Submitter's Name: W. Billie
City/State: Arlington, VA

Registrant ID: 1799
Name: Harry Holmes
City/State: New York, NY
Railroad: NY Railroad
Position: Waiter
Years of Service: 1944-1958
Submitter's Name: Donald
City/State: Albuquerque, NM

Registrant ID: 1804
Name: Willie Ben Holmes
City/State: Asheville, NC
Railroad: Southern Railroad, Norfolk Southern Railway

Position: Sleeping Car Porter
Years of Service: 1947-1974
Submitter's Name: Debora
City/State: Asheville, NC
Comments: Our father died November 9, 2001 at that time he was one of the two remaining Pullman Porters in western North Carolina. During his employment he received several acknowledgements for customer service and dedication to Norfolk Southern Railway.

Registrant ID: 1801
Name: Rufus E. Holmes
City/State: Chicago, IL
Railroad: Pullman Company and Rock Island Railroad
Position: Pullman Porter
Years: Circa 1943-early 1960's
Submitter's Name: Esther J
City/State: Country Club Hills, IL
Comments: My dad loved this job and took great pride in his work. During World War 2, I remember my dad being gone for long periods of time and my mother and I going downtown to the station to see him briefly and bring him clean clothes.

Registrant ID: 1797
Name: Ernest O Holmes
City/State: Erie, CO
Railroad: Pullman Rail Car Company
Position: Pullman Porter
Years of Service: 1942-1969
Submitter's Name: Gregory
City/State: Erie, CO
Comments: Father worked out of Denver Colorado.

Registrant ID: 1805
Name: Willie Mack Holmes
City/State: Winnsboro, SC
Position: Chef
Years of Service: 1925-1937
Submitter's Name: Shirley
City/State: Philadelphia, PA

Registrant ID: 1800
Name: Johnny Holmes
City/State: New York, NY

Railroad: The Silver Meter
Submitter's Name: Hallie Jean
City/State: Saluda, VA
Comments: He worked on the train going from New York to Florida from 1920's 1940's or 1950's according to my father Joshua Holmes who is now 87 years old.

Registrant ID: 1806
Name: William Fleming Holsey
City/State: New York, NY
Railroad: Pennsylvania
Position: Waiter
Years of Service: 1920-1944
Submitter's Name: Denyce
City/State: Oakland, CA
Comments: My grandfather worked on the Penn. railroad his entire career. He passed before I was born. My father often talks about his father's experiences, many were degrading. While traveling, the waiters often had to stay in "colored" quarters.

Registrant ID: 1807
Name: Albert Holt
City/State: St. Louis, MO
Railroad: St. Louis-NY-Boston.

Submitters: James, John, and Tom
City/State: St. Louis, MO

Registrant ID: 1808
Name: Alfred Holt
City/State:
Railroad: New York Central
Position: Pullman Porter
Submitter's: Beverly Ann

Alfred Holt

Registrant ID: 1809
Name: Eugene Holt
City/State: Cincinnati, OH
Position: Porter
Submitter's Name: Mary
City/State: Cincinnati, OH
Comments: Worked 38 years

Registrant ID: 1811
Name: Joseph Holt
City/State: Washington, DC
Position: Porter
Years of Service: Circa 1940's-70's. Retired in 1975

Submitter's Name: Johnny
City/State: Calpeper, VA

Registrant ID: 1812
Name: Lawrence Reynolds Holt
City/State: Harlem, NY
Railroad: New York Central
Position: Pullman Porter
Years of Service: 1911 - 1957
Submitter's Name: Brian
City/State: Raleigh, NC
Comments: His first run was from New York (Grand Central Station) to Asheville NC...He was affiliated with James Reese Europe and the New York Clef Club during this time. He was drafted in June of 1917 and served in the New York 369th Infantry (Harlem Hell fighter)

Registrant ID: 1813
Name: Reynolds Holt
City/State: Bronx, NY
Railroad: He did the run from NYC (Grand Central Station) to Canada
(I think Toronto)
Service: Circa 1910- 1920's
Submitter's Name: Pam
City/State: Raleigh, NC

Registrant ID: 1815
Name: Theodore King Hood
City/State: Chicago, IL
Railroad: Service for Chicago
Position: Dining car waiter or Pullman Porter
Years of Service: 1929-1933
Submitter's Name: DORA
City/State: Los Angeles, CA
Comments: I was a child at the time, but my mother met him while he worked on the train.

213

Registrant ID: 1814
Name: Chester Hood
City/State: Washington, DC
Railroad: Seaboard
Position: Dining Car Waiter
Years: Circa1949-1959
Submitter's Name: Carol
City/State: Washington, DC
Comments: My recollection of my father's job with Seaboard Railroad is a joyous one! My father would travel to New York for his "run" from New York to Miami where he served as a Dining Car Waiter/Maitre d'. We knew this was a job to be proud of, and my father was.

Registrant ID: 1817
Name: Obie Hooker
City/State: Chicago, IL
Railroad: Burlington
Position: Dining Car Waiter
Submitter's Name: Melody
City/State: Chicago, IL
Comments: My uncle spoke about the lifelong friends that he made and his lifelong experiences, and that he was able to travel and make friends all over the country which he reminisced about fondly until the end of his life. He also talked about the politicians that

Registrant ID: 1819
Name: Obazine Hooks
City/State: AL
Railroad: California Zephyr and The Santa Fe Railroad
Position: Sleeping Car Porter
Years of Service: circa 1950-60
Submitter's Name: Linda
City/State: Powder Springs, GA.

Comments: I remember my father being very proud to be a Sleeping Car Porter. During that time, it was a job that carried much prestige in the African American communities.

Registrant ID: 1821
Name: Charles B. Hopkins
Position: Sleeping Car Porter
Years of Service: Retired1940's
Submitter's Name: Faye H.

Registrant ID: 1825
Name: Philip Hopkins
City/State: St. Louis (Kinlock), MO
Railroad: Illinois Central, New York Central,
Position: Sleeping Car Porter
Years of Service: Late 1890's through 1950's
Submitter's Name: Philip
City/State: Sun City, CA

Registrant ID: 1822
Name: Charlie Hopkins
City/State: St. Louis (Kinlock), MO
Railroad: Illinois Central, and The New York Central
Position: Sleeping Car Porter
Years of Service: 1890-1930's
Submitter's Name: Philip
City/State: Sun City, CA
Comments: His run was Missouri Kansas & Texas

Registrant ID: 1834
Name: Clem H Horton
City/State: Louisville, KY
Railroad: Central Railroad Dyersburg TN,38024,
Position: Exgans
Years of Service: 1972-1973

Registrant ID: 1833
Name: Barry Horton
City/State: Chicago, IL
Position: Pullman Porter
Submitter's Name: Christopher
City/State: Jersey City, NJ
Comments: I wish I could tell you more about my grand father but I don't have much to tell. He was married to a Willie Bell Collins (maiden name) in Chicago. He normally traveled to New York, New Orleans, California and Chicago.

Registrant ID: 1835
Name: Kyle House
City/State: TX
Position: Tracks
Years of Service: 1930's
Submitter's Name: Wanell
City/State: Dallas, TX
Comments: All information was received from the Ike House Guardianship Report from the Veterans Administration.

Registrant ID: 1836
Name: Arthur Houston
City/State: IL
Position: Pullman Porter
Years of Service: 1940's until
Submitter's Name: Catherine
City/State: San Jose, CA
Comments: Arthur Houston was my uncle, and I visited him regularly in Chicago, Illinois, and sometimes listened to some of his stories he shared about while he was on the road working. The only tangible thing I have right now is a picture of him in his porter uniform .

Registrant ID: 1840
Name: Daniel Howard
Railroad: New York Central
Position: Pullman Porter
Submitter's Name: Mabel`
City/State: Boyd, MD
Comments: Buried in Illinois,

Registrant ID: 1843
Name: Leo Howard
City/State: Chicago, IL
Position: Porter
Years of Service: 1930-1940's
Submitter's Name: Sharron E.
City/State: Indianapolis, IN
Comments: I am his granddaughter

Registrant ID: 1841
Edward Marshall Howard
City/State: Charlottesville, VA
Railroad: Chesapeake & Virginia
Position: Pullman Porter
Years of Service: 40+
Submitter's Name: Linda
City/State: Providence, RI
Comments: Edward Howard is deceased. He died in 1988. Born 1900 Charlottesville, VA. His widow received a RR pension for his time of service up until her death in 1996.

Registrant ID: 1844
Name: Willie James Howard
City/State: Warrensville Heights, OH
Railroad: New York Central
Position: Pullman Porter
Years of Service: 1944-1963
Submitter's Name: Ramona
City/State: Warrensville Heights OH

Comments: This is my father who is now deceased. However I do know that he made very little money. He usually ran the rail from New York City to Chicago.

Registrant ID: 1845
Name: Alphonso Howell
Position: Pullman Porter
Service: Circa 1937-1950
Submitter's Name: Doris
City/State: St. Louis , MO

Registrant ID: 1846
Name: Benjamin Howell
Position: Pullman Porter
Service: Circa 1937-50
Submitter's Name: Doris
City/State: St. Louis , MO

Registrant ID: 1847
Name: John Henry Howell
City/State: Chattanooga, TN
Railroad: Pullman Rail Car Co.
Position: Pullman Porter
Years of Service: 1935-1950
Submitter's Name: Doris
City/State: St. Louis , MO
Comments: My Great-uncle

Registrant ID: 1848
Name: Alphonso Howell
City/State: Detroit, MI
Railroad: Pullman Rail Car Co.
Position: Pullman Porter
Years of Service: 1935 - 50
Submitter's Name: Doris
City/State: St. Louis , MO
Comments: My Great-uncle

Registrant ID: 1850
Name: Otha Howelton
City/State: MN
Railroad: Soo Line

Position: Chef and Porter
Years of Service: 1940's
Submitter's Name: Cheryl
City/State: Minneapolis, MN

Registrant ID: 1851
Name: Robert Howelton
City/State: MN
Railroad: Great Northern
Position: Waiter
Years of Service: 1940-1950's
Submitter's Name: Cheryl
City/State: Minnesota, MN
Comments: I don't think they knew he was black because he was fair skinned and not many were allowed to be waiters at that time.

Registrant ID: 1852
Name: Benny Hubbard
City/State: Cleveland, OH
Position: Pullman Porter
Years of Service: 1919-1927
Submitter's Name: Mattie
City/State: Cleveland, OH

Registrant ID: 1853
Name: Willie Hubbard
City/State: Washington, DC
Position: Waiter, Porter
Years of Service: 50's to 60's
Submitter's Name: Terri
City/State: Washington, DC
Comments: He was originally from Lynchburg, Virginia

Registrant ID: 1854
John D. "Johnnie" Hudson
City/State: Peoria, IL
Railroad: Rock Island Railroad, Burlington Railroad, CSX
Position: Track maintenance, Gang Foreman

216

Service: May18, 1953 - 1990
Submitter's Name: Rose
City/State: Peoria, IL

Registrant ID: 1855
Name: John Leonard Huffman
City/State: North, SC
Position: Maintenance Worker
Submitter's Name: Bernice
City/State: North, SC

Registrant ID: 1859
Name: Frank L. Hughes
City/State: MI
Position: Porter
Years of Service: 20's & 30's
Submitter's Name: Sarah
City/State: Detroit, MI

Registrant ID: 1856
Name: Edgar Hughes
City/State: Washington, DC
Position: Porter or Waiter
Years of Service: 1920s to 40s
Submitter's Name: Peggy
City/State: Washington, DC
Comments: I don't remember
too much about him, but Edgar
Hughes was my great uncle. He
was married to my
grandmother's sister. I
remember his white uniform with
gold trimmings and gold buttons.
He was brown skin and balding
with white hair and so very
dignified

Registrant ID: 1861
Edwards Donald Hughes II
City/State: Elkgadge, MD
City/State: Elkgadge, MD
Comments: Worked as a
Pullman Porter until he went into
business for himself.

Registrant ID: 1862
Name: Sandie H. Hugle
City/State: Murfreesboro, TN
Railroad: Pacific Lines-Nashville,
TN
Position: Pullman Porter
Service: Late 1920-
To the Mid 1930's
Submitter's Name: Valerie
City/State: Kenosha, WI
Comments: He was a member of
NAACP & member of the
Brotherhood Of the Sleeping Car
Porters labor union. There are
several letters from union
meetings. Disputing the salaries
and working conditions. The
great works of A Philip Randolph.

Registrant ID: 1863
Name: James Hulbert
City/State: TN
Position: Porter
Years of Service: Circa 1920s
Submitter's Name: Marguerite
City/State: Washington, DC
Comments: My father's life. He
was born in Greenville,
Mississippi, lived in Memphis,
Tennessee as a young man. He
attended Morehouse College in
Atlanta and later did work
toward his doctorate at Columbia
University.

Registrant ID: 1864
Name: Henry Humbles
City/State: St. Louis, MO
Railroad: Norfolk and Western
Position: Pullman Porter
Years of Service: 1940-1970
Submitter's Name: Michael
City/State: St. Louis , MO

Registrant ID: 1866
Name: Montie Humphrey
City/State: Los Angeles, CA
Railroad: Southern Pacific
Years of Service: 1924-1971

Registrant ID: 1865
Name: James A. Humphrey
City/State: AL
Position: Porter
Years of Service: 1950-1970
Submitter's Name: Alan O
City/State: Clinton TWP, MI

Registrant ID: 1872
Name: Shanta Hunt
City/State: AL

Registrant ID: 1870
Name: Charles E. A. Hunt
City/State: Cincinnati, OH
Comments: Pullman Porter
Instructor according to
"Cincinnati Colored Citizens" Pg
253 author Wm Dabney
published 1926.

Registrant ID: 1871
Name: Owen Sr. Hunt
City/State: Memphis, TN
Railroad: Illinois Central
Position: Pullman Porter
Years of Service: 40's-60'
Submitter's Name: Francis
City/State: Menphis, TN
Comments: He was my
Grandfather

Registrant ID: 1874
Name: Walter Hunt
City/State: New York, NY
Railroad: Pennsylvania RR
Position: Dining Car Waiter
Years of Service: 1943 to 1970

Submitter's Name: Michele
City/State: Winston-Salem, NC
Comments: My father worked on
the railroad before I was born
(1952). He took care of 5 children
and gave the best of the best to
all his children even after my
mother died in 1958. He enjoyed
his work.

Registrant ID: 1876
Name: Owen Hunt, Sr.
City/State: Memphis, TN
Railroad: Illinois Central
Position: Pullman Porter
Years of Service: 40 Years
Submitter's Name: Francis

Registrant ID: 1878
Name: Walter L. Hunt, Sr.
City/State: MI, AL
Railroad: Pennsylvania
Position: Dining Car Waiter
Years of Service: 1941-1970
Submitter's Name: Laura
City/State: New York, NY
Comments: My father retired as
the supervisor of the Dining Car
Dept. He passed away on April
18, 1993.

Registrant ID: 1880
Name: Carl Hunter
Submitter's Name: Lawrence

Registrant ID: 1879
Name: Alonzo Hunter
City/State: AL
Railroad: New York Central
Position: Sleeping
Car Porter Porter
Years of Service:
Approx 25 years
Submitter's Name: Catina

City/State: Calumet city, IL
Comments: My great-grandfather

Registrant ID: 1881
Name: Claude Hunter
City/State: El Paso, TX
Railroad: Southern Pacific and the Texas Pacific
Position: Pullman Porter
Years of Service: Approx 192-60
Submitter's Name: Claudette
City/State: Grandview, NY
Comments: At the time of this submission Claude Hunter is 93 years old. This application is being completed by his daughter, Claudette.

Registrant ID: 1882
Name: Henry Hunter
City/State:St.Clair Stites Township, IL
Railroad: St. Louis Car Works
Position: Pullman Porter
Years of Service: 1911-1922
Submitter's Name: Vivian
City/State: Martinez, GA
Comments: Henry Hunter, my great-grandfather was one of the first Pullman Porter's to work for either St. Louis Car Works, or Terminal Railroad, or the American Car and Foundry. He also worked for the Amour Meat Packing Co. In 1922, Henry was murdered by the police.

Registrant ID: 1883
Name: Hiram Ephraim Hunter
City/State: NY
Railroad: New York
Position: Pullman-Porter
Years of Service: over 25 years

Submitter's: Marie and Renee
City/State: Virginia Beach , VA
Comments: My grandfather worked as an a Pullman porter in the early 1900's. He was born 11/11/1890. I still have the Pullman porter pin he received for his(25 year pin) He must have worked for the railroad between 2/03/1927 - He served in World War I.

Registrant ID: 658
Name: Horace C. Hunter Sr.
Railroad: Pennsylvania
Position: Pullman Porter
Years of Service: 40's
Submitter's Name: Horace
City/State: Poughkeepsie, NY
Comments: Was my father. My Dad told many stories about working on the railroad and about riding the trains before working on them.

Registrant ID: 1885
Name: Harry Huntsberry
City/State: Oakland, CA
Position: Cook or Dining Car Waiter
Years of Service: Mid 1940's
Submitter's Name: Latanya
City/State: Southfield, MI

Registrant ID: 1887
Name: Eugene Hurley
City/State: Chicago, IL
Position: Chef
Years of Service: 1940-1983
Submitter's Name: Bobbie
City/State: Chicago, IL

Registrant ID: 1889
Name: Bremond Hutchins
City/State: New York, NY
Railroad: Pennsylvania RR
Position: Bartender
Years of Service: 1944-1969
Submitter's Name: Diane
City/State: Dallas, TX

Registrant ID: 1891
Name: James Hutchinson Jr.
City/State: New Orleans, LA
Railroad: Milwaukee Railroad,
New York Central, Illinois
Central, Pacific
Position: Pullman Porter
Years of Service: 1922-1967
Submitter's Name: James
City/State: LA
Comments: My father worked
out of Chicago, for 45 years. I
remember when I was a boy, my
father took me with him to the
union hall of the Brotherhood at
39th Street and Drexel Ave. I
also remember Mr. Webster and
his son.

Registrant ID: 1892
Name: Maurice Hutner
City/State: AL
Position: Porter
Years of Service: 1925 - 1932
Submitter's Name: Joan
City/State: Poughkeepsie, NY

Registrant ID: 1893
Name: Sylvania Hyman
City/State: Washington, D.C..,
Railroad: Atlantic Coast Lines
And the New Haven & Hartford
Position: Cook
Years of Service:
1925-1928 (Atlantic)

1930-1947 (New Haven)
Submitter's Name: Carole
City/State: MD

Registrant ID: 1894
Name: Clarence Hyte
City/State: IL
Position: Porter
Submitter's Name: Jessye
City/State: Chicago, IL
Comments: My grandfather,
Clarence Hyte, was a Pullman
Porter. He retired from service 50
years ago.

Registrant ID: 1895
Name: Hector I.T
City/State: Cincinnati, OH
Railroad: Pullman Company
Position: Pullman Porter

Registrant ID: 1896
Name: Martin Reginald India
City/State: Saline, LA
Years of Service: 1968-86
Submitter's Name: Negro Shady
Grove A.I.D.S Fund
City/State: Saline, LA

Registrant ID: 1897
Name: Edward Ingram
City/State: Middletown, DE
Years of Service: 1930's - 40's
Submitter's Name: Niki
City/State: Wilmington, DE

Registrant ID: 1898
Name: Haywood Irving
City/State: St. Louis, AL
Years of Service Circa 1925-1930
Submitter's Name: Tina
City/State: St. Louis , AL
Comments: My father told us
stories about working on the
railroad and traveling through

Texas and Mexico on the railways. I don't have alot of information about his time working on the railways because he did not talk a lot.

Registrant ID: 1900
Name: Benjamin Isaac
City/State: Los Angeles, CA
Railroad: California Line
Position: Porter
Years of Service: 1930's

Registrant ID: 1901
Name: John Iverson
Position: Sleeping Car Porter
Submitter's Name: Lee B
Comments: Friend

Registrant ID: 1902
Name: Clarence Izard
City/State: Pine Bluff, Arkansas,
Railroad: Cottonbelt
Position: Pullman Porter
Years of Service: 50 plus years
Submitter's Name: Frances
City/State: Brown Deer, WI
Comments: My uncle celebrated his 100th birthday on October 22, 2001. His mind is razor sharp.

Registrant ID: 1930
Name: Tonya Jackson
City/State: Buffalo, NY

Registrant ID: 1910
Name: Eddie Jackson
Position: Pullman Porter
Years of Service: Over 25
Comments: He ws a member of the B.S.C.P.

Registrant ID: 1924
Name: O.B. Jackson
Position: Pullman Porter
Years of Service: Over 25
Comments: He was a union member

Registrant ID: 1923
Name: Mariah Jackson
City/State: Gary, IN
Railroad: Pullman Company
Position: Beautician
Years of Service: 12yrs

Registrant ID: 3423
Name: Andrew Sanders
City/State: Pittsburgh, AL
Railroad: Penn. Railroad
Position: Sleeping Car Porter
Years of Service: 1945
City/State: AL
Comments: Also uncle Dave Kirkley also Porter also Joe Davis Conductor Penn RR

Registrant ID: 1927
Name: Roger Jackson
City/State: Boston, MA
Railroad: Merchant L&T Business mains car
Position: Waiter and Pullman Porter
Years of Service: 45 Plus
Submitter's Name: Liz
City/State: Boston, MA
Comments: Worked over 45 years thru WWII He died at age 85.

Registrant ID: 1908
Name: Donald Jackson
City/State: AL
Railroad: Southern Pacific
Position: Pullman Porter

Years of Service: Circa 1950-1965
Submitter's Name: Joyce
City/State: Bowie, MD

Registrant ID: 1912
Name: Harold A. Jackson
City/State: Toronto, Canada,
Railroad: Porter
Years of Service: 1954-58
Submitter's Name: Fern
City/State: Brooklyn, NY

Registrant ID: 1917
Name: John Jackson
City/State: New Orleans, LA
Railroad: City of New Orleans
Position: Pullman porter
Submitter's Name: Marlene
City/State: Chicago, IL
Comments: He worked on the City of New Orleans Run during 1949.

Registrant ID: 1904
Name: Allan Jackson
City/State: Carson, CA
Railroad: Atlantic Coastline
Position: Car Cleaner
Years of Service: 40 years
Submitter's Name: Wilbur
City/State: Chicago, IL
Comments: Met one of the Ringling Bros. Said to be John Ringling.

Registrant ID: 1920
Name: John Willie Jackson
City/State: Chicago, IL
Railroad: Santa Fe / Chicago & North Western
Position: Pullman Porter
Years of Service: 33
Submitter's Name: Michael

City/State: Chicago, IL
Comments: I had the privilege of going with my father to the downtown Chicago office and, I had the chance of hear what I can recall as the most dynamic speaker I have ever heard. That speaker was Mr. A. Phillip Randolph.

Registrant ID: 1909
Name: Ed Jackson
City/State: Chicago, IL
Position: Porter
Years of Service: 20 years
Submitter's Name: Brenda
City/State: Chicago, IL
Comments: Grandfather

Registrant ID: 1906
Name: Alonzo Jackson
City/State: Omaha, NE
Position: Porter
Submitter's Name: Ms. Grace
City/State: Cleveland, OH

Registrant ID: 1926
Name: Ralph M. Jackson
City/State: Evanston, IL
Railroad: Burlington
Position: Dining Car Waiter
Years of Service: 30
Submitter: Frank P. (III)
City/State: Columbia, MD
Comments: Ralph Jackson was my maternal grandfather who work for Burlington Railroad out of Chicago, Illinois (Union Station). He traveled from Chicago to Denver, Co. at least once a week. He did this as long as I can remember until he retired in the late 1960's.

Registrant ID: 1929
Name: Scott Jackson
City/State: Columbus, OH
Railroad: Pennsylvania
Position: Dining Car
Waiter in Charge
Service: 1911-1944 (33 years)
Submitter's Name: Robert R.
City/State: Columbus, OH
Comments: Scott Jackson died
on September 8, 1957. He was
survived by his wife Alma who
died in December 1960, his sons,
Scot Jackson (now deceased
also) and Robert R. Jackson who
currently lives in Columbus
Ohio.

Registrant ID: 1913
Name: Henry Jackson
City/State: Gary, IN
Position: Brakeman and a
Dining Car Waiter
Years of Service: 45 years
Submitter's Name: Charles
City/State: Gary, IN

Registrant ID: 1921
Name: Leslie Jackson
City/State: Grand Rapid, MI
Position: Cook/Signal & Tracks
Years of Service: 1943-1967
Submitter's Name: Mary
City/State: Grand Rapids, MI

Registrant ID: 1903
Name: Adolph Jackson
City/State: Chicago, IL
Position: Porter, Assistant
Conductor, and Acting
Conductor.
Years of Service: From 1930
until his retirement in the early
40's

Submitter's Name: Olden
City/State: Mesa, AZ
Comments: My Father was a
member of the Sleeping Car
Porter's union. He routes were
from New Orleans Louisiana,
Seattle, New York, California,
and East Coast cities, performed
duties as Acting Conductor on
several lines.

Registrant ID: 3367
Charles Rteny Mamos Jackson
City/State: Nashville, TN
Submitter's Name: Carolin
City/State: Nashville, TN
Comments: My Father

Registrant ID: 1931
Name: Troy Jackson
City/State: CA
Position: Waiter or Chef
Submitter's Name: Elaine
City/State: Norwalk, CA
Comments: Mr. Jackson was my
cousin.

Registrant ID: 1907
Name: Andrew J Jackson
City/State: Pittsburgh, PA
Railroad: Pennsylvania
Position: Pullman Porter
Years of Service: 1945
Submitter's Name: Andrew J.
City/State: Pittsburgh, PA
Comments: Identification card
#4665 my father was employed
for about 10 years

Registrant ID: 1919
Name: John Jackson
City/State: Los Angeles, CA
Submitter's Name: Sheila
City/State: Reisterstown, MD

Registrant ID: 1911
Name: George Dewey Jackson
City/State: St. Paul, MN
Position: Porter
Years of Service: 1923-1970
Submitter's Name: Ventress L.
City/State: St. Paul, MN

Registrant ID: 1916
Name: John Jackson
City/State: Tampa, FL
Railroad: Silver Meteor et al
(many others Via the Pullman
Company, from1930's - 1970's)
Position: Pullman Porter
Years of Service: 1930's-70's,
Submitter's Name: Delores
City/State: Tampa, FL
Comments: My grandfather,
John Jackson (deceased),
formerly of 2210 E. 15th Ave.,
Tampa, Fl. 33605, worked on
the railroad for many years
during the 1930's, 1940's,
1950's, 1960's and retired in the
early 1970's. He was a Pullman
Porter during those years.

Registrant ID: 1932
Name Anderson Jackson Hulbert
City/State: Denver, CO
Railroad: Rio Grande
Years of Service: 1900's
Submitter's Name: Lee
City/State: Denver, CO

Registrant ID: 1934
Name: Isaac James
Railroad: Pullman Company
Position: Webster
Years of Service: 1924-194
Submitter's Name: Ramsey

Registrant ID: 1935
Name: Albert James
City/State: Baltimore, MD
Railroad: Baltimore & Ohio
Position: Pullman Porter
Years of Service: 1918-1948
Submitter's Name: Kenneth
City/State: Baltimore, MD
Comments: During the early
days when efforts were underway
to organize the union, Pullman
Porter meetings were held in my
home at 1822 Madison Avenue,
Baltimore, Maryland.

Registrant ID: 1943
Name: Thomas James
City/State: Chicago, IL
Railroad: Chicago to California
Position: Pullman Porter
Service: late 50's early 60's
Submitter's Name: Golda
City/State: Chicago, IL
Comments: Thomas James is
not a blood relative of mine, he
was my godfather and is now
deceased. When he traveled I
would stay with his wife
Gertrude James. He traveled
between Chicago and California
and maybe New York.

Registrant ID: 1939
Name: Robert D. James
Position: Porter
Years of Service: Circa 1943 - 60
Submitter's Name: Kennie M.
City/State: Chicago, IL

Registrant ID: 1944
Name: Warrick C. James
Position: Porter/Club Car
Years of Service: Circa 1943-61
Submitter's Name: Coreane
City/State: Ecorse, MI

Registrant ID: 1938
Name: Ralaf James
City/State: Morison, SC
Years of Service: 1960-73
Submitter's Name: Margaret
City/State: Florener, SC

Registrant ID: 1942
Name: Sumpter James
City/State: Madison, FL
Submitter's Name: Stanley
City/State: Madison, FL

Registrant ID: 1936
Name: Arthur James
City/State: St. Paul, MN
Railroad: Great Northern Pacific
Railroad
Position: Pullman Porter
Years: Approx 1925-1957
Submitter's Name: Robin
City/State: St. Paul, MN
Comments: Arthur James
Howard was a Pullman Porter
and one of the first African
American men to settle in St.
Paul, Minnesota. He worked for
the Great Northern Pacific for 35
year and lived near the historic
Rondo Avenue located in the
largest black neighborhood in

Registrant ID: 79
Name: Henry James Agee
City/State: Columbus, OH
Railroad: Pullman Company
Position: Pullman Porter
Years of Service: 1889-1914
Submitter's Name: Angee

Registrant ID: 1947
Name: Oscar James Webb
City/State: Chicago, IL
Position: Pullman Porter

Years of Service: 1929-1971
Submitter's Name: Webb

Registrant ID: 1949
Name: Henry Jamison
City/State: AL
Position: Porter
Submitter's Name: Olga Frank
City/State: New Orleans, LA

Registrant ID: 1952
Name: Timothy Jefferies
City/State: Chattanooga, TN
Position: Not sure.
Years of Service: Not sure.
Submitter's Name: Vicki
City/State: Winston-Salem, NC
Comments: Timothy Jefferies
was my great uncle, my fathers
mother's brother. I believe my
great uncle continued to live in
Chattanooga.

Registrant ID: 1954
Name: James Jefferson Mason
City/State: Chicago, IL
Railroad: Santa Fe and
the Super Chief
Position: Pullman Porter
Years of Service: 47 Years
Submitter's Name: Kathin
City/State: Chicago, IL
Comments: Lived 1898-1969 he
had Ten children.

Registrant ID: 1956
Name: Rufus Jefferson, Sr.
City/State: FL
Railroad: Pullman Company
Position: Pullman Porter
Submitter's Name: Kimberly
Years of Service: 34 years
City/State: Hinesville, GA

Comments: My Grandfather worked for the Pullman Company, which provided service to the Atlantic and Pacific Coastlines. I remember him telling me that he once met A.Philip Randolph and how it was a privilege. I am very proud of my Grandfather and the service he provided.

Registrant ID: 1957
Name: James Jeffery
City/State: Philadelphia, PA
Railroad: Silver Meteor-Silver Star
Position: Dining Car Waiter
Years of Service: 1920's/30's – and then 1960's/70's
Submitter's Name: Meridel
City/State: Fort Washington, PA
Comments: My father has been deceased since August 1988. I know that he worked for approximately 50 years and retired in the late 1960's or very early 1970's. I am not sure exactly when he was hired but I would suspect the 1920's or 30's.

Registrant ID: 1958
Name: Wade Jeffreys
City/State: Roanoke, VA
Railroad: Norfolk & Western (out of Roanoke, Virginia)
Position: Pullman Porter
Years of Service: 1940-75
Submitter's Name: Keith
City/State: Martinsburg, WV
Comments: My grandfather enjoyed every experience of his work on the railroad, especially the camaraderie with his fellow Pullman Porters relationships

which existed until his death in 1981.

Registrant ID: 1964
Name: L.D. Jenkins
Position: Pullman Porter
Years of Service: Over 25
Comments: B.S.C.P.

Registrant ID: 1985
Name: Sidney Jenkins
City/State: Columbus, OH
Railroad: Pullman Company
Position: Pullman Porter
Years of Service: 1942-1943

Registrant ID: 1959
Name: Edward Jenkins
City/State: Schenevus, NY
Railroad: TBA
Position: Pullman Porter
Years of Service: 1913 to 1965
Submitter's Name: Gordon
City/State: Baltimore, MD

Registrant ID: 1966
Name: Mathew Jenkins
City/State: Philadelphia, PA
Position: Chef
Years of Service: 1946
Submitter's Name: C.B
City/State: Chicago, IL

Registrant ID: 1963
Name: George A. Jenkins
City/State: College Park, GA
Position: Porter
Years of Service: 1946-1954
Submitter's Name: George A.
City/State: Dorchester, MA
Comments: My father, a former Pullman Porter, at the time of this submittal is almost 82 years of age. Several of his friends

were Porters when we lived in Harlem in New York City in the 1960's and 1970's.

Registrant ID: 1960
Name: Gayden Jenkins
City/State: Little Rock, AR
Railroad: Rock Island and Missouri- Pacific
Position: Pullman Porter
Years of Service: 1938-1962
Submitter's Name: Euleta
City/State: North Little Rock, AK
Comments: This was a job that my father truly loved. He was a Pullman Porter when I was born so I am uncertain about the exact date that his employment began.

Registrant ID: 1988
Name: Louis V. Jennings
City/State: Chesterfield, MO
Railroad: The Pullman Company Chicago, Central District Central Station. Chicago, Ill.
Position: Porter
Years of Service: 1943-1970
Submitter's Name: Richard
City/State: Chesterfield, MO
Comments: My father traveled as a Porter from coast to coast during my childhood. I remember him getting his uniform ready and packing his clothing for long trips. He talked about his experiences like seeing the Grand Canyon.

Registrant ID: 1986
Name: Ernest M. Jennings
City/State: Jamaica, NY
Railroad: Pennsylvania RR
Position: Waiter
Service: Approx 1945- 1965

Submitter's Name: Wendell
City/State: Cleveland, TN
Comments: My Grandfather always came home in his uniform, and I remember seeing some of his poster's and calendars of the railroad he worked for.

Registrant ID: 1987
Name: George Jennings
City/State: DC
Position: Pullman Porter
Submitter's Name: Donna
City/State: Washington, DC
Comments: My father worked on the railroad as a Pullman porter in the 1950's (maybe before). He did some long distance trips to California during that time.

Registrant ID: 1989
Name: William Jerome Thomas
City/State: Chicago, IL
Railroad: Amtrak
Position: Pullman Porter
Years of Service: 20yrs 1938-1958
Submitter's Name: Velma
City/State: Chicago, IL

Registrant ID: 1993
Name: LeRoy Jetton
City/State: Chicago, IL
Position: Porter

Registrant ID: 1994
Name: Persico John
City/State: Mosinee, Wisconsin
Railroad: Pullman Company
Position: Porter
Years of Service: 45-57

Registrant ID: 1995
Name: B.W. Johns
Position: Pullman Porter
Years of Service: Over 25

Registrant ID: 2058
Name: Walter L. Johnson
City/State: Baltimore, MD
Railroad: B & O
Position: Pullman Porter

Registrant ID: 2028
Name: John Johnson
City/State: Jacksonville, FL
Railroad: Seaboard or Atlantic
Coast Line
Position: Pullman Porter

Registrant ID: 2042
Name: R.J. Johnson
Position: Pullman Porter
Years of Service: Over Plus

Registrant ID: 2055
Name: W.E. Johnson
Position: Pullman Porter
Years of Service: Over 25

Registrant ID: 1996
Alexander Calvin Johnson
City/State: Miami, FL
Position: Pullman Porter
Years of Service: 1950-1981
Submitter's Name: Cora S.

Registrant ID: 2017
Name: Hayes M. Johnson
City/State: New Canton, VA
Position: Laborer/Truck Driver
Years of Service: 1941-1963

Registrant ID: 2060
Name: William Johnson
Position: Pullman Porter

Years of Service:
1930's-1940's
Submitter's Name: Dr. Essie
Comments: Uncle

Registrant ID: 2075
Name: Roy E Johnson
Railroad: Pullman Company
Position: Pullman Porter
Years of Service: 1917-1965
Submitter's Name: Johnson

Registrant ID: 2002
Name: Claude Johnson
City/State: Killeen, Texas
Railroad: MKL & Missouri
Pacific
Position: Pullman Porter
Years of Service: 1917-1962
Comments: Son of a Porter

Registrant ID: 2065
Name: William C. Johnson
City/State: Roanoke, VA
Position: Cook
Years of Service: 10 Years

Registrant ID: 2022
Name: James W. Johnson
City/State: Atlanta, GA
Position: Dining Car Waiter
Years of Service: 1945-1954
Submitter's Name: Gloria
City/State: GA

Registrant ID: 2059
Name: Water Mathews Johnson
City/State: Charleston SC
Railroad: Atlantic Coastline RR
Position: Pullman Porter
Years of Service: 1919-1939
Submitter's Name: Debbi
City/State: Acworth, GA
Comments:Grandfather

worked for 20 years retired in 1939 Passed 2 years later Tuberculosis.

Registrant ID: 2014
Name: Eugene F. Johnson
City/State: AL
Railroad: Southern
Position: Dining Car Waiter
Submitter's Name: Arthur e.
City/State: Atlanta, GA

Registrant ID: 2037
Name: Luther Johnson
City/State: Decatur, GA
Railroad: Southern Railways/Southern Cresent
Position: Dining Car Waiter
Years of Service: 30+ Years
Submitter's Name: Pamela
City/State: Atlanta, GA
Comments: Luther Johnson was my grandfather and as far back as I can remember he worked for the Southern Railroad. On "the road" as he would call it. I can remember he would go on trips for days at a time and my grandmother would always help him pack for the trips

Registrant ID: 2062
Name: William Johnson
City/State: Atlanta, GA
Position: Pullman Porter
Years of Service: 20 years
Submitter's Name: Sharron
City/State: Atlanta, GA
Comments: Newspaper article in Atlanta Daily World indicated Mr. Johnson was one of the first blacks to retire as a Porter

Registrant ID: 2061
Name: William Johnson

City/State: Omaha, NE
Railroad: Union Pacific
Position: Dinning Cart Waiter
Years of Service: 1948-1965
Submitter's Name: Renata
City/State: Atlanta, GA
Comments: He went from Omaha to California route for many years. He put his tips in his napkins and taught his children math lessons with them.

Registrant ID: 2038
Name: Paul Milton Johnson
City/State: New York, NY
Position: Dining Car Waiter
Years of Service: 1941-1944
Submitter's Name: Lorraine
City/State: Aurora, CO

Registrant ID: 2035
Name: Lonnie Johnson
City/State: Boston, MA
Railroad: Texas and Pacific Railroad (or something similar)
Position: Pullman Porter
Years of Service: Circa1938-58
Submitter's Name: Velma
City/State: Boston, MA
Comments: My father worked on the railroad as a Pullman Porter. He traveled all over this country before his marriage, and continued until I was a young girl. He later went into business for himself.

Registrant ID: 2018
Name: Hence Johnson
City/State: AL
Position: Porter
Submitter's Name: Steven
City/State: Boston, MA

Registrant ID: 2044
Name: Roy E. Johnson
City/State: Bronx, NY
Railroad: New York Central
Position: Pullman Porter
Years: 1920's thru 1960's
Submitter's Name: Leslie
City/State: Bronx, NY
Comments: My Grandfather was a college graduate. He was originally from North Carolina and went to College at Bennett College. This job provided a means for him to take care of his five children and wife. My grandfather taught me many things and instilled a sense of pride and thirst for knowledge.

Registrant ID: 2057
Name: Wallace Johnson
Position: Porter
Years of Service: Circa 1920-1930
Submitter's Name: Edwina M.
City/State: Brooklyn, NY

Registrant ID: 2020
Name: Henry H. Johnson
City/State: New York, NY
Position: Porter/Waiter
Years of Service: 1907-1914
Submitter's Name: Edwina M.
City/State: Brooklyn, NY

Registrant ID: 2066
Name: William F. Johnson
City/State: Charlottesville, VA
Position: Day Coach Porter
Years of Service: 1939-1962
Submitter's Name: Mary J.
City/State: Charlottesville, VA

Registrant ID: 2029
Name: Johnnie Johnson
Position: Pullman Porter
Years of Service: 1948-1965
Submitter's Name: Betty
City/State: Chicago, IL

Registrant ID: 2051
Name: Ulysses S. Johnson
City/State: Chicago, IL
Railroad: Illinois Central
Position: Sleeping Car Porter
Years of Service: 1943-1948
Submitter's Name: Marvouneen
City/State: Chicago, IL

Registrant ID: 2001
Name: Cicero J. Johnson
City/State: Atlanta, GA
Railroad: Southern RR
Position: Pullman Porter
Years of Service: 1944 -1960
Submitter's Name: Gloria
City/State: East Point, GA

Registrant ID: 2049
Name: Theophilus Johnson
City/State: Shreveport, LA
Position: Pullman Porter
Years of Service: Early 1920's
Submitter's Name: Juanita
City/State: Ewing, NJ
Comments: Theophilus Matthew Johnson was my great-uncle. He was one of the first black dentist in the state of Louisiana. As a student at Meharry Medical College, he was able to help pay for his education by working as a Pullman Porter on the train during his summer.

Registrant ID: 2008
Name: Elwood Johnson

City/State: Kansas city, MO
Position: Dining Car Waiter
Years of Service: Before I was born until about 1950
Submitter's Name: Aaron
City/State: Flint, MI
Comments: I'm not sure of the rail line, but I know he was based out of Wichita Kansas. Some where in the back of my mind I think I heard my mother say Southern Pacific. He went from Wichita to California. I can't remember exactly. He was my Grandfather

Registrant ID: 2054
Name: Vernell Johnson
City/State: Macomb, MS
Railroad: Pullman Company
Position: Pullman Porter
Years of Service: 1940-1969
Submitter's Name: Vernell
City/State: Flossmoor, IL
Comments: My Father was a member of the Brotherhood Of Sleeping Car Porter from 1940 until Amtrak took over.

Registrant ID: 2005
Name: David Johnson
City/State: Washington, DC
Railroad: Southern
Position: Pullman Porter
Years of Service: Approx- 30 Yrs
Submitter's Name: Anna
City/State: Forestville, MD
Comments: I really think my father took pride in his job. I do remember him complaining, about the numerous times he was called "boy" or awakened in the middle of the night to tend to a white passengers senseless requests.

Registrant ID: 2067
Name: William Walter Johnson
City/State: Gardena, CA
Railroad: Wabash Railroad
Position: Dinning Car Waiter
Years of Service: 1912-1933
Submitter's Name: Margo
City/State: Gardena, CA

Registrant ID: 2003
Name: Cletus Johnson
City/State: Indianapolis, IN
Position: Porter
Years of Service: Late 1930's
Submitter's Name: Don
City/State: Indianapolis, IN

Registrant ID: 2031
Joseph Kenneth Johnson
City/State: Laurelton, and Queens, New York
Railroad: New York Central
Position: Pullman Porter
Years of Service: 1930-1961
Submitter's: Rosalind Serena
City/State: Laurelon and Queens, New York
Comments: This entry is for my late father, Joseph Kenneth Johnson, who passed away June 26, 1991. He worked with A. Philip Randolph with the Sleeping Car Porters union.

Registrant ID: 2011
Name: Ernest Jacobs Johnson
Position: Cook, Dining Car
Submitter's Name: Marquerito
City/State: Louisville, KY

Registrant ID: 2033
Name: Leeaner Johnson
City/State: Robbins, IL
Position: Car Cleaner
Submitter's Name: Chandra
City/State: Midlothian, IL
Comments: Leeanner Johnson is my great grandmother. She will be 102 years old in August 2002. The railroad was the only job she ever had and worked there for at least 30 years. She retired from there.

Registrant ID: 2026
Name: John Johnson
City/State: Dallas, TX
Railroad: Unknown-Home base was Oakland CA.
Position: Pullman Porter
Years of Service: 1949-50
Submitter's Name: William
City/State: Montgomery, AL
Comments: As I understand John Pressley Johnson Sr. served as a Pullman Porter operating out of Oakland CA. He did not have regular runs but ran "Wild" as he related his experiences to me.

Registrant ID: 2063
Name: William Johnson
City/State: Oklahoma City, OK
Railroad: FRISCO
Position: Pullman Porter
Years of Service: 1946-1953
Submitter's Name: William
City/State: Montgomery, AL
Comments: William E. Johnson Sr's home base was Oklahoma City, Oklahoma. During his initial service he assisted in transporting troops throughout

the U,S. During the early 1950s his service was limited primarily to a regular run on the FRISCO LINE.

Registrant ID: 1997
Name: Archie Johnson
City/State: New Orleans, LA
Railroad: Southern Pacific
Position: Pullman Porter
Years of Service: 28
Submitter(s): Debra C. John
City/State: New Orleans, LA
Comments: I am the granddaughter of Mr. Archie Samuel Johnson. He lived in New Orleans and worked as a Pullman Porter for Southern Pacific Railroad.

Registrant ID: 2009
Name: Ernest Johnson
City/State: New York,
Years of Service: Retired 1947
Submitter's Name: John
City/State: New York,
Comments: Worked out of New York

Registrant ID: 2048
Name: Shirley Johnson
City/State: Chicago, IL
Position: Porter
Submitter's Name: Christopher
City/State: Olympia Fields, IL

Registrant ID: 2016
Name: George H. Johnson
Position: Pullman Porter
Submitter's Name: Gloria
City/State: Philadelphia, PA

Registrant ID: 1998
Name: Bert Johnson
City/State: Pleasantville, NJ
Railroad: NJ Line Central

232

Position: Waiter
Years of Service: 1940-1950
Submitter's Name: Mariet
City/State: Pleasantville, NJ

Registrant ID: 2046
Name: Samuel Johnson
City/State: Jersey City, NJ
Railroad: Pennsylvania
Position: Dining Car Waiter
Submitter's Name: Carol
City/State: Reston, VA
Comments: My grandfather Samuel Johnson was a waiter for over 45 years for the Pennsylvania railroad. His run was from New York to Washington DC.

Registrant ID: 2034
Name: Leon Johnson
City/State: New Orleans, LA
Submitter's Name: Joan
City/State: Springdale, MD

Registrant ID: 2015
Name: George Johnson
City/State: St. Louis, MO
Railroad: Union Station
Position: Porter
Years of Service: 35 years
Submitter's Name: Naomi
City/State: St. Louis , MO
Comments: George O. Johnson was a porter for Union Station, located in St. Louis, Missouri. Employment date 6/26/1922. He worked between 30-35 long dedicated years. D.OB. 10-24-1892, deceased mid 1960's.

Registrant ID: 2019
Name: Henry Johnson
City/State: AL

Position: Waiter
Years of Service: 1947-1960
Submitter's Name: Debra
City/State: St. Paul, MN

Registrant ID: 2032
Name: Landy Johnson
City/State: AZ
Railroad: Southern Pacific
Position: Dinning Car (Chef)
Years of Service: 15
Submitter's Name: Rita
City/State: Tucson, AZ
Comments: My father was the Chef Cook for the Southen Pacific Railroad. He Lived in Tucson, Arizona then he and his brother relocated to Pasadena California. His Brother Percy B. Johnson and my father Landy C. Johnson trips were from Los Angeles. Californa, New Orleans.

Registrant ID: 2007
Name: Elmo Johnson
City/State: St Louis, MO
Railroad: Missouri Pacific
Position: Waiter in Charger
Years of Service: 42 years
Submitter's Name: Elmo
City/State: Wentzville, MO
Comments: Elmo L. Johnson was my Father, He was also elected President of the DINING CAR LOCAL, I don't remember the number of the Local. He died in 1977.
Thank You very much for creating this registry.

Registrant ID: 2023
Name: John Johnson
City/State: Chicago, IL
Position: Porter

Years of Service: 1930's
Submitter's Name: Keely
City/State: Wheaton, IL

Comments: Being a porter gave my great-grandfather the opportunity to see the country. The position also afforded him to purchase land in Baldwin Michigan. I was told by Yvonne Little (Malcolm X's sister) that many black porters purchased lake front property in Baldwin Michigan. In the 1930's, this area was a well-known resort owned and operated by blacks. The land was relatively inexpensive and affordable to porters.

Registrant ID: 2030
Name: Joseph Edward Johnson
City/State: Wilmington, DE
Railroad: Pennsylvania
Submitter's Name: Leesa
City/State: Wilmington, DE

Registrant ID: 2068
Name: Robert Johnson
City/State: New York, NY
Position: Dining Car Waiter
Submitter's Name: Dorothy
City/State: New Haven, CT
Comments: He worked on the trains that ran from New York to Florida from 1930 until 1945 Mr. Johnson died in 1949

Registrant ID: 2069
Name: Al'grie Johnson Martino
City/State: Philadelphia, PA
Railroad: Pullman Company

Registrant ID: 2071
Name: Johnnie Johnson Sr.
City/State: CA
Railroad: Santa Fe
Position: Mail and Baggage Handler
Years of Service: 1950-1971
Submitter's Name: Sharon
City/State: Compton, CA

Registrant ID: 2074
Nathaniel W. Johnson, Sr.
City/State: Slidell, LA

Registrant ID: 2077
Name: M. Jolley
City/State: North Little Rock, Arkansas

Registrant ID: 2150
Name: Alfred L. Jones, Sr.
City/State: Knoxville, TN
Railroad: L & N Railroad
Position: Porter
Submitter(s): Dr. Howard V.
City/State: Ann Arbor, MI

Registrant ID: 2079
Name: Andrew Jones
City/State: LA
Position: Pullman Porter
Years of Service: 1920's – 1930
Submitter's Name: Dorothy
City/State: IL
Comments: Took care of paper work for the porters on the train.

Registrant ID: 2086
Name: Bozie Jones
City/State: Chicago, IL
Railroad: Illinois
Position: Chef

Years of Service: 1951-81
Submitter's Name: Robert J.
City/State: Marietta, GA

Registrant ID: 2087
Name: Calilwell Jones
City/State: Pompano Beach,
Florida
Railroad: Burke County
Position: Porter
Years of Service: 1915-1917
Submitter's Name: Rosemary
City/State: Popano Beach, FL
Comments: Wagnes Brod,
Georgia.

Registrant ID: 2090
Name: Charles Jones
City/State: Oakland, CA
Position: Pullman Porter
Submitter's Name: Ronnie D.
City/State: San Bernardino, CA
Comments: This was my
Grandfather, who is now
deceased, so I am unable to
share very much information.
Talking with him over the years
at one time, I just happened to
mention to him that belonged to
the A. Philip Randolph Institute,
then he tells me that he knew "
Asa " and that he used to belong
to the " porters " union! Think I
wasn't surprised to learn that!
We would talk occasionally about
his experiences on the railroad
and how it shaped his life. He
died many years ago and is
buried in Oakland. May God rest
his soul! I do miss him.

Registrant ID: 2151
Name: Charles H Jones, Sr.
Railroad: Southern Pacific

Position: Waiter
Submitter's Name: Jennie B
Comments: A Friend

Registrant ID: 2091
Name: Charles H. Jones
City/State: AL
Railroad: Southern Railway
Position: Dining Car Waiter
Years of Service: 15 Years
Submitter's Name: Gloria
City/State: Houston, TX
Comments: My father was a
dining car waiter on the
Southern Railroad. He is now
deceased. I am not certain about
the years he worked on the
Southern Railroad. I do
remember his run was from
Washington DC to Nashville TN.
He worked prior to World War II.

Registrant ID: 2089
Name: Charles Jones
Submitter's Name: Fran Cena
City/State: Jamaica, NY

Registrant ID: 2092
Name: Cleveland Jones
City/State: Woodlands, CA
Railroad: Southern Pacific
Position: Porter
Years of Service: 1952-1969
Submitter's Name: Pamela
City/State: Woodlands, CA

Registrant ID: 2095
Name Emmett Jones
City/State: Ennis, TX
Position: Turned trains around
at the end of the line
Years of Service: Retired 1954
Submitter's Virginia, Margo
City/State: Sacramento, CA

Comments: Emmett James was my grandfathers first cousin

Registrant ID: 2094
Name: Emmitt Jones
City/State: El Paso, TX
Railroad: Pullman Company
Position: Pullman Porter
Years of Service: 1920 - 1950
Submitter's: Thomas Henry
City/State: Seattle, WA
Comments: My uncle worked as Pullman Porter between El Paso, Texas, and Silver City, New Mexico, and later on between El Paso and Albuquerque, NM. He was instru-mental in getting my grandfather to move to Albuquerque in 1927 from Brenham Texas to start work.

Registrant ID: 2096
Name: Floyd Jones
City/State: NC
Railroad: Pennsylvania Railroad
Position: Dining Car Porter
Years of Service: 1945 - 1961
Submitter's Name: Leslie
City/State: New York, NY
Comments: Several of my dad's brothers also worked for the railroad We are the Rhues, descendants of escaped enslaved people who went to Canada through the Underground Railroad. My dad's father, William Rhue and his wife, Electa Robbins, lived in the escaped slave settlement of North Buxton, Ontario, Canada. Oral tradition says that "Rhue" was the name of the French Canadian abolitionist who

befriended my ancestors and, as was the custom, the escaped enslaved often changed their names once in Canada to confuse the bounty hunters. Oral tradition also says that the original male Rhue was an escaped slave from the miles plantation in Maryland.

Registrant ID: 2097
Name: G. R. Jones
Position: Porter/In Charge
Years of Service: 1941-1961
Submitter's Name:
Dr. G. Daniel
City/State: Wyncote, PA

Registrant ID: 2100
Name: Gip Jones
City/State: Toccoa, GA
Submitter's Name: Irene
City/State: Oxon Hill, MD
Comments: My grandfather has died but he worked for the railroad. My grandmother Zemmie Jones received his benefits. She has since died also.

Registrant ID: 2103
Name: Harry Jones
City/State: Chicago, IL
Position: Cook
Years of Service: 1936-1952
Submitter's Name: Sylvia S.
City/State: Chicago, IL

Registrant ID: 2108
Name: Harry Henry Jones
City/State: Cincinnati, OH
Position: Dining Car Waiter
Years of Service: 1917-1944
Submitter's Name: Louis
City/State: Cincinnati, OH

Registrant ID: 2102
Name: Harry Jones
City/State: New Orleans, LA
Position: Porter
Years of Service: 1925-1940's
Submitter's: Shirley Gettridge
City/State: New Orleans, LA
Comments: Harry's mother Theresa Jones (Mi Mare) came over on a slave ship in 1855 at the age of 10. She was a native of Ethiopia (Abyssinia) she died in 1952 at the age of 107. Through oral history she passed the story of the voyage to on the Atlantic Ocean to America in to slavery. Harry was my grandfather.

Harry Jones

Registrant ID: 2109
Name: Henry Jones

City/State: Albuquerque, NM
Railroad: AT&SF Railroad
Position: Train Porter/Brakeman
Years of Service: 1929 - 1957
Submitter's: Thomas, Henry
City/State: Seattle, WA
Comments: Grandfather was a member of Brotherhood of Sleeping Car Porters but worked as a Train Porter-Brakeman (name given to avoid paying same wages as white counterparts) for Santa Fe Railroad. Worked New Mexico Division from Albuquerque to La Junta, Colorado.

Registrant ID: 2110
Name: Herman Jones
Railroad: NY Central
Years of Service: 1921-1962
Submitter's Name: Fran Cena
City/State: Jamaica, NY

Registrant ID: 2112
Name: Hillma Jones
City/State: Jamaica, NY
Railroad: NY Central
Years of Service: 1921-1962
Submitter's Name: Fran Cerra
City/State: Jamaica, NY

Registrant ID: 2114
Name: Ike Jones
Railroad: Santa Fe
Years of Service: 44 Years
Submitter's Name: Ms.
City/State: Chicago, IL

Registrant ID: 2116
Name: Ike Jones
City/State: Chicago, IL

Railroad: Santa Fe
Years of Service: 44 Yrs
City/State: Chicago, IL

Registrant ID: 2120
Name: James A. Jones
City/State: Westland, MN
Railroad: Chicago Northwestern
Position: Yard Clerk
Years of Service: 1966-1967

Registrant ID: 2117
Name: James Jones
City/State: AL
Position: Pullman Porter
Years : Circa 1928 to 1940
Submitter's Name: Amie
City/State: Palmdale, CA
Comments: James Jones is my great-grandfather and I know that he worked mostly in Colorado and Kansas, and left his five young children after the death of his wife for life on the railroad. He was very proud of his career as a Porter.

Registrant ID: 2118
Name: James Jones
City/State: KY
Railroad: L&N
Position: Pullman Porter and Dining Car Waiter
Years : late 50's thru 1972
Submitter's Name: L'Tanya
City/State: Newark, NJ

Registrant ID: 2134
Name: Joseph Jones
City/State: Lumine, SD
Position: Porter
Years of Service: 1950-1960
Submitter's Name: Pricilla
City/State: Lumine, SD

Registrant ID: 2121
Name: James S Jones
City/State: Brooklyn, NY
Railroad: Penn Station
Position: Pullman Porter
Years of Service: 45
Submitter's Name: Yvette
City/State: Jersey City, NJ
Comments: My father retired from the railroad around 1957. He worked out of Penn Station on the New York to Miami, Florida line. In later years he worked on the Silver Meteor from New York to Los Angeles, Ca. up until the time of retirement. He met and married Bessie Chandler who also worked in the system.

Registrant ID: 2149
Name: Jasper Jones, Jr.
City/State: Catonsville, MD
Railroad: Baltimore Ohio
Years of Service: 50's-60's
Submitter's Name: Carrie
City/State: Catansville, MD
Comments: My Grandfather

Registrant ID: 2124
Name: John E. Jones
City/State: Fort Worth, TX
Railroad: T & P
(Texas & Pacific)
Position: Pullman Porter
Years of Service: 40
Submitter's Name: Delmar
City/State: Albuquerque, NM
Comments: For over forty years, John E. Jones was a part of a dapper group of distinguished black gentlemen. The Pullman Porters. He traveled the Texas and Pacific Railroad runs, when

train riding was in it's heyday. From 1922 to 1962.

Registrant ID: 2125
Name: John H. Jones
Position: Pullman Porter
Years of Service: 25 Years
Comments: B.S.C.P.

Registrant ID: 2122
Name: John Jones
City/State: Chicago, IL
Railroad: Rock Island Railroad
Position: Pullman Porter
Years of Service: 43 Years
Submitter's Name: Mary
City/State: Chicago, IL
Comments His run was from Chicago to LA

Registrant ID: 2129
Name: Jonas Jones
City/State: New York, NY
Position: Porter
Submitter's Name: Donna
City/State: San Francisco, CA
Comments: My great uncle appears on the 1920 census as a Porter.

Registrant ID: 2130
Name: Joseph Jones
City/State: Jamaica, NY
Position: Pullman Porter, and a Dining Car Waiter
Submitter's Name: Joseph
City/State: Spring Hill, FL
Comments: My grandfather worked on the Silver Meteor run from New York to Miami. He retired at age and died in 1963.

Registrant ID: 2126
Name: Johnny Jones

City/State: AL
Submitter's Name: Jackie
City/State: Auburn, WA

Registrant ID: 2132
Name: Joseph Jones
City/State: MO
Railroad: Pullman Co.
Position: Pullman Porter
Submitter's Name: Paul
City/State: Crete, IL

Registrant ID: 2131
Name: Joseph Jones
City/State: Chicago, IL
Railroad: California Zephyr and the Burlington
Position: Sleeping Car Porter
Submitter's Name: Lauri
City/State: Chicago, IL
Comments: Joseph "Bonnie" Jones was my uncle. Although he retired shortly after I was born (around 1960), I still remember the stories that he told us, and the stories that my mother and her sisters re-told us after Uncle Bonnie died.

Registrant ID: 2135
Name: Mauion D Jones
City/State: Atlanta, GA
Railroad: Norfolk/southern
Years of Service: 1930's-1965
Submitter's Name: Sonje L
City/State: Atlanta, GA
Comments: Grandfather

Registrant ID: 2136
Name: Milton J. Jones
Position: Pullman Porter
Years of Service: 25 Years
Comments: B.S.C.P.

Registrant ID: 2137
Name: Milton W. Jones
City/State: Chicago, IL
Railroad: Pullman-Santa Fe/Amtrak
Yearse: 1942 till late 1960's
Submitter's Name: Milton W
City/State: Chicago, IL

Registrant ID: 2138
Name: Norman Jones
Railroad: Pullman Company
Position: Cook
Years of Service: 1940's
Submitter's Name: Davis

Registrant ID: 2119
Name: James Willie Jones
City/State: PA
Position: Porter
Years of Service: 1940's
Submitter: Clarence Jr.
City/State: Columbia, SC

Registrant ID: 5004
Employee Name: Parrish Jones
City/State: Chicago, IL
Railroad: Pullman Company
Position: Sleeping Car Porter
Submitter's Name: Aaron
City/State: Detroit, MI
Comments: He was my father's uncle. He was also a Porter Inspector.

Registrant ID: 2142
Name: Robert E. Jones
City/State: Brooklyn, NY
Position: Station Master, Conductor, Ticket Taker, Claims Analysis
Years of Service: 1939-1979
Submitter's Name: Patricia
City/State: Fairburn, GA

Registrant ID: 2143
Name: Royal Jones
City/State: New Orleans, LA
Position: Porter-Cook
Years of Service: 1940's
Submitter's Name: Lena M.
City/State: Atlanta, GA
Comments: Because of my father's exposure to the northern cities my father realized the many opportunities available to Black's outside of the south. My parents left their home of New Orleans, LA to start a new life in Boston, MA in the late 40's.

Registrant ID: 2145
Name: Searse Jones
City/State: Chicago, IL
Position: Sleeping Car Porter
Submitter's Name: Searse E
City/State: Chicago, IL
Comments: Father and Grandfather from Columbus MI Path were Pullman Porters.

Registrant ID: 2144
Name: Samuel Jones
City/State: Jacksonville, FL
Railroad: Jacksonville Terminal
Position: Baggage And Mail Porter, Redcap
Years: 1940's,1950's, 1960
Submitter's Name: Stephanie
City/State: Corona, NY
Comments: My uncle, Mr. Samuel Jones born October 20,1898 - passed away Sunday Febuary 28,1981, at the age of 83. Uncle Jones was an unsung hero who lobbied most of his life for Civil Rights. He fought for the rights of others from City Hall to the steps of the Capital.

My uncle, a self-educated man, was helpful in starting a local school established mainly for the early education of former slaves and filed suits against segregated sleeping cars on the nation's railroads and against school desegregation.

Registrant ID: 2147
Name: Thomas Jones
Railroad: El Paso
Submitter's: Lawrence, Lars

Registrant ID: 2148
Name: Warrick C. Jones
City/State: St Lois District, MO
Position: Porter-Club Car
Years of Service: 1943-1961
Submitter's Name: Warrick C.
City/State: Ecorse, MI

Registrant ID: 2073
William Truitt Sr. Johnson,
City/State: Waycross, GA
Railroad: Atlantic Coast Line and Amtrak
Position: Porter and Dining Car Waiter
Years of Service: 1940's
Submitter's Name: Shirley E.
City/State: Barnwell, SC
Comments: My father was a very hardworking, dedicated man and committed to his duties as a Pullman porter and dining car waiter. He was not educated in the formal mode, but was a very smart man. He was frequently laid off of his job, but he was an enterprising.

Registrant ID: 2152
Name: Bryant Jordan

City/State: Smiths, AL
Railroad: Central Of Georgia
Position: Carpenter Station
Years of Service: 1927-1953
Submitter's Name: Stacey
City/State: Silver Spring, MD
Comments: My grandfather worked for the railroads. He passed before I was born. I recently asked my father about his father's experiences working on the railroad and he had very few words

Registrant ID: 2154
Name: Burrell Jordan III
City/State: Aurora, NC
Railroad: Southern Railroad
Position: Pullman Porter
Years of Service: 1950-1975
Submitter's Name: Burrell
City/State: Charlotte, NC
Comments: My mother Lillian A. Jordan was President of the lady' auxiliary for the Porters in N.C. Mr. Randolph would stay at our house when he was in town for meetings. The last time I saw Mr. Randolph in 1960 at Maryland State College I was a freshman.

Registrant ID: 2157
Name: Robert Jordan, Jr.
City/State: South Haven, MI
Railroad: Illinois Central, Santa Fe, Milwaukee
Position: Dining Car Waiter
Years of Service: 1944-48
Submitter's Jo Ann, Jordan
City/State: Chicago, IL

Registrant ID: 2155
Name: Burrell Jordan, Jr.
City/State: Charlotte, NC

Railroad: Southern
Position: Sleeping Car Porter
Years of Service: 1941 to 1972
Submitter's Name: Alfredine
City/State: Southfield, MI
Comments: My mother was the president of the women's auxiliary. Mr. Randolph slept in our home when he came through Charlotte with Mr. McLaurin one of his assistants. This was in the early 50's. My father, Burrell Jordan Jr. traveled all over the United States.

Registrant ID: 2161
Name: Stanley S. Joseph
Railroad: New Orleans
Years of Service: 1940's
Submitter's Name: R.
City/State: New Orleans, LA

Registrant ID: 2159
Name: Stander S Joseph
City/State: New, LA
Railroad: New Orleans
Years of Service: 1946
Submitter's Name: Rhea
City/State: New, LA

Registrant ID: 2162
Name: James Joye
City/State: Brooklyn, NY
Position: Porter
Years of Service: 1935-1952
Submitter's Name: Sherry
City/State: Laurelton, NY

Registrant ID: 2163
Name: Lester Jules
City/State: Chicago, IL
Position: Pullman Porter
Years of Service: 1940's
Submitter(s) Ida, Lorraine, and Linda
City/State: Minneapolis, MS
Comments: Uncle

Registrant ID: 2165
Name: Charles E. Juniel
City/State: Aurora, CO
Position: Chair Car Waiter
Years of Service: 1961-1968

Registrant ID: 2166
Name: Lycurtis Junior
City/State: Milwaukee, WI
Railroad: L&A (Louisiana & Arkansas Railroad) and Miland Valley Railroad
Position: Track Layer
Years of Service: 1940's
Submitter's Name: Carol
City/State: Milwaukee, WI

Registrant ID: 2168
Name: Sidney Justice
City/State: Washington, DC
Years of Service: Early 1900s
Submitter's Name: Katherine
City/State: Phoenix, AZ
Comments: He was born a in 1855. He is listed as a 14 year old house servant in the home of a Rowan County, NC lawyer on the 1870 census.

Registrant ID: 2167
Lewis Harold (L.H.) Justice
City/State: Washington, DC
Years of Service: Around 1905
Submitter's Name: Katherine
City/State: Phoenix, AZ
Comments: He was the son of a Pullman Porter. He was born in 1882 in Charlotte (Mecklenburg County), NC. He retired to Charlotte after years of working

in the Northern US. My father's oldest living first cousin has more information.

Registrant ID: 2169
Name: Frank Juzang
Railroad: Pullman Company
Position: Pullman Porter
Years of Service: 1940-1960
Submitter's Name: Juzang

Registrant ID: 2171
Name: George W. Kates
City/State: NJ
Railroad: New York Central
Position: Pullman Porter
Submitter's Name: Edward
City/State: Plainfield, NJ

Registrant ID: 2170
Name: Albert S. Kates
City/State: AL
Railroad: New York Central
Position: Pullman Car Porter
Years of Service: Over 30 years
Submitter's Name: Edward
City/State: Plainfield, NJ
Comments: My grandfather received Christmas cards from the old movie star Dorothy Lamour for years.

Registrant ID: 2173
Name: Raymond Keaton
City/State: Old Fort, NC
Railroad: Southern Railroad
Position: Dining Car Cook and later Pullman Porter
Years of Service: 1955-1982
Comments: My father was based out of Asheville, NC. He retired from the railroad in the 1980's.

Registrant ID: 2174
Name: George Keeling
City/State: Evanston, IL
Railroad: Amtrak
Position: Pullman Porter
Years of Service: 38
Submitter's Name: Georgiana
City/State: Columbia, MD

Registrant ID: 2175
Name: Darius Keene
City/State: Philadelphia, PA
Railroad: Pennsylvania RR
Position: Dining Car Waiter
Years of Service: 1915-1917
Submitter's Name: Joseph
City/State: Mt. Laurel, NJ
Comments: He is my father. He related many railroad stories about his runs from Philadelphia to Pittsburgh, PA. Including one, which involved the train that hit the stalled car of a PRR vice president and propelling the car through the air and before landing.

Registrant ID: 2176
Name: George W Keener
City/State: N/A, OR
Railroad: Union Pacific
Position: Porter
Years of Service: 1920 - 1969
Submitter's Name: James F
City/State: Los Angeles, CA
Comments: He was my grand dad all he talked about was railroad he was a railroad man until the end.

Registrant ID: 2177
Name: Chester Keller
City/State: AL
Railroad: Railway Express

Position: Clerk
Submitter's Name: Jeanne
City/State: Chicago, IL

Registrant ID: 2178
Name: James J. Kellum
City/State: California
Railroad: Santa Fe, Southern Pacific, Union Pacific, Western Pacific at various times.
Position: Pullman Porter
Years : 1935-1969 34 Years
Submitter's: James R. & Letitia Reginald, Michael, Winifred, and Karolyn.
City/State: Sacramento, CA
Comments: James Writes: Over the years my mother his wife Isabel used to regale his six children so that he could talk about his "rail-roading" experiences I know that his easy going, and professional manner made him a friend to countless travelers. He retired in 1969, but was still receiving Christmas cards, from former passengers with whom he had worked over the years. Letitia Writes: My dad worked the most years of his career for the Santa Fe Railroad on the Super Chief for one and traveled from Richmond, California. to Chicago for many years at least twice a month. 'My brothers and sisters all have found memories of my fathers employment.

Registrant ID: 2184
Name: Nick Kelly
City/State: Birmingham, AL
Railroad: Burlington
Years of Service: 1937-1973

Submitter's Name: Margaret
City/State: Burningham, AL

Registrant ID: 2179
Name: Albert Kelly
City/State: Boston, MA
Railroad: New York Central
Position: Dining Car Waiter and a Porter
Years of Service: 1929-1966
Submitter's Name: Herman
City/State: Laurel, MD
Comments: My mother shares the stories of the discrimination that my grandfather and the other Sleeping Car Porters were subjected to, and how they preserved. He must have been doing relatively well for that era he owned a rather large home in the Dorchester area.

Registrant ID: 2183
Name: Nathan Kelly
City/State: Denver, CO
Railroad: Colorado & Southern
Position: Dining Car Waiter
Years of Service: 190?-1927
Submitter's Name: Kathleen
City/State: Los Angeles, CA
Comments: My grandfather Nathan Kelly worked as a dining car waiter for Colorado & Southern railroad until he died f in 1927. I did not know Nathan as he died long before I was born, and I only know about his position with the railroad as a result of genealogy research.

Registrant ID: 2185
Name: Wallace Kelly
City/State: Asheville, NC
Railroad: Southern Railway

Position: Laborer, Car Cleaner, Pullman Porter and outstanding salesman for the Pullman Company (May 1948 see his story and picture in the Pullmans national news letter)
Years of Service: 1909 - 1959
Submitter's Name: Najeeullah
City/State: Riverdale, GA
Comments: I have a local Asheville NC newspaper clipping with pictures and cover story about Wallace Kelly's retirement from the Railroad. I have also started an amazing family history study build up around Wallace and other Siblings.

Registrant ID: 2180
Name: Alonso Monroe Kelly Sr.
City/State: San Diego, CA
Railroad: Michigan Central
Years of Service: 1920-1955
Submitter's Name: Mildred
City/State: San Diego, CA
Comments: Worked for 35 years

Registrant ID: 2181
Name: Lee Kelly
City/State: Springfield, MA
Railroad: Between LA and CA
Position: Porter, Cook
Years: Started before 1934
Submitter's Name: Betty
City/State: Springfield, MA
Comments: My dad worked on this RR before 1934.

Registrant ID: 2186
Name: Henry Kelly   C
City/State: Manhattan, NY
Railroad: B & W
Baltimore/Washington Line
Position: Dining Car Waiter

Years of Service: 1930s-40s
Submitter's Name: Richard
City/State: Bronx, NY
Comments: My father was 96 at the time of his death.

Registrant ID: 2186
Name: Samuel James Kelly Sr.
City/State: Jacksonville, FL
Railroad: Seaboard and Atlantic Coastline
Position: Pullman Porter
Years of Service: 1908-1953
Submitter's Name: Charles H
City/State: Jacksonville, FL
Comments: When he retired at age 70, he was the #1 Pullman Porter on the seniority list in the District. He was a charter member of the Brotherhood of Sleeping Car Porter in the Jacksonville, Florida area.

Registrant ID: 2186
Name: William Henry Kelly, Sr.
City/State: Hempstead, NY
Railroad: Oyster Bay Club Car, Long Island Railroad, NY
Position: Porter and Machinist
Submitter's Name: Jean
City/State: East Orange, NJ
Comments: I was born in 1928 and as far back as I can remember, my father worked for the railroad, during the early years in the Oyster Bay Club Car, a private section of the railroad. In later years he worked at Sunnyside Yard in Queens, NY and at the machine shop in Jamaica.

Registrant ID: 2186
Name: Paul Kelsey

City/State: Detroit, MI
Railroad: Wabash Cannonball
Position: Cook
Years of Service: 1948 -1969
Submitter's Name: Yvonne
City/State: Eastpointe, MI
Comments: My grandfather
(Paul e. Kelsey) now deceased, I
remember him talking how he
worked as a porter and cook on
the Wabash Cannonball train.
He died in 1971.

Registrant ID: 2187
Name: Hamilton Kemp
City/State: St. Paul, MN
Railroad: Pullman Company
Position: Pullman Porter
Years of Service: 1937-1969
Submitter's Name: Hamilton
City/State: Warrenville, IL
Comments: A.Philip Randolph
was his Hero.

Registrant ID: 2188
Name: Lucius Kennebrew
Railroad: Chicago South Shore
South Bend Railroad (Electric)
Michigan City, Indiana
Position: Station Porter; Janitor
and Ticket Agent
Years of Service: 1951 to 1981
Submitter's Name: Harriette
City/State: Ft.Washington, MD
Comments: Working on the
railroad was a part of him. He
could have written a book about
the people he had met, items he
found, and the stories he heard.
My parents moved to the Washington
D.C. area to be near my family.

Registrant ID: 2191
Name: William Kennedy
Railroad: L & N

Position: Porter
Years of Service: 1940-1970
Submitter's Name: Ruth
City/State: Berea, KY

Registrant ID: 2190
Name: Gustavus Kennedy
City/State: MN
Submitter's Name: Dennis
City/State: St. Paul, MN

Registrant ID: 2192
Name: Lee Keys
City/State: Houston, TX
Railroad: The Pullman Co.
Position: Porter
Years of Service: 1920-1947
Submitter's Name: Aaron L.
City/State: Plainfield, NJ
Comments: Mr. Keys was my
uncle. He was killed in a train
crash in 1947. The following is
from the Pittsburgh Courier,
dated Saturday, March 8, 1947.
The accident occurred on Friday,
February 28, 1947.A 58 year old
Pullman porter, Lee Keys, of
Houston, Texas rode to his death
trying vainly to halt a runaway
Pennsylvania Railroad Sleeping
Car on a wild three and one-half
mile dash down a mountain
grade, last Friday before dawn.
The car reached a top speed of
50 miles an hour, before it finally
crashed into a hillside. Mr. Keys
was pinned in the smashed end
of the car, and died. For 3 miles
he had tried to save his
passengers, but his efforts were
in vain. Eleven persons were
injured.

Registrant ID: 2194
Name: I. E. Kimbro
Position: Pullman Porter
Years of Service: Over 25 Years

Registrant ID: 2195
Name: Gary Kimbrough
City/State: Chicago, IL
Railroad: Amtrak
Years of Service: 1973-Present
Submitter's Name: Gary
City/State: Chicago, IL

Registrant ID: 2196
Name: Anthony Kinan
City/State: Jacksonville, FL
Railroad: Silver Meter and the
Orange Blossom
Position: Pullman Porter
Years of Service: circa 1920's
Submitter's: Clotillda
City/State: Poughkeepsie, NY
Comments: Anthony Kinan was
my Great Uncle on my mother's
side. My great Grandmother's
children also worked for the
same Railroad from Florida to
New York. Eddie Sylvester Kinan
Pullman Porter Les Kinan,Mail
Car Clinton Kinan - Cook
Alfred Kinan – Pullman

Registrant ID: 2197
Name: John L Kincade
City/State: Lake Village, AR
Railroad: Missouri Pacific
Position: Pullman Porter
Years: Circa 1925 -1945
Submitter's Name: Joseph W
City/State: Eudora, AR
Comments: I use to sit and
listen to my uncle talk about his
experinces,working long hours
for twenty-five cents a day,and

all the humiliation and
degradation that went along with
it. Blacks did,not like him
because he was a white black
boy and the whites didn't like
him either.

Registrant ID: 2198
Name: Edgar JR King
City/State: Cincinati, OH
Position: Chef and Porter
Years of Service: 1940
Submitter's Name: Salahuddin

Registrant ID: 2203
Name: Robert Edward King
City/State: NY
Railroad: Baltimore & Ohio
Position: Pullman Porter
Submitter's Name: Barbara
City/State: Baltimore, MD

Registrant ID: 2204
Name: Rufus King
City/State: Calumet City, IL
Railroad: Santa Fe
Position: Dinning Car Waiter
Years of Service: 1943-1964
Submitter's Name: Phyllis
City/State: Calumet City, IL
Comments: There differences
made between the fair skin
dining car waiters and the darker
skin Pullman porters. As a child
my father always told me to get
an education because I am a
dark skin black woman. Also
how union workers were the
most important workers.

Registrant ID: 2201
Name: Jeff King
City/State: Saint Louis, MO
Railroad: Pullman Company

Position: Porter
Years of Service: 1935 1960
Submitters: Alvin and Jeanine
City/State Memphis &
Nashville, TN
Comments: Jeanine Writes: My grandfather passed away when I was really young. Didn't get much information from him prior to his passing.

Registrant ID: 2200
Name: Henry King
City/State: Hartford, CT
Railroad: Hartford-New Haven-New York RR
Position: Cleaner
Years of Service: 1915-39
Submitter's Name: Priscilla
City/State: Philadelphia, PA

Registrant ID: 2199
Name: Fitz King
City/State: New York, NY
Railroad: New York Central
Position: Carmen Worker (Car Cleaner)
Years of Service: 1927-1961**Submitter's:** Marilyn
City/State: Staten Island, NY
Comments: My father worked for the New York Central for 34 years, and never took a day off sick. Deceased

Registrant ID: 2202
Name: Robert Ander King
City/State: Inkster, MI
Position: Porter
Submitter's Name: Gwendolyn
City/State: Washington, DC
Comments: Only knowledge is being told by parents that he worked on the railroads as a

porter. I believe it was on the east coast. Both parents are deceased and I have no records.

Registrant ID: 2206
Name: Thomas Kirce, Sr.
City/State: FL
Railroad: Seaboard Coastline
Position: Pullman Porter
Years of Service: 1948-1952
Submitter's Name: Elizabeth
City/State: Jacksonville, FL
Comments: My father died January, 1972 in Jacksonville, FL, my mother is also deceased. I am the youngest of the siblings, As a child, I do remember how handsome he looked in the uniform.

Registrant ID: 2207
Name: James G. Kirk, Sr.
City/State: AL
Railroad: Northern Pacific
Position: Dining Car Waiter And waiter-in-charge
Years of Service: 1913-63
Submitter's: Beverly
City/State: Seattle, WA
Comments: My father, was one of the organizers of the Dining Car Waiters Union, Local 516, in St. Paul, Minnesota, in 1937. A history of his years on the railroad is recorded in the book "Seven Stars & Orion: Reflections of the Past"

Registrant ID: 2208
Name: Aaron Kirkland
City/State: MI
Years of Service: 1500's
Submitter's Name: Lisa
City/State: Detroit, MI

Registrant ID: 3933
Name: Lewis Thomas
City/State: Stone Mountain, GA
Position: Pullman Porter
Years of Service: 1863-1969
Submitter's Name: Karla M
City/State: Stone Mountain, GA

Registrant ID: 2210
Name: Lewis Thomas Klugh
Position: Pullman Porter
Years of Service: 1863-1969
Submitter's Name: Karla M.
City/State: Stone Mountain, GA

Registrant ID: 2213
Name: Thomas Knight
City/State: Detroit, MI
Railroad: Detroit Line
Position: Pullman Porter
Years of Service: Pre 1917
to approx 1930
Submitter's Name: Carole

Registrant ID: 2212
Name: Jimmy Knight
Position: Pullman Porter

Registrant ID: 2214
Name: Horace Knowles
City/State: Gary, IN
Railroad: Santa Fe
Position: Waiter
Years of Service: 1972

Registrant ID: 2217
Name: Lee Knox
City/State: AL
Railroad: Illinois Central
Position: Porter
Years of Service: 1907-1962
Submitter's Name: Ruby
City/State: Chicago, IL
Comments: He was well

respected by his peers and
other workers. If you mention his
name to other railroad employees
regardless of color, they knew
who you were referring to. At
retirement, he was given a gold
pass.

Registrant ID: 2218
Name: Willis Knox
City/State: New Orleans, LA
Railroad: Southern Pacific
Position: Pullman Porter
Years of Service: 1920's - 1937
Submitter's Name: Adrienne
City/State: Los Angeles, CA

Registrant ID: 2219
Name: Joseph Knox, Sr.
City/State: Los Angeles, CA
Railroad: Southern Pacific
Position: Dining Car Waiter
Years of Service:1920's - 68
Submitter's Name: Adrienne
City/State: Los Angeles, CA

Registrant ID: 2220
Name: Robert Koger Sr.
City/State: Manhattan, NY
Railroad: New York Central
Position: Pullman Porter
Years of Service: 31yrs
Submitter's Name: Naeema
City/State: Staten Island, NY

Registrant ID: 2221
Name: Thomas Kunghet
City/State: Detroit, MI
Railroad: Detroit line B& W
Chicago to Detroit Run.
Position: Porter
Submitter's Name: Carla
City/State: Detroit, MI
Comments: Grandfather

Registrant ID: 2226
Name: William Kyle
City/State: AL
Railroad: Burlington
Position: Cook -Kitchen worker
Years of Service: 1940's-70's
Submitter's Name: Bernard
City/State: New Rochelle, NY
Comments: My dad was a cook and kitchen worker on the Burlington Railroad. He frequently traveled from Chicago (home base) to Los Angeles. My Father died in 1996.

Registrant ID: 2223
Name: E.W. Kyle
Position: Porter
Years of Service: 1920's - 30's
Submitter's Name: Mary Agnes
City/State: Norman, OK

Registrant ID: 2224
Name: Ruben Kyle
City/State: Houston, TX
Railroad: Pullman Company
Position: Sleeping Car Porter
Years of Service: 1930-1970
Submitter's Name: Kurt
City/State: Pittsburgh, CA
Comments: Houston Texas Chicago Illinois I just remember my mother talking about her uncle that was a Pullman porter. He was also a union organizer. He was From Houston Texas. My mother would talk about her travels between Houston and Chicago and how he would always take very good care of her.

Registrant ID: 2227
Name: Nathaniel Kyles
City/State: Decatur, GA
Position: Porter
Years of Service: 50's
Submitter's Name: Christine
City/State: Decatur, GA
Comments: He lived in Chicago

Registrant ID: 2229
Name: Wilmer "Burt" Lacy
City/State: Fort Worth, TX
Railroad: Texas & Pacific
Position: Pullman Porter
Years of Service: 31
Submitter's Name: Almita
City/State: Chicago, IL
Comments: I found old pictures of my father, mother & myself attending a Brotherhood convention in Chicago around 1945 or 46. I also remember my mother taking my dad to work at the "yards." I would get on the train with him and help him get the cars ready before the train pulled into the main station to board passengers. My job was to place the covered soap bars and the white hand towels in the bathrooms and to make sure that his shoe polishing kit was neat. Lots of memories that were important to me.

Registrant ID: 2231
Name: John William Lacy JR.
City/State: Richmond, VA
Railroad: RF&P
Position: Pullman Porter
Years of Service: 10 plus
Submitter's Name: Geraldine
City/State: Glen Allen, VA

Registrant ID: 2233
Name: Alfred Ladner
City/State: Poplarville/Hillsdale, MS
Railroad: New Orleans
Position: Fireman
Years of Service: 1900
Submitter's Name: David
City/State: Renton, WA
Comments: John Ladner (my grand-uncle) would be the only one of the four who may have still been working when the Union was formed. Alfred's death certificate in 1917 listed his occupation as a fireman, which would have been very unusual in Jim Crow days in Mississippi.

Registrant ID: 2236
Name: Edwin Ladner
City/State: Poplarville-Hillsdale, MS
Railroad: New Orleans
Position: Porter
Years of Service: 1900
Submitter's Name: David
City/State: Renton, WA

Registrant ID: 2237
Name: Jesse Ladner
City/State: Poplarville-Hillsdale, MS
Railroad: New Orleans
Position: Porter
Years of Service: 1900
Submitter's Name: David
City/State: Renton, WA

Registrant ID: 2239
Name: John Ladner
City/State: Poplarville- Hillsdale, MS

Railroad: New Orleans
Position: Porter
Years of Service: 1900
Submitter's Name: David
City/State: Renton, WA
Comments: John Ladner (my grand-uncle) would be the only one of the four who may have still been working when the Union was formed. Alfred's death certificate in 1917 listed his occupation as a fireman, which would have been very unusual in Jim Crow days in Mississippi.

Registrant ID: 2240
Name: Robert Cullie LaFaye
City/State: Danville, IL
Railroad: Seaboard Coastline
Position: Pullman Porter
Years of Service: 1933-1969
Submitter's Name: Maggie
City/State: Danville, IL

Registrant ID: 2242
Name: Peter William Lamar
Railroad: Southern, Atlantic Coastline
Position: Pullman Porter
Years of Service: 1920-1977
Submitter's: Carolyne, Peter and Lamar
City/State: Memphis TN and Burke,VA
Comments: Peter and Lamar Write: My grandfather was an active member of the Brotherhood of Sleeping Car Pullman Porters. He was secretary of the local chapter and attended many national conventions.

Registrant ID: 2243
Name: Percy Lambert
City/State: Jamaica, NY
Railroad: Pennsylvania
Position: Chef
Years of Service: 1924 to 1967
Submitter's Name: Herbert
City/State: New York, NY
Comments: Percy who was my grandfather worked with his cousins and brothers on the railroad also. They served in the capacity of Cooks and Waiters. In 1947, The Lambert's, combined devoted a total of 143 years of combined service and continued long after that.

Registrant ID: 2245
Name: Robert M. Lambert
City/State: Selden, N.Y., NY
Railroad: Pennsylvania R. R.,
Position: Waiter
Years: Approx. 1927 thru 1952
Submitter's Name: Gloria m.
City/State: Sun City, AZ
Comments: He hated it till his dying day. It was so humiliating for him but he had a family to support, he never had anything good to say about his job the treatment the pay, or the long hours away from home.

Registrant ID: 2246
Name: J.L. Landrum
Position: Pullman Porter
Years of Service: Over 25

Registrant ID: 2247
Name: Paul T. Landry
City/State: Ft. Washington, MD
Railroad: Illinois Central
Position: Porter

Years of Service: 1940-1946
Submitter's Name: John
City/State: Ft, Washington, MD

Registrant ID: 2248
Name: Henry Lane
City/State: Jonestown, MS
Railroad: Yazoo & Mississippi Valley Railroad, and Illinois Central
Position: Brakeman and a Porter
Years: 1910 through 1940
Submitter's Name: Cassandra
City/State: Milwaukee, WI
Comments: My Great-grandfather was also a member of the Association of Colored Railway Trainmen in the mid 1920's. I was told that he was very active with both organizations. He was able to travel quite a bit due to his job as a train porter.

Registrant ID: 2250
Name: Clarence A. Lane Jr.
Railroad: Santa Fe
Position: Waiter
Years of Service: 1938-1946
Submitter's Name: Marianne
City/State: Chicago, IL
Comments: From what I remember he always came home with great stories of the rich and famous people that he had served on the Super Chief and The Chief but most of the time he was on the Super Chief.

Registrant ID: 2252
Name: Teackle Lansey, Jr.
City/State: Baltimore, MD
Railroad: B&O
Position: Dining Car Waiter

Years of Service: Circa1933-41
Submitter's Name: Sheryl
City/State: Baltimore, MD
Comments: The waiter experience must not have been a pleasant one since my father spoke little of it, but he worked for the B&O, on the run from Baltimore to Chicago. This job was performed while he was a student at, the then, Morgan State College.

Registrant ID: 2253
Name: Alphonso F Lars
City/State: Chicago, IL
Position: Mail Clerk Fed Government
Years of Service: 1913- 60's
Submitter's Name: Janice S
City/State: Chicago, IL
Comments: *Grandfather forced into retirement in 82,83 died at the age of 101*

Registrant ID: 2254
Name: Jerry Lars
City/State: Shreveport, LA
Position: Worked On Section
Years of Service: 1950-1955
Submitter's Name: Lora Lee
City/State: Memphis, TN

Registrant ID: 2255
Name: John Lasker
City/State: Conway, AR
Railroad: Missouri Pacific
Position: Pullman Porter
Years: 1930s to late 1940s
Submitter's Name: Marzella
City/State: Aurora, CO
Comments: My grandfather is now deceased.

Registrant ID: 2256
Name: Hugh Page Lassiter
City/State: New York City, NY
Railroad: Grand Central Station
Position: Porter in Charge
Years : 47 years of service
Submitter's Name: Myles
City/State: Burlington, NJ
Comments: My great grandfather, according to a New York Newspaper article about his retirement, written by James H. Hogans, states the following: "He was the most dynamic and picturesque personality without a doubt.

Registrant ID: 2257
Name: William H. Laster
City/State: TN
Railroad: L&N Railroad
Position: Cook
Years of Service: Early 1940'S
Submitter's Name: Jerry
City/State: Cleveland, OH
Comments: Deceased. My father was a cook on the rail line that ran mostly to the southern part of the country and to the lower parts of Ohio. He worked there for about twenty years. Our home was in a place called Cowan, Tennessee.

Registrant ID: 2258
Name: Darrell Lathan
City/State: Dolton, IL
Railroad: Amtrak
Position: Train Attendant, Chief on Board, Sleeper Attendant
Years of Service: 17 Years

Registrant ID: 2261
Name: LeRoy Latt
City/State: AL
Position: Cook
Years: 1930's early 1940's
Submitter's Name: Mary
City/State: Lathrup, VA

Registrant ID: 2260
Name: Clarence Latt
Position: Pullman Porter
Years of Service: 1930-40's
Submitter's Name: Mary
City/State: Lathup Village, MI

Registrant ID: 2262
Name: Mr. Isiah Lausen
City/State: Fayetteville, NC
Position: Sleeping Car Porter
Years of Service: 1932
Submitter's Name: Mr Llyod
City/State: Fayettville, NC

Registrant ID: 2263
Name: Ike Lauson
Position: Sleeping Car Porter
Submitter's Name: Louis

Registrant ID: 2264
Name: Robert Laususe
City/State: St. Louis, MO
Railroad: Pullman Co.   Wabash
& Mo. Pacific
Position: Pullman Porter
Years of Service: 1942 - 1968
Submitter's Name: Adrienne
City/State: Detroit, MI

Registrant ID: 2265
Name: Robert L Laususe
City/State: St, Louis, MO
Railroad: Kansas City, Florida
Position: Pullman Porter
Years of Service: 1942-1967

Submitter's Name: Robert L
City/State: St. Louis , MO
Comments: Callen who is 85yrs
old was a Pullman Porter and,
the first who became a state
senator.

Registrant ID: 2266
Name: Octave (Frank) LaVigne
City/State: New Orleans, LA
Position: Pullman Porter
Years of Service: 1940's
Submitter's: Ida Lorraine and
Linda
City/State: Minneapolis, MS
Comments: Uncle

Registrant ID: 4173
Edward Walkins Lawing Jr.
City/State: Asbury Park, NJ
Railroad: Norfolk Raid Line
Years of Service: 1940-1963
City/State: Asbury Prk, NJ
Comments: His sister registered
him.

Registrant ID: 2271
Name: Edward W Lawings
City/State: Lansing, MI
Years of Service: 1945
Submitter's Name: Alison
City/State: Lansing, MI

Registrant ID: 2272
Name: Herman Lawless
City/State: LA
Railroad: Illinois- Central
Position: Pullman Porter
Years of Service: 1940-49
Submitter's Name: Philip M.
City/State: New Orleans, LA

Registrant ID: 2273
Name: Philip Lawless Jr.

City/State: AL
Railroad: Southern-Pacific
Position: Pullman Porter
Years of Service: 1940-46
Submitter's Name: Philip Me.
City/State: New Orleans, LA

Registrant ID: 2268
Name: Leo Jason Lawrence
City/State: DE
Railroad: New York Central to Florida
Position: Pullman   Porter
Years of Service: 1929 -1972
Submitter's Name: Karen
City/State: Brockton, MA
Comments: He is deceased. They tried extremely hard to prevent my uncle from taking the only job that he was allowed to do that also let him travel.

Registrant ID: 2275
Name: Charles Lawrence
City/State: Detroit, MI
Railroad: Pennsylvania, B & O and C&O R. R.
Position: Pullman Porter
Years of Service: 1930 to 1965
Submitter's Name: Aaron
City/State: Detroit, MI
Comments: So I am told, my dad was one of the first, Porters.

Registrant ID: 2275
Name: Charles Lawrence
City/State: Detroit, MI
Railroad: Pennsylvania, B & O and C&O R. R.
Position: Pullman Porter
Years of Service: 1930 to 1965

Registrant ID: 2276
Name: Joel Laws

City/State: AL
Railroad: New York Central
Position: Pullman Porter
Years: Approx 1925-1965
Submitter's Name: Melvin
City/State: Coppell, TX

Registrant ID: 2277
Benjamin William Lawson
City/State: Dallas, TX
Railroad: The M,K, & T
Position: Porter
Years of Service: 1914-44
Submitter's Name: Marc Ira
City/State: Atlanta, GA
Comments: My Grandfather's home was in Dallas, Texas. He worked for the Missouri, Kansas City, Texas Railroad as a Porter for 27 years, until 1944.

Registrant ID: 2281
Name: not sure (my grandmohter's brother) Lawson
City/State: Chicago, IL
Railroad: The Empire Builder
Position: Sleeping Car Porter
Years of Service: Circa Mid 1930's until his death in the early 1940's
Submitter's Name: Larry
City/State: Chicago, IL
Comments: My uncle and and his sister , my grandmother Mattie Lawson were from Central Texas. Fayette or La Grange County.

Registrant ID: 2282
Name: U N Lawson
City/State: Cincinnati, OH
Submitter's Name: Barbara
City/State: Columbus, OH

Comments: He was killed at work, on the railroad tracks. His widow was my father's aunt, Opal Atwater Lawson Sweeney. She is also deceased.

Registrant ID: 2280
Name: Isiah Lawson
Position: Porter
Submitter's Name: Lloyd s.
City/State: Fayetteville, NC

Registrant ID: 2278
Name: Henry Lawson
City/State: Chicago, IL
Railroad: Gulf Mobile and Ohio
Position: Pullman Porter
Years of Service: Approx 32
Submitter's Name: Carolyn
City/State: Spanaway, WA
Comments: My father was a porter in the early 1940's and he retired in the 70's. The last run that I remember he had was from Chicago to the King Street station in Seattle. He did receive a railroad retirement pension.

Registrant ID: 2279
Name: Ike Lawson
Position: Porter
Submitter's Name: Lois
City/State: Syracuse, NY

Registrant ID: 2284
Name: Milton Layne
City/State: Huntington, W.V.A
Railroad: Pullman Company
Position: Pullman Porter
Years of Service: 1930-40-50
Submitter's Name: Layne

Registrant ID: 2285
Name: Wendell L Leach

City/State: Redlands, CA
Railroad: Line unknown
Years of Service: 1863-1969
Submitter's Name: Carolina
City/State: Redlands, CA
Comments: He was my grandfather. Not sure about the dates, but his runs were Boston-Chicago

Registrant ID: 2286
Name: Raymond Leach JR.
City/State: Ashville, NC
Railroad: Southern Railway
Years of Service: 1935-1965
Submitter's Name: Gary
City/State: Cincinnati, OH
Comments: My uncle was on the train for President Roosevelt's train tour.

Registrant ID: 2287
Name: Edward D. Lead, Sr.
City/State: Buffalo, NY
Railroad: NY Central
Position: Dining Car Waiter
Years of Service: 1905-1934
Submitter's Name: Florence L.
City/State: Buffalo, NY
Comments: He was my father

Registrant ID: 2288
Name: Don Leak
City/State: MD
Railroad: Seaboard Coastline
Position: Cook
Years of Service: 1944 - 1963
Submitter's Name: Angel
City/State: Lanham, MD
Comments: Daddy, loved the East coast route. He loved the kitchen. Cooking was his passion, with the huge pots, true stainless steel and heavy metal

utensils. Though the work area seemed relatively small (I remember getting a tour). All the cooks wore crisp, white jackets.

Registrant ID: 2289
Name: Wendell Leath
City/State: Alliance, OH
Railroad: Pullman Company
Position: Car Reprm
Years of Service: 1950-1985

Registrant ID: 2290
Name: Walter Per LeDoux-Hunt
City/State: Winston-Salem, NC
Railroad: Pennsylvania RR
Position: Waiter
Years of Service: 1943-1970
Submitter's Name: Michelle
City/State: Winson Salem, NC

Registrant ID: 2296
Name: William Lee
City/State: AL
Railroad: New York Central
Position: Sleeping Car Porter
Years of Service: Circa 1920s -26
Submitter's Name: Eva
City/State: Columbus, NJ

Registrant ID: 2292
Name: James David Lee
City/State: NY
Railroad: Pennsylvania RR
Position: Dining Car Waiter
Years of Service: 1922-1935
Submitter(s): James
City/State: Concord, CA
Comments: We are not sure of the exact dates because my parents are deceased and there's no one who can supply me with the exact information.

Registrant ID: 2297
Name: William A. Lee
City/State: Pittsburgh, PA
Years of Service: 1950-1959
Submitter(s) Name: Dorcas
City/State: Ocoee, FL
Comments: William was my father

Registrant ID: 2291
Name: Emmerson Lee
City/State: New Orleans, LA
Railroad: Illinois Central
Position: Waiter
Years of Service: 1939-1941
Submitter's Name: Deborah
City/State: Sacramento, CA
Comments: While working on the train he had an injury.

Registrant ID: 2293
Name: Joseph Lee
City/State: Stockton, CA
Railroad: New York Central System/ Illinois Central
Position: Dining Car Waiter
Years of Service: 1937-1954
Submitter's Name: Virginia
City/State: San Jose, CA

Registrant ID: 2294
Name: Rayfield Lee
City/State: Washington, DC
Railroad: Amtrak
Position: Pullman Porter
Years of Service: 1920-1930
Submitter's Name: Joyce
City/State: Washington, DC
Comments: Rayfield Lee is my father, who has been deceased since May 1977. He was born March 22, 1900 and worked for Amtrak, before it was called Amtrak. He worked as a

Pullman Porter to support his way through Howard University School of Music. He successfully graduated.

Registrant ID: 2298
Name: John Lee Dunn
City/State: Park Forest, IL
Railroad: Santa Fe Illinois Central
Position: Pullman Porter
Years of Service: 1930-1970
Submitter's Name: Deborah
City/State: Park Forest, IL
Comments: Father

Registrant ID: 2300
Name: John Lee Linder
City/State: Birmingham, AL
Railroad: L&N RR TCI RR
Position: Switchman/Coopler
Years of Service: 1909-1940
Submitter's Name: Linder

Registrant ID: 2301
Name: Lace Lee McNeal
City/State: Marston, NC
Railroad: Seaboard
Years of Service: 1957
Submitter's Name: Mable
City/State: Marshton, NC

Registrant ID: 2302
Name: Johnny Lee Pace
City/State: Cincinnati, OH
Railroad: Pullman Company
Submitter's Name: Lee Pace

Registrant ID: 2303
Name: Willie Lee Smith
City/State: Akron, OH
Submitter's Name: Helen
City/State: Atron, OH

Registrant ID: 2304
Name: Joseph Henry Lee, Sr.
City/State: TX
Railroad: Texas and Pacific RR
Position: Dining Car Waiter and Stewart
Years: Circa 1910 to 1944
Submitter's Name: Virginia K.
City/State: New York, NY
Comments: My grandfather, Joseph H. Lee, Sr. or "Papa Joe" as he was affectionately called because he was so nice and an inspiration to all who worked with and around him. He was responsible for getting my dad, Joseph Henry Lee, Jr. employed as a Dining Car Waiter.

Registrant ID: 2305
Name: James Leek
City/State: Gary, IN
Submitter's Name: Dorothy J.
City/State: Hilton Head Island, South Carolina

Registrant ID: 2306
Robert "Bobby" Lee-Wade
Position: Cook
Years of Service: 1935-1941
Submitter's Name: James W.
City/State: Roanoke, VA

Registrant ID: 2308
Name: Robert Lemon
City/State: Cincinnati, OH
Railroad: C & O Railroad
Position: Dining Car Waiter
Years of Service: 42 years
Submitter's Name: Ralph
City/State: Atlanta, GA
Comments: He was a Union Representative.

Registrant ID: 2309
Name: Warren G Leonard
City/State: Chicago, IL
Railroad: Pennsylvania RR
Position: Dinning Car Waiter
Years of Service: 42-48
Submitter's Name: Warren G
City/State: Chicago, IL

Registrant ID: 2310
Name: Cynthia Lessington
City/State: AL
Submitter's Name: Cynthia
City/State: AL

Registrant ID: 2311
Name: Grover Lester
Position: Pullman Porter
Years of Service: 1940-1958
Submitter's Name: Vivette K.
City/State: Cleveland, OH

Registrant ID: 2312
Name: Kirby Leufroy, Sr.
City/State: New Orleans, LA
Railroad: Louisville & Nashville Railroad Co
Position: Pullman Porter
Years: Sept.1940- August 1973
Submitter(s): Mitchel and Kirby, Jr.
City/State: Cerritos CA and Seattle,Washington
Comments: Mitchel Writes: Some of his most proud moments was moving soldiers from camp to camp at the start of world II until he was called duty Kirby, Jr.Writes: 'He was fluent in French. Once he served two French Canadian Priests who were traveling to the Canadian border.

Registrant ID: 2318
Name: Thaddeus, V Lewis
City/State: Calumet City, IL
Railroad: Santa Fe
Position: Locomotive Engineer
Years of Service: 25 years
Submitter's Name: Barbara, J
City/State: Calumet City, IL
Comments: My husband was one of the first African American locomotive engineers at Santa Fe Railroad.

Registrant ID: 2314
Name: Eugene Lewis
City/State: Chicago, IL
Railroad: Illinois Central
Position: Pullman Porter
Years of Service: 25 or more
Submitter's Name: Gloria
City/State: Chicago, IL
Comments: Uncle Gene was a tall, stately gentleman who took pride in his job. As a child I had no idea of The Struggle but I was proud of him because of the way he carried himself. He is deceased but is still one of my favorite relatives.

Registrant ID: 2320
Name: Tom Lewis
City/State: Sturgis, MS
Position: Porter
Years: 48 years
Retired early 1940's.
Submitter's Name: Felicia
City/State: Laurelton, NY
Comments: Tom Lewis was my "great uncle". His grandmother was born a slave. His parents purchased 32 acres of land in Mississippi. Soon after, his father died. Being the only male

in the family he secured a job as a Porter to pay the property taxes.

Registrant ID: 2319
Name: Thomas L. Lewis
City/State: The Bronx, NY
Railroad: Pennsylvania RR
Position: Dinning Car Waiter - Pullman Porter
Years of Service: Circa 1914-63
Submitter's Name: Irma
City/State: Smithville, NJ
Comments: My father, born 9/14/1893 began as a Dining Car Waiter when he was 16. He lied about his age and told them at the time that he was 18. When he was fired a short time later, he hired on as a Pullman Porter and remained employed with the Pullman Company where he retired.

Registrant ID: 2316
Name: Lloyd Lewis
City/State: OK
Railroad: Frisco
Position: Porter
Submitter's Name: Richard
City/State: Springfield, MO

Registrant ID: 2317
Name: Nathaniel Lewis
City/State: Triangle, VA
Railroad: New York City
Position: Dining Car Waiter
Submitter's Name: Laverne
City/State: Triangle, VA

Registrant ID: 2321
Name: James E Lewis, Sr.
City/State: Chicago, IL
Railroad: Pullman Co.

Position: Pullman Porter
Years of Service: 1928 to 1965
Submitter's Name: Erick
City/State: St. Paul, MN

Registrant ID: 2322
Name: Searse Lian Dean
City/State: Chicago, IL
Years of Service: Approx 36-yrs.
Submitter's Name: Connie
City/State: Chicago, IL
Comments: My father was working at age 65.

Registrant ID: 2323
Name: Andrew Life Carter
City/State: Pittsburgh, PA
Railroad: Penn. Railroad
Position: Sleeping Car Porter
Years of Service: 10yrs
Submitter's Name: Geraldine
City/State: Pittsburgh, PA
Comments:
Andrew was my father

Registrant ID: 2325
Name: William Liipsha
City/State: Indianapolis, IN
Railroad: Super Chief/ Chg LA
Position: Porter/ waiter
Years of Service: 1930-1950
Submitter's Name: Mrs. Beatrice M.
City/State: Indianapolis, IN
Comments: Uncle

Registrant ID: 2326
Name: Wayman L. Lindsay, Sr.
City/State: Indianapolis, IN

Registrant ID: 2327
Name: William Lindsey
City/State:
Railroad: New York Central

Position: Pullman Porter
Years of Service: Circa 1941-68
Submitter's Name: Jasper
City/State: Detroit, MI

Registrant ID: 2328
Name: Love Lee Linen
City/State: Shaker
Heights, Ohio
Years of Service: 1940-1969
Submitter's Name: Kathryn
City/State: Shaker
Heights, OH
Comments: My father worked
over 29 years.

Registrant ID: 2330
Name: Thomas Robert Little
City/State: Chattanooga, TN
Railroad: Southern Railroad
Position: Pullman Porter
Years of Service: 1939-58
Submitter's Name: Barbara
City/State: Chattanooga, TN

Registrant ID: 2329
Name: Bennie Little
City/State: Linden, AL
Railroad: L&N
Position: Trackman
Years of Service: 20 YRS.
Submitter's Name: Tommie
City/State: Chicago, IL
Comments: My father repaired
and laid track in North Florida in
the late 40,s through the 50,s
an into the 60,s retired in 1962.

Registrant ID: 2331
Name: William Little, Jr.
Position: Dining Car Waiter
Years of Service: 1930's
Submitter's Name: Edith
City/State: Galesburg, IN

Registrant ID: 2984
Name: Jesse Bee Littlejohn, Sr.
City/State: AL
Railroad: Katy Railroad
Position: Mail loader
Years of Service: 1950's
Submitter's Name: Vivian
City/State: Waco, TX
Comments: My father worked
for the Katy Railroad in Waco, TX
for more than 10 years in
addition to owning his own
bakery. His family consisted of
eight children so working more
than one job was a necessity for
him. I have always admired my
father for the sacrifice he made
for his family.

Registrant ID: 2334
Name: Dewey Littleton
City/State: AL
Railroad: Santa Fe
Position: Dining Car Porter
Years of Service: 1930s
Submitter's Name: Dismay
City/State: Chicago, IL

Registrant ID: 2336
Name: Leather Lloyd
City/State: Portland, OR
Railroad: Union Pacific
Years of Service: 1942-1944

Registrant ID: 2335
Name: Chester Lloyd
City/State: S. Euclid, OH
Submitter's Name: Abdul
City/State: S Euclid, OH

Registrant ID: 2337
Name: Emmett Lockett
City/State: Macon, GA

Railroad: MDS-Macon, Duben & Savannah Line
Position: Pullman Porter
Years of Service: 1920-1935
Submitter's Name: Mary
City/State: Woodbridge, VA
Comments: My dad's memories of his fathers job.

Registrant ID: 2338
Name: Joseph W. Loftin
City/State: PA
Railroad: Pennsylvania R.R.
Position: Pullman Porter, (Private Car Porter U.S. Steel Mr. Ben Fairless)
Years of Service: 1942 - 1957
Submitter's Name: Joseph
City/State: Arlington, TX
Comments: My father, Joe, as he was known, worked for the Pennsylvania Railroad for approximately 15 years as a Pullman Porter where he distinguished himself by rising to become one of those men chosen to work on a private car. He truly enjoyed his tenure with the railroad

Registrant ID: 2339
Name: Phil Lofton
Railroad: Texas & Pacific
Years of Service: Early 1900's
Submitter's Name: Alma

Registrant ID: 2340
Name: John Logan
City/State: Washington, DC
Railroad: Baltimore-Ohio
Position: Pullman Porter
Years of Service: 1870-early 1900's
Submitter's Name: Nadine
City/State: Fort Washington, MD

Comments: I am John Francis Logan's great-granddaughter. He died before I was born but, my mother always spoke about him. She said that he was away from home a lot but, provided a good-living for his wife and 10 children. He was very close to the church.

Registrant ID: 2342
Name: Arthur Logwood
City/State: Oakland, CA
Railroad: Pullman Company
Position: Electrical Apprentice
Years of Service: 1929 - 1943
Submitter's Name: Elaine
City/State: Oakland, CA
Comments: My father, Arthur Logwood was employed by the Pullman Company in July of 1929 to May 1st 1936. In March of 37 he was an Electrical Helper Apprentice, after completing his apprenticeship he was made a Journeyman and worked in that capacity until 1943.

Registrant ID: 2343
Name: Edward Lomax
City/State: IL
Railroad: Illinois Central
Submitter's Name: James C.
City/State: Champaign, IL

Registrant ID: 2344
Name: George London
City/State: Chicago, IL
Submitter's Name: Jacquelyn
City/State: Galveston, TX
Comments: My uncle was a porter on the railroad. He is now deceased.

Registrant ID: 2345
Name: Hernan Wesley Loney Sr.
City/State: Richmond, VA
Railroad: RF&P
Position: Pullman Porter
Years of Service: 40+
Submitter's Name: Minnie
City/State: Richmond, VA
Comments: Late husband . His route was Richmond to Detroit Michigan.

Registrant ID: 2348
Name: John Long
City/State: CO
Railroad: Amtrak
Position: Cook
Years of Service: 40 yrs
Submitter's Name: Vernon
City/State: Denver, CO
Comments: My uncle was a very good man. he live in Denver Colorado for about 60yrs. He died in 1999.

Registrant ID: 2349
Name: Emuel Long Sr.
City/State: MO
Railroad: Pennsylvania RR
Position: Sleeping Car Porter
Years of Service: 40 plus years
Submitter's Name: Emulex
City/State: Olivette, MO
Comments: All the documents that I remember seeing showed his name as E.W. Long . My father died in 1998 at age of 92.

Registrant ID: 2351
Name: Charles Lott
City/State: CA
Railroad: Santa Fe
Position: Porter

Comments: Charles l. Lott was my cousin. He retired some time in the 1970's and from what I understand worked for the railroad for most of his life.

Registrant ID: 2352
Name: Clarence Lott
Position: Pullman Porter
Submitter's Name: Mary
City/State: MI

Registrant ID: 2353
Name: John Louden
City/State: Greenwood, SC
Railroad: Seaboard Railroad
Position: Sleeping Car Porter
Years of Service: 19 Years
Submitter's Name: Bessie
City/State: Philadelphia, PA
Comments: My father loved the railroad. He really admired trains. He also loved meeting people.

Registrant ID: 2354
Name: Cherry Lovell
City/State: Brooklyn, NY

Registrant ID: 2356
Name: Willie James Lovett
City/State: Savannah, GA
Railroad: Central of Georgia
Position: Pullman Porter
Years of Service: 40 years
Submitter's: Mrs. Emma Lou
City/State: Jackson, NJ
Comments: I am the daughter of Mr. Willie James Lovett. My name is Mrs. Emma Lou Lovett-Gray, and I would like to acknowledge my father's years of service with the railroad.

Registrant ID: 3221
Name: Addison Loving
City/State: Camden, NJ
Railroad: Pennsylvania Railroad
Position: Porter
Submitter's Name: Donald
City/State: Hillcrest Heights, Maryland
Comments: I am afraid this is all the information I can provide.

Registrant ID: 2358
William Grant Sr. Lowery
City/State: PA
Position: Short Order Cook
Years of Service: 1918-20's
Submitter's Name: Harriett C.
City/State: Pittsburgh, PA
Comments: Wife

Registrant ID: 2363
Name: Walter Lucas
City/State: East Elmhurst, NY
Railroad: New York Central
Position: Waiter
Years of Service: 1950's
Submitter's Name: Valid
City/State: Forestville, MD
Comments: My mother has kept his time cards from the railroad and other memorabilia.

Registrant ID: 2362
Name: James Lucas
City/State: NY
Railroad: The Pennsylvania RR
Position: Dining Car Waiter
Years of Service: 1930-1937
Submitter's Name: Erica
City/State: Mount Vernon, NY

Registrant ID: 2361
Name: Greene Lucas
City/State: AL

Railroad: Pullman Co.
Grand Central, New York
Position: Porter
Years of Service: Began 6/25/25..Ended circa 1962-64
Submitter's Name: Ranke
City/State: Staten Island, NY
Comments: My late great-grandfather, Greene W. Lucas, worked for the Pullman Company from 6/25/25 until his retirement around 1962-64. He passed in the late 1970's. He was a graduate of Morris Brown College. Our family still has his Pullman Company ID card.

Registrant ID: 2364
Name: W.B. Lugrand
Position: Pullman Porter
Years of Service: Over 25

Registrant ID: 2365
Name: Percy Lumpkin
City/State: Oakland, CA
Position: Pullman
Submitter's Name: Stanley
City/State: New Orleans, LA

Registrant ID: 2367
Name: John Luster
Railroad: Hummingbird
Position: Pullman Porter
Submitter's Name: Dr Essie
Comments: Cousin

Registrant ID: 2366
Name: Charles Luster
Position: Pullman Porter
Years of Service: 30's
Submitter's Name: Dr Essie
Comments: Cousin

Registrant ID: 2374
Benjamin Franklin Lyman
City/State: Cincinnati, OH
Railroad: The Pullman Co.
Position: Pullman Porter
Years: Circa 1950's-70-
Submitter's Name: Affiances
City/State: Chicago, IL
Comments: I do not know when my father was hired by the Pullman Company. I can remember when he became a Porter in Charge. He always took pride in his job; and consequently, my siblings and I felt good about our dad's employment

Registrant ID: 2376
Name: Charles Lynch
Railroad: Pullman Company
Position: Boiler Man
Submitter's Name: Pope

Registrant ID: 2377
Archie Guilford Lyons, Sr.
City/State: AL
Railroad: Lehigh Valley RR
Position: Redcap
Years of Service: 1922- 1944
Submitter's Name: JoAnne
City/State: Mitchellville, MD
Comments: My Grandfather, Archie Guilford Lyons, Sr. worked at the Lehigh Valley Railroad Station in Buffalo, NY.

Registrant ID: 2379
Name: Reodie Mabon
City/State: MI
Position: Cook
Years of Service: 1939-43
Submitter's Name: Emily M.
City/State: Ypsilanti, MI

Registrant ID: 2381
Name: George Mace
City/State: Edwards, MS
Railroad: Started in Chicago. Then worked line from Minneapolis to Seattle.
Position: Porter
Years of Service: 35
Comments: George Mace is my elder cousin and I am registering him. He still lives in Mississippi and is 104 years old. You may contact him through me with the information I have supplied.

Registrant ID: 2395
Name: Thornton Mack
City/State: Chicago, IL
Position: Chef
Years of Service: 1947-1984
Submitter's Name: S.
City/State: Cleveland, OH

Registrant ID: 2388
Name: Dennis Mack
City/State: Decatur, GA
Railroad: Southern Railway
Position: Pullman Porter, And a Mail Porter
Years of Service: 1943-1967
Submitter's Name: Miranda
City/State: Decatur, GA
Comments: My father had many interesting stories to tell about his life as a Pullman Porter and a Mail Porter. He was the father of 14 children and some of the lessons and values he taught us originated from his experiences with Southern Railway.

Registrant ID: 2391
Name: Mr. Louis M Mack
City/State: New Orleans, LA

Railroad: Illinois Central
Position: Baggage Carrier
Submitter's: Mrs. Rose Mack
City/State: Parker, CO

Registrant ID: 2399
Name: Millard Mack JR
City/State: Willingboro, NJ
Railroad: Penn. Railroad
Position: Club Car Porter
Years of Service:1920's-60's
Submitter's Name: Millard
City/State: Willingboro, NJ

Registrant ID: 2400
Name: Doniphan Mackay
City/State: Oakland, CA
Railroad: Southern Pacific/San
Joaquin Daylight
Position: Pullman Porter
Years of Service: 1950-68
Submitter(s): Frederick, Melvin
City/State: Oakland, CA
Comments: Frederick Writes:
My father began working as a
Pullman Porter in Omaha
Nebraska in the 1950's. He
moved to Oakland and
worked as a Pullman Porter on
the Southern Pacific/San
Juaquin Daylight. Th route that
he worked was from Oakland to
Los Angeles and Oakland to
Nevada. He did this for two
decades. My father died in 1968
in the Southern Pacific Railroad
Hospital Fell Street, San
Francisco, and California.
Melvin Writes: My Father was a
Porter on the Southern Pacific
railroad for 28 years. I used to
ride with him all over California
before he passed in 1969.

Registrant ID: 2401
Name: Joseph B Mackey Sr.
City/State: Philadelphia, PA
Railroad: Pullman Railroad
Position: Cook
Years of Service: 1900--1925
Submitter's Name: John
City/State: Yeadon, PA
Comments: My grandfather was
a cook for private cars that
traveled long distance. He cooked
for the actress Lillian Russell
and other notables. His son
Joseph Jr. was a Sleeping Car
Porter for the Pullman
Corporation

Registrant ID: 2402
Name: Henry James MacMakin
City/State: TX
Railroad: Pullman began in
Dallas Texas ended in Illinois
Position: Pullman Porter
Years of Service: Circa 1930-50
Submitter's Name: Geraldine
City/State: Chicago, IL
Comments: My late uncle
learned to be very attentive to
customers needs, always seeking
to pleasantly be of service to
them as though he was still
waiting on them in the Sleeping
Car or Dining Car. Henry
MacMakin began working in a
drug store near 45th & Indiana

Registrant ID: 2404
Name: Thomas G. Macon
City/State: Chicago, IL
Railroad: The Pullman Co.
Position: Porter
Submitter's Name: William
City/State: Albany, NY

Comments: I have my uncles ID badge from the Pullman Company. On the Front is his photo, and on the back is his height, weight, hair and eye color. there is a handwritten ID # on the back

Registrant ID: 2405
Name: Will Macon
City/State: Montgomery, AL
Position: Porter
Submitter's Name: Dorothy
City/State: Bronx, NY
Comments: This was my grandfather. I was about 5 years old, but remember him with his blue suit and cap, and my father told me where he worked. He had to be away from home for long periods of time while working on the railroad.

Registrant ID: 2407
Name: Lewis Mack Madden
Position: Car Cleaner
Years of Service: 1930's-50's
Submitter's Name: Sue
City/State: Flower Mound, TX

Registrant ID: 2410
Name: John J. Madison
City/State: Brooklyn, NY
Position: Porter
Years of Service: thru 1933
Submitter's Name: Dorothy
City/State: Brooklyn, NY

Registrant ID: 2408
Name: Charles Madison
City/State: New Rochelle, NY
Submitter's Name: Loretta
City/State: New Rochelle, NY

Comments: My is the contact person for her father, Charles Madison who worked on the railroad as a Dinning Car Cook.

Registrant ID: 2411
Name: Major
City/State: Chicago, IL
Position: Dining Car Waiter
Years of Service: 1944-1945
Submitter's Name: Vivian I.
City/State: Chicago, IL

Registrant ID: 2412
Name: Carl Makle
City/State: Birmingham, AL
Railroad: Beuswmen Pullman
Position: DCW
Years of Service: 1943-1964
Submitter's Name: Charles E
City/State: Birmingham, AL

Registrant ID: 2413
Name: Oscar W. Mallory
City/State: New York, NY
Years of Service: 1939-80

Registrant ID: 2414
Name: William G.Mallory
City/State: Cairo, IL
Railroad: Illinois Central
Position: Pullman Porter, Brakeman
Years of Service: 20+ Years
Submitter's Name: Karen
City/State: New Berlin, WI

Registrant ID: 2416
Name: William and Resale Malone
City/State: Jacksonville, FL
Railroad: Seaboard Coastline
Position: Car Porter and Mechanic

Years of Service: 1950-1970
Submitter's Name: Essie
City/State: Jacksonville, FL
Comments: My mother and
father both worked and retired
from the railroad.

Registrant ID: 2417
Name: Edgar W. Mandeville
City/State: Corona,, NY
Railroad: Pennsylvania RR
Position: Dinning Car Waiter
Years of Service: 1929-1947
Submitter's Name: David
City/State: Silver Spring, MD

Registrant ID: 2419
Name: Edward Mapp
City/State: New York, NY
Position: Pullman Porters and
Dining Attendants
Years of Service: 30's to 50's

Registrant ID: 2418
Name: Charles Mapp
City/State: St. Albany, NY
Position: Bartender
Submitter's Name: Barbara J.
City/State: GermanTown, TN

Registrant ID: 2420
Name: Mr. Ellie Sr. Mapson
City/State: Cleveland, OH
Railroad: N.Y.C.R.R Lindale
Roundhouse
Position: Roundhouse Turntable
Boilermaker
Years of Service: 1934-1959
Submitter's Name: Mr. Ellie
City/State: Cleveland, OH

Registrant ID: 2421
Name: James Arnold Marble
City/State: Little Rock, AR

Position: Pullman Porter
Submitter's Name: Dawn
City/State: Buffalo,, NY

Registrant ID: 2423
Name: John Marison
City/State: AL
Railroad: Union Station in
Charleston, SC.
Years of Service: 1900's
Submitter's Name: Marvin
City/State: North Charleston,
South Carolina
Comments: The station was
located in Charleston South
Carolina, and it was burned
down around 1930's

Registrant ID: 2430
Name: Lillie Marshall
City/State: Matteson, IL
Position: Pullman Porter
Submitter's Name: Jesse
City/State: Birmingham, AL

Registrant ID: 2426
Name: Charles Marshall
City/State: New York, NY
Position: Pullman Porter
Submitter's Name: Yolanda
City/State: Hialeah, FL
Comments: I only know that my
great-grandfather (born around
1882) worked as a Porter for the
Pullman Company during the
1930 census.

Registrant ID: 2431
Name: William Marshall
City/State: Chicago, IL
Submitter's Name: Doris
City/State: South Bend, IN

Registrant ID: 2432
Name: W. H. Marshbank
Position: Pullman Porter
Years of Service: 25 Years
Comments: B.S.C.P union member.

Registrant ID: 2439
Name: Robert Martin
City/State: Camden, MS
Railroad: Santa Fe
Position: Waiter
Years of Service: 1961, 1962
Comments: I was a college student attending a black college. I thoroughly enjoyed the work in that it gave me the opportunity to travel to the West Coast, meet people and most of all I earned money to continue my education. My dad was a former Pullman car porter .

Registrant ID: 2436
Name: Leonard martin
City/State: Grand Rapids, MI
Position: Porter
Submitter's Name: Neighbor
City/State: MI

Registrant ID: 2435
Name: Joseph G Martin
City/State: Chicago Hits, IL
Railroad: NYC
Position: Pullman Porter
Years of Service: 1933-1973
Submitter's Name: Juju & Jo
City/State: Chicago Hts, IL

Registrant ID: 2447
Name: Solomon Martin
City/State: Beaumont, TX
Railroad: Southern Pacific
Position: Waiter

Years of Service: 1945 to approximately 1956
Submitter's Name: Cynthia
City/State: Fairfield, CA

Registrant ID: 2448
Name: Solomon Martin
City/State: IL
Railroad: Burlington
Position: Pullman Porter
Years: Before 1938 until 1965
Submitter's Name: Valerie
City/State: Matteson, IL
Comments: He was hired as a part-time employee for the Burlington Railroad during World War II. He eventually was hired as a full-time employee and worked on the Empire Builder. This train connected Chicago to Seattle. My grandfather would go out for 8-day runs. We would drop him off and pick him up at Union Station in Chicago. He told my grandmother that he waited on Mahalia Jackson (she didn't tip very well. He retired in 1965, and died in 1972.

Registrant ID: 2445
Name: Smith Martin
City/State: AL
Railroad: Union Pacific
Position: Dining Waiter
Years of Service: 1945-1955
Submitter's Name: Marcellus
City/State: Oakland, CA
Comments: I remember as a kid, my father and my grandfather, also a waiter, and others in Denver, Colorado telling stories about things that happened on the road.

Registrant ID: 2437
Name: Percy Martin
City/State: Philadelphia, PA
Railroad: Pennsylvania RR
Position: Pullman Porter
Years of Service: 1924 to 1968
Submitter's Name: Dwight
City/State: Philadelphia, PA
Comments: The enclosed information is regarding my father, Percy P. Martin. My father held the position of Pullman Porter. The documentation that is available to me notes his hiring date as May 1922, and a retirement date of May 1968. I have calculated he had 44 years of service.

Registrant ID: 2449
Name: William R. Martin
City/State: Roswell, SD
Railroad: Penn. Railroad
Position: Pullman Porter
Years of Service: 1924-1964
Submitter's Name: James
City/State: Rosuell, SD

Registrant ID: 2433
Name: Fidel A. Martin
City/State: CA
Railroad: Pullman
Position: Dining Car Attendant/Porter
Years of Service: 1933-1959
Submitter's Name: Tom
City/State: San Jose, CA
Comments: Survived two terrible train wrecks. In the early years, he would be gone for three weeks at a time (roundtrip plus layovers), an absentee father. There was a large contingent of Filipino busboys

and porters who worked for Pullman also.

Registrant ID: 2453
Name: Elias Morris Martini
City/State: Seattle, WA
Railroad: Northern Pacific
Position: Waiter
Years: Not sure when he began, but worked until his death in 1938
Submitter's Name: Mark
City/State: CA
Comments: Elias Martini was my great uncle.

Registrant ID: 2464
Name: John Homer Mason
City/State: Keyser, WV

Registrant ID: 2458
Name: Henry Mason
City/State: Chicago, IL
Railroad: Union Pacific, Milwaukee Road, Amtrak
Position: Pullman Porter, Buffet & Bar Attendant
Years of Service: 1952 - 1979
Submitter's: Jerome & James
City/State: Atlanta, GA
San Lorenzo, & CA
Comments: My father retired from duty in 1979 due to illness, sadly he passed away December 1993.

Registrant ID: 2468
Name: Julius Mason
City/State: Chicago, IL
Railroad: Pullman Rail Car Co.
Position: Pullman Porter
Years of Service: 30 Yrs
Submitter's Name: James
City/State: Chicago, IL

Comments: He was my uncle

Registrant ID: 1139
Name: James J Mason
City/State: Chicago, IL
Railroad: Santa Fe
Position: Pulliam Porter
Years of Service: Circa1921-64
Submitter(s: James J. &
Katherine
City/State: Grand Rapids &
Chicago, MI & 'IL
Comments: He was the father of
Ten children, I am the elder, and
well remember the debate
between my father and mother
reference his joining the union.
He always told us children about
the wonderful Movie stars he met
and had the pleasure of serving.

Registrant ID: 2461
Name: Howard James Mason
City/State: DE
Railroad: Baltimore Ohio
Position: Waiter
Years of Service: 1936-l971
Submitter's Name: Delores
City/State: Hyattsville, MD
Comments: My Father would tell
me horror stories about the way
black men were treated, and the
places he had to stay were he
called the quarters. He attended
Delaware State College and the
only job he could get a the time
was on the B & O Railroad

Registrant ID: 2455
Name: Ashley Mason
City/State: NY
Railroad: New York Central

Position: Pullman Porter
Years of Service: 1930's-60's
Submitter's Name: Grace
City/State: Palmdale, CA
Comments: Ashley S. Mason
(died December 23, 1970) he was
my great uncle. When his wife
passed I was given a small box
full of documents including but
not limited to letters of
recognition and service pins from
the Pullman Company, copies of
the Negro Traveler he (Ashley S.
Mason appears on the cover of
one of them.

Registrant ID: 2456
Name: Freddie Mason
City/State: Chicago, IL
Railroad: Illinois Central RR
Position: Waiter, Waiter-in-
Charge, Trainman
Years: 45 years (1938 -1982)
Submitter's Name: Frederick
City/State: South Holland, IL
Comments: As far as I know my
dad was a well respected Dining
Car Waiter-In-Charge for many
years on the Illinois Central City
of Miami, City of New Orleans,
and the Green Diamond. Later
in his career he took a position
as a trainman for the local
Chicago line by the Illinois
Central.

Registrant ID: 2469
Name: Harry Massengill
City/State: Minneapolis, MN
Railroad: Pullman Company
Position: Pullman Porter
Years of Service: 1930-1963
Submitter's Name: Massengill
Johnson

Registrant ID: 2470
Name: Arned Sr. Master
Railroad: Pullman Company
Position: Pullman Porter
Years of Service: 1921-1963
Submitter's Name: Arned

Registrant ID: 2333
Name: Humphrey T. Mates
City/State: Springfield, OH
Position: Porter
Years of Service: 1925-1966
Submitter's Name: Mrs. Edith
City/State: Detroit, MI

Registrant ID: 2478
Name: Willie Mathews
Position: Porter
Years of Service: 1920's
Submitter's Name: Alma
Comments: My husband is deceased.

Registrant ID: 2477
Name: Clarence Mathews
City/State: IL
Position: Pullman Porter
Years of Service: 1946 to 1970
Submitter's Name: Joyce
City/State: Hazel Crest, IL
Comments: My uncle Clarence worked as a Pullman Porter on the El Capitan train, going to Los Angeles.

Registrant ID: 2480
Name: Clarence Mathews, Sr.
Submitter's Name: Elliott A.
City/State: Chicago, IL
Registrant ID: 2482
Name: Oscar Matley
Railroad: NW Rail Road
Position: Porters
Years of Service: 1930-1940

Registrant ID: 2486
Name: Wilson Matley
Railroad: N W Railroad
Position: Waiter
Years of Service: 1934-1970
Submitter's Name: Zella
City/State: Homewood, IL

Registrant ID: 2488
Name: Wilson Mattey
City/State: Homewood, IL
Railroad: NW Rail Road
Position: Waiters/Porters
Years of Service: 1930-1940
Submitter's Name: Zeela
City/State: Homewood, IL
Comments: Father is Wilson worked as Dining Car waiter 1934-1970.

Registrant ID: 2489
Name: Wilson Mattey
City/State: Homewood, IL
Railroad: NW Rail Road
Position: Waiters
Years of Service: 1930-1940
Submitter's Name: Zeela
City/State: Homewood, IL
Comments: Father is Wilson worked as Dining Car waiter 1934-1970.

Registrant ID: 2494
Name: Joseph Glenn Mathews
City/State:
Railroad: New York Central
Position: Cook and Waiter
Years: Approx 1945 - 1953
Submitter's Name: Stephanie
City/State: Chicago, IL
Comments: He was my father. He died in the 1970s.

Registrant ID: 2490
Name: Calvin B. Mathews
Position: Pullman Porter
Years of Service: Approx 40Yrs
Submitter's Name: Lillie
City/State: Florence, AL

Registrant ID: 2492
Name: Charles Mathews
City/State: MO
Years of Service: 1930's-1971
Submitter's Name: Jeanette
City/State: St. Louis , MO

Registrant ID: 2495
Name: B.S. Mattison
Position: Pullman Porter
Years of Service: Over 25
Comments: He was a member of the 'B.S.C.P.

Registrant ID: 2497
Name: Mr. Maberry
City/State: Detroit, MI
Railroad: Southern Railroad
Position: Dining Car Waiter
Years of Service: 1938 -
Submitter's Name: Eleanor
City/State: Detroit, MI

Registrant ID: 2498
Name: James Mayers
City/State: Whitmire, SC
Position: Porter
Years of Service: 1902-1913
Submitter's Name: Amanda
City/State: Whimire, SC

Registrant ID: 2499
Name: William Mayes
Railroad: Pullman Company
Position: Engine Worker
Years of Service: 1930-1940

Submitter's Name: Chappell

Registrant ID: 2506
Name: Alex McCall
City/State: New Orleans, LA
Railroad: Jacksonville, FL - New Orleans, LA
Position: Pullman Porter
Years of Service: 1920-1940
Submitter's Name: Jewell
City/State: Pachuta, MS
Comments: I only know the information that I was told as a child. He worked on the train line from Jacksonville, FL to New Orleans, LA

Registrant ID: 2507
Name: William S.McCallum
City/State: LA
Railroad: L&N Railroad
Position: Pullman Porter
Years of Service: 1920 to 1956
Submitter's Name: Trygve
City/State: New Orleans, LA
Comments: He traveled out of New Orleans to New York on the L&N line. Also New Orleans to St. Louis on the L&N line.

Registrant ID: 2508
Name: Norris McCoy
City/State: Kansas City, MO
Railroad: San Francisco
Position: Dinner Car Waiter
Years of Service: late 40s to the early 60s
Submitter's Name: Michael
City/State: St. Louis , MO
Comments: I rarely saw my father and did not know what type of work he did when I was a child.

Registrant ID: 2509
Name: George McCray Sr.
City/State: AL
Railroad: Santa Fe
Position: Pullman Porter
Years of Service: 1925 to 1955
Submitter's Name: Janice
City/State: Chicago, IL

Registrant ID: 2513
Name: Andrew Mc Ginnis
City/State:
Railroad: Union Pacific
Position: Sleeping Car Porter
Years of Service: 1956-1968
Submitter's Name: Kimberly
City/State: Norwalk, CA
Comments: This gentleman
was my uncle whom I adored
and he played a major role in
getting my father a job on the
railroad. He was a gentle giant in
our family and every one loved
him.

Registrant ID: 2515
Name: Thomas Mc Lauren
City/State: East ST Louis, IL,
Railroad: Illinois Central
Position: Pullman Porter
Years: Approx 1938 -1968
Submitter's Name: Genoa
City/State: Chicago, IL
Comments: Honored at
retirement by presentation of
silver engraved bowl celebrating
his service to the railway
industry.

Registrant ID: 2516
Arthur Clarendon Mc Watt
City/State: MN
Position: Porter
Years of Service: 1920-1952

Submitter's Name: Arthur
City/State: St. Paul, MN

Registrant ID: 2517
James Washington Mc Wherter
City/State: Mrirfreesbord, TX
Position: Porter
Years of Service: 1940-60s-
Submitter's Name: Ollie
City/State: Mrirfreesbord, TX

Registrant ID: 2518
Name: Houston McAllister
City/State: NY
Position: Waiter
Years of Service: 1926-1974
Submitter's Name: Delores R.
City/State: Chicago, IL

Registrant ID: 2520
John Thomas McAllister, Sr.
City/State: NY
Railroad: Pennsylvania RR
Position: Head Dining Car
Waiter
Years of Service: 1910 - 1960
Submitter's Name: Arlene
City/State: Rockaway Beach,
NY

Registrant ID: 2521
Name: DeWitt Macao McCaleb
City/State: OH
Railroad: New York Central
Position: Waiter - In – Charge
and Bartender
Years of Service: I929 - 1965
Submitter's Name: Ms. Norma
City/State: Cincinnati, OH
Comments: My father worked
for the railroad during the Great
Depression,he had a law degree
and worked as a waiter in order
to care for a wife and three

children. His base was Chicago,even though he lived in Cincinnati, which meant he had to ride all the way to Chicago.

Registrant ID: 2525
Name: James Albert McClain
City/State: AL
Railroad: Penn Central
Position: Sleeping Car Porter
Submitter's Name: Lillian
City/State: Palm Coast, FL
Comments: My father was a Pullman Porter on the Penn. railroad. That had to be in the thirties or early forties.

Registrant ID: 2526
Name: Alex McClaron
City/State: Corona,
Position: Secretary of Union
Submitter's Name: Edward
City/State: Corona,
Comments: Father

Registrant ID: 2527
Name: George S. McClellan
City/State: Jacksonville, Fl
Railroad: Pullman Company
Position: Pullman Porter
Years of Service: 1941-1977

Registrant ID: 2528
Name: Andrew Mc Clendon
City/State: CA
Position: Dining Car Waiter And Cook
Years: Approx 1929-1949
Submitter's Name: Jacqueline
City/State: Wilmington, CA
Comments: Deceased 1957

Registrant ID: 2529
Name: Rever McCloud

City/State: Omaha, NE
Railroad: UP
Position: Red Cap
Years of Service: 38
Submitter's Name: J.
City/State: Oakland, CA
Comments: Retired from the railroad after 38 years of service.

Registrant ID: 2531
Name: Joseph Barnes McCormick
City/State: Birmingham, AL
Railroad: Southern
Position: Pullman Porter
Years of Service: 1927-28
Submitter's Name: Joseph
City/State: Marietta, GA
Comments: My grandfather's run was from Birmingham to New York City. He died in in 1930 when I was 1 (one) year old. The little I know about him and his occupation I was told by my mother.

Registrant ID: 2532
Name: Andy McCottry McDonald
City/State: Charleston, SC
Railroad: Pullman Company
Years of Service: 1930-1958
Submitter's Name: McCottry Smith

Registrant ID: 2534
Name: Procter McCovey
City/State: Denver, CO
Submitter's Name: Vera
City/State: Flint, MI
Comments: There is not a lot I can give you about my Grandfather. My mother lost contact with him because he had to move to Denver Colorado

because of his asthma being so bad. My mother has since died as well thre is no other sourse of information.

Registrant ID: 2536
Name: Hence McCowin
City/State: Gary, IN
Railroad: Union Pacific
Position: Dinning Car Waiter
Years of Service: 1940-1968
Submitter's Name: Richard
City/State: Gary, IN
Comments: Father worked out of Omaha died while he was still an employee.

Registrant ID: 2538
Name: Henry McCoy
Railroad: Santa Fe and Amtrak
Position: Dining Car Waiter and Bartender
Years of Service: Approximately 1925-1979
Submitter's Name: Henrika
City/State: Chicago, IL

Registrant ID: 2539
Name: Robert McCoy
City/State: Pittsburgh, PA
Railroad: Pennsylvania RR
Position: Dining Car Waiter
Years of Service: 1920'S
Submitter's Name: Theodore
City/State: Chicago, IL

Registrant ID: 2537
Name: Charles McCoy
City/State: AL
Railroad: Rock Island Railroad
Position: Porter
Years of Service: 1950 - 1960
Submitter's Name: Vivian
City/State: Hercules, CA

Comments: I'm not sure about the years of service. I don't have access to my father's records. He worked for Rock Island Railroad even after they discontinued passenger service.

Registrant ID: 2540
Name: Howard James McCray
City/State: El Paso, TX
Railroad: Southern Pacific
Position: Pullman Porter
Years of Service: 1947 - 1963
Submitter's Name: Juanita
City/State: El Paso, TX
Comments: Route was from El Paso, Texas to Pecos, Texas and points beyond. He was one of 15 local African-American men working on the Southern Pacific and the Santa Fe Railroads.

Registrant ID: 2541
Name: Samuel McCray
City/State: New York, NY
Submitter's Name: Deidra
City/State: New York, NY

Registrant ID: 2543
Name: Richard T. McDade
City/State: Jellico, TN
Years of Service: 1930's
Submitter(s): Shirley,Grace
City/State: Milwaukee, WI

Registrant ID: 2544
Milton Lindsey McDaniels, Sr.
City/State: Lakewood, CA
Position: Pullman Porter
Submitter's Name: Milton
City/State: Lakewood, CA

Registrant ID: 2546
Lonnie Walter Mc Donald

Position: Pullman Porter
Years of Service: 1940-1959
Submitter's Name: Jeannette
City/State: Cerritos, CA
Comments: Lonnie Walter McDonald was my grandfather. He passed away when I was only six years old.

Registrant ID: 2545
Name: Lonnie Mc Donald
City/State: AL
Railroad: Union Pacific/Santa Fe
Position: Pullman Porter
Years of Service: 1940-1959
Submitter's Name: Jeannette
City/State: Cerritos, CA
Comments: This is information on my grandfather. I am not sure of the exact dates of service.

Registrant ID: 2547
Name: Elijah Mc Duffie
City/State: Boston, MA
Position: Porter
Years of Service: 1923-39
Submitter's Name: Gloria
City/State: Madison, IL
Comments: He was my father

Registrant ID: 2548
Name: Kiah (JD) Mc Elroy
City/State: Newton, MS
Position: Pullman Porter
Years of Service: Early 1900's
Submitter's Name: Theresa
City/State: East Lansing, MI
Comments: He was my great uncle that worked for the railroad.

Registrant ID: 2550
Name: Walter Mc Elroy
City/State: MN

City/State: Foster City, CA

Registrant ID: 2552
Name: Bland Mc Ferren
City/State: Chicago, IL
Position: Dining Car Waiter
Years of Service: 1936-1966
Submitter's Name: Louis
City/State: Philadelphia, PA

Registrant ID: 2553
Name: F.A. McGee
Position: Pullman Porter
Years of Service: Over 25
Comments: B.S.C.P. member

Registrant ID: 2557
Name: Walter McGhee
City/State: IL
Position: various
Submitter's Name: Ruby
City/State: Detroit, MI
Comments: He was my husband.

Registrant ID: 2558
Name: Hoy McGill
City/State: Minneapolis, MN
Railroad: Burlington Northern and Amtrak
Position: Cook and train attendant
Years of Service: 1965 - 1975
Submitter's Name: Hoyt
City/State: Minneapolis, MN
Comments: My father was hired as a private business car cook for the Northern Pacific Railroad after retiring from the U.S. Army as a cook. Northern Pacific Railroad and the Great Northern Railroad merged forming the Burlington Northern Railroad. Around 1970, the U.S

government acquired all passenger service in the USA forming Amtrak. Hoy McGill died on June 26,1997 at the age 81. Among the many celebrities he met and served aboard the trains were James Brown. Muhammad Ali and Duke Ellington.

Registrant ID: 2559
Name: Russell McGinnis
City/State: AL
Railroad: Southern Pacific
Position: Chair Car Porter
Years of Service: 33
Submitter's Name: Adrian
City/State: El Paso, TX
Comments: I never heard my father (deceased) complain about going to work. I know it was very hard, demanding work. Yet, we always had food on our table. I currently have some memorabilia from his many years as a porter. His work ranged over a wide area.

Registrant ID: 2560
Name: James McGoings
City/State: MD
Submitter's Name: Michael
City/State: Fort Washington, MD
Comments: He was my father

Registrant ID: 2561
Name: Elridge McHenry Farris
City/State: Pittsburgh, PA
Railroad: Penn. Railroad
Position: Sleeping Car Porter
Submitter's Name: Geraldine
City/State: Pittsburgh, PA
Comments: My father in-law

Registrant ID: 2565
Name: Alexander McIntosh

City/State: Hollis, NY
Railroad: New York Central
Position: Pullman Porter for the Commodore Vanderbilt
Years of Service: 30 years
Submitter's Name: Alice
City/State: Hollis, NY
Comments: I can remember visits from A. Philip Randolph to our home on Convent Avenue in NYC; such a gentleman; the treatment changed dramatically once unionization took place. Even as a child I can remember my father praising Asa's efforts and ultimate success.

Registrant ID: 2567
Name: John S. McLver Sr.
City/State: Chicago, IL
Railroad: Union Pacific
Position: Pullman Porter
Years 32 (1927 to 1959)
Submitter's Name: John S.
City/State: Chicago, IL
Comments: He was my father. He worked from Chicago to the west cost on the North Westen,UP & The Burling Northern. They would bid on the Line they wanted to work. The man with the most seniority would get the bid. The longer the train ride the more money the men made.

Registrant ID: 2570
Name: Ramsom Mckay
City/State: Chicago, IL
Position: Porter
Submitter's Name: Joslyn
City/State: Chicago, IL
Comments: Granddaughter

Registrant ID: 2569
Name: Norman McKay
City/State: Pass Christian, MS
Railroad: L&N
Position: Pullman Porter
Years of Service: 1930's- 40's
Submitter's Name: Shawn
City/State: Spotslyvania, VA
Comments: My Uncle Norman said, he would work the lines from the Mississippi to as far west to California, and also east and north up to New York. My Uncle passed away at 90 years old with a good mind and at peace in May of 1987. Interesting to note, my mother was just telling me she can remember him talking about Dr. Carver whom he called the "Peanut Man" getting on the train in Tuskeegee, Alabama to go and "Beg for money, for research!"

Registrant ID: 2571
Name: Claborne McKneel
City/State: AL
Railroad: Milwaukee Road
Position: Pullman Porter
Years of Service: 55
Submitter's Name: Susan
City/State: Milwaukee, WI

Registrant ID: 2572
Name: John McKinnel Oneal
City/State: St. Paul, MN
Position: Porter
Years of Service: 1800-1959
Submitter's: Ana and Ora Lee
City/State: St. Paul, MN

Registrant ID: 2575
Name: Washington Mckinney

City/State: Chicago, IL
Railroad: Santa Fe/Amtrak
Position: Waiter, Sleeping Car Porter, Steward
Years of Service: 1947 - 1987
Submitter's Name: Daryl
City/State: Chicago, IL

Registrant ID: 2576
Name: Thomas McKinney Sr.
City/State: Holly Springs, MS
Railroad: Frisco Railroad (maybe short for San Francisco)
Position: Repairman for rails and tracks
Years of Service: Worked 47 years.Retired in the 1950's
Submitter's Name: Donna
City/State: Austell, GA
Comments: Thomas McKinney, Sr. was my maternal great-grandfather. He retired in the 1950's after 47 years of service. Shortly before he retired a motor car had run over one of his legs. He passed in 1966. I am fortunate to have 5 generations living on both sides.

Registrant ID: 2577
Name: Charles McKinnley
City/State: Memphis, TN
Railroad: Santa Fe Railroad
Position: Cook/Dishwasher
Years of Service: 1963-1969

Registrant ID: 2578
Name: James Leroy McKnight
City/State: AL
Railroad: Santa Fe
Position: Head Waiter
Years of Service: 1941 to 1950
Submitter's Name: Jennie
City/State: Fillmore, CA

Comments: My father worked on the train that took the troops from Ohio to California. He was stationed in Ohio and would be gone five days and return for two days during the second World War. At times we did not know where he was going.

Registrant ID: 2580
Name: Charlie McLaddie
City/State: Augusta, GA
Railroad: Atlantic Coast Line
Position: Pullman Porter
Years of Service: 1940's
Submitter's Name: Laverte
City/State: Augusta, GA
Comments: He went from New York to Augusta Ga., that was his route.

Registrant ID: 2581
Name: Jackson McLean
City/State: South Orange, NJ
Railroad: Seaboard Railway co
Years of Service: 1926-1970
Submitter's Name: Patricia
City/State: South Orange, NJ
Comments: Grandfather. His brother Anderson Nowde Seaboard 1926-1972

Registrant ID: 2582
Name: George McLendon
City/State: Daytona Beach, FL
Railroad: Pullman Company
Position: Locomotive Fireman
Years of Service: 1952-1960

Registrant ID: 2584
Name: Leonard "Pop" McLendor
City/State: Chicago, IL
Railroad: Pullman Company
Position: Pullman Porter

Years of Service: 1942-1962

Registrant ID: 2588
Name: Augusta (Gus) McMillian
Railroad: Pullman Company
Position: Pullman Porter
Years of Service: 1945-1955
Submitter's Name: Jone

Registrant ID: 2586
Name: Augusta McMillian
City/State: St. Louis, MO
Position: Porter
Submitter's Name: Maureen
City/State: St. Louis , MO

Registrant ID: 2589
Name: Albert N.McMinn
City/State: Chicago, IL
Years of Service: circa 1930's
Submitter's Name: Barbara
City/State: Chicago, IL
Comments: Uncle by marriage

Registrant ID: 2590
Name: Ernest McNeeley
City/State: Chicago, IL
Railroad: Northwestern RR
Position: Pullman Porter
Years of Service: 1929-69
Submitter's Name: Zelia
City/State: Chicago, IL

Registrant ID: 2592
Name: Lacy Lee McNeil
City/State: Hamlet, NC
Railroad: He was my Grandfather
However, my knowledge is limited. I only know that he worked the East coast and lines between Raleigh N.C. and Richmond VA
Position: Porter

Years of Service: Early 1900's
Submitter's Name: William M.
City/State: Raleigh, NC
Comments: I know my Grandfather as a proud man but of course some of his experiences were very humiliating because of the time period.

Registrant ID: 2593
Name: Gaston McNorton
City/State: Cincinnati, OH
Railroad: Louisville & Nashville and Florida.
Position: Waiter
Years of Service: 1940-1960
Submitter's Name: Simon
City/State: Chicago, IL
Comments: Gaston McNorton was my cousin, Gaston died in 1968 at the age of 68

Registrant ID: 2594
Name: David D. McPheeters, Sr.
City/State: Cincinnati, OH
Position: Pullman Porter
Years of Service: 1917-1964
Submitter's Name: Irma M.
City/State: Cincinnati, OH

Registrant ID: 2600
Name: Daniel Mc Poride
City/State: Desoto, TX
Railroad: Illinois Central
Position: Porters
Years of Service: 20's-60's
Submitter's Name: Jimmie
City/State: Desoto, TX
Comments: Great Uncle

Registrant ID: 2601
Name: Edward McQuirter
Position: Pullman Porter
Years of Service: 25 Plus

Comments: B.S.C.P union member.

Registrant ID: 2603
Name: Rufus Mc Rae
City/State: Wilmington, NC
Railroad: Atlantic Coastline
Position: Fireman
Years: 1940s' thru late 50s'
Submitter's Name: Melvin
City/State: Richmond, VA
Comments: Mr. McRae was a fireman and was instrumental in introducing me into the railroad industry. I am a Conductor with AMTRAK since 1973. Although Mr. McRae was not a relative of mine he was a surrogate grandfather who also was a neighbor and helped raise me.

Registrant ID: 2608
Name: Cornelius Mc Sween
City/State: Harlem, NY
Railroad: whatever was going through North Carolina (Hamlet) or nearby at the time.
Years : Circa1920-s to 1950's
Submitter's Name: Ervina
City/State: Queens Village, NY

Registrant ID: 2606
Name: Clemmie Mc Sween
City/State: Queens, NY
Railroad: whatever was going through North Carolina (Hamlet) or nearby at the time.
Years of Service: Circa 1920's-50's
Submitter's Name: Ervina
City/State: Queens Village, NY

Registrant ID: 2609
Name: Frank McSween Jr.

City/State: Toms River, NJ
Position: Pullman Porter
Years of Service: 30-50
Comments: I am submitting this information for him he is the only one still alive. I don't have all of the details but they were definitely there from all of the stories I heard as a little girl.

Registrant ID: 2610
Name: Frank Mc Sween Sr.
City/State: Marston/Hamlet, NC
Railroad: whatever was going through North Carolina (Hamlet)
Years: Circa 1920's 50's
Submitter's Name: Ervina
City/State: Queens Village, NY
Comments: He was my grandfather, several of my uncles also worked on the railroad. That was the only decent work available for African-American men during that time period. They were very proud of their jobs.

Registrant ID: 2612
James Washington McWherter
City/State: East Saint Louis, IL
Railroad: Pullman Company
Position: Sleeping Car Porter
Years of Service: 1924-1960
Submitter's: Iris . Lewis, Ollie
City/State: Chesterfield, MO
Comments: My father worked out of the Union Station in St Louis Missouri until he retired. He lived only about Six months after retiring. I knew all of the Pullman Porters in East St. Louis, Illinois where I grew up. I have many warm memories of

him. Iris stated: "My father, James W. McWherter, was a member of the Sleeping Car Porter union for years, and worked as a Pullman porter for approximately 36 years. Because of the teaching and foundation given to us by my father, we have achieved some degree of success in our careers. I am one of his 7 children which are all still alive. My father emphasized education, and integrity to his children. He would have been proud to know that all of his children have went on to become professionals, and I believe, people of character. I am an attorney with licenses in Texas, Illinois, and several other federal venues, my 2 sisters both hold master degrees, one brother previously served as assistant police chief in Centerville, Illinois, another brother retired from general motors in Detroit, and a sister taught at Grambling University, and currently works for the United States government at Redstone Arsenal, Huntsville, Alabama."

Registrant ID: 2613
Name: Oscar Mc Williams
City/State: Beckville, TX
Railroad: Santa Fe Railroad
Position: Track Worker
Years of Service: 25 Years
Submitter's Name: Sandra
City/State: Glenn Heights, TX
Comments: He's dead now, but he worked on the railroad for years. He was my grandfather. The train track ran in front of my grandfather house. When I was a

young girl I would watch my grandfather leave early every Monday morning and return Friday evening.

Registrant ID: 2614
Name: Jerry Mead
City/State: Philadelphia, PA
Position: Porter
Years of Service: 1942-46
Submitter's Name: Lillie
City/State: Philadelphia, PA
Comments: Daughter of a Porter

Registrant ID: 2615
Name: Larry Meade
City/State: Grand Blanc, MI
Railroad: Amtrak
Position: Sleeping Car Porter aka On-Board-Service-Attendant
Years of Service: June 1973-76
Comments: I am very grateful to have been associated with the men who spent their entire careers as Pullman Porters. They took me under their wings and taught me the ropes as a Sleeping Car Porter (Mr. Rahn Workcuff of Minneapolis, MN,in particular.

Registrant ID: 2616
Name: Horace Mealing
City/State: Chicago, IL
Railroad: Santa Fe - El Captain Route Chicago to San Francisco
Position: Porter
Submitter's Name: Janeen
City/State: Missour City, TX
Comments: My grandfather (deceased) retired from the railroad in the early 1970's.

Registrant ID: 2622
Name: Richard Meek
City/State: Knoxville, TN
Submitter's Name: Edith
City/State: Manfield, OH

Registrant ID: 2621
Name: Fred Meek
City/State: New York, NY
Submitter's Name: Edith
City/State: Manfield, OH

Registrant ID: 2624
Name: Everett Menzie
Position: Porter
Submitter's Name: Marion

Registrant ID: 2625
Name: James H. Mercer
City/State: VA
Railroad: My Grandfather James H. Mercer:Norfolk, Va.to New York
Position: Pullman Porter
Years of Service: 1928-1935
Submitter's Name: Cindy
City/State: New York, NY
Comments: This is so wonderful and I'm proud to be a part of this project! Thank you! Cindy

Registrant ID: 2626
Name: Benjamin Meredith
City/State: New York, NY
Submitter's Name: Bomani
City/State: Winston-Salem, NC
Comments: I don't have any additional information about my great-grandfather's experiences working on the railroad. my great-grandfather's worked as Pullman Porter.

Registrant ID: 2627
James Walter Meriwether
City/State: KY

Position: Porter
Years of Service: 30's - 50's
Submitter's Name: Keith Eric
City/State: Louisville, KY
Comments: Worked for many years as a Porter on the railroad. He moved his family from Clarksville, TN to Memphis, TN to Louisville, KY because of his railroad work. We believe he was employed until 1959.

Registrant ID: 2629
Name: John Merritt
City/State: Oakland, CA
Position: Dining Car Chief
Submitter's Name: Narvelle
City/State: Erie, CO

Registrant ID: 2630
Name: John Albert Meriwether
City/State: Oakland, CA
Railroad: Southern Pacific
Position: Dinning Car Waiter, Dining Car Steward
Years of Service: 1940 to 1968
Submitter's: Colleen & Paul
City/State: Shreveport, LA Oakland, California.
Comments: Met many friends on the railroad. Met many famous people while working for southern pacific, Lucille Ball and many others.

Registrant ID: 2632
Name: Ernest Meshack
City/State: CA
Railroad: Southern Pacific
Position: Sleeping Car Porter
Years: Approx 1944 to 1970
Submitter's Name: Diane
City/State: Richmond, CA

Comments: My father told us many times about being in Atlanta, GA with $70 in his pocket and could not buy a sandwich because of his race; the time he tried to buy a newspaper, but was told "niggers can't read".

Registrant ID: 2634
Name: Walter Meyers Metcalfe
City/State: Fullerton, CA
Position: Porter
Years of Service: Early to Mid 1900's
Submitter's Name: Alice
City/State: Fullerton, CA

Registrant ID: 2635
Name: Rasmus Mgee
City/State: Chicago, IL
Position: Pullman Porter
Years of Service: Up to 1929 the year he died
Submitter's Name: Robert
City/State: Chicago, IL

Registrant ID: 2637
Name: Albert Mickens Mgee
City/State: Pittsburgh, PA
Railroad: Pennsylvania Central
Position: Pullman
Years of Service: 1945-1975
Submitter's Name: Gloria
City/State: Bradenton, FL

Registrant ID: 2638
Name: Grant Mickins
City/State: Jacksonville, FL
Railroad: Seaboard Coastline
Position: Pullman Porter
Years of Service: 1917-1961
Submitter's Name: Laura
City/State: Jacksonville, FL

Comments: He was my father. His run was Chicago St Louis East Coast originally out of Jacksonville worked for 44 years.

Registrant ID: 2640
Name: Charles Middleton
City/State: TX
Railroad: Unknown-He worked the south and eastern part of US
Position: Pullman Porter
Years of Service: 1942-43
Submitter's Name: Charles
City/State: San Antonio, TX
Comments: It was during the war. He was rejected from military service and required to work on the railroad.

Registrant ID: 2641
Name: Alfonso Middleton
City/State: Detroit, Michigan
Railroad: Pullman Company
Position: Track Builder
Years of Service: 1863-1950
Submitter's Name: Bedrick

Registrant ID: 2642
Name: Berney Miles
City/State: Cincinnati, OH
Position: Pullman Porter
Years of Service: 1922 -
Submitter's Name: Charles
City/State: Cincinnati, OH

Registrant ID: 2660
William David "Dave" Miller
City/State: DC
Railroad: Pullman Co./C&O/B&O Railroad & AMTRAK
Position: Pullman Car Porter - Amtrak trainer/evaluator
Years of Service: 40

Submitter's Name: J
City/State: MD
Comments: Was a union Steward and Local union President. He was inspired by the late A. Phillip Randolph, who visited Miller's Washington, DC home and family. Providing historic research and narrative information about the Brotherhood of Sleeping Car Porters.

Registrant ID: 2655
Name: Robert H. Miller
City/State: Chicago, IL
Position: Pullman Porter
Years of Service: Circa 1930's
Submitter's Name: Barbara
City/State: Chicago, IL
Comments: He was my father

Registrant ID: 2656
Name: Vernon Miller
City/State: Niles, MI
Railroad: New York Central and Penn Central
Position: Dining Car Waiter
Years of Service: 37 years
Submitter's Name: Claudette
City/State: Chicago, IL

Registrant ID: 2657
Name: Vernon Lee Miller
City/State: Niles, Michigan
Railroad: Pullman Rail Car Co.
Position: Dining Car Waiter
Years of Service: 1940's-1950's
Submitter's Name: Claudette Chg & Elenore Wash D.C
City/State: Chicago, IL
Comments: He was our father

Registrant ID: 2659
Name: William Miller
City/State: IL
Railroad: New York Central and Penn Central
Position: Dining Car Waiter
Years of Service: Circa 1932-1968
Submitter's Name: Norris
City/State: Fremont, CA
Comments: Bill Miller was my dad. He was a Dining Car Waiter on the New York Central until it was taken over by Penn Central. Eventually, he had to take medical leave until retirement due to hernia's from lifting the heavy trays.

Registrant ID: 2644
Name: Birce Miller
City/State: Louisville, KY
Position: Pullman Porter
Years of Service: 1950-1980
Submitter's Name: Harriet
City/State: Louisville, KY

Registrant ID: 2651
Name: Matthew Miller
City/State: IL
Railroad: New York Central
Position: Waiter
Submitter's Name: Audrey
City/State: Matteson, IL
Comments: My father went to work shortly after World War I he worked until his death in 1937. I don't know the exact year he started. My Uncle also worked for railroad and my older brother.

Registrant ID: 2646
Name: George Miller

City/State: Jersey City, NJ
Railroad: Erie Lackawanna-- Belford 99 Car and the Jersey Central
Position: Special Chef for the Railroad President
Years of Service: 47
Submitter's Name: Leslie
City/State: Mt.Vernon, NY
Comments: My Grandfather, George Miller served as Special Chef to the Belford 99 owner George Baker and past Presidents G.W. Maxwell and Perry M. Shoemaker. Mr. Miller was loved and respected by all. He was a dedicated and loyal employee of the railroad.

Registrant ID: 2647
George Arthur Lee Miller
City/State: NY
Railroad: Pennsylvania R. R.
Position: Porter
Submitter's Name: Harold B.
City/State: New York, NY
Comments: My father, as a young man, experienced a great opportunity to travel and raise his children in New York City.

Registrant ID: 2653
Name: Noble Miller
City/State: Tyler, TX
Railroad: Southern Pacific
Position: Porter
Submitter's Name: Kashan
City/State: Oakland, CA
Comments: I wish I could give you more but my relative is deceased.

Registrant ID: 2648
Name: Joe Miller

City/State: Tyler, TX
Railroad: Cotton Belt
Position: Storeman
Submitter's Name: Kashan
City/State: Oakland, CA
Comments: Relative deceased

Registrant ID: 2645
Name: Ferdinand Miller
City/State: AL
Submitter's Name: Ethel M.
City/State: Orange, New Jersey, NJ

Registrant ID: 2650
Name: Levi Miller
City/State: Philadelphia, PA
Position: Track Worker
Years of Service: 1920's
Submitter's Name: Jacqulyene
City/State: Philadelphia, PA

Registrant ID: 2662
Name: Reuben Miller Jr.
City/State: Tyler, TX
Railroad: Cotton Belt
Position: Warehouseman
Submitter's Name: Kashan
City/State: Oakland, CA

Registrant ID: 2665
Name: Oliver A. Millet
City/State: AL
Railroad: Southern Pacific
Position: Lounge Car Porter
Years of Service: 1905 - 1945
Submitter's Name: Ann
City/State: Orinda, CA
Comments: My father ran on the Del Monte Express, San Francisco to Pacific Grove, CA for 37 years. When he retired the car was named OLIVER MILLET

after him as a tribute to his excellent service....the only employee in the history of Southern Pacific to have a car.

Registrant ID: 2666
Name: Curtis Mills
City/State: Mount Vernon, NY
Railroad: Pennsylvania RR
Position: Porter/mail porter
Years of Service: 1940-1960
Submitter's Name: Donna
City/State: Bronx, NY
Comments: My father remembers marching in Harlem with Rev. Adam Clayton Powell to force big employers and corporations to hire Black people. He then got the job at the railroad.

Registrant ID: 2667
Name: Joe Mills
City/State: Compeville, KY
Railroad: L&N RR
Position: Labor Machine Operator
Years of Service: 1942-1975
Submitter's Name: Mills

Registrant ID: 2668
Name: William Mills
City/State: Elmont, NY
Railroad: Atlantic Coast Line
Position: Pullman Porter
Years of Service: 1922-1959
Submitter's Name: William
City/State: Elmont, NY
Comments: He was a member of the new York executive board Brotherhood Of Sleeping Car Porters.

Registrant ID: 2669
Name: James Milner
City/State: Philadelphia, PA
Railroad: Pennsylvania & Redding
Position: Dinning Car Porter
Submitter's Name: Barbara
City/State: Philadelphia, PA
Comments: Grandfather

Registrant ID: 2671
Name: Connie Milson
City/State: AL
Railroad: El Paso
Years of Service: 1977's
Submitter's Name: Lawrence
City/State: AL

Registrant ID: 2676
Name: Willie Milter
City/State: Junction City, KS
Railroad: Erie Lackawanna
Position: Sleeping Car Porter
Years: Circa 1930's-54
Submitter's Name: Dorothy
City/State: Junction City, KS
Comments: Grandfather retired in 53's

Registrant ID: 2679
Name: Mr. Mims
City/State: Upper Marlboro, MD
Position: Pullman Porter
Years of Service: 1932-1962
Submitter's Name: A. Bradley

Registrant ID: 2678
Name: Bobby Mims
City/State: Unknown - last known was Pasadena, CA, AL
Railroad: Santa Fe Railway
Position: Porter
Years of Service: late1940's-50's
Submitter's Name: Kimberly

City/State: Garland, TX

Registrant ID: 2679
Name: Brodley A Mims
Position: Sleeping Car Porter
Years of Service: 1932-1962
Submitter's Name: Brodley A
City/State: Upper Malboro, MD
Comments: Grandfather

Registrant ID: 2681
Name: James Mingo
City/State: Philadelphia, PA
Years of Service: 1940s-1950s
Submitter's Name: Cyndi
City/State: Philadelphia, PA
Comments: It was my (uncle) Grandpa, James Mingo.

Registrant ID: 2682
Name: Arthur Levi
City/State: Great Falls, MT
Railroad: Great Northern
Years: Approx 1948 to 1953
Submitter's Name: Linda Joyce
City/State: Bellevue, WA
Comments: My father is deceased. He passed away Sept. 6, 1997. I can't remember the exact dates that he worked for Great Northern.

Registrant ID: 2707
Name: Simon Mitchell
Railroad: Pullman Rail Car Co.
Position: Sleeping Car Porter
Years of Service: 30yrs
Submitter's Name: H Mark
Comments: Simon was my uncle. Rout was from Honce to Columbus Mississippi.

Registrant ID: 2689
Name: Charles Mitchell

City/State: St. Louis, MO
Railroad: Wabash
Position: Dining Car Waiter
Years: 1935 Retired 1969
Submitter's Name: Lynn
City/State: Bethlehem, PA
Comments: Mr. Swann's father was a railroad employee before him. He quit high school in the 9th grade and went to work as a waiter. He never took a sick day and, he had one job all his adult life. He always told us to make sure you were called by your correct name.

Registrant ID: 2700
Name: Harry S. Mitchell
City/State: Washington, DC
Position: 2nd Cook
Years of Service: 1948-1951
Submitter's Name: Mary
City/State: Bronx, NY

Registrant ID: 2683
Name: Ben Henry Mitchell
Railroad: B & O Railroad
Position: Porter
Years of Service: 1968 -
Submitter's Name: Charles
City/State: Brooklyn, NY

Registrant ID: 2697
Name: Fannie Mae Mitchell
Railroad: B & O Railroad
Position: Porter
Years of Service: 1968-
Submitter's Name: Charles
City/State: Brooklyn, NY

Registrant ID: 2696
Name: Ernest T. Mitchell
Position: Train Attendant
Years of Service: 1942-1983

Submitter's Name: Julia
City/State: Chicago, IL
Registrant ID: 2705
Name: Lloyd Mitchell
City/State: Dallas, TX
Railroad: Union Terminal
Position: Baggage Porter
Submitter's Name: Vickie
City/State: Dallas, TX
Comments: He worked for the railroad for many years and white 18 & 19 years olds were hired to spite him. He was extremely intelligent and knew everything there was to know from scheduling to maintenance of the equipment. Unfortunately because of the racist conditions he could not advance.

Registrant ID: 2692
Name: Edgar E. Mitchell
City/State: Cleveland, OH
Railroad: New York Central
Position: Pullman Porter
Years of Service: 1930-1968
Submitter's Name: Gary
City/State: Dothan, AL
Comments: As far as I can remember my uncle worked on the New York Central Line, but he also worked other lines that went south from Cleveland before I was born. in 1949

Registrant ID: 2709
Name: William "Will" Mitchell
City/State: Jacksonville, FL
Position: Pullman Porter
Years: mid 1920's
Submitter's Name: J'Neane
City/State: Jacksonville, FL
Comments: " Will" was my grandmother's father.

Registrant ID: 2694
Name: Edward Mitchell
City/State: New Orleans, LA
Position: Pullman Porter
Years of Service: 1940's
Submitter's: Ida Lorraine and Linda
City/State: Minneapolis, MS
Comments: Uncle

Registrant ID: 2690
Name: Daniel Webster Mitchell
City/State: Montgomery, AL
Position: Porter
Years of Service: 1937-66
Submitter's Name: Willodean
City/State: Montgomery, AL

Registrant ID: 2710
Name: William B. Mitchell
City/State: OK
Submitter's Name: Gregory
City/State: San Francisco, CA

Registrant ID: 2712
Name: Chester A. Mitchell Sr.
City/State: Atlanta and Athens, GA
Railroad: Southern Railroad
Position: Pullman Porter
Years of Service: 1-3 years
Submitter's Name: Kathryn
City/State: Chicago, IL
Comments: My grandfather, Chester A. Mitchell, Sr. was a Pullman Porter. We don't have much information about his experiences, but we do know he worked for the Southern Railroad in Georgia for a short period between 1910 to 1917. My father says he resigned because of the racism.

Registrant ID: 2715
Name: Kenneth Mizes
City/State: Chicago, IL
Railroad: Union Pacific
Position: Pullman Porter
Submitter's Name: Wesley
City/State: Chicago, IL

Registrant ID: 2716
Name: Eugene Mobley
City/State: Jacksonville, FL
Railroad: Fruit Growers Express
Position: Mechanic
Years of Service: 27
Submitter's Name: Willie Mae
City/State: Jacksonville, FL

Registrant ID: 2720
Name: Charles Henry Monroe
City/State: Nashville, TN
Submitter's Name: Carolyn

Registrant ID: 2721
Name: Lee Monroe
City/State: IL
Railroad: Pullman
Position: Porter
Submitter's Name: Lynda
City/State: Chicago, IL

Registrant ID: 2725
Name: Willie Monroe Sr.
City/State: VA
Railroad: Chesapeake & Ohio
Position: Porter
Years of Service: 1940s
Submitter's Name: Willie
City/State: El Cajon, CA
Comments: My father retired from the C&O Railroad. He was employed out of Richmond, Va. I do know he possibly made runs from Richmond to Chicago. I

have very little information about
his time with the railroad.

Registrant ID: 2726
Name: Yvonne Monterio
City/State: Louisville, KY
Railroad: L N railroad
And Cottontail Ohio
Position: Pullman Porter
Years: 30 years 6 months
Submitter's Name: Robert
City/State: Louisville, KY
Comments: My mother always
told me that when she attended
Kentucky State college she would
go and meet the train and her
father would through money off
the train to her as it passed
through.

Registrant ID: 2733
Name: Charles Montgomery
City/State: Chicago, IL
Position: Porter in Dining Car
Years of Service: 1930's - 1950's
Submitter's Name: Robert E.
City/State: Chicago, IL
Comments: He will be 82 years
old, the 18th of Feb

Registrant ID: 2734
Name: Otis Montgomery
City/State: Waxhaw, NC
Railroad: Southern Railroad
Position: Laid tracks
Years of Service: Approx 40 Yrs
Submitter's Name: Georgia
City/State: Pikesville, MD

Registrant ID: 2735
Name: Hutella (Mack) Monts
City/State: Little Rock, AK

Position: Chef
Years of Service: 1949-50
Submitter's Name: Kenneth
City/State: Houston, TX

Registrant ID: 2736
Name: George Moody
City/State: Chicago, IL
Railroad: The Pullman Company
and Amtrak
Position: Pullman Porter
Years of Service: 1939 - 1979
Submitter's Name: Thaddeus
City/State: Chicago, IL
Comments: My grandfather
started at the age of 14 working
for the railroad. Amtrak made
him retire in 1979. He told me
many great stories about A.
Philip Randolph.

Registrant ID: 2741
Name: David E Mooney
City/State: St. Louis, Mo, MO
Railroad: Wabash/Golden Eagle
Position: Pullman Porter
Years of Service: 1952-1961
Submitter's Name: Alverta
City/State: St. Louis , MO
Comments: Worked the St.
Louis to Chicago to Detroit route
frequently, out of Union Station
in St. Louis Missouri.

Registrant ID: 2743
Name: Cleveland Moore
City/State: St. Louis, MO
Railroad: Missouri Pacific
Position: Car Cleaner
Years: 25 YRS 1941-1966
Submitter's Name: Percy
City/State: St. Louis, MO

Registrant ID: 2744
Name: Dorsey Moore
City/State: AL
Position: Pullman Porter
Submitter's Name: Ellena
City/State: Oak Park, MI
Comments: I have no information concerning Dorsey Moore other than information that he was a Pullman Porter. He had five children with Ella Mae White. Their names are Harold, Marie, Gwendolyn Louise, Lucy Catherine and Betty Jane.

Registrant ID: 2747
Name: Eugene Moore
City/State: Atlanta, GA
Railroad: The Pullman Co.
Position: Porter- In-Charge
Years of Service: 1944-1955

Registrant ID: 2761
Name: Otho L. Moore
City/State: Indianapolis, IN
Railroad: Pullman Co., Pennsylvania RR, AMTRAK
Position: Porter, Attendant
Years of Service: 1942-1989

Registrant ID: 2762
Name: Robert Moore
City/State: AL
Position: Pullman Porter
Years of Service: 1937-1941
Submitter's Name: Ellen
City/State: Capitol Heights, MD

Registrant ID: 2763
Name: Rudolph Moore
City/State: North Branford,CT
Railroad: NY Central and the Atlantic Coastline Railroad

Position: Dining Car Waiter
Years of Service: New York Central 1948-1949
Atlantic Coastline 1950-1952
Registrant ID: 2767
Name: Sotho L. Moore
City/State: Indianapolis, IN
Position: Pullman Porter
Years of Service: 1942-1969

Registrant ID: 2769
Name: Thorton Moore
City/State: Anderson, IN
Position: Porter
Submitter's Johnnie
City/State: Anderson, IN

Registrant ID: 2753
Name: James Moore
City/State: CA
Railroad: Western Pacific
Position: Dining Car Waiter
Years of Service: Approximately 30 years retired
Submitter's Name: Queen E.
City/State: Oakland, CA

Registrant ID: 2760
Name: John Ester Moore
City/State: LA
Railroad: Union Pacific RR
Years of Service: 1949-1966
Submitter's Name: Annie
City/State: Shreveport, LA
Comments: My father worked on the railroad from 1949-1966. He died on the job in Green River, Wyoming. His home base was Salt Lake City, Utah to Los Angeles, CA. He often told us that he did various jobs i.e. shined shoes, made beds, carried luggage, etc.

Registrant ID: 2774
William Henry, Sr. Moore
City/State: AL
Railroad: Rock Island
Position: Dining Car Waiter
Years of Service: 1894 - 1940
Submitter's Name: Marie
City/State: Tuskegee, AL
Comments: Additional relatives
who are deceased: Alfred G.
Moore who worked in Round
House in Manly Iowa from about
1921-1972; others were all
Dining Car Waiters - Gage C.
Moore (father)1924-1934;
Booker W. Moore from about
1930-1972; Aaron E. Moore circa
1940

Registrant ID: 2748
Name: Harold Moore
City/State: Zion, IL
Railroad: Chg South
Submitter's Name: Pat
City/State: Zion, IL

Registrant ID: 2777
Name: Joseph E. Moore
City/State: Chicago, IL
Railroad: Burlington
Position: Pullman Porters
Years of Service: 1938-1978
Submitter's Name: Joseph E.
City/State: Chicago, IL

Registrant ID: 2777
Name: Jackie B.Morehead
City/State: Little Rock, AR
Years of Service: 1967-1994
Submitter's Name: M.L.
City/State: Little Rock, AR

Registrant ID: 2782
Name: Richard Morgan

City/State: Lithonia, GA
Railroad: Burlington Northern
Position: Dining Car Waiter
Years of Service: 1969-1970
Comments: I worked on the
railroad during the summer
months (June-September). This
allowed me to earn funds to help
finance my college education.
The two summers I worked were
in 1969 and 1970.during the fall,
I attended the University of
Georgia.

Registrant ID: 2779
Name: Albert Morgan
City/State: Chicago, IL
Railroad: Santa Fe Railroad
Position: Buffet Porter
Years of Service: 1937-1942
Submitter's Name: Stephanie
City/State: Chicago, IL

Registrant ID: 2780
Name: Charlie Morgan
City/State: Detroit, MI
Position: Porter
Years of Service: Early 1900's
Submitter's Name: Edda
City/State: Detroit, MI
Comments: Lived and worked
out of Mississippi.

Registrant ID: 2784
Name: Robert A. Morgan
City/State: AL
Railroad: Ogden,UT, Kansas City
MO
Position: Cook and Dining Car
Waiter
Years of Service: 1895-1917
Submitter's Name: Monique
City/State: Fairburn, GA

Comments: We know that he died in 1917 and was in his early thirties so the dates of service are and estimated date. (Ogden, UT)

Registrant ID: 2785
Name: Wilbert O.C. Morgan
City/State: Temple Hills, MD
Railroad: B & O
Position: Pullman Porter
Years of Service: 1963-1964
Submitter's Name: Linda
City/State: Temple Hills, MD

Registrant ID: 2786
Name: Ross L. Morgan Sr.
City/State: AL
Railroad: New York Central
Position: Pullman Porter
Years of Service: 1924 -1954
Submitter's Name: Ross L.
City/State: Richmond, VA

Registrant ID: 2787
Name: William
City/State: St. Louis, MO
Railroad: Wabash-Norfolk-Western
Position: Waiter-in-Charge
Years of Service: 1940-1967
Comments: I enjoyed it very much, as I met a lot of different people and traveled quite a lot.

Registrant ID: 2792
Name: H.L Morris
Railroad: El Paso
Submitter's: Lawrence, Lars

Registrant ID: 2798
Name: William Morris
City/State: Philadelphia, PA
Years of Service: 1922-1935

Submitter's Name: William
City/State: NJ

Registrant ID: 2791
Name: Frank Morris
City/State: NY
Position: Porter
Submitter's Name: Margurite
City/State: Hampstead, NY

Registrant ID: 2790
Name: Benjamin F. Morris
City/State: AL
Railroad: Santa Fe
Position: Pullman Porter
Submitter's Name: Paul W.
City/State: Las Vegas, NV
Comments: My father also ran on the road from Kansas City, Missouri to Chicago, Ill on the Super Chief. He was a Pullman Porter in the 50's.

Registrant ID: 2805
Elvatus Cromwell Morris Sr.
City/State: W Monroe, LA
Railroad: Union Pacific
Position: Porter
Submitter's Name: Jeanie
City/State: Winnetka, CA
Comments: Not sure of much other than that our Grandfather was a Porter in his early days approx in his 19-20 year window. Per our mother he left home in search of other work, from the Spearsville, LA area in circa (1910). The line then was Union Pacific.

Registrant ID: 2806
Name: Carl John Morris Sr.
City/State: Chicago, IL
Railroad: Illinois Central

Position: Pullman Porter
Years of Service: 43 years
Submitter(s): Shirley Jean
City/State: Chicago, IL

Registrant ID: 2800
William "Bill" Henry Morris
City/State: Norfolk, VA
Railroad: Pennsylvania RR
Position: Pullman Porter
Submitter's Name: Alveta V.
City/State: Norfolk, VA
Comments: My grandfather died
before I was born and I am not
sure of his dates of employment.
My mother was born in 1902 and
he was already working with
there. He was quite well known
by older Norfolkians. His route
was the train bound for NYC.
He was a Steward.

Registrant ID: 2797
Name: Percy Morris
City/State: Philadelphia, PA
Railroad: pa railroad
Position: Pullman Porter
Years of Service: 1930's or 40's
until retirement.
Submitter's Name: Brenda
City/State: Roosevelt, NY
Comments: He was my uncle.
He is now deceased. All my life I
remember him in his uniform
coming home from trips

Registrant ID: 2794
Name: Mr. Morris
City/State: Shreveport, LA
Railroad: Union Pacific
Position: Pullman Porter
Submitter's Name: Annie

City/State: Shereport, LA
Comments: Father
Registrant ID: 2807
Name: Walter F. Morris Jr.
City/State: Portland, OR
Railroad: SDNS/USPS
Position: Waiter
Years of Service: 1937-42

Registrant ID: 2810
Name: James Morrison
City/State: Bristol, VA
Railroad: Norfolk & Western
Position: Red Cap, Porter, Mail
& Freight Loader
Years of Service: Retired Oct
31, 1977 after 35 years
employment
Submitter's Name: William
City/State: Bristol, TN
Comments: Worked out of
various cities primarily in VA:
Christiansburg, Radford,
Pulaski, Marion, Narrows,
Pearisburg; but most of his time
was spent in Roanoke & Bristol.
Now retired on a pension.

Registrant ID: 2808
Name: David Morrison
City/State: Marion, SC
Position: Motorman
Years of Service: 1959-1985
Submitter's Name: Darnell
City/State: Marion, SC

Registrant ID: 2811
Name: Louis Edward
Railroad: Seaboard
Position: Head Waiter
Years of Service: 1920's-1947
Submitter's Name: Helen
City/State: OH

Registrant ID: 2813
Name: Nathaniel Morton
City/State: Little Rock, AR
Railroad: Rock Island
Club Car Waiter, and Porter
Years of Service: 1941-1970
Submitter: Nathaniel Chicago IL
And Phyllis Vallejo, CA
Comments: My dad hired on in
Little Rock around 1941. He
moved to Chicago when the Little
Rock commissary closed
(1946).Eventually moved into the
personnel office. Retired about
1970.

Registrant ID: 2815
Name: William W. Morton
Position: Red Cap
Years of Service: 1930
Submitter's Name: H.W.
City/State: Cincinnati, OH

Registrant ID: 2817
Name: James Mosby
City/State: Richmond, VA
Railroad: Seaboard Coastline
Position: Private Car Porter
Years of Service: 30 years from
appox 1946-1976
Submitter's Name: Carlton
City/State: Los Angeles, CA
Comments: My Father is now
deceased. The last position he
held for the majority of the time
with the railroad was "Private
Car Porter" for the President of
Seaboard Coastline Railroad.
With a 4th grade education, he
worked his way up through the
ranks.

Registrant ID: 2818
Name: Wilbur J. Mosby

City/State: Richmond, VA
Railroad: Seaboard Coastline
Railroad and Amtrak
Position: Pullman Porter
Years of Service: 1942 to 1978
Submitter's Name: Gloria
City/State: Lynchburg, VA
Comments: My father, Wilbur J
Mosby who is deceased, was very
active with The Brotherhood of
Sleeping Car Porters in
Richmond. While he enjoyed the
traveling his job provided, he did
not like the discrimination he
faced when he had to layover in
certain towns.

Registrant ID: 2823
Name: John Mosee
City/State: Philadelphia, PA
Position: Pullman Porter
Years of Service: 1903-1944
Submitter's Name: George
Comments: My grandfather

Registrant ID: 2825
Name: Lee Mosley, Sr..
City/State: AL
Railroad: Southern
Position: Pullman Porter
Years of Service: 1943 to 1957
Submitter's Ermell (Mosley)
City/State: Chattanooga, TN
Comments: Mr. Mosley is
deceased. The information was
input for his daughter by Al
Seals.

Registrant ID: 2835
Name: Mittie D. Moss
City/State: Detroit, MI
Railroad: Pullman Company
Position: Coach cleaner
Years of Service: 1943-1953

Submitter's Name: Hunter

Registrant ID: 2828
Name: Henry Alexander
Position: Personal Attendant to Franklin Roosevelt
Years of Service: 1939-1943
Submitter's Name: Rosella

Registrant ID: 2827
Name: Benjamin Suen Moss
City/State: AL
Position: Pullman Porter
City/State: AL

Registrant ID: 2832
Name: Mittie Moss
City/State: Detroit, MI
Railroad: Pullman Company
Position: Coach Cleaner
Years of Service: 1943-1953
Submitter's Name: Lori
City/State: Detroit, MI
Comments: My grandmother worked cleaning coach cars for the Pullman Company in 1943 until 1953 when she retired at 65 years.

Registrant ID: 2830
Name: James B. Moss
City/State: East Orange, NJ
Railroad: Pennsylvania
Position: Sleeping Car Porter
Years of Service: Approx.-28
Submitter's Name: Ray A.
City/State: East Orange, NJ
Comments: James B. Moss, my father worked as a Pullman Porter on the Pennsylvania railroad, and supervised a Pullman crew, as we were told. During his employment with the Pennsylvania railroad, he would work anywhere the line went.

Registrant ID: 2836
Name: John Motler
Railroad: N W Railroad
Position: Porter
Submitter's Name: Zella
City/State: Homewood, IL

Registrant ID: 2840
Name: Jalin Motley
Railroad: NW Rail Road
Position: Porters
Years of Service: 1930-1940

Registrant ID: 2841
Name: Westley Motley
Railroad: NW Rail Road
Position: Porters
Years of Service: 1930-1940

Registrant ID: 3386
Name: Lunis Mounter
City/State: OH
Railroad: Seaboard
Position: Waiter
Years of Service: 1920-1947
Submitter's Name: Helen
City/State: OH

Registrant ID: 2842
Name: Thomas Mungen
Atlantic & Seaboard Coastline
Position: Dining Car Waiter
Years: 11-1937 - 12-1978
Submitter's Name: Mary
City/State: Jacksonville, FL
Comments: Mr. Mungen's employment began November 1937 with the Railway Express (under Railroad Retirement) before becoming a Dining Car Waiter with Atlantic Coastline.

He continued work after the merger of Atlantic with Seaboard Coastline.

Registrant ID: 2844
Name: James Murphy
City/State: Montgomery, AL
Railroad: Pullman Company
Position: Pullman Porter
Years of Service: 1950
Submitter's Name: Murphy

Registrant ID: 2846
Name: William O. Murphy Sr.
City/State: Washington, DC
Railroad: Southern Railroad
Position: Pullman Porter
Years of Service: 34 Years
Submitter's Name: William
City/State: DC

Registrant ID: 2845
Name: John W.Murphy Sr.
City/State: Chicago, IL
Railroad: Peremarqeete Line
Position: Pullman Porter
Years of Service: 1943
Submitter's Name: John W.
City/State: Chicago, IL

John W.Murphy Sr.

Registrant ID: 2848
Name: Henry Murell, Jr.
City/State:
Position: Pullman Porter
Submitter's Name: Maxine
City/State: Bronx, NY
Comments: My father was a Pullman porter for a while when I was young and he was hardly home, but when he came home it was a very special time for my family.

Registrant ID: 2849
Name: Henry Murell, Jr.
City/State: AL
Position: Pullman Porter
Submitter's Name: Maxine
City/State: Bronx, NY

Registrant ID: 2852
Name: Strat Myers
City/State: Bakersfield, AL
Railroad: Union Pacific RR
Position: Shop Helper
Years of Service: 1944-1950
Submitter's Name: Larry E.
City/State: Carson, CA

Registrant ID: 2854
Name: Walter Robert Myers
City/State: Richmond, VA
Railroad: The Pullman Co.
train between NY & VA
Position: Porter
Years of Service: Early 1900's
up to about the late 1940's
Submitter's Name: Alice
City/State: Fullerton, CA
Comments: I don't have much
info regarding my grandfather.
My Mother and Aunt told me
that he worked up until
retirement. We are not sure his
exact dates but believe
somewhere in the early 1900's
up to about late 1940's.

Registrant ID: 2850
Name: Arthur Myers
City/State: Siegling, SC
Railroad: Unknown - he went
from Jacksonville, FL up North
Position: Pullman Porter
Years of Service: 1920 - 1949
Submitter's Name: Rachelle
City/State: Oak Ridge, TN

Comments: Arthur Myers was
my grandmothers uncle. My
grandmother is decease now but
my mother and two aunt that are
96 and 98 years old always
talked about him. And they
always said, "He was the first
Pullman Porter from South
Carolina".

Registrant ID: 2851
Name: Lyman Myers
City/State: St Paul, MN
Railroad: Northern Pacific
Position: Waiter
Years of Service: 1938-40
Submitter's Name: Leora
City/State: San Francisco, CA

Registrant ID: 2855
Name: William Maynard
City/State: St. Louis, MO
Railroad: B & O & Penn
Years of Service: 1936-1966
Submitter's Name: Nancy

Registrant ID: 1198
Name: Carl Edwards Nakle
Position: Dinning waiter
Years of Service: 1932-1968

Registrant ID: 2857
Name: Leslie Nash
City/State: Clifton, NJ
Railroad: Lackawanna
Position: Pullman Porter
Submitter's Name: Jean
City/State: Montclair, NJ
Comments: My Dad worked as a
Pullman Porter for I believe at
least 40 years and in his travels
"on the road" met many
wonderful people of all races who
became great family friends.

Many of his closest friends were fellow workers.

Registrant ID: 2858
Name: Leon B. Nash Sr.
City/State: Kansas City, MO
Railroad: Last was Burlington
Position: Sleeping Car Porter
Years of Service: 1934-75
Submitter's Name: Leon B
City/State: Lawton, OK
Comments: My Dad was hired in Shreveport, La and worked on the then Kansas City Southern until 1945 when we moved to Kansas City, Mo.

Registrant ID: 2859
Name: Leslie A. Nash Sr.
City/State: AL
Railroad: Lackawanna
Position: Porter
Years of Service: 1925-1965
Submitter's Name: Cheryll
City/State: Montclair, NJ
Comments: Many of the people that I knew as my grandfather's friends were people he worked with on the railroad. His trips usually emanated from Hoboken, NJ. He would usually be away 4 or 5 days and sometimes longer when he had to do what he called "dead head."

Registrant ID: 2860
Name: Joseph A. Nathan
City/State: Philadelphia, PA
Railroad: Pennsylvania RR
Submitter's Name: Inez
City/State: Bronx, NY
Comments: My Grandfather has been dead for more then 30 years. I used to visit him during the summer. I remember him being buried with his union pin on. In January 2002 during Ken burns jazz series on PBS my gradfather was seen on one of the tapes walking with Mr. Randolph. I remember him talking about the El Presidente and the trains that ran from the North East Corridor all the way to Florida. Thank you so much for this.

Registrant ID: 2866
Name: Everette Neal
City/State: AL
Position: Pullman Porter
Years of Service: 1920-1940
Submitter's Name: Jennie
City/State: Los Angeles, CA

Registrant ID: 2871
Name: Nathaniel Neal
City/State: NJ
Railroad: Pennsylvania RR
Position: Dining Car Chef
Years: 1930s through 1950s**Submitter's Name:** Gayle
City/State: Plainfield, NJ
Comments: My grand uncle resided in Jersey City, NJ while employed on the railroad. His brother, Clifford Neal also worked as a Pullman Porter.

Registrant ID: 2864
Name: Cecil Cornelias Neal
City/State: Saint Paul, MN
Railroad: Burlington Northern and Union Pacific
Position: Red Cap
Years of Service: 1947-1972
Submitter(s): Darren, Allen
City/State: Saint Paul, MN

Registrant ID: 2861
Name: Bishop Neal
City/State: Saint Paul, MN
Burlington Northern and union Pacific
Position: Pullman Porter
Years of Service: 1947-1970
Submitter's Name: Darren
City/State: Saint Paul, MN

Registrant ID: 2870
Name: Joe Neal
City/State: St. Louis, MO
Railroad: Work for various railroads out of Memphis, TN
Position: Pullman Porter
Years of Service: 1939-1960
Submitter's Name: Helen
City/State: St. Louis , MO

Registrant ID: 2873
Name: George L. Neely
City/State: Chicago, IL
Years of Service: 1906-58
Submitter's: Mark Anthony
City/State: Pataskala, OH
Comments: I had three uncles that worked on the railroad during the early 20's as porters: One other family member Horse Smith year 1913 Metropolis, IL
1. George L Neely   Home town: Metropolis, IL Year:1906
2. James H. Neely   Home town: Metropolis, IL

Registrant ID: 2875
Name: James Nelson
City/State: Miami, FL
Railroad: Florida East Coast
Position: Porter
Years of Service: 1934-1956

Registrant ID: 1247
Name: Roddy Eugene Nelson
City/State: Hamlet, NC
Railroad: Pullman Company

Registrant ID: 2878
Name: Robert Nelson
City/State: Chicago, IL
Position: Porter
Submitter's Name: Regina
Comments: Uncle

Registrant ID: 2879
Name: Harold Nevels
City/State: Savannah, GA
Railroad: Seaboard Coastline
Submitter's Name: Annette
City/State: Atlanta, GA
Comments: My identical twin uncles, Harry & Harold Nevels, worked as Pullman Porters. I have a picture of one of them in a Pullman uniform. My father, Samuel Arthur Nevels, worked for the Seaboard Coastline Railroad as a laborer in Savannah, Georgia.

Registrant ID: 2880
Name: Richard Nevius
Railroad: Pennsylvania RR
Position: Dining Car Waiter
Submitter's Name: Patricia
City/State: Philadelphia, PA
Comments: My grandfather was a Pullman Porter during the early 1900's. His full name was Richard Henry Nevius and he lived in Brooklyn, New York at the time. There is a story that a wealthy passenger, liked my grandfather so much that, he gave him a life insurance policy.

Registrant ID: 2885
Name: Harry R.L. Newman
City/State: Indianapolis, IN
Railroad: IL Central
Position: Porter
Years of Service: 1935-1939

Registrant ID: 2888
Name: Claude C. Newsom, Sr.
City/State: Murfreesboro, TN
Railroad: L&N/St. Louis
Position: Porter
Submitter's Name: Ernest B.
City/State: Minfreesbord, TN

Registrant ID: 2894
Name: J.C. Nichols
Position: Pullman Porter
Years of Service: 25 Plus
Comments: He was a union member

Registrant ID: 2892
Name: Dave Nichols
City/State: Detroit, MN
Railroad: Pullman Rail Car Company
Position: Porter
Submitter's Name: Betty
City/State: Detroit, MN

Registrant ID: 2891
Name: Bennie Nichols
City/State: TX
Railroad: Santa Fe
Position: Pullman Porter
Submitter's Name: Cheryl
City/State: Missouri City, TX

Registrant ID: 2893
Name: Herman Nichols
City/State: Oklahoma, OK
Railroad: SANTA-FE
Position: Pullman Porter

Years of Service: 1939-1953
Submitter's Name: Laurin
City/State: Oklahoma, OK
Comments: He was a member of the BSCP union.

Registrant ID: 2895
Name: Sanders Nicholson
City/State: New Orleans, LA
Railroad: City of New Orleans
Position: Porter
Submitter's Name: Tamra
City/State: Wheaton, IL
Comments: I have been told that my great-great-grandfather, ran a boarding house in New Orleans for Pullman porters.

Registrant ID: 2897
Name: Edgar Daniel Nixon
City/State: Montgomery, AL
Position: Pullman Porter
Submitter's Name: Taybar
City/State: Killeen, TX
Comments: Better known as E.D. Nixon was a Civil Rights Leader, he served as a Pullman Porter for 41 years. His life extended from 1899-1987. He is my Great Uncle. His Portrait is on the 3rd floor of the Alabama Department of Archives and History Museum.

Registrant ID: 2898
Name: Robert Noble
City/State: Port Gibson, MS
Illinois Central & Gulf Rail Road
Position: Car man
Years of Service: 1972-1975

Registrant ID: 2899
Name: Walter Nobles

302

City/State: Detroit, MI
Railroad: Pullman Company
Position: Janitor
Years of Service: 1950-1980
Submitter's Name: Reese

Registrant ID: 2901
Name: Sallie Noel
City/State: Washington, DC
Railroad: Pullman Company
Years of Service: 30-40
Submitter's Name: Hall Collins

Registrant ID: 2900
Name: Charles R. Noel
City/State: Baltimore., MD
Railroad: B&O
Position: Waiter and Steward
Years of Service: 1930+
Submitter's Name: Bettie
City/State: Naples, FL
Comments: My Dad worked in the Dining Car for over 30yrs and traveled all over America. He was a really handsome and intelligent man and spoke of his job as an elite position for a Black man of that era.

Registrant ID: 2906
Name: Leroy Noisette
City/State: NY
Railroad: Penn, Railroad
Position: Porter Captain Supervisor
Years of Service: 1940-1970
Submitter's Name: Judith
City/State: Jamaica, Queens, NY
Comments: He was my father, he was the last supervisor they had at Penn Railroad.

Registrant ID: 2907
Name: John Noldon
City/State: Brooklyn, NY

Railroad: New York Central
Position: Pullman Car Porter/Club Car Attendant
Years of Service: 1934-1965
Submitter's Name: Ronald
City/State: Sayreville, NJ

Registrant ID: 2914
Name: R. W. Norris
Position: Pullman Porter
Years of Service: 25 Plus Yrs

Registrant ID: 2915
Name: Will Norris
City/State: Tennille, GA
Railroad: Georgia Southern
Position: Porter
Years of Service: 1919-1930
Submitter's Name: TF
City/State: Augusta, GA

Registrant ID: 2916
Name: Henry Northcross
Railroad: Erie Line
Submitter's Name: Winston
City/State: Columbia, SC

Registrant ID: 2918
Name: Anderson Nowden
Railroad: Seaboard Railway Co.
Years of Service: 1926-1972
Submitter's Name: Patricia
City/State: South Orange, NJ
Comments: Brother of Jackson McLean

Registrant ID: 2919
Name: James O McDonald, Sr.
City/State: Popular Bluff, MO
Railroad: Union Pacific
Position: Pullman Porter
Years of Service: 1929-69
Submitter's Name: Angela
City/State: St. Louis , MO

Registrant ID: 2921
Name: Edgar Odom
City/State: Jacksonville, FL
Railroad: Amtrak
Position: Pullman Porters
Submitter's Name: Robert
City/State: Jacksonville, FL

Registrant ID: 2925
Name: Robert Officer
Position: Pullman Porter
Years of Service: Over 25

Registrant ID: 2927
Name: Marshall Ogilvie
City/State: Shreveport, LA
Railroad: Texas and Pacific
Position: Pullman Porter
Years of Service: 1910's-40's
Submitter's Name: Violet
City/State: Seattle, WA

Registrant ID: 2929
Name: Frank Oliver
Position: Pullman Porter
Years of Service: Over 25 s
Comments: B.S.C.P union
member

Registrant ID: 2930
Name: John Q. Oliver
City/State: Chicago, IL
Railroad: Rock Island
Position: Dining Car
Years of Service: 1940-1960
Submitter's Name: Mary Ellen
City/State: Chicago, IL
Comments: Father

Registrant ID: 2932
Name: Wallace Oliver
Railroad: Milwaukee & St. Paul
Position: Porter

Years of Service: Unknown start
date until 1968
Submitter's Name: Constance
City/State: Whitecloud, MI
Comments: Mr. Olivier worked
as a Porter for a very long time

Registrant ID: 2928
Name: Carl Oliver
City/State: Williamfroth, NJ
Position: Porter
Years of Service: 1800's - 1908
Submitter's Name: Juanita
City/State: Wiliamforth, NJ
Comments: Great Great Uncle
form Hakifnz Ctn VA

Registrant ID: 2933
Name: Anselmo Orozco
City/State: Compton, CA
Position: Laborer
Years of Service: 1950-1956

Registrant ID: 2936
Name: Victor Otayson
City/State: Indianapolis, IN
Railroad: Pullman Company

Registrant ID: 2943
Name: Anthony W. Overstreet
City/State: Chicago, IL
Years of Service: 37 Years
Submitter's Name: Elva L
City/State: Chicago, IL
Comments: Husband

Registrant ID: 2946
Name: Henry A. Overstreet
City/State: OH
Railroad: Cincinnati Union
Terminal
Position: Pullman Porter
Submitter's Name: Marian
City/State: Cincinnati, OH

Registrant ID: 2940
Name: Anthony Overstreet
City/State: Chicago, IL
Railroad: Santa Fe
Position: Pullman Porter
Years of Service: 39 years
Submitter's Name: Donna
City/State: Country Club Hills, IL

Registrant ID: 2948
Name: Hulet DeWit Overton
City/State: Jacksonville, FL
Position: Dining Care Waiter
Submitter's Name: Deidra
City/State: Ft Washington, MD
Years of Service: Circa 1917-60
Comments: I am not sure when he worked, but he was born in 1897 in S.C. and died in 1965 in Jacksonville, Florida

Registrant ID: 2955
Name: Clell Owens
Railroad: Santa Fe
Position: Porter
Years of Service: 1918 – 1959

Registrant ID: 2962
Name: Herman Owens
Railroad: Santa Fe
Position: Porter
Years of Service: 1918 - 1959

Registrant ID: 2965
Name: Maceo Owens
Railroad: Santa Fe
Position: Porter
Years of Service: 1918 – 1959

Registrant ID: 2971
Name: William Owens
City/State: Stockton, CA
Railroad: Santa Fe

Position: Porters
Years of Service: 1918 - 1959
Submitter's Name: Barbara
City/State: Dayton, OH
Comments: My mother, Olene Owens Haynes' father and 5 brothers all worked for the railroad. Her father, William Owens worked for the railroad back in 1918 when they lived in Oklahoma. Her brothers, Lilias, Herman, Clell, Maceo and Howard worked for the Santa Fe.

Registrant ID: 2970
Name: Sidney L. Owens
City/State: Little Rock, AR
Railroad: Missouri Pacific
Position: Pullman Porter
Years of Service: 3
Submitter's Name: Charlene E.
City/State: Granada Hills, CA

Registrant ID: 2972
Name: Yeoman Silvan Owens
City/State: IL
Railroad: The Pullman Company Chicago Station
Position: Pullman Porter
Years : Uncertain - 1940's
Submitter's Name: Elon
City/State: Harvey, IL

Registrant ID: 2961
Name: Hayden Owens
City/State: IL
Railroad: The Pullman Company Chicago North District C&NW Stations
Position: Pullman Porter
Years of Service: Until 1943
Submitter's Name: Elon
City/State: Harvey, IL

Comments: I have the original employment card issued to my father issued 04/15/1943 Employed: 03/01/1943 DOB: 01/31/1907 The Pullman Company Chicago North District C & N W Station Chicago, Ill

Registrant ID: 2953
Name: Augustus Owens
City/State: Minneapolis, MN
Railroad: Northern Railroads
Position: Pullman Porter
Years of Service: Circa 1910-27
Submitter's Name: Alyce
City/State: Jackson, TN
Comments: I was toldby other family members that he worked with Randolph on uniting the Sleeping Car Porters.

Registrant ID: 2967
Name: Sam Henry Owens
City/State: Sacramento, CA
Railroad: Railroad Pullman Co. Southern Pacific
Position: Pullman Porter
Years of Service: 1944
Submitter's Name: Phyllis A.
City/State: Las Vegas, NV
Comments: My uncle Sam worked from Los Angeles Railroad Station and traveled all over this country. He was traveling with the Railroad as late a 1950's

Registrant ID: 2985
Name: Harold Palmer
City/State: Paris, TN
Railroad:Pullman Co. Chicago, IL was his home base.
Position: Dining Car Waiter

Years of Service: Prior to WWII,and a few years after.
Submitter's Name: Edith
City/State: Agoura Hills, CA
Comments: He and his brother, Cecil Palmer, worked as waiters together for a short time out of Chicago, IL. He may have worked prior to 1941. He served in the Army during WWII. He may have also worked on the railroad after he was honorably discharged from the Army.

Registrant ID: 2980
Name: Cecil Palmer
City/State: Toledo, OH
Railroad: I am not certain, but Chicago was his home base.
Position: Dining Car Waiter
Years of Service: Mid 1920s thru the early 1950s.
Submitter's Name: Edith
City/State: Agoura Hills, CA
Comments: Our father worked for over 20 years on the railroad. We remember many stories regarding the struggle for fair treatment. He spoke highly of A. Philip Randolph. Our mother would take us to meet the train at the Toledo, Ohio, station as it was passing through the city.

Registrant ID: 2476
Name: Edward Palmer
Railroad: Bangor & Aroostook
Position: Porter
Years of Service: 1900-1910
Submitter's Name: Barbara
City/State: Philadelphia, PA

Registrant ID: 2986
Name: Louie Palmer Sr.

City/State: Chicago, IL
Position: Porter
Years of Service: 1920
Submitter's Name: Louie
City/State: Chicago, IL

Registrant ID: 2987
Name: H.C. Palmer Sr.
City/State: MI
Position: Porter
Years of Service: 1940-1950
Submitter's Name: Sharon
City/State: Detroit, MI

Registrant ID: 2357
Name: Charles Parham
City/State: Magnolia, NJ
Railroad: Pennsylvania RR
Position: Pullman Porter
Years Circa 1937-1967
Submitter's Name: LeRoy
City/State: Clinton, MD
Comments: Was Poter-in-charge
for last 3 years of service.

Registrant ID: 450
Name: Johnny Parham
City/State: Atlanta, GA
Railroad: Seaboard Rail Road
Position: Dining Car Waiter
Years of Service: 1939-1962
Submitter's Name: Johnny
City/State: New York, NY
Comments: My father worked on
the railroad for 23 years. He
passed away in 1989. His career
in the railroad ended when he
was seriously injured in a train
wreck.

Registrant ID: 2995
Name: Leon Paris
City/State: Aurora, CO
Railroad: Union Pacific

Position: Waiter- in Charge
Years of Service: 1943-1972
Comments: I enjoyed the
experience of working and
traveling on the railroad.

Registrant ID: 2993
Name: Edward Paris
City/State: Bronx, NY
Railroad: New York Central
Position: Porter
Years of Service: 1920 to 1932
Submitter's Name: William
City/State: Bronx, NY

Registrant ID: 2997
Name: Edward H. Paris Sr.
Railroad: New York Central
Position: Porter
Submitter's Name: William R.
City/State: Bronx, NY

Registrant ID: 2998
Name: Field Parish
City/State: Greenville, MS
Railroad: Illinois Central
Position: Pullman Porter
Years of Service: 1942 -1975
Submitter's Name: Debra
City/State: Brandywine, MD
Comments: My Dad suffered
many racial incidents to provide
for his family of 11 children in
Mississippi. He endured because
he loved his family and God. As
of today he is 91 years old and in
good health.

Registrant ID: 3000
Name: Claude F. Parker
Railroad: Pullman Company
Position: Porter
Submitter's Name: Riley

Registrant ID: 3001
Name: Daniel H. Parker
City/State: AL
Submitter's Name: Betty
City/State: AL

Registrant ID: 2999
Name: Chicken Parker
City/State: AL
Position: Pullman Porter
Submitter's Name: Hazel
City/State: Cameron, NC

Registrant ID: 3008
Name: William H. Parker
City/State: DC
Railroad: Pullman
Company/The Washington
Terminal Company
Position: Chair Car Porter and
Head Car Supplier
Years of Service: 1922-1965
Submitter's Name: James
City/State: Greenwood, SC

Registrant ID: 3007
Name: Ulysses Parker
City/State: Louisville, KY
Railroad: L&N
Position: Outside rail worker
Years of Service: 1937 to 1941
Submitter's Name: Marjorie
City/State: Louisville, KY
Comments: Ulysses Parker
worked around the clock on
several occasions until he
developed Tuberculosis. He
worked in snow, rain, sleet and
freezing temperatures without
proper clothing. He was my
father. He left my mother with
eight children to raise. My
mother had to fight very hard to
raise their children.

Registrant ID: 4207
George Washington Parker
City/State: Marianna, FL
Position: Pullman Porter
Years of Service: 50's-60's
Submitter's Name: Anita Marie
City/State: Sanford, FL
Comments: Uncle George would
say the white people would call
him George not knowing they
were not offending him because
George was his name.

Registrant ID: 3002
Name: Elijah Parker
City/State: Richmond, VA
Position: Porter
Years of Service: 40 years
Submitter's Name: Vermeadia
City/State: Wilmington, DE

Registrant ID: 3009
Name: Elijah Parker Sr.
City/State: Richmond, VA
Position: Pullman Porter
Years of Service: 20 Years
Submitter's Name: V
City/State: Wilmington, DE

Registrant ID: 3013
Name: Mr. Parks
City/State: Jefferson, MO
Position: Pullman Porter
Years of Service: 1935-1970
Submitter's Name: Dr. Arnold

Registrant ID: 3014
Name: Thomas Ranfort Parks
City/State: DC
Railroad: Baltimore and Ohio
Submitter's: Carolyne, DeVore
City/State: Brookline, MA

Registrant ID: 3012
Name: Frank Parks
City/State: Chicago, IL
Railroad: Pullman Rail Car Co
Position: Pullman Porter
Years of Service: Circa 1940's-70's
Submitter's Name: Barbara
City/State: Chicago, IL
Comments: Uncle by marriage

Registrant ID: 3017
Name: Lucien Parrish
City/State: Philadelphia, PA
Railroad: Philadelphia
Position: Porter
Years of Service Early 1900's-40
Submitter's Name: Andrea
City/State: Charlottesville, VA
Comments: Lucien Parrish was
my Great-Grandfather. I am
researching my family tree, and
am looking for information on his
occupation as a Porter .

Registrant ID: 3016
Name: Edward J.Parrish
City/State: Franklin, TN
Position: Porter
Years of Service: 1945-46
Submitter's Name: Elease
City/State: Franklin, TN
Comments: Summer program in
Canada

Registrant ID: 3018
Name: Grant Pascall
City/State: Springfield, MO
Railroad: Frisco
Position: Head Waiter-in Charge
Years of Service: 1941- 1983
Submitter's Name: Rebecca
City/State: Colorado Springs,
CO

Registrant ID: 3020
Name: Walter Patillo
Railroad: Santa Fe
Years of Service: 1943-1970
Submitter's Name: Ms Judith
Comments: Father, worked for
27yrs

Registrant ID: 3019
Name: James Patillo
City/State: Little Rock, AR
Position: Porter
Years of Service: 1920's
Submitter's Name: Verl
City/State: Chicago, IL
Comments: James Patillo was
my grandfather. My mother,
Mary Catherine Patillo
Brengettcy (also deceased, said
he was a Pullman Porter in Little
Rock, Arkansas.

Registrant ID: 3028
Name: T.T.Patterson
Submitter's Name: Aldington

Registrant ID: 3027
Name: Samuel Patterson
City/State: AL
Railroad: Norfolk & Western
Position: Pullman Porter
Years: Circa 1902 - 1940
Submitter's Name: Naomi
City/State: Baltimore, MD
Comments: Samuel Patterson
was my great uncle, and is now
deceased. His date of birth is
unknown. He lived at 2607
Middle Street, Norfolk, Virginia.
He ran from Norfolk, Virginia to
Cincinnati, Ohio. He was a
Pullman Porter.

Registrant ID: 3023
Name: John Patterson
City/State: Montgomery, AL
Railroad: L & N Railroad
Submitter's Name: Helen
City/State: Hubbard, OH

Registrant ID: 3024
Name: Lincoln Patterson
City/State: AL
Railroad: Southern Pacific
Position: Lineman
Years of Service: 1910-1940
Submitter's Name: Linda
City/State: San Jose, CA
Comments: My father started
working for the Southern Pacific
Railroad in White River,
Arkansas. He Retired in Omaha,
Nebraska.

Registrant ID: 3022
Name: Issac Patterson
City/State: KY
Railroad: Southern Line
to the East Coast
Position: Porter
Submitter's Name: Brenda L.
City/State: Woodbridge, VA
Comments: As a child I rode the
train to South Carolina with my
Grandmother Hattie B. Jordan
from D.C. She would get a pass
for us to ride since grandpa was
retired from the railroad. I also
rode the train from D.C. to New
York.

Registrant ID: 3029
Name: Robert B. Paul
City/State: Wichita, KS
Submitter's: Yeye Akilimali
Funua

City/State: Adeyipo Village,Via
Ibadan,Nigeria, AL

Registrant ID: 3030
Name: C.J. Payne
Position: Pullman Porter
Years of Service: Over 25
Comments: B.S.C.P member.

Registrant ID: 3031
Name: Delores Peacell
City/State: Tampa, FL

Registrant ID: 3035
Name: Willard Pearcy
City/State: Knoxville, TN
Submitter's Name: Edith
City/State: Manfield, OH

Registrant ID: 3037
Name: Willie Edward Pearse
City/State: Rockingham,, NC
Position: Pullman Porter
Years of Service: 1943-1968
Submitter's Name: Julius O
City/State: Freeport, NY

Registrant ID: 3038
Name: William "Red " Pearson
City/State: Boston, MA
Position: Porter
Submitter's Name: Robert
City/State: Easton, MA
Comments: My grandfather was
a black porter they called him
red for short. I am adding this to
your profile.

Registrant ID: 3040
Name: William Louis Pearson
Position: Porter
Years of Service: 1944-1955
Submitter's Name: Caroline
City/State: Yonkers, NY

Registrant ID: 3043
Name: Henry Pellom
City/State: Oakland, CA
Railroad: Santa Fe and Southern Pacific
Position: Porter
Years of Service: 1943 -1970
Submitter's Name: Clara
City/State: Sparks, NV
Comments: My uncle made quite a few good friends while working as a Porter and continued to keep in touch with them until his death.

Registrant ID: 3045
Name: Bailey Pendergrass
City/State: AL
Railroad: the Atlantic Coast Line and the Pennsylvania RR
Position: Porter
Years of Service: Approximately 1920-1941
Submitter's Name: Omega
City/State: Silver Spring, MD

Registrant ID: 3046
Name: Edward Penny
City/State: AL
Railroad: Seaboard Railroad
Position: Porter
Years of Service: 1950's-thru the early 1970's
Submitter's Name: Amelia
City/State: Corona Hills, CA
Comments: My Great grandfather, Rev. Edward Penny was a Porter for Seaboard Railroad in Tallahassee, Fl. Grandfather passed away July 17, 1993, at the age of 83. I can recall him explaining to me the racial prejudice he endured everyday, just so he could support his family.

Registrant ID: 3054
Name: Gus Peoples
Position: Pullman Porter
Years of Service: Over 25
Comments: B.S.C.P member

Registrant ID: 3050
Name: Elyvan Peoples
City/State: Indianapolis, IN
Railroad: Amtrak
Position: Sleeping Car Porter
Years of Service: 1942-1976

Registrant ID: 3058
Name: Willie C. Peppers
City/State: St. George, SC
Years of Service: 1935-1937
Submitter's Name: Alice
City/State: Ladson, SC

Registrant ID: 3062
Name: Sherryl Morgan Perkins
City/State: Kirkland, WA
Railroad: Union Pacific RR
Position: Pullman Porter
Years of Service: 1955-58

Registrant ID: 3061
Name: Jonas Perkins
City/State: Harvey, IL
Railroad: Pullman Co then New York Central
Position: Porter
Years of Service: 1930 1963
Submitter's Name: Jonas
City/State: Fredericksbrg, TX
Comments: My dad Mr. Gordon Parks worked on the road in the 1930's

Registrant ID: 3060
Name: James Anderson Perkins
City/State: Kansas City, MO
Railroad: CBQ Burlington, Burlington Northern & Amtrak
Position: Porter (Chair car), Waiter (Supervisor) Bartender
Years: 35 years 1937-1972
Submitter(s) Name:
James, Bernard
City/State: Kansas City, MO
Comments: His picture is in a book or magazine, Amtrak Trains & Travel by Patrick Dorin. Copyright 1979 by Superior Publishing Co. Seattle, Washington. Page 98. Library Of Congress.

Registrant ID: 3067
Name: Lawrence Perpener
Submitter's Name: Lawrence

Registrant ID: 3068
Name: Samuel Perrino
City/State: Atlanta, GA
Railroad: Georgia Pacific
Position: Dining Car Waiter
Years of Service: 35 years
Submitter's Name: Clifford
City/State: Houston, TX

Registrant ID: 3069
Name: Elmo Perry
City/State: Kansas City, MO
Railroad: Chicago, Burlington and Quincy
Position: Pullman Porter
Years of Service: Over 10 years
Submitter's: Tina & Tonya
City/State: Kansas City, MO
Comments: My father would say it was very very hard the way they worked. He has two friends

living that are in their 90's. Mr. Ragsdale, my father's friend for over 65 years, rode on my father's train to boot camp for World War II. He lives directly across the street.

Registrant ID: 3070
Name: Frank W. Perry
City/State: PA
Railroad: Pennsylvania
Position: Baggage Man
Years of Service: 1937-1960
Submitter's Name: Gladys
City/State: Wheaton, IL
Comments: Niece

Registrant ID: 3075
Name: Richard Perry
City/State: AL
Railroad: Penn Central and or Illinois Central
Position: Waiter/Short order Cook
Submitter's Name: David
City/State: Chicago, IL
Comments: He was my uncle.

Registrant ID: 3073
Name: Joseph Perry
City/State: AL
Railroad: Milwaukee Railroad
Position: Buffet Attendant
Years of Service: 1924
Submitter's Name: Karen
City/State: Chicago, IL

Registrant ID: 3071
Name: George Perry
City/State: TX
Railroad: Texas and Pacific RR
Position: Chef Cook
Years: Circa 1939-Dec 1959
Submitter's Name: Pamela

City/State: Fort Worth, TX
Comments: The gentleman is my father and he passed away when I was only nine years of age. I do remember my father would be gone for several days at a time, he would travel from Ft. to Louisiana to New York and back home.

Registrant ID: 3078
Name: Albert Person-Blount
Position: Porter
Submitter's Name: Richard T.
City/State: Los Angeles, CA

Registrant ID: 3081
Name: James Peters
City/State: Baltimore, MD
Years: Early 50's retired 80's
Submitter's Name: Diane
Comments: Neighbor

Registrant ID: 3079
Name: George Peters
Railroad: Southern Pacific
Position: Cook
Years of Service:
Between the 20's and 30's
Submitter's Name: Gloria
City/State: Monrovia, CA

Registrant ID: 3082
Name: Hayes Petrie
City/State: Chicago, Ill.,
Submitter's Name: Ernest T.
City/State: Phoenix, Arizona

Registrant ID: 3084
Name: William Petter Cooper
City/State: Coco, FL
Railroad: Chesapeake and Ohio
Position: Pullman Porter
Years of Service: 1948-1950

Submitter's Name: Dr Essie
City/State: Coco, FL
Comments: Brother

Registrant ID: 3085
Name: Isaac Pharr
City/State: Omaha, NE
Position: Pullman Porter
Submitter's Name: J.
City/State: Oakland, CA
Comments: Started to work in about 1920 - his run was out of Cleveland and New Orleans Information supplied by his 90 year old son in law.

Registrant ID: 3087
Name: Romeo Philips
City/State: Portage, MI

Registrant ID: 3098
Name: Ralph Phillips
City/State: Atlanta, GA
Railroad: Southern Pacific
Years of Service: 1930-1969
Submitter's Name: Henrietta
City/State: Atlanta, GA

Registrant ID: 3099
Name: Ralph Franklin Phillips
Position: Red Cap
Years of Service: 25 Years
Submitter's Name: Gayle
City/State: College Park., GA

Registrant ID: 3088
Name: Artis Phillips
City/State: AL
Railroad: Santa Fe
Position: Chair Car Attendant
Submitter's Name: Ann
City/State: Los Angeles, CA

Registrant ID: 3092
Name: Jessie "Jess" Phillips
City/State: Peoria, IL
Railroad: Rock Island Railroad
Position: Track department
Maintenance of Way
Years of Service: 1953 --
Submitter's Name: Rose
City/State: Peoria, IL

Registrant ID: 3089
Name: James Phillips
City/State: AL
Railroad: Pullman Co.
Position: Pullman Porter
Years of Service: 1930 – 1979
Submitter's Name: Romeo E.
City/State: Portage, MI
Comments: My father, prior to
his retirement, became a Porter-
in-Charge.

Registrant ID: 3101
Name: Thomas Philpot
City/State: Roxbury, MA
Position: Porter
Years of Service: 1942-1962
Submitter's Name: Alicia
City/State: Roxburry, MA
Comments: Daughter

Registrant ID: 3102
Name: Frank Pickens
City/State: St. Louis, MO
Railroad: Frisco
Position: Dinning Car Waiter
Years of Service: Approx 15
Submitter's Name: Frances
City/State: Las Vegas, NV

Registrant ID: 3105
Name: Letcher Pickens Jr.
Railroad: Frisco
Position: Dinning Car Waiter
Years of Service: Approx 10

Submitter's Name: Frances
City/State: Las Vegas, NV

Registrant ID: 3106
Name: Wayne Pickett
City/State: Quincy, MA
Position: Porter

Registrant ID: 3107
Name: James Pierce
Position: Pullman Car Porter
Years of Service: 1890-1915
Submitter's Name: T.
City/State: Athens, GA

Registrant ID: 3108
Name: R. Eugene Pincham
City/State: Chicago, IL
Railroad: Santa Fe Railroad
Position: Dining Car Waiter
Years of Service: 1945

Registrant ID: 3110
Name: Charles J.Pinckard
City/State: AL
Railroad: Milwaukee Railroad
Position: Buffet Attendant
Years of Service: 1930-1949
Submitter's Name: Karen
City/State: Chicago, IL
Comments: My dad's experience
on the rail road helped him to
start his own successful
restaurant chain in Chicago,
Prince & Joy. Deceased

Registrant ID: 3109
Name: Albert Pinckard
City/State: AL
Railroad: Milwaukee Railroad
Position: Buffet Attendant
Years of Service: 1930-1949
Submitter's Name: Karen
City/State: Chicago, IL

Registrant ID: 3111
Name: Trillman (Brother) Piner
City/State: Buffalo, NY
Railroad: Buffalo NY Central
Position: Waiter
Years of Service: 1941-1943
Submitter's Name: Shirley
City/State: Buffalo, NY

Registrant ID: 3113
Name: Robert Pitner
City/State: Chicago, IL
Railroad: Pullman Company
Position: Pullman Porter
Years of Service: 1943-1969
Submitter's Name: Barbara
City/State: Chicago, IL

Registrant ID: 3114
Name: Walter Pitts
City/State: CA
Railroad: Southern Pacific
Position: Dining Car Waiter
Years of Service: 1938-1989
Submitter's Name: Walda
City/State: Richmond, CA
Comments: My father and grandfather were both dining car waiters on the Southern Pacific Railroad. My Dad, who passed away in August 2000, worked 41 years from the railroad and retired from there. We grew up listening to many stories of the railroad days.

Registrant ID: 3115
Name: Enies Plowden
City/State: Mullins, SC
Railroad: Baltimore/Ohio
Position: Dining Car Waiter
Years of Service: 1942-1976
Comments: I am filling this out for Mr. Plowden who at the tiime

of this submission is 93 years old. He is still driving and reads two newspapers a day. He lives by himself in a retirement Apt.. He served Mary Mcleod Bethune.

Registrant ID: 3118
Name: Samuel E. Plummer
City/State: Philadelphia, PA
Position: Pullman Porter
Years of Service: 1943-1961
Submitter's Name: Pam
City/State: Philadelphia, PA
Comments: Worked for 18yrs Deceased 1978

Registrant ID: 3119
Name: Adolphus Polite
City/State: New York, NY
Railroad: New York Central
Position: Dining Car Waiter
Years: Approx 1942 thru 1951
Submitter's Name: Craig
City/State: Westport, CT
Comments: This is my father.

Registrant ID: 1424
Name: Cox Gillespie-Poll, Sr.
City/State: Detroit, MI
Railroad: Tenn. Railroad
Position: Porter
Years of Service: 6 Years
Submitter's Name: Eleanor E.
City/State: Detroit, MI

Registrant ID: 3120
Name: Lee Pollard
City/State: GA
Position: Porter
Years of Service: 1920-1940
Submitter's Name: Lileigh
City/State: Emerville, GA

Registrant ID: 3122
Name: Eugene Pollock
City/State: E. St. Louis, IL
Position: Pullman Porter
Submitter's Name: Mary
City/State: Anderson,, IN
Comments: He worked out of the St. Louis

Registrant ID: 3123
Name: Isaiah Mercer Poole
City/State: PA
Position: Porter
Years of Service: 1946-1956
Submitter's Name: Raymond L.
City/State: Roslyn, PA
Comments: Son

Registrant ID: 3126
Name: Erskin Porham
City/State: Sacramento, CA
Railroad: St Louis
Position: Pullman Porter
Years of Service: 1930-1950
Submitter's Name: Theodore V
City/State: Sacramento, CA

Registrant ID: 3134
Name: Florzell Porter
Submitter's Name: Charles

Registrant ID: 3135
Name: Frank Porter
City/State: Asheville, NC
Position: Pullman Porter
Years of Service: late 40's-60's
Submitter's Name: Doris
City/State: Atlanta, GA
Comments: The only information I have currently is that he was a Pullman Porter for most of his life. Born in Union County, SC and lived in Asheville, NC with wife. (note: I

am a family researcher, researching his grandfather, James Porter and Frank Porter's father.

Registrant ID: 3131
Name: Earnest Porter
City/State: Chicago, IL
Railroad: Union Station
Position: Sleeping Car Porter
Years of Service: 1943-1964
Submitter's Name: Charles
City/State: Chicago, IL
Comments: At the time of this submission Earnest Porter was born Feb. 10th, 1900, and is one-hundred and two years old. Wife, Mrs. Lonnie Porter passed away in 1987. Mr. Porter had five children, two sons, three daughters (born in this order): Thomas, Alfred, Mary Lue (Mother of Charles).

Registrant ID: 3133
Name: Edgar Porter
City/State: Cincinnati, OH
Railroad: Pullman Company
Position: Pullman Porter
Years of Service: 1942 - 1970
Submitter's Name: Beverly
City/State: Cincinnati, OH
Comments: My father was honored at the Union Terminal where his uniform was on display.

Registrant ID: 3127
Name: Amstead T. Porter
City/State: Harrisburg,, PA
Railroad: Pennsylvania Railroad And Conrail
Years of Service: 1945 to 1984
Submitter's Name: Marcus L.

City/State: Dayton,, OH
Comments: My brother-in-law is deceased (October 29th,

Registrant ID: 3129
Name: Charles Porter
City/State: Lynn, MA
Years of Service: 1911
Submitter's Name: Lorna
City/State: Lynn, MA

Registrant ID: 3138
Name: Mr. Oliver R. Porter
City/State: New Orleans, LA
Railroad: Sunset Limited
Position: Pullman Porter
Years of Service: l952
City/State: New Orleans, LA
Comments: My father, belonged to the Brotherhood of Sleeping Car Porters.

Registrant ID: 3136
Name: Jeremiah Porter
City/State: Warrensville, OH
Position: Engineer
Years of Service: 1960-1965
Submitter's Name: Simon
City/State: New York, NY

Registrant ID: 3137
Name: Lafayette Porter
City/State: Chicago, IL
Position: Car Inspector
Years: 07/1946 - 08/1978
Submitter's Name: Debee
City/State: Woodridge, IL
Comments: I am so pleased and encouraged to become a part of this historic event. I thank you for remembering the men of this era. God bless you and success.

Registrant ID: 3139
Name: Joseph E. Porter Jr.
City/State: Los Angeles, CA
Railroad: Penn Central and Mousourri Pacific
Position: Dining Car Waiter
Years of Service: 1941-1946
Submitter's Name: Carolyn

Registrant ID: 3140
Name: Cecil B.Potts
City/State: IL
Railroad: Chicago North Dist. C&NV station
Position: Pullman Porter
Years of Service: 20 plus
Submitter's Name: Debra
City/State: Chicago, IL
Comments: He moved to Chicago from Oklahoma City in the early 1920s. My father's employment with the Pullman Company (per his ID) began August 1942. He worked 20 plus years. He shared his experiences with friends.

Registrant ID: 3141
Name: Joseph Potts
City/State: Portsmouth, VA
Railroad: N.Y. Central Rail
Position: Sleeping Car Porter
Years: May 1932 to June 1963
Submitter's Name: Ronald
City/State: Skippack, PA
Comments: As a child I remember him telling me that he travel from N.Y.C. to Chicago and than on to California. And that I should see the western part of the U.S and how beautiful it is. He said the people were always nice to him.

Registrant ID: 3143
Name: Samuel L. Powe
City/State: Centralia, IL
Railroad: Pullman Company
Position: Laborer
Years of Service: 70-80
Submitter's Name: McClain

Registrant ID: 3144
Name: William Powell
City/State: MD
Railroad: B&O
Position: Maintenance of Way
Laborer and Trackman
Years of Service: 1935-1962
Submitter's Name: Jacqueline
City/State: Brentwood, MD
Comments: My grandfather,
William Powell Jr., began
working for the B & O Railroad
in June 1935, and continued to
do so until furloughed for the
last time on January 5, 1962.
He worked as a maintenance of
way laborer and trackman.

Registrant ID: 3145
Name: William Randolph Powell
Railroad: B & O
Position: Dining Car Waiter &
Pullman Porter
Years of Service: 30 Years
Submitter's Name: Doris J.
City/State: Hampton, VA

Registrant ID: 3149
Charles Maceo Powell Sr.
City/State: Cincinnati, OH
Railroad: Southern Railway
Position: Pullman Porter
Years of Service: 3 years
Submitter's Name: Brenda
City/State: Cincinnati, OH

Registrant ID: 3150
Name: Jasper Pratt
Railroad: Pullman Company
Position: Porter
Years of Service: 1944-1952
Submitter's Name: Murray

Registrant ID: 3151
Name: Mr.Prayron
City/State: Atlanta, GA
Position: Porter
Submitter's Name: Debbie
City/State: Atlanta, GA
Comments: Porter stated as
fathers occupation on her birth
certificate.

Registrant ID: 3152
Name: Paul Prebble
City/State: MI
Position: Bartender
Submitter's Name: Constance
City/State: White Cloud , MI
Comments: Brother-in-law

Registrant ID: 3155
Name: Carlton Presley
City/State: Jacksonville, FL
Position: Waiter
Years of Service: 40 Years
Submitter's Name: Doris
City/State: Chicago, IL

Registrant ID: 3158
Name: Joseph Lee Preston
City/State: Lawrenceville, GA
Railroad: Seaboard
Position: Porter
Years of Service: 50 Years
Submitter's Name: Joseph L Jr.
City/State: Lawrenceville, GA

Registrant ID: 3157
Name: Joseph Preston

City/State: AL
Railroad: Sea Board Coastline
Position: Pullman Porter
Years of Service: 50
Submitter's Name: Joseph
City/State: Lawrenceville, GA
Comments: Was involved in train wreck.

Registrant ID: 3159
Name: Kenneth Pretlow
City/State: Arial, NJ
Position: Electrician
Years of Service: 1912-1965
Submitter's Name: Ron
City/State: Philadelphia, PA

Registrant ID: 3165
Name: W. T. Price
Position: Pullman Porter
Years of Service: Over 25
Comments: B.S.C.P union member.

Registrant ID: 3162
Name: Douglas Price
City/State: Shaker Heights, Ohio
Railroad: Pullman Company
Position: Pullman Porter
Years of Service: 1944-1945

Registrant ID: 3164
Name: Louis Price
Railroad: Southern Railway Atlanta,Georgia
Position: Chef
Years of Service: 38 Years
Submitter's Name: Linda
City/State: Atlanta, GA
Comments: My Dad loved working on the train. As a child,

I remember the excitement of taking the train for summer vacations. In 1978, My Dad was killed when the Southern Crescent derailed in Virginia. He was the oldest chef for the company. He was photographed in several ads for the "Trains Magazine. I am currently writing a book on his life and his hard work and dedication to the railroad.

Registrant ID: 3163
Name: George Price
City/State: Los Angeles, CA
Railroad: Union Pacific RR
Position: Waiter
Years of Service: 30 years
Submitter's Name: Agnes
City/State: Las Vegas, NV
Comments: His dad also worked on the Union Railroad as a Pullman Porter

Registrant ID: 3166
Name: Walter Price
City/State: Dallas, TX
Position: Pullman Porter
Years of Service: Circa 1920'S-50'S
Submitter's Name: Styles
City/State: Oakland, CA

Registrant ID: 3167
Name: James Primous
City/State: Memphis, TN
Railroad: Santa, Fe, Union Pacific, Ill. Central
Position: Pullman Porter
Years of Service: 1944----1956
Submitter's Name: Commodore
City/State: Collierville, TN

Registrant ID: 3168
Name: Lawrence Prince
City/State: Washington, DC
Railroad: The Pullman Co.
Position: Porter
Years : 1916 - death in 1966
Submitter's Name: Richard
City/State: Oxon Hill, MD
Comments: According to what I have been able to glean from information that I received from the Railroad Retirement Board; my Grandfather began employment with the Pullman Company at age 21 in 1916, although they were unable to verify his date of birth through records. I understand, from conversation with a relative, my Grandfather put his age up, in order to obtain work once he came to Washington, DC.

Registrant ID: 3170
Name: Ulysses Providence
City/State: Harrisburg, PA
Submitter's Name: Charles
City/State: Twinsburg, OH
Comments: I believe that Ulysses's father John Providence and brother Julius aka Jesse-Jessie Providence also worked as Pullman employees.

Registrant ID: 4208
George Washington Pruitt
City/State: NY, NY
Position: Pullman Car Porter
Years of Service: 1928-1964
Submitter Name: Swanston V

Registrant ID: 3178
Name: Richard Prutt
City/State: Chicago, IL

Railroad: Chicago-Ca Line
Position: Pullman Porter
Years of Service: 20's-30's
Submitter's Name: Johnny
City/State: Chicago, IL
Comments: Grandfather I live in the house he bought in 1922

Registrant ID: 3183
Name: Charles L. Pryor
City/State: Chicago, IL
Position: Waiter
Years of Service: 1939-1971
Submitter's Name: Shirley

Registrant ID: 3185
Name: Eugene Pryor
City/State: Columbus, OH
Submitter's Name: Marilee
City/State: Conley, GA

Registrant ID: 3179
Name: Bent T. Pryor
City/State: Chicago, IL
Position: Porter
Years of Service: 1950-1960
Submitter's Name: Suetta
City/State: Detroit, MI

Registrant ID: 3184
Name: Edward Pryor
City/State: Chicago, IL
Position: Porter
Years of Service: 1949-1960
Submitter's Name: Suetta
City/State: Detroit, MI
Comments: Brother

Registrant ID: 3186
Name: James Pryor
City/State: Memphis, TN
Railroad: Train was called City of New Orleans-ran between Memphis and Chicago

Position: Pullman Porter
Submitter's Name: Loretha
City/State: St. Louis , MO

Registrant ID: 3189
Name: Paul Pugh
City/State: Chicago, IL
Railroad: Santa Fe Railroad
Position: Waiter

Registrant ID: 3188
Name: Drexel Pugh
City/State: St. Paul, MN
Railroad: Northern Pacific
Position: Dining Car Waiter
Years of Service: 30 years
Submitter's Name: Kathleen
City/State: Chicago, IL
Comments: My father passed in January 2001. He worked on the railroad from 1950 to 1980.

Registrant ID: 3190
Name: Earskin Pullearm
City/State: MO
Railroad: Pullman Co.worked out of St. Louis Mosourri.
Position: Pullman Porter
Years: Approx 1930 - 1950
Submitter's Name: Theodore
City/State: Sacramento, CA
Comments: My Grandfather went wherever the Pullman Car went. He stayed in the Pullman Porter Lounges while he was on the road.

Registrant ID: 3191
Name: Frank Pullen
City/State: Enfield, NC
Railroad: Pullman Company
Position: Pullman Porter
Years of Service: 1890-1900
Submitter's Name: Evelyn

City/State: Philadelphia, PA

Registrant ID: 3192
Name: Booker T. Pullen Sr.
City/State: NC
Position: Switchman
Years of Service: 1935-1940
Submitter's Name: Booker T.
City/State: Garner, NC

Registrant ID: 3193
Name: Wilbert Pulliam, Sr.
City/State: Baltimore, MD
Railroad: B & O
Position: Dining Car Waiter
Years of Service: 1940 - 1960
Submitter's Name: Milena
City/State: Owings Mills, MD
Comments: My father, Wilbert Pulliam Sr., worked on the B &O railroad as a dining car waiter for many years. He loved his work and had many stories to tell us about the famous people he met while traveling with the railroad between his Maryland to New York route.

Registrant ID: 3194
Name: Jesse Purdie
City/State: AL
Railroad: Erie Lackawanna
Position: Porter
Years of Service: Approx 30
Submitter's Name: Nellie
City/State: Brooklyn, NY

Registrant ID: 3196
Name: Joseph E Purter Jr.
City/State: Los Angeles, CA
Railroad: Pennsylvania and Mo Pacific
Position: Dining Car Waiter
Years of Service: 1940-1946

Submitter's Name: Carolyn
City/State: Los Angeles, CA
Comments: He was my father

Registrant ID: 3204
Name: Bosie Queen
City/State: Chicago, IL
Position: Porter
Years of Service: 1925-1965
Submitter's Name: Alma
City/State: PA

Registrant ID: 3200
Name: James Qualls, Sr.
City/State: Denver, CO
Railroad: Union Pacific
Position: Porter Car Waiter
Submitter's Name: Linda
City/State: Denver, CO

Registrant ID: 3202
Name: Oscar Quarles
City/State: MI
Position: Waiter
Submitter's Name: Connie
City/State: Los Angeles, CA

Registrant ID: 3205
Name: Percy Quick
City/State: East Orange, NJ
Position: Steward
Years of Service: 1930's
Submitter's Name: Debra R.
City/State: San Diego, CA
Comments: My grandfather
worked for the railroad. He lived
in East Orange, N.J. The 1930
census shows him to be 54 years
old in 1930. I know he retired;
he worked on the railroad and he
used to take my mother and her
brother, to the secret union
meetings.

Registrant ID: 3206
Milton Douglas Quigless, Sr.
City/State: Raleigh, NC
Railroad: Milwaukee
Position: Porter/Dining Car
Waiter
Years of Service: 1927-1933
Submitter's Name: Milton

Registrant ID: 3207
Name: Stilton Quizles
City/State: Raleigh, NC
Railroad: Seattle
Position: Porter & DCW
Years of Service: 1927-1933
Submitter's Name: Mildon
City/State: Raleigh, NC

Registrant ID: 3208
Name: Louis Raiford
City/State: Las Vegas, NV
Submitter's Name: Olvin
City/State: New Rochelle, NY

Registrant ID: 3212
Name: William Ramsey
City/State: MS
Railroad: Alabama Great
Southern
Position: Fireman
Years of Service: Circa 1910- 1926
Submitter's Name: Jonnie
City/State: Stone Mountain,
Georgia
Comments: William "Boss" was
my grandfather.

Registrant ID: 3210
Name: John Quincy Ramsey
City/State: Chattanooga, TN
Position: Pullman Porter and
Years of Service: 1940's
Submitter's Name: Charlotte
(grand daughter) , Calvin (son)
City/State: Wesley Hills, NY

Comments: My Grandfather worked as a Pullman Porter shortly after the second world war. for many years.

Registrant ID: 3211
Name: Waylon Ramsey
City/State: Tuskegee, AL
Position: Pullman Porter/ Waiter
Years of Service: 1940's
Submitter's Name: Charlotte
City/State: Wesley Hills, NY
Comments: My great uncle worked for the Railroad in the forties, according to my father. He and his brother, John Quincy of Chattanooga both worked shortly after the second world war.

Registrant ID: 3213
Name: Finnley Randolph
City/State: Wanderbel, CT
Submitter's Name: Finnley
City/State: Wanderbel, CT

Registrant ID: 3214
Name: Leon Ransom
City/State: Zanesville, OH
Railroad: I'm not sure
Position: Pullman Porter
Years of Service: 1922-1923
Submitter's Name: Kathryn H.
City/State: Carrboro, NC
Comments: My grandfather was a Pullman porter before entering Ohio State University Law school. He graduated from there with honors and went on to teach at Howard University. There is currently a chair named in his honor at the University. My grandmother, Willa or Billy Ransom ran a boarding house

with her mother in the early 1900-1923 for the Pullman company. Her maiden name was Carter. Her mother was Fannie Crowe

Registrant ID: 3215
Name: Robert D. Ransom
City/State: Albany, NY
Railroad: New York Central
Position: Pullman Porter
Years of Service: 1933-1957
Submitter's Name: Doris G.
City/State: Hamden, CT
Comments: Robert D. Ransom was my uncle, married to Loraine E Ellington of Winston-Salem, NC

Registrant ID: 3217
Name: Rufus Raspberry
City/State: Kansas City, MO
Position: Chair Car Attendant
Years of Service: 1943-1952
Submitter's Name: Julia
City/State: Los Angeles, CA
Comments: Daughter

Registrant ID: 5005
Name: N.P. Ray
Position: Pullman Porter
Years of Service: Over 25
Comments: He was a union member

Registrant ID: 3220
Name: Donald Ray
City/State: Chicago, IL
Railroad: Amtrak Railroad
Position: Waiter, Porter, Bartender
Years of Service: 1972 - 1983

Comments: My experience with the railroad was great. I met many people, traveled all over the country, experienced different cultures and learned more about life and the world. At the time I was young and the experiences were eye opening which broadened my prospective.

Registrant ID: 3225
Name: Willie Ray
City/State: Baltimore, MD
Railroad: Camden Yard Station Baltimore MD
Position: Pullman Porter
Years of Service: 1920 - 1950
Submitter's Name: Nora
City/State: Baltimore, MD
Comments: My father worked on the railroad until an accident claimed his left leg. He did not leave their employ until 1950 even though the accident occurred in 1923.

Registrant ID: 3222
Name: Walter David Ray
City/State: Chicago, IL
Position: Porter
Years of Service: 1949-1954
Submitter's Name: Robert
City/State: Oak Park, IL

Registrant ID: 3226
Name: Ely Rae
City/State: Atlanta, GA
Railroad: Atlanta and West Point
Submitter's Name: Johnetta
City/State: Decatur, GA
Comments: My Grandfather died while working on the railroad. His death was due in

part to a lack of quick and timely medical services.

Registrant ID: 3228
Name: Charles Readus
City/State: Chicago, IL
Railroad: Illinois Central
Position: Dining Car Waiter
Years of Service: Approx 40
Submitter's Name: Frank
City/State: Apple Valley, MN
Comments: Mr. Readus passed in 1996. His last position was with Illinois Central before retirement. He was with their commuter system in Chicago. His position as a Dining Car Waiter ended with the introduction of Amtrak.

Registrant ID: 3229
Name: John Reco
Submitter's Name: Robert

Registrant ID: 3233
Name: Frank Earl Reed
Railroad: Great Northern
Position: Ding Car Porter
Years of Service: Two (2) years
Submitter's Name: Ms. Frankie
City/State: Columbia, MD
Comments: My father ran on the Great Northern Railroad as a means to earn money to finish his pharmacy degree at the University of Kansas. His run was from St. Paul, MN to Seattle, WA. He, my father, always spoke of the experience.

Registrant ID: 3234
Name: Elton Reeder Sr.
City/State: Oakland, CA
Railroad: Southern Pacific

Position: Waiter
Years of Service: 1946-61
Submitter's Name: Elton Jr.
City/State: Oakland, CA
Comments: My father moved to California from New Orleans, after Pearl Harbor, to work in the Richmond, Calif. Ship Yards. Later became a Waiter with Southern Pacific. Got married to Verona E. Featherstone also of New Orleans. Raised three successful children.

Registrant ID: 3236
Name: Addis Reese
City/State: Cincinnati, OH
Railroad: L & N Railroad
Position: Pullman Porter
Submitter's Name: Linda
City/State: Cincinnati, OH

Registrant ID: 3237
Name: Richard Reese
City/State: Cincinnati, OH
Railroad: B&O Railroad
Position: Pullman Porter
Years of Service: 1949
Submitter's Name: Linda
City/State: Cincinnati, OH

Registrant ID: 3238
Name: George Reese Sr.
City/State: Cincinnati, OH
Railroad: B&O
Years of Service: 40's - 1960
Submitter's Name: Marjean
City/State: Cincinnati, OH

Registrant ID: 3239
Name: James Reeves
City/State: Chicago, IL

Registrant ID: 3240
Name: Jerome Revees
City/State: South Field, MI
Position: Porter
Years of Service: 40 Years**Submitter's Name:** John
City/State: South field, MI

Registrant ID: 3242
Name: William Reid
City/State: Suffolk, VA
Railroad: Norfolk & Western
Position: Cook
Years of Service: 1902-1935
Submitter's Name: Elsie
City/State: Suffolk, VA
Comments: Grand-daughter Osceola writes: I am writing this for my mother whose name is given above. William Clarence Reid (4/9/1888 - 1/17/1950) was my grandfather who worked as a Cook on the railroad. My mother who is now 81 years old remembers her father working for the company.

Registrant ID: 3243
Name: William Reid
City/State: Suffolk, VA
Railroad: Norfolk &western
Position: Waiter
Years of Service: 35 to 40yrs
Submitter's Name: Laurell
City/State: Virginia Beach, VA
Comments: He was also was a laborer in Suffolk, VA for Norfolk & Western Railroad starting about 1932. Living survivor is my mother, daughter of Mr. Wm. Clarence Reid (nick name Bill or Chum)

Registrant ID: 3244
Name: William Reledge
City/State: IN
Position: Porter
Years of Service: 1940-1963
Submitter's Name: Geraldine
City/State: Gary, IN
Comments: My grandfather

Registrant ID: 3245
Name: Frank Render
City/State: AL
Railroad: Southern
Position: Pullman Porter
Years of Service: 1940's- 50's
Submitter's Name: Toni
City/State: Lithonia, GA

Registrant ID: 3246
Name: John Rentie
City/State: Seattle, WA
Railroad: R. R.B. No 9632
Position: Pullman Porter
Years of Service: 1937 - 1941
Submitter's Name: Janette
City/State: Seattle, WA
Comments: John Wesley
Rentie Born Feb 11,1916 Died
May 18, 1986 Married to Edna
(Ross) Rentie June 14, 1942 in
Everett WA Mrs. Rentie also died
May 18, 1986 Survived by
Janette Louise Rentie, only
daughter born 07/29/1954

Registrant ID: 3248
Name: Charles Reynolds
City/State: MO
Railroad: Union Pacific
Position: Dining Car Waiter
Years: 1940'S-1960'S
Submitter's Name: Larry
City/State: Kansas City, MO

Registrant ID: 3249
Name: John L. Rhodes
City/State: CA
Railroad: Rock Island
Colorado Springs
Position: First African American
Brakeman
Years of Service: 1900's-1932
Submitter's Name: Jennie
City/State: M.V, CA
Comments: The African
American Brakeman

Registrant ID: 3251
Name: James Rhone
City/State: RI
Position: Pullman Porter
Submitter's Name: Ellen
City/State: Bayonne, NJ
Comments: My grandfather,
James Baron Rhone, worked on
the railroad, many years ago. I
know he was originally from
Newbern, North Carolina, but I
believe his home would have
been listed in Providence, Rhode
Island.

Registrant ID: 3253
Name: John Rhone
City/State: Dallas, TX
Position: Sleeping Car Porter &
Dinning Car Waiter
Years: 1930 to August 1951
Submitter's Name: ILene
City/State: Dallas, TX
Comments: My father passed
away when I when I was seven
months old. I have been told a
story of how his friends would
assist my family after his death.
I met a man by the name of Mr.
Childs, who was maybe as old as
100 that was a close friend of my

father's and worked side by side with him.

Registrant ID: 3255
Name: Wendell Rhue
City/State: CA
Railroad: Pullman Co.
Position: Dining Car Waiter
Years of Service: Circa 1940's-50's
Submitter's Name: Candace
City/State: Los Angeles, CA

Registrant ID: 3254
Name: Thomas Howard Rhue
City/State: AL
Railroad: Union Pacific,
City of Los Angeles
Position: Waiter
Years of Service: 1944 - 1958
Submitter's Name: Thomas
City/State: Los Angeles, CA
Comments: Several of my dad's brothers also worked for the railroad and their descendants are registering with the museum also. We are the Rhues, descendants of escaped enslaved people who went to Canada through the Underground Railroad. My dad's father, William Rhue and his wife, Electa Robbins, lived in the escaped slave settlement of North Buxton, Ontario, Canada. We trace the Rhue side of the family in Canada to the mid-1800s and have recently discovered a wedding certificate on the Robbins side of the family dated 1804. Oral tradition says that "Rhue" was the name of the French Canadian abolitionist who befriended my ancestors and, as was the custom, the escaped enslaved often changed their names once in Canada to confuse the bounty hunters. Oral tradition also says that the original male Rhue was an escaped slave from the Miles Plantation in Maryland.

Registrant ID: 3259
Name: Oresterous Rice
Position: Cook
Years of Service: 20-30 Years
Submitter's Name: Ruth
City/State: Berea, KY

Registrant ID: 3257
Name: Lucious T. Rice
City/State: Bronx, NY
Position: Porter
Years of Service: 1946-50
Submitter's Name: Mrs. Yvette
City/State: Bonx, NY

Registrant ID: 3262
Name: Axan Richards
Submitter's Name: Charles

Registrant ID: 3273
Name: Joseph Richardson
City/State: New Orleans, LA
Railroad: Illinois Central
Years of Service: Approx.20-25
Comments: Mr. Richardson was my step grandfather and he died when I was a child.
Unfortunately I have no knowledge of his experiences.

Registrant ID: 3280
Name: Owen Jr.Richardson Jr.
City/State: Arkron, OH
Railroad: Pullman Company
Position: Porter
Years of Service: 1938-1944

Registrant ID: 4209
Name: George Washington Richardson
Railroad: Pullman Company
Position: Sleeping Car Porter
Submitter's Name: Richardson

Registrant ID: 3264
Name: Daniel Richardson
City/State: Cross, SC
Years of Service: 1930's - 40's
Submitter's Name: Kenneth
City/State: Brooklyn, NY

Registrant ID: 3267
Name: Henry Richardson
City/State: Carson, CA
Position: Cook and Server
Years of Service: 1943-1955
Submitter's Name: Joan
City/State: Carson, CA

Registrant ID: 3266
Name: Frank G. Richardson
City/State: Cleveland, OH
Position: Pullman Porter
Years of Service: 52 Years
Submitter's Name: Joseph S.
City/State: Cleveland, OH
Comments: My father was hired by the Pullman company when he was 17 years old. He died in 1932. At that time he was the oldest porter in service, he has been a porter for 52 years. He worked up to two weeks before his death...A Philip Randolph came to our home.

Registrant ID: 3277
Name: Robert Willis Richardson
City/State: Mt Vernon,
Position: Sleeping Car Porter
Years of Service: 1913-1918

Submitter's Name: Bob S
City/State: Mt Vezaon,
Comments: Attended Dillard University while working as Pullman Porter. We appreciate and were very proud of article that appeared in Ebony Magazine Feb 02-or 03

Registrant ID: 3274
Name: Percy Richardson
City/State: Berkeley, CA
Position: Waiter
Submitter's Name: Laurel
City/State: Oakland, CA

Registrant ID: 3270
Name: James Henry Richardson
City/State: Springfield, MA
Position: Pullman Porter
Years: Approx 1917 to 1929
Submitter's Name: Carolyn
City/State: Springfield, MA
Comments: Born in Buford, S C. Mother was Mary (Johnson) Richardson. Father was Sam Richardson. James was married to Minnie Christine (Sims) He had a sister Rebecca born 1832 died 1924, Rachel born after 1832 and a brother Robert born 1834.

Registrant ID: 3265
Name: Elvin E. Richards
City/State: San Antonio, TX
Railroad: Southern Pacific
Position: Pullman Porter
Years of Service: 1943-1970
Submitter's Name: Simmie T.
City/State: Waterbury, CT
Comments: My uncle Elvin's work was on a train running from San Antonio to the

Midwest, and from San Antonio to Los Angeles and Oakland, Ca.

Registrant ID: 3279
Name: Sammie Richardson Sr.
City/State: Marshall, TX
Railroad: Texas & Pacific
Position: Built boxcars, watered engines
Years of Service: 1940-1950
Submitter's: Leslie Nicole
City/State: Indianapolis, IN
Comments: Sammie was my grandfather July 3, 1917 - Jan 6, 1973 My grandmother Velma (Lee Cypress) Richardson Williams is 81.

Registrant ID: 3281
Name: Percy Ricks
City/State: Tuscumbia, AL
Railroad: Southern Railway
Position: Machine operator (4 yrs), fireman (45 yrs.), engineer
Years of Service: 51 years
Submitter's Name: Sonja
City/State: Davis, CA
Comments: My grandfather was a witness in the historical supreme court case of the Scottsboro Boys vs. Alabama. He was the train operator. Mr. Ricks was also the 1st Black Engineer for Southern Railway in the late 1960's. He was also a minister of Church.

Registrant ID: 3283
Name: Williams Arthur Ricks
City/State: Philadelphia, PA
Railroad: Pennsylvania RR
Position: Porter
Years of Service: 1933-1969
Submitter's Name: Diane

City/State: East Orange, NJ

Registrant ID: 3285
Name: Clifford A. Ridgeway
City/State: Seattle, WA
Railroad: I don't know exactly - I Think it was Western RR
Position: Sleeping Car Porter
Years of Service: At least 40
Submitter's Name: Ann
City/State: Columbus, OH
Comments: He was originally from Columbus, Ohio, as I am, and at some time moved to Denver, Colorado. Then some time after that, moved to Seattle Washington. He retired in the circa 1950's, 60's.

Registrant ID: 3289
Name: Samuel David Riggins
City/State: Cincinnati, OH
Position: Pullman Porter
Years of Service: 1941-57
Submitter's Name: Janice
City/State: Cincinnati, OH
Comments: Daughter

Registrant ID: 3291
Name: James Laverne Robbins
City/State: AL
Railroad: Canadian Pacific RR
Position: Pullman Porter
Years of Service: 1940 - 1979
Submitter's Name: Connie
City/State: Ontario , Canada
Comments: Stanley Grizzle Raymond Lewis (ran in the British Empire games and the 1932 63 Palmerton Sq Olympics)

Registrant ID: 3292
Name: Robert Robbins
City/State: Philadelphia, PA

Railroad: Pennsylvania
Position: Cook, Waiter
Years of Service: 1900-1945
Submitter's: Norman &
Kimberly
City/State: Philadelphia, PA
Comments: Norman states: Per oral history passed down through the years my grandfather worked on the rails as a Cook and or Dining Car Waiter. It was said that he had worked for the Pennsylvania Railroad and also worked on private cars that were attached to the main train. 'Kimberly Writes: I am not sure of his position but he (my great-grandfather) worked on the Eastern Shore to Chicago line. I believe he was some type of engine worker. He traveled up and down the east coast for many years.

Registrant ID: 3296
Name: Shirlene
City/State: Lamaring, MI
Railroad: Pullman Company

Registrant ID: 3293
Name: Myles Roberson
City/State: Lima, OH
Railroad: Pullman Company
Position: Pullman Porter
Years of Service: 1924-1964
Submitter's Name: Downton

Registrant ID: 3295
Name: Roye Roberson
Submitter's Name: Marguerite
City/State: Louisville, KY

Registrant ID: 3304
Name: William Roberts
Railroad: Pullman Company
Position: Porter
Years of Service: 1924-1930
Submitter's Name: Roberts

Registrant ID: 3303
Name: Samuel G. Roberts
City/State: Roanoke, VA
Railroad: Norfolk and Western
Submitter's Name: Craig
City/State: Detroit, MI

Registrant ID: 3305
Name: Willie Roberts
City/State: Fort Worth, TX
Railroad: Texas & Pacific
Position: Chef And
Dining Car Waiter
Years of Service: Not sure, he retired. Died in 1995 at age 90
Submitter's Name: Wilhelmina
City/State: Fort Worth, TX
Comments: It gave him the chance to travel around the country, see the world that he may not have been able to see on his on. His children and wife as well. He really enjoyed the work that he did. We heard some great stories.

Registrant ID: 3298
Booker T. (Eddie) Roberts
City/State: TX
Railroad: Union & Southern Pacific
Position: Pullman Porter and a Dining Car Waiter
Years of Service: 1939-1962
Submitter's Name: Annie Mary
City/State: Houston, TX

Comments: My father was born Booker T. Roberts but, during his many trips across the U.S. in the early 1940s, several Southern Belles commented on his name and good looks, after he completed his run he was informed that the "T" in his name had to be changed.

Registrant ID: 3300
Name: Dennis Presley Roberts
City/State: PA
Position: Waiter
Submitter(s): Denise Roberts
City/State: Stone Ridge, NY
Comments: My grandfather (deceased) worked as a waiter, on the New York New Haven and Hartford line - from about 1900 to the 1940's. He died in 1948, three years after retiring.

Registrant ID: 3306
Name: Ardee Robertson
City/State: Bay Minette, AL
Railroad: Gulf Mobile, L&N; Illinois Rock Island
Position: Pullman Porter
Years of Service: 1945-1953
Submitter's Name: Mildred
City/State: Bay Minette, AL

Registrant ID: 587
Name: Andrew Brown Robinson
City/State: Clinton, SC
Position: Sleeping Car Porter
Submitter's Name: Arlene
City/State: Clinton, SC
Comments: Andrew was my uncle. He worked out of Harlem, NY

Registrant ID: 3308
Name: John W. Robertson

City/State: NY
Railroad: Pennsylvania Railroad
Position: Dining Car Waiter
Years of Service: 1930-1971
Submitter's Name: Michele D.
City/State: Brooklyn, NY
Comments: My grandfather died September,1981. He retired from the Pennsylvania Railroad/Amtrak in 1971. In the 1960's he was transferred to the rail yards in Sunnyside, N.Y. where he worked until his retirement.

Registrant ID: 3309
Name: Joseph
City/State: Columbia, SC
Railroad: Erie Line
Submitter's Name: Shields
City/State: Columbia, SC

Registrant ID: 3327
Name: Percy Harry Robinson
City/State: Wichita, KS
Position: Pullman Porter
Submitter's Name: Nelson

Registrant ID: 3326
Name: Lenwood Robinson
City/State: Clinton, SC
Position: Dining Car Waiter

Registrant ID: 3332
Name: Walter Robinson
Railroad: El Paso
Years of Service: 1977's
Submitter's Name: Lawrence Lars

Registrant ID: 3311
Name: Amos Robinson
Railroad: L&N RR
Position: Boiler

Years of Service: 1924-1968
Submitter's Name: Ativie

Registrant ID: 3333
Name: William Robinson
Position: Pullman Porters
Years of Service: 1918
Submitter's Name: Evelyn

Registrant ID: 3331
Name: Walter Robinson
Submitter's Name: Lawrence

Registrant ID: 3324
Name: Lee Ray Robinson
City/State: Jacksonville, FL
Railroad: Atlantic Coastline
Railroad which became Seaboard
Coastline Railroad which
became Amtrak
Position: Waiter
Years of Service: 1960's-90's
Submitter's Name: Pearl
City/State: Atlanta, GA

Registrant ID: 3330
Name: Thomas Riley Robinson
City/State: Chicago, IL
Railroad: Illinois Central
Position: Dinning Car Waiter
Years: Approx. 1924-1928
Submitter's Name: Leandrian
City/State: Carson, CA
Comments: Thomas Robinson
contracted Bilateral Labor
Pneumonia and died at Illinois
Central Hospital on March 12,
1928.

Registrant ID: 3310
Name: Aliven L. Robinson
City/State: Chicago, IL
Submitter's Name: Aliven L Sr
City/State: Chicago, IL

Registrant ID: 3318
Name: Clarence Robinson
Position: Porter
Years of Service: 35
Submitter's Name: Delia Gray
City/State: Chicago, IL
Comments: My uncle's run was
from Washington DC west and
south.

Registrant ID: 3325
Name: Lenwood Robinson
City/State: Clinton, SC
Position: Sleeping Car Porter
Submitter's Name: Arlene
City/State: Clinton, SC

Registrant ID: 3321
Name: Foy Lee Robinson
City/State: AL
Railroad: The Pullman Company
Burlington Northern/Amtrak
Position: Pullman Porter
Years of Service: 1946 - 1987
Submitter's Name: Edward Lee
City/State: Federal Way, WA
Comments: My father due to his
age was probably one of the last
"True" Pullman Company
Employees, he started June 6,
1946 and retired from Amtrak in
1987.

Registrant ID: 3323
Name: Jesse Robinson
City/State: Decatur, AL
Position: Pullman
Submitter's Name: Cassie
City/State: Georgetown, KY

Registrant ID: 3315
Name: Benjamin Perry Robinson
City/State: Pine Bluff, AR
Railroad: Union Pacific

Position: Pullman Porter
Years of Service: 1880 to 1896
Submitter's Name: Sylvester
City/State: Greenwood, SC
Comments: He work in Arkansas on the railroad and move to Chicago in 1897. His granddaughter is my mother she is still lives in Chicago.

Registrant ID: 3319
Name: Douglas Robinson
Railroad: Penn Railroad
Years of Service: 1921-1962
Submitter's Name: Fran Cena
City/State: Jamaica, NY

Registrant ID: 3328
Name: Samuel Robinson
Railroad: Penn Rail Road
Years of Service: 1921-1962
Submitter's Name: Fran Cen
City/State: Jamaica, NY

Registrant ID: 4197
Name: Solom Warren Robinson
City/State: Jonesboro, GA
Railroad: Pullman Porter
Position: Waiter
Years of Service: 1940's
Submitter's Name: C.
City/State: Jonesboro, GA
Comments: Grandmother Bessie Harris was a cleaning woman for the Pullman Porters.

Registrant ID: 3329
Name: Solomon Robinson
City/State: PA
Railroad: Pennsylvania RR
Position: Waiter
Years of Service: 1946 - 1952
Submitter's Name: M. Arthur
City/State: Lund, Sweden, NY

Comments: I remember him taking us on the train between New York and Philadelphia, and he showed his employment card and the conductor never charged him for the ticket. Many of the cooks and waiters who were his friends, oftern visited him.

Registrant ID: 3334
Name: Oliver L. Robinson Sr.
City/State: Chicago, IL
Registrant ID: 3338
Name: Daniel Rodgers
Position: Porter
Submitter's Name: Zella
City/State: Homewood, IL

Registrant ID: 3339
Name: Frank Rodgers
Railroad: N W Railroad
Position: Porter
Submitter's Name: Zella
City/State: Homewood, IL

Registrant ID: 3340
Name: Napoleon Rodgers Sr.
City/State: St. Louis, MO
Position: Pullman Porter
Years of Service: 1937-1956
Submitter's Name: Nathaniel
City/State: Florissant, MO

Registrant ID: 3347
Name: Robert Rodgers
City/State: Chicago, IL
Railroad: Pullman Company
Position: Pullman Porter
Years of Service: 1942-1966
Comments: I worked as a Pullman Porter from 1942 until 1966, I was able to travel all over the United States.

Registrant ID: 3342
Name: Daniel Rodgers
Railroad: NW Rail Road
Position: Porters
Years of Service: 1930-1940

Registrant ID: 3343
Name: Frank Rodgers
Railroad: NW Rail Road
Position: Porters
Years of Service: 1930-1940

Registrant ID: 3348
Name: Robert M. Rodgers
City/State: Bolingbrook, IL
Railroad: Pullman Rail Car Co
Submitter's Name: Robert M.
City/State: Bolingbrook, IL

Registrant ID: 3341
Name: Charles Rodgers
City/State: Memphis, TN
Railroad: Pullman Company
Position: Pullman Porter
Years of Service: 1919 -1950's
Submitter's Name: Odella
City/State: Chicago, IL
Comments: My Grandfather helped secretly collect money from workers to help fund the starting of the union in Memphis Tenn.

Registrant ID: 3345
Name: Kahn Rodgers
City/State: Jacksonville, FL
Position: Pullman Porter
Years of Service: In the 50's
Submitter's Name: Ethel R.
City/State: Darlington, SC

Registrant ID: 3350
Name: David Rollerson Sr.
City/State: Omaha, NE

Railroad: Union Pacific RR
Position: Dining Car Porter
Years of Service: 20
Comments: Despite the sometime unfair treatment, I found the time I spent with the railroad a sound and productive way to support myself and family to a better lifestyle.

Registrant ID: 3351
Name: Peter Rollins
City/State: Phoenix, IL
Position: Porter
Years of Service: 1950's-1970's
Submitter's Name: Darrell
City/State: Harvey, IL

Registrant ID: 3352
Name: Percy Rolls
City/State: Wheeling, WV
Railroad: Canadian National Railway (CNR)
Position: Pullman Porter
Years: Approx 1911 - 1953
Submitter's Name: Frankie
City/State: Vallejo, CA
Comments: My Dad was born in Wheeling West Virginia around 1894. He was a Black American who naturalized as a Canadian sometime during his service with the CNR. His route was from British Columbia, Canada to Ontario, Canada.

Registrant ID: 3353
Name: Adolphus Rooker
City/State: Dalton, GA
Railroad: Southern Railroad
Position: Dining Car Waiter
Years of Service: 1940-1960
Submitter's Name: Johnnie
City/State: White Plains, NY

Comments: This was my father and he is deceased. His nickname on the railroad was "young blood".

Registrant ID: 3354
Name: George Rooker
City/State: Dalton, GA
Railroad: Southern Railroad
Position: Brakeman
Years of Service: 1890-1940
Submitter's Name: Johnnie
City/State: White Plains, NY
Comments: This was my grandfather and then my father Adolphus Rooker was a Dining Car Waiter from approximately 1940-1960 on the Southern Railroad. My grandfather told many "ghost" stories regarding his experience on the railroad.

Registrant ID: 3355
Name: Charles Rose
City/State: San Antonio, TX
Railroad: Missouri Pacific/ International Great Northern
Position: 1870-1879 Messenger,1879-1882 Brakeman,1882-1886 Fireman,1886-1888 Baggage porter,1888-1928 Train porter
Years of Service: 1870-1928
Submitter's Name: Rose
City/State: Adkins, TX
Comments: 1870-1879 he was in Houston, Texas. 1879-1882 he was in Palestine, Texas. He moved to San Antonio, Texas in 1888. He retired with a pension in 1928.

Registrant ID: 3356
Name: William Rose

City/State: Atlanta, GA
Railroad: Retired/Seaboard
Position: Chef
Years of Service: 42 yrs late 1800's thru early 1900's
Submitter's Name: Claudiette
City/State: Detroit, MI
Comments: My grandfather told me that he carried keys to the food pantry and that he cooked for presidents of the railroads in their private train cars.

Registrant ID: 3359
Name: Samuel S. Ross
City/State: St. Paul, MN
Railroad: Northern Pacific
Position: Waiter - Dinning Car
Years of Service: 1938 - 1963
Submitter's Name: Sandra
City/State: Toronto, Ontario, Canada M6K 1P9 --- formally of USA, MN
Comments: Working on the railroad gave my father the opportunity to buy a home, a car and provide for his children. He also worked on the railroad at a time when Black men home from the road, dressed well, and were very well respected. Proud men.

Registrant ID: 3360
Name: Edmond Rosser
City/State: Lynchburg, VA
Railroad: Lynchburg, VA
Position: Porter
Submitter's Name: June
City/State: Lynchburg, VA
Comments: My grandfather, (Edmund Rosser) was a Porter that helped people on and off trains when they came to Lynchburg, VA in the 1800's.

Registrant ID: 33
Name: Joseph Irvin Rosse
City/State: Lynchburg, VA
Railroad: Lynchburg, VA
Position: Dining Car Waiter
Years of Service: 1950's
Submitter's Name: June
City/State: Lynchburg, VA
Comments: His route was up and down the eastern states.

Registrant ID: 3361
Harvey Franklin Rountree
City/State: AL
Railroad: Pennsylvania/Silver Metro
Position: Dining Car Waiter
Years of Service: Prior to World War 2
Submitter's Name: Louise
City/State: Salisbury, NC

Registrant ID: 3362
Name: Carey G. Rouse
City/State: Chicago, IL
Position: Porter
Years of Service: 1930-35
Submitter's Name: Gwendolyn
City/State: Gwinn, MI

Registrant ID: 3364
Name: Fred Royal
City/State: Kansas City, MO
Railroad: Santa Fe Railroad
Position: laborer, unloading trains
Years: 1943 through 1979
Submitter's Name: Jackie
City/State: Toluca Lake, CA
Comments: My dad unloaded and cleaned trains, he had several positions as a laborer for Santa Fe Railroad.

Registrant ID: 3363
Name: Andrew B. Royal
City/State: Washington, DC
Railroad: Denver to Chicago
Position: Dining Car Porter
Years of Service: 1930's
Submitter's Name: George C.
City/State: Washington, DC

Registrant ID: 3365
Name: Gus Royal Jr.
City/State: Richmond, VA
Railroad: Richmond, F & Potomac
Position: Pullman Porter
Submitter's Name: Davis
City/State: Richmond, VA

Registrant ID: 3369
Name: Finney Rudolph
City/State: CT

Registrant ID: 3370
Name: Howard Ruffin
City/State: Merdian, MS
Railroad: Southern Railway
Position: Carmen
Years of Service: 1944 1970
City/State: AL
Comments: My grandfather was very proud of his position on the railroad as a coachman.

Registrant ID: 3372
Name: Fred C. Rush
Submitter's Name: Marquerito
City/State: Louisville, KY

Registrant ID: 3377
Name: William Russell
City/State: Portland, OR
Railroad: Union Pacific
Position: Waiter
Years: 1943 to 1978   35 years

Comments: The conditions we had to live under while on the road were hell! We had to sleep in the dining car after we cleaned up after the passengers. When we had a layover, we had to stay in run down hotels. During that era African-Americans had a very difficult time.

Registrant ID: 3373
Name: Faye Russell
City/State: Inkster, MICH
Railroad: Pullman Company
Position: Clerk
Years of Service: 10yrs

Registrant ID: 3376
Name: William Russell
City/State: Pittsburgh, PA
Railroad: Pennsylvania;
And Baltimore & Ohio
Position: Porter, Dining Car Waiter
Years of Service: 1940's-1960
Submitter's Name: Khalil
City/State: Atlanta, GA
Comments: He repaired watches for other Pullman Porters

Registrant ID: 3375
Name: William Russell
City/State: Chicago, IL
Railroad: B & O Capital Limit
Position: Dining Car Waiter
Years of Service: 40+
Submitter's Name: Barbara
City/State: Chicago, IL

Registrant ID: 3378
Name: Norris Rutherford
City/State: Louisville, KY
Submitter's Name: Julius B.
City/State: Louisville, KY

Comments: Worked 20 years:Other descendants Rose Atlanta GA, Ben Reeder Louisville KY

Registrant ID: 3379
Name: Eddie Rye, Sr.
City/State: Seattle, WA
Submitter's Name: Jackie
City/State: Seattle, WA

Registrant ID: 3380
Name: William J, Jr Sabbath
City/State: St Louis, MD
Position: Pullman Porter
Years of Service: 1966
Submitter's Name: Sabbath

Registrant ID: 3381
Name: Earl Sadler
City/State: Shreveport, LA
Position: Porter-KCS
Years of Service: 1942-1970
Submitter's: Wanda Jean
City/State: Moreauville, LA

Registrant ID: 3382
Name: Dozier Salley
City/State: AL
Railroad:Out of Charleston SC
Position: Porter
Years of Service: 1937
Submitter's Name: Mildred
City/State: Hamden Ct, CT
Comments: My grandfather Dozier Salley is no longer living he was my mother's father. I always remember my mother speaking of her father working for the railroad. My father gave me the date of 1937. I know he worked there for many years.

Registrant ID: 3383
Name: Isaac Salley
City/State: Seattle, WA
Position: Pullman Porter
Years of Service: Prior to 1956
Submitter's Name: Feloneze
City/State: Seattle, WA
Comments: I found out that my uncle was a porter via Census Information found at the University of Washington in Seattle. I was a student at the time and was just looking through census material. He and his brother Sylvester were both porters. Thank you so much for this reguistry.

Registrant ID: 3384
Name: A.C. Salley
Railroad: Santa Fe Railroad
Position: Pullman Porter
Years: June 1928 - July 1967
Submitter's Name: Phillip
City/State: Dallas, TX

Registrant ID: 3388
Joseph Addison Sampson
Position: Waiter
Years of Service: Circa 1930-1941
Submitter's Name: Linson J.
City/State: Chicago, IL

Registrant ID: 3387
Haywood Wesley Sampson
City/State: Wilmington, AL
Railroad: Atlantic Coast Line
Position: Fireman
Years of Service: 1910-1959
Submitter's Name: Margaret S.
City/State: Wilmington, NC
Comments: My father was born in Duplin County, January 1891.

He started my interst in history by the time I was in third grade.

Registrant ID: 3389
Name: Edward Sander
Railroad: Chicago
Position: Dining Car Waiter
Years of Service: 1940's
Submitter's Name: Delois J.
City/State: Chicago, IL

Registrant ID: 3390
Name: Jasper Sander
Position: Sleeping Car Porter
Years of Service: 1930-1935
Comments: Grandfather

Registrant ID: 3391
Name: Carl Sanders
City/State: Bossier City, LA
Submitter's Name: David E.
City/State: Houston, TX

Registrant ID: 3392
Name: Dave Sanders
City/State: CA
Position: Dining Car Waiter
Years of Service: 1946-1958
Submitter's Name: Lorraine
City/State: Los Angeles, CA

Registrant ID: 3395
Name: Elder Sanders
City/State: AL
Railroad: Southern Pacific
Position: Cook
Years Circa: 1924- 1950
Submitter's Name: James
City/State: Oakland, CA
Comments: My dad, Elder Sanders worked on trains for Southern Pacific for many years. He ran on trains from Oakland, California to Portland, Oregon;

Chicago, Illinois; Ogden, Utah; Los Angeles, California. He also worked on special trains from the West Coast to The Kentucky Derby and finally worked on a private car, (The Doctors Car), that went to different cities and stayed for awhile, so that the Doctor could give workers medical attention. He was a member of the Cooks and Waiters Union, located on Peralta Street, Oakland, California."

Registrant ID: 3425
Name: Edgar Saunders
City/State: Chicago, IL
Position: Pullman Porter
Years Circa 1940 - 1952
Submitter's Name: Sasha
City/State: Olympia Fields, IL
Comments: Mr. Saunders was my father.

Registrant ID: 3394
Name: Edward Sanders
City/State: New Orleans, LA
Position: Pullman Porter
Years of Service: 1930-40
Submitter's: Phyllis Walker
City/State: Roswell, GA
Comments: My Grandfather worked from New Orleans

Registrant ID: 3402
Name: George Julis Sanders
City/State: Los Angeles, CA
Position: Cook
Years of Service: 1930-1945
Submitter's: Margaret Ann
City/State: Los Angeles, CA

Registrant ID: 3400
Name: George Sanders

Position: Cook/porter
Years of Service: 1905-1920's
Submitter's Name: Sanders

Registrant ID: 3407
Name: James Thomas Sanders
City/State: Omaha, NE
Railroad: Union Pacific
Position: Pullman Porter
Submitter's Name: Susan
City/State: Jackson, MS
Comments: My grandfather traveled from Omaha to the West Coast.

Registrant ID: 3409
Name: Jesse Sanders
City/State: NY
Railroad: New York Central RR
Position: Dining Car Waiter
Years: Circa 1932-1935
Submitter's Name: Mary L
City/State: Buffalo, NY
Comments: Since I was a small child when Dad worked on the railroad, all that I can remember is that he talked about Chicago's "El" that ran by his hotel window when he "deadheaded" there.

Registrant ID: 3410
Name: Jonas Sanders
City/State: Merrillville, IN
Years of Service: 1920's
Submitter's Name: Percy
City/State: Merriville, IN

Registrant ID: 3411
Name: Satch Sanders
City/State: Warrensiville HTs, OH
Railroad: Pullman Company
Position: Cook
Years of Service: 1965-1969

Registrant ID: 3414
Name: Sheridan B. Sanders
City/State: Chicago, IL
Railroad: Pullman Co. later with Amtrak
Position: Dining Car Waiter
Years of Service: 1958 to 1989 (Retired from Amtrak
Submitter's Name: Dimitri L.
City/State: Huntington Beach, CA
Comments: He died in 1998

Registrant ID: 3426
Name: Gus Saunders
City/State: IL
Railroad: Illinois Central
Position: Pullman Porter and Waiter
Years of Service: 1940's
Submitter's Name: Warner
City/State: Chicago, IL
Comments: When I was a child, my father would occasionally take me with him on short trips of one day...I remember seeing him working as both a Pullman Porter and waiter on the trains. I always had dimes to spend because so many of his tips were dimes.

Registrant ID: 3427
Name: Powell Saunders
City/State: Bluefield, WV
Railroad: Norfolk and Southern
Position: Porter and Brakeman
Years of Service: 1955-1991
Submitter's Name: Latosha
City/State: Charlotte, NC

Registrant ID: 3429
Name: Frank Savage
City/State: NY
Railroad: Southern
Position: Pullman Porter

Years of Service: Circa 1899-1930
Submitter's Name: Diane
City/State: Greensboro, NC
Comments: I cannot remember the name of the railroad, but it ran from New York down through North Carolina. Both my grandfather, and his brother were Pullman Porters.

Registrant ID: 3430
Name: John Anthony Savage
City/State: NY
Railroad: Southern
Position: Pullman Porter
Years of Service: Circa 1899-1930
Submitter's Name: Diane
City/State: Greensboro, NC

Registrant ID: 3433
Name: Alphonso F. Saville
Position: Mail Clerk
Years Circae: Early 1900's late 50's
Submitter's Name: Janice S.
City/State: Chicago, IL

Registrant ID: 3436
Name: Hugh Sawyer
City/State: Harrisburg, PA
Position: Porter
Submitter's Name: Harold
City/State: Detroit, MI

Registrant ID: 3440
Name: William H. Sayles
City/State: Everett, MA
Submitter's Name: Beverly
City/State: Natick, MA
Comments: William was born 1865 died 1929. This documentation came from an old

newspaper clipping that belonged to a Mr. J. A. Roth, superintendent of North Station, who attended his funeral, as well as a Mr. George Price, supervisor of Porters, who spoke on their behalf at the funeral.

Registrant ID: 3437
Name: Napoleon Sayles
City/State: AL
Railroad: Santa Fe/Amtrak
Position: Dining Car Waiter
Years of Service: 1941-1976
Submitter's Name: Sandra
City/State: Shreveport, LA
Comments: My uncle retired in 1976. He died in 1987.

Registrant ID: 3443
Name: Gerald Scarborough
City/State: Chicago, IL
Railroad: Burlington Northern
Position: Maintenance
Years of Service: 2 years
Submitter's Name: Barbara, J
City/State: Calumet City, IL

Registrant ID: 3444
Name: James Scarfer
City/State: College Park, GA
Railroad: Southern Railroad
Position: Sleeping Car Porter
Years of Service: 1942- until layoff during the depression
Submitter's Name: Rossy
City/State: College Pk, GA
Comments: My father was laid of in 1943 during depression. He retired on disability in 1964.

Registrant ID: 3446
William Arthur Sr. Schell
City/State: Chicago, IL

Railroad: SR. ILL Central
Position: Porter
Years of Service: 30 yrs
Submitter's Name: Jackie
City/State: Park Forest, IL

Registrant ID: 3447
Name: Willis Schumacher
City/State: Kansas City, MO
Position: Pullman Porter
Submitter's Name: Leslee
City/State: Springfield, IL

Registrant ID: 3498
Name: Will Scott
City/State: Atlanta, GA
Position: Pullman Porter
Submitter's Name: Virgil M.
City/State: Atlanta, GA
Comments: My grandfather worked Circa from1926 to the mid 1950's. His routes were from the South to North and occasionally went west from Atlanta. My reference for this information was my father who is now deceased.

Registrant ID: 3489
Name: Julius Scott
City/State: New Jersey, NJ
Position: Porter
Years of Service: 1935-1978
Submitter's Name: Margie
City/State: Birmingham, AL
Comments: My Uncle

Registrant ID: 3460
Name: Crys Scott
City/State: New York, NY
Position: Porter
Years of Service: 1930-1969
Submitter's Name: Marjie
City/State: Birmingham, AL

Registrant ID: 3453
Name: Charles Scott
City/State: Buffalo, NJ
Railroad: NY Central Rail road
Years of Service: Retired 1964
Submitter's Name: Lynda
City/State: Buffalo, NJ
Comments: Grandfather worked for 43yrs died in 1982. He was an early supporter of the BSCP union.

Registrant ID: 3458
Name: Charles S. Scott
Railroad: NY Central Railroad
Years of Service: 43 Years
Submitter's Name: Lydia
City/State: Buffalo, NY

Registrant ID: 3480
Name: James (JB) Scott
City/State: Oak Park, IL
Railroad: Milwaukee Railroad
Position: Pullman Porter
Years of Service: 10-42 - 1968
Submitter's Name: Joan
City/State: Chicago, IL

Registrant ID: 3491
Name: Julius Caesar Scott
City/State: Jersey City, NJ
Railroad: New York Central
Position: Pullman Porter
Years of Service: 1929 to 1960
Submitter's Name: Carolyn
City/State: East Orange, NJ
Comments: My dad was very proud to work as a Pullman Porter for NY Central. He performed his job with diligence and pride. He received a letter from Herbert Hoover commending him for the fine service shown him by my Dad.

Registrant ID: 3493
Name: Linus J. Scott
City/State: Gary, IN
Railroad: Pullman Company Chicago West District
Position: Pullman Porter
Years of Service: 1941 to 1969
Submitter's Name: Noah L.
City/State: Gary, IN
Comments: When the railroad took over the sleeping cars I worked for Santa Fe Railroad and Amtrak until 1975. I had very good experiences while working for the company. I enjoy traveling to different places within the US.

Registrant ID: 3497
Name: Sport Scott
City/State: Jacksonville, FL
Railroad: Amtrak
Position: Sleeping Car Porter
Years of Service: 30 plus years
Submitter's Name: Patricia
City/State: Jacksonville, FL
Comments: Sport Arzolia Sylvester Scott, my grandfather passed away February 1991.

Registrant ID: 3492
Name: Leroy B. Scott
City/State: Perris, CA
Railroad: New York Central, Illinois Central, Pennsylvania
Position: Club Car Attendant
Years of Service: 1940-46
Submitter's Name: Celwyn
City/State: Kent, WA
Comments: It was my first job and although we only made $72.00 a month I got the opportunity to travel and see a

lot of different cities and experience many exciting things.

Registrant ID: 3459
Name: Clarence Scott
City/State: AL
Position: Porter
Years: 1930's and early 1940's
Submitter's Name: Mary
City/State: Lathrup, VA

Registrant ID: 3449
Name: Amos Scott
City/State: Chicago, IL
Railroad: Illinois Central RR
Position: Pullman Car Porter
Years of Service: 25 Years
Submitter's Name: Dolores
City/State: Markham, IL

Registrant ID: 3471
Name: Harry Scott
City/State: New York, NY
Position: Sleeping Car Porter
Submitter's Name: Michelle
City/State: New York, NY

Registrant ID: 3455
Name: Charles C. Scott
City/State: Mineral, VA
Railroad: Pullman Company
Position: Pullman Porter
Years of Service: 1941-1958
Submitter's Name: Harry W.
City/State: Port Jefferson
Station, New York
Comments: My uncle Charles informed me that Pullman Porters all worked for the Pullman Company not for the railroad companies. When the Pullman Co. went out of business- railroads) started hiring black porters directly.

There were no regular hours; job assignments could be from one week to three weeks. Porters kept a record of the hours they worked, a copy went to the local hiring hall; a copy to the Pullman Company; and the porter kept the third copy. Some porters were Porter- in-charge, others were Pullman conductors. Porters sometimes were posted to station duty." While out on the road and between runs, the Pullman office would lodge porters with either the YMCA or private homes. My father worked for the Pullman CO.

Registrant ID: 3478
Name: Henry L. Scott
City/State: Detroit, MI
Position: Pullman
Submitter's Name: Ronald K.
City/State: Rowlett, TX

Registrant ID: 3473
Name: Harry James Scott
City/State: Bronx, NY
Railroad: New York Central
Position: Waiter -in-charge
Years of Service: Over 30yrs
Submitter's Name: Margaret
City/State: Stone Mountain, GA
Comments: My father Harry J. Scott passed away on July 7,1972. He was a waiter-in-charge on New York Central Railroad for over 30 yrs. According to his army papers on enlistment, in the Army 1918 his vocation was waiter. My brother and I enjoyed many trips on the railroad. Of course these were trips from New York going

north. What an adventure, and being so proud that Dad was in charge. Smile. We took trips until we became teenagers and then we thought we were too mature. Thank you for this privilege

Registrant ID: 3475
Name: Henry Scott
Position: Track Layer
Years of Service: 1917-1928
Submitter's Name: Tamu
City/State: Union City, GA

Registrant ID: 3501
Name: George W. Scott, Sr.
City/State: Richmond, VA
Railroad: Chesapeake & Ohio
Position: Brakeman
Years of Service: 1900-1940
Submitter's Name: Robert H.
City/State: Philadelphia, PA

Registrant ID: 3503
Name: Marion Scruggs
City/State: Hollis, NY
Railroad: Seaboard Coastline
Position: Dining Car Waiter
Years of Service: 1946-1967
Submitter's: Marvin and Sharon
City/State: Hollis, NY
Comments: Sharon Writes: My father and the men he worked with truly represented a brotherhood. They called my father "Sarge" or "Scruggs." As a very young child, they always impressed me with the way they seemed to look out for each other.

Registrant ID: 3504
Name: Joseph Scudder
City/State: Shreveport, LA
Position: Fireman
Years of Service: 1934-1974

Submitter's Name: Linda
City/State: WI
Comments: My Grandfather

Registrant ID: 3507
Name: Willie (W W) Seals
City/State: Chattanooga, TN
Railroad: Southern
Position: Pullman Porter
Years of Service: 1943 to 1957
Submitter's Name: Al L
City/State: Chattanooga, TN
Comments: My father,W.W. Seals, is 89 years old and may be the sole surviving porter in Chattanooga. He has countless stories about his experiences. He would welcome an opportunity to share them.

Registrant ID: 3508
Name: Arthen W. Sean
City/State: Elgin, IL
Railroad: Penn. Rd
Position: Porter
Years of Service: 1911for 40yrs Then returned 1951
Submitter's: Arthen W Jr..
City/State: Elgin, IL
Comments: He was my father. His mother was a maid in Florida

Registrant ID: 3510
Name: Johnny L. Sears
Railroad: B & O and L & N
Position: Porter
Years of Service: 1928-1952
Submitter's Name: Jonnie
City/State: Cincinnati, OH
Comments: Began working at the age of 14. He was fired in 1952 for seating and elderly black couple in the rear of White only.

Johnny L. Sears

Registrant ID: 3514
Name: Edward Clarence Sease
City/State: Columbia, SC
Railroad: Southern
Years of Service: 1929-1950
Submitter's Name: Geneva
City/State: Columbia, SC

Registrant ID: 3518
Name: Hernan "Trucky" Seean
City/State: Patts, PA
Railroad: B&D, P&E,
Position: Sleeping Car Porter
Years of Service: 1920-1930

Submitter's Name: Bethy
City/State: Patts, PA
Comments: Grandfather

Registrant ID: 3515
Name: Leo Seay
City/State: Chicago, IL
Position: Porter
Years of Service:
Circa 1944 - 1984
Submitter's Name: Stephenye
City/State: Annapolis, MD

Registrant ID: 3523
Name: Frank Sellers, Sr.
City/State: DC
Railroad: Baltimore & Ohio
Position: Dining Car Waiter
Years of Service: 1935-1955
Submitter's Name: Frank J.
City/State: Chicago, IL
Comments: My father during
one period of his employment
worked on what was called the
"Presidential Special" which was
the special train used by
President Franklin D. Roosevelt
when he traveled outside of
Washington, D.C. He was a
Dining Car Waiter on this train.

Registrant ID: 3525
Name: LeRoy Joseph
Shackelford, II
City/State: Chicago, IL
Position: Porters
Submitter: Leroy Joseph III
City/State: Chicago, IL

Registrant ID: 3526
Name: Oscar Shamberger
City/State: Chicago, IL
Railroad: Pullman Railcar Co.
Position: Porter
Years of Service: 1938
Submitter's Name: Gwendolyn
City/State: Chicago, IL
Comments: I know very little. He owned a home in Morgan Park. None of his children to my knowledge worked for the railroad. His trips were to Mobile Alabama, I'm told. He was my grandfather. His wife's name was Annie McDole from Alabama.

Registrant ID: 3530
Name: Walter Edward
City/State: AL
Position: Pullman Porter
Submitter's Name: Carol A.
City/State: Ajax, AL
Comments: My father was proud member of the Sleeping Car Porters of Canada. I think it is important to include the Canadians who worked as porters. The African Canadians who worked, as porters would not have made the gains they did without the example set by A. Philip Randolph.

Registrant ID: 3529
Name: Hubert Sharp
Railroad: Penn Railroad
Years of Service: 1921-1962
Submitter's Name: Fran Cen
City/State: Jamaica, NY

Registrant ID: 3536
Name: Hubert Sharpe

City/State: Pittsburgh, PA
Railroad: Pennsylvania, Pittsburgh Lake Erie
Position: Porter
Years of Service: 1923
Submitter's Name: Anthony
City/State: Hamburg, NY
Comments: My grandfather Hubert St. Clair Sharpe was killed in 1923 when the train he was working on left the tracks near Franklin, PA. He was working a run from Buffalo to Pittsburgh.

Registrant ID: 3540
Name: Frank Shaw
City/State: Los Angeles, CA
Railroad: Southern Pacific, Oakland Chicago
Submitter's Name: Frank
City/State: Los Angeles, CA

Registrant ID: 3538
Name: Eugene "Jim" Shaw
City/State: La Grange, NC
Railroad: Norfolk Southern
Position: Pullman Porter
Years of Service: 37
Submitter's Name: Eugene
City/State: New York, NY

Registrant ID: 3544
Name: William Sheffield
City/State: Hot Springs, AR
Railroad: Missouri Pacific/Hot Springs To Little Rock
Position: Pullman Porter
Submitter's: Grant Sheffield
City/State: Kansas City, KS
Comments: All I Knew, that he had a run between Hot Springs and Little Rock Arkansas. He, has Two sons in Richmond Va.

and one in Topeka Kansas.
Deceased

Registrant ID: 3547
Name: Jim Shelby
City/State: Chicago, IL
Submitter's Name: Denise
City/State: Chicago, IL
Comments: Lived in Chicago, he passed in 1958 while making last run from Chicago to Las Angeles.

Registrant ID: 3548
Name: Willie Lee Shelmon
City/State: Chattanooga, TN
Railroad: Southern
Position: Pullman Porter
Years of Service: 1939-1964
Submitter's Name: William
City/State: Lathrup Village, MI
Comments: He really enjoyed his work and took great pride in the service he was providing. His train route of travel was back and forth between Chattanooga and Cincinnati was a very rewarding experience for him.

Registrant ID: 3549
Name: Daniel Shelton
Submitter's Name: Regina
Registrant ID: 3555
Name: Oscar Shelton
City/State: Washington,, DC
Position: President, Brotherhood of Sleeping Car Porters, Chapter in Washington, DC
Years of Service: Circa1920-1955 received a 35 year pin at retirement
Submitter's Name: William
City/State: Seabrook,, MD
Comments: Minimal amount of information known. I

understand that he was very active in the "Brotherhood". As the family genealogist/historian, I am currently researching his activities. Oscar Wise Shelton was born 1895 or 1896 and died July 12, 1977.

Registrant ID: 3556
Name: James H. Shelton, Sr.
City/State: Washington, DC
Position: Instructor
Years of Service: 1933-1969
Submitter's Name: Joel P.
City/State: Washington, DC

Registrant ID: 3558
Captain. Charles Shephard
Railroad: Northern Pacific
Submitter's Name: Joan
City/State: St. Paul, MN

Registrant ID: 3563
Name: George Sherman Sr.
City/State: Detroit, MI
Railroad: Pennsylvania
Position: Pullman Porter
Years of Service: 1920-1927
Submitter's Name: Dorothy
City/State: Detroit, MI

Registrant ID: 3564
Name: Moses Shields
City/State: Bronx, NY
Railroad: Santa Fe Southern Contential Route
Position: Pullman Porter
Years of Service: He retired in the late 50's
Submitter's Name: Shields
City/State: Arverne, NY

Registrant ID: 3566
Name: Chester Shipps

City/State: Springfield, MO
Railroad: Frisco Railroad
Position: Porter Breakman

Registrant ID: 3565
Name: Chester Shipps
City/State: Springfield, MO
Railroad: Frisco Railroad
Position: Porter Breakman
Submitter's Name: Cecilia
City/State: St. Louis , MO
Comments: My Dad, Chester W.
Shipps will celebrate his 91st
Birthday, on July 27, 2002. My
dad has a very good memory,
and able to travel, while he's in
good health. His company
Shipps Electric is over 57 years
old, and he still works off and on
his business.

Registrant ID: 3567
Name: Edmond A. Shirley
City/State: Louisville, KY
Position: Pullman Porter
Years of Service: 1945-1950

Registrant ID: 3570
Name: Squire Shores
City/State: MO
Position: Porter
Submitter's Name: Jean
City/State: Chicago, IL
Comments: I have another
relative, George Shores who also
worked as a porter on the
railroad.

Registrant ID: 3574
Name: Ulysses Short, Sr.
City/State: New Orleans, LA
Railroad: Pullman, Co.
Position: Pullman Porter
Years of Service: 30 Years

Submitter's Name: Melisande
City/State: New Orleans, LA
Comments: My grandfather was
a lifetime employee of the
Pullman, Co, as were my great-
uncle,my father, my uncle,many
cousins and family friends.
During the early sixties, the
company sent my grand-father to
Mexico, to help train their
Porters, as he spoke very good
Spanish.

Registrant ID: 3579
Name: Willie Clyde Shy Sr.
City/State: Toledo, OH
Submitter's Name: Willie Clyde
City/State: Toledo, OH

Registrant ID: 3580
Name: John J. Sickley McIver
City/State: Chicago, IL
Railroad: Northwestern
Position: Porter
Years of Service: 1940-1960
Submitter's Name: Jean
City/State: Chicago, IL

Registrant ID: 3585
Name: Joseph Simmons
City/State: Birch, VA
Railroad: Santa Fe-Carolina
Position: Porter
Years of Service: 1929-1928
Submitter's Name: Neal
City/State: Burk, VA

Registrant ID: 3583
Name: Benjamin Simmons
City/State: East Orange, NJ
Position: Track Worker
Years of Service: 1940-48
Submitter's Name: Gwendolyn
City/State: East Orange, NJ

Registrant ID: 3589
George Benjamin SimmonsSr.
City/State: Amite, LA
Railroad: Pullman Company
Chicago Central District
Position: Pullman Porter
Years of Service: 1943-1946
Submitter's Name: Sharon
City/State: Chicago, IL
Comments: We have my
grandfather's uniform, coffee
holder, and time sheets.

Registrant ID: 3591
Name: Paul Simms
City/State: Wilson, NC
Position: Porter
Years: Early 30's -40's
Submitter's Name: Velma
City/State: Wilson, NC
Comments: Uncle Paul was a
Porter, I believe on the Seaboard
Train Company. I heard so
much about his travels from city
to city and state to state as a
youngster. He was my
grandmother's brother (Gertrude
Simms Hoskins).

Registrant ID: 3593
Name: David Simpson
City/State: Harrisburg, AL
Position: Porter
Years of Service: 1929-1941
Submitter's Name: Cootie
City/State: IL

Registrant ID: 3600
Name: Hernan Sims
City/State: Leaborn, OH
Railroad: B&O
Years of Service: 1914
Submitter's Name: Byid

Registrant ID: 3598
Name: C. D. Sims
City/State: Kansas City, CA
Railroad: Santa Fe
Position: Sleeping Car Porter
Years of Service: Circa 1938-
1950
Submitter's Name: William C.
City/State: Los Angeles, CA
Comments: C. D. Sims (my
uncle) was a Sleeping Car Porter
from the earliest days of my
memory until I was in high
school. His run was from
Kansas City to somewhere in
Kansas (Emporia?); it was a day
trip, and he often treated my
brothers and I to a trip.

Registrant ID: 3601
Name: John Henry Sims
City/State: Salem, OR
Position: Spikel
Years of Service: 1966-67
Submitter's Name: Henry Dell
City/State: Salem, OR

Registrant ID: 3606
Name: Rodney R. Sims Sr.
City/State: Chicago, IL
Railroad: Santa Fe Railroad
Position: Linen Man / Dining
Car Waiter / Pantry Man /
Lounge Car Attendant
Years of Service: 1943- 1982
Comments: It was hard work
with long hours but it afforded
me the opportunity to raise a
family and send four children
through college.

Registrant ID: 3607
Name: Charles Singleton, Sr.

City/State: Columbia, SC

Registrant ID: 3609
Name: Thomas Henry Sisney
City/State: Nashville, TN
Railroad: L & N
Position: Pullman Porter
Years of Service: Circa 1940-1946 **Submitter(s):** Janice
City/State: Nashville, TN
Comments: My father's line was called the Dixie Flyer from Nashville to Florida I believe. Please note that my father is deceased the above address is where we lived while he worked for the railroad.

Registrant ID: 3611
Name: Henry Skeeter
City/State: Suffolk, VA
Years of Service: Early 1900's
City/State: AL
Comments: All I know is my Grandfather was a Porter in the early half of the 1900's.

Registrant ID: 3618
Name: George A. Slade
City/State: AL
Position: Pullman Porter
Years of Service: 1916-1970
Submitter's Name: Elizabeth A.
City/State: Washington , D.C.
Comments: Daughter

Registrant ID: 3621
Name: Ernest Slaughter
City/State: Landover, MD
Railroad: Seaboard Coastline And Amtrak
Position: Pullman Porter
Years of Service: 1951-1983
Submitter's Name: Vanessa

City/State: Forestville, MD
Comments: My father is now deceased but he took great pride in wearing his uniform and serving the public. My uncle and brother both also worked for the railroad. My family and I still travel by train and on occasion we will meet current railroad employees who knew them and still speak of them in high regards. During his career he mostly worked the route that took him to Canada and the route that took him to New Orleans.

Registrant ID: 3624
Name: Willie Spencer Slaughter
City/State: Tacoma Park, MD
Position: Waiter
Years of Service: 1940's-1970
Submitter's Name: Wilmatine
City/State: Tacoma Park, MD

Registrant ID: 3623
Name: Ernest L. Slaughter
Submitter's Name: Wilmatine
City/State: Tacoma Park, MD

Registrant ID: 3625
Name: Benjamin Slaus
City/State: Los Angeles, CA
Railroad: California Line
Position: Pullman Porter Porter
Years of Service: 1936-
Submitter's Name: Benjamin
City/State: Los Angeles, CA
Comments: Chg 98 years old

Registrant ID: 3628
Name: Gerald Sleigh
City/State: New York, NY
Railroad: Pennsylvania

Position: Waiter
Years of Service: 1929-1960

Registrant ID: 3629
Name: Gerald Elliot Sleigh
City/State: New York, NY
Railroad: Pennsylvania RR
Position: Dining Car Waiter
Years of Service: 1942-1970
Submitter(s): Geraldine and Denise
City/State: New York, NY
Comments: Geraldine Writes: My father worked during the years when black people were treated as second-class citizens. He experience prejudice every time he went to work. But he raised his girls to look beyond the color of a person skin, to look at the color of ones character. 'Denise Writes: Pres. Of Penn Railroad was involved closely with A. Philip Randolph.

Registrant ID: 3630
Name: Thomas Sloan
City/State: Bakersfield, CA
Railroad: Southern Pacific
Position: Carried luggage
Submitter's Name: Beverly
City/State: Sacramento, CA
Comments: My husband's great grandfather was a porter. I remember hearing about it from my husband's grandmother. She said he traveled all the time.

Registrant ID: 3632
Name: C.J.Sloss
Position: Pullman Porter
Years of Service: Over 25
Comments: He was a member of the union.

Registrant ID: 3641
Name: Willie Nathan Small
City/State: Palatka, FL
Submitter's Name: Rudy
City/State: Deltona, FL

Registrant ID: 3639
Name: Elmer Small
City/State: New Orleans, LA
Railroad: L & N & Crescent
Position: Sleeping Car Porter
Years of Service: 1919-1967
Submitter's: Judy, Lois, Louis,Rhea
City/State: Gulfport MS, Syracuse NY, Oakland, CA
Comments: Judy states: My grandfather born January 16, 1902 died in 1984. he ran from new Orleans to new York. We aren't certain of the years, but we think he retired in 1966 - '67. His twin brother, Alvin small, was also a Pullman porter who ran from new Orleans to California. 'Rhea Writes: Elmer Small and other Pullman Porters worked as conductors without conductors' pay. A lawsuit was filed against the Pullman company and was won.The Pullman Porters won the lawsuit and were paid the back money owed them.

Registrant ID: 3633
Name: Alvin Small
City/State: New Orleans, LA
Railroad: Sunset Limited
Position: Pullman Porter
Submitter's Name: Judy
City/State: Gulfport, MS
Comments: My uncle died in 1991. We think he retired in

1967-'68. He ran from New Orleans to California. His twin brother, Elmer small, my grandfather were both Pullman porters. Their DOB was Jan16,1902.

Registrant ID: 3637
Name: Ceasar Small
City/State: New Orleans, LA
Position: Pullman Porter
Submitter's Name: Cheri
City/State: Warrensville Heights, OHio
Comments: Ceasar was my great uncle

Registrant ID: 3643
Name: Henry Smallwood
City/State: Petersburg, PA
Position: Dining Car Waiter
Years of Service: 1947-1969
Submitter's Name: Ann
City/State: Petersburg, PA
Comments: My Father

Registrant ID: 3650
Name: Alphonso Rex Smith
City/State: AL
Position: Red Cap
Years of Service: 1930-1936
Submitter's Name: Lillian
City/State: Philadelphia, AL
Comments: Widow

Registrant ID: 3723
Name: Arthur Smith Sr.
City/State: AL
Years of Service: Until 1968
Submitter's Name: Arthur S.
City/State: AL

Registrant ID: 3652
Name: Augustus Smith
City/State: Norfolk, VA

Railroad: Seaboard R R.
Position: Pullman Porter
Years of Service: 1947 - 1959
Submitter's Name: William A.
City/State: Mechanicsville, VA
Comments: My father traveled between Portsmouth, VA. and Miami, FL. He was a Porter for a few years and then he worked as a porter for the vice-president of Seaboard R. R.(Mr. Simpson) traveling on a private car. My father died in 1959. Everyone called him Gussie.

Registrant ID: 3653
Name: Bradley Smith
City/State: Washington, DC
Railroad: Washington, DC
Position: Private car assignments
Submitter's Name: Gladys
City/State: Washington, DC
Comments: Mostly, he was assigned to private car service. There were tantalizing stories told throughout the generations of such luminaries as the Prince of Wales, J.P. Morgan, and General Pershing, among others.

Registrant ID: 3656
Name: Briller Smith
City/State: El Paso, TX
Railroad: T&NO
Position: Pullman Porter
Submitter's Name: Cecilia
City/State: Las Vegas, NV
Comments: We are not quite sure when my grandfather began his service as a porter. He met his last wife on the train as he was working, and they married in 1925. He retired in 1955.

Registrant ID: 3657
Name: Carson K. Smith
City/State: Chicago, IL
Position: Porter
Submitter's Name: Mable S.
City/State: Chicago, IL
Comments: He was my brother

Registrant ID: 3662
Name: Curtis H. Smith
City/State: Bronx, NY
Railroad: New York Central
Position: Dining Car Waiter
Years of Service: 1945 to 1951
Submitter(s): Denise
City/State: Bronx
Submitter Tara
City/State: Jamaica, NY
Comments: He was featured in
Ebony Magazine, June 1947
issue. The title of the article was
Around the Clock with a
freshman Dining Car Waiter. I
told my aunt that I read about
the Pullman Porter Museum and
would like to submit his name.
His wife Thelma is still living.

Registrant ID: 3666
Name: Eugene Smith
City/State: IL
Railroad: The Pullman Co.
Position: Sleeping Car Porter
Years of Service: 1920-1963
Submitter's Name: Tracye E.
City/State: Chicago, IL
Comments: He was a staunch
member of the Brotherhood of
Sleeping Car Porters. He
routinely brought his children to
union offices when he paid his
dues or handled other union
business. His son, Richard

Eugene Smith won a Pullman
Scholarship to attend IIT.

Registrant ID: 3664
Name: Eugene
City/State: AL
Position: Porter
Years of Service: Early 1900's
Submitter's Name: Gregory
City/State: Flossmoor, IL
Comments: Lived in Chicago.

Registrant ID: 3667
Name: Golden W.Smith
City/State: Los Angeles,, CA
Railroad: California Zephyr: City
of Los Angeles; San Francisco
Chief
Position: Porter
Years: May 1910-Jan 1955
Submitter's Name: Dolores J.
City/State: Chicago,, IL
Comments: Worked 44 years, 8
month; he was never late and
only missed one-half of a run to
California due to a train wreck in
which all passengers and crew
were taken to the hospital for
observation. The Chicago
Defender Newspaper wrote an
article on my grandfather.

Registrant ID: 3668
Name: Henry Smith
City/State: NC
Position: Porter
Years of Service: 1941-45
Submitter's Name: Joan
City/State: Whiteville, NC

Registrant ID: 3669
Name: Issac M. Smith
Position: Porter
Years of Service: 1889-1937

Submitter's Name: William
City/State: Denver, CO
Comments: Issac was my uncle

Registrant ID: 3671
Name: James Smith
City/State: Simi Valley, CA
Submitter's Name: Rodney
City/State: Arlington, TX
Comments: Mr. Smith was a dining car waiter, and he has fascinating stories about his years as a dining car waiter. I have listened for hours about how professional and courteous he and his fellow waiters were in spite of hostile racism.

Registrant ID: 3672
Name: James Smith
City/State: Cleveland, OH
Railroad: Pennsylvania
Position: Pullman Porter
Years of Service: 43
Submitter's Name: Thomas
City/State: Cleveland, OH
Comments: During World War II, he stayed on a troop train with soldiers and was gone for months at a time. He was father to seven sons and often told us stories of his experiences as a Pullman Porter.

Registrant ID: 3729
Name: James I. Smith Jr.
City/State: Belgit, WA
Position: Conductor
Years of Service: 1970-2001
Submitter's Name: Ike
City/State: Beloit, WI

Registrant ID: 3673
Name: James Edward Smith

City/State: Cincinnati, OH
Railroad: Big Four
Position: Porter
Years of Service: 1925-1930
Submitter's Name: JE
City/State: Cincinnati, OH
Comments: Hard work ..little pay.

Registrant ID: 3676
Name: John Thomas Smith
City/State: AL
Position: Pullman
Submitter's Name: Walter L.
City/State: Chicago, IL

Registrant ID: 3677
Name: Joseph Lee Smith
Position: Waiter/Porter
Years: Circa 1940-1969
Submitter's Name: Audrey
City/State: Carson, CA

Registrant ID: 3680
Name: Joyce N Smith
Railroad: Pullman Company
Position: Laid Railroad Ties
Years of Service: 1954-1956
Submitter's Name: Foster

Registrant ID: 3675
Name: John Smith
City/State: DC
Position: Porter
Years of Service: 1900's
Submitter's Name: Alicia
City/State: Roxbury, MA
Comments: He was my maternal grandmother's second husband and she lived in dc for many years while he worked there, she was a housekeeper for a then prominent attorney, Karl Flocks,

Chainbridge Road, NW, that's all I remember.

Registrant ID: 3682
Name: Julius Edward Smith
City/State: Richmond, VA
Railroad: RF&P
Position: Pullman Porter
Years of Service: Approx 4 years prior to retirement
Submitter's Name: Doris
City/State: Richmond, VA
Comments: J. E. Smith (JE as he was called) worked from Richmond to New York and Winston Salem and back to New York to Richmond. I am his only living granddaughter he was a fine and kind man. My sister and I helped to clean and change the berths as little girls.

Registrant ID: 3683
Name: Lawrence C. Smith
City/State: Memphis,, TN
Railroad: Union Pacific
Position: Dining Car Waiter
Years of Service: 1943 to 1971
Submitter's Name: Laurice
Comments: Lawrence C. Smith is deceased; died on Feb. 19, 2001. My Dad had mostly good experiences for the railroad. He ran on the Los Angeles to Chicago route and had the opportunity to meet many celebrities, such as Frank Sinatra, Pearl Bailey, Edward R. Murrow.

Registrant ID: 3684
Name: Mack Smith
City/State: Washington, DC
Railroad: Seaboard out of Humlet NC to NY to FL

Position: Dining Car Waiter
Submitter's Name: Donald
City/State: Washington, DC
Comments: Grandfather, moved from Hamlet NC to Spartanburg, 3-4 sons and 4 daughters.

Registrant ID: 3685
Name: Mr. Smith
Railroad: Union Pacific
Position: Dining Car Waiter
Years Retired 1958 or 1968
Submitter's Name: Laurice
City/State: Memphis, TN

Registrant ID: 3687
Name: Osey Smith
City/State: AK
Railroad: Pullman Co
Texas & Pacific
Position: Pullman Porter
Submitter's Name: Latrice

Registrant ID: 3688
Name: Ralph Smith
City/State: El Paso, TX
Railroad: Southern Pacific
Position: Chair Car Porter
Years: late 40's to 1976
Submitter's Name: Cecilia
City/State: Las Vegas, NV
Comments: My father (deceased in 1996) was very active with the union in El Paso. He served as Sec'y-Treasurer for quite a while. My mother has a large group photo of him with other attendees at a convention in Chicago. Mr. Randolph was in the photo as well.

R.C. Smith

Registrant ID: 3698
Name: R.C. Smith
City/State: Buffalo, NY
Position: Pullman Porter
Submitter's Name: Ronald
City/State: Chicago, IL
Comments: R. C. was my father

Registrant ID: 3689
Name: Richard Smith
City/State: Chicago, IL

Registrant ID: 3691
Name: Robert Smith
City/State: IL
Submitter's Name: Marilyn
City/State: Elmhurst, IL

Registrant ID: 3692
Name: Robert P. Smith
City/State: New York, NY

Position: Pullman Porter
Years of Service: I believe some time in the 1920's
Submitter's Name: Hugh
City/State: Jacksonville, NC
Comments: He was married to a woman named Emma Rosa Robinson in the Bronx or Manhattan New York. In my research from a letter I found out that he died in a train accident and his wife received his pension.

Registrant ID: 3694
Name: Roman Smith
City/State: MN
Railroad: Great Northern
Position: Pullman Porter
Years of Service: 1940-1955
Submitter's Name: Cheryl
City/State: Minneapolis, MN

Registrant ID: 3701
Name: Steward Smith
City/State: Cincinnati, OH
Railroad: C&O
Position: Pullman Porter
Years of Service: 1949-1961
Submitter's Name: Gail
City/State: Cincinnati, OH
Comments: He was my grandfather. He worked for the railroad for 12 years. He passed away on train in 1961.

Registrant ID: 3702
Name: Stewart Smith
City/State: Cincinnati, OH
Railroad: Pullman Company
Position: Pullman Porter
Years of Service: 1923-1963
Submitter's Name: Baker

356

Registrant ID: 3708
Name: Sylvester Smith
City/State: Cincinnati, OH
Railroad: All
Position: Pullman Porter
Years: 1940- to-1955
Submitter's Name: William
City/State: Burien, WA
Comments: My father worked on all trains, in all 48 states.

Registrant ID: 3709
Name: Talbot Smith
Position: Pullman Porter
Years of Service: 1917 - Retirement
Submitter's Name: Elrath P.
City/State: Chicago, IL

Registrant ID: 3710
Name: Thomas Smith
City/State: Cincinnati, OH
Position: Pullman Porter
Submitter's Name: Charles
City/State: Cincinnati, OH

Registrant ID: 3712
Name: Walter Smith
City/State: Birmingham, AL
Position: Sleeping Car Porter
Years of Service: Approx 1939 to 1945 during World War II. Intermittently after that into the 1950's. **Submitter(s):** Rose
City/State: Birmingham, AL
Comments: Walter Smith was my father, born July 26, 1899 and died June 1994. (The address given for him is where he lived during the time he worked for Pullman.) He was not young enough to be drafted into the military. The US government required him to hold a "defense"

job and that is how he ended up becoming a Pullman Porter. "I have been to all 48 states," he'd say. He enjoyed his years as a porter and the only down side to it was being away from his wife and children. He did speak about the prejudice but never belabored it. He would tell interesting stories about fellow workers and passengers. Sometime he would be gone for so long that I'd think he was just one of the many soldiers I'd seen on the street. His Pullman hat is a family treasure.

Registrant ID: 3730
Name: Walter L. Smith Sr.
City/State: Chicago, IL
Railroad: NY Central
Position: Waiter/
Pullman Porter
Years of Service: 1941-1956
Submitter's: Barbara, and Burham
City/State: Chicago, IL
Comments: Also Preston Barrett he was my uncle. Years that he worked for the railroad are unknown.

Registrant ID: 3716
Name: William Smith
City/State: Philadelphia, PA
Railroad: 30th Street Station
Position: Pullman Porter and a Red Cap
Submitter's Name: Teresa
City/State: Dothan, AL
Comments: My Grandfather started out as a Pullman Porter but was later laid off and then he got hired as a Red Cap. He was

also Secretary to the Auxiliary of the Railroad Brotherhood for the 30th Street Station in Philadelphia.

Registrant ID: 3718
Name: Willie Lee Smith
City/State: Akron, OH
Submitter's Name: Helen

Registrant ID: 3713
Name: Whitfield Smith
City/State: Redlick, MS
Position: Pullman Porter
Years of Service:
Submitter's Name: Taunya
City/State: Ridgeland, MS
Comments: I don't know the years my grandfather worked as a Pullman Porter, he is now deceased but it is something we talked about often. It had to have been in the late 30's early 40's because my father was young and of school age.

Registrant ID: 3738
Name: Clarence C. Smothers
City/State: IL
Position: Porter
Years of Service: 1922-1928
Submitter's Name: Shirley A.
City/State: Country Club Hills, IL

Registrant ID: 3740
Name: Contella Eugene Snelling
City/State: AL
Railroad: St. Louis - Francisco
Position: Train Porter
Years of Service: 1890-1937
Submitter's Name:
George/Caroline
City/State: St. Louis , MO

Registrant ID: 3742
Name: Dennis Snipe
City/State: Chicago, IL
Position: Porter
Years of Service: 1950
Submitter's Name: Ruth
City/State: Southfield, MI
Comments: My uncle is deceased. He used to stop in Detroit when they had a lay-over. I was very young at the time but I remember him telling our family stories about working in the dining car. My grandfather also worked for the railroad. His name was Raymond Snipe.

Registrant ID: 3746
Name: Ernest Snowden
City/State: Macon, GA
Railroad: Seaboard Railroad
Position: Fireman
Years: Mid 1920's to 1950's
Submitter's Name: Pearl
City/State: Atlanta, GA
omments: Ernest Snowden was one of four brothers who made a career working for the railroad. His brothers were Andrew, Booker T., and Roosevelt Snowden. Deceased

Registrant ID: 3743
Name: Andrew Snowden
City/State: Savannah, GA
Railroad: Seaboard Railroad
Position: Fireman
Years: Mid 1920's to 1950's
Submitter's Name: Pearl
City/State: Atlanta, GA
Comments: Andrew Snowden was one of four brothers who made a career working for the railroad. His brothers were

Ernest, Booker T., and Roosevelt Snowden. Deceased

Registrant ID: 3745
Name: Booker T. Snowden
City/State: Savannah, GA
Railroad: Atlantic Coastline Railroad which became Seaboard Coastline which became Amtrak
Position: Trainman-Conductor
Years: 1940's to 1976
Submitter's Name: Pearl
City/State: Atlanta, GA
Comments: My brother, Booker T. Snowden, was one of the first African-American conductors on a passenger train. In fact, he initiated a lawsuit for seniority placement. The lawsuit had not yet been resolved at the time of his passing. 'Booker T. was one of four brothers who had a career working on the railroad. His brothers were Ernest, Andrew, and Roosevelt. Deceased

Registrant ID: 3751
Name: Roosevelt Snowden
City/State: Savannah, GA
Railroad: Atlantic Coastline
Position: Fireman
Years of Service: 1920's-70's
Submitter's Name: Pearl
City/State: Atlanta, GA
Comments: My father, was one of four brothers who established a career on the railroad. His brothers were Ernest, Andrew, and Booker T. Snowden. Deceased

Registrant ID: 3759
Name: Virginias Southallsat
City/State: LA, CA

Railroad: 1933-1968
Submitter's Name: Christian
City/State: LA, CA
Comments: Worked for 35 years

Registrant ID: 3761
Name: John Spann
City/State: St. Louis, MO
Railroad: New York Central
Position: Sleeping Car Porter
Years of Service: 1949-1965
Submitter's Name: Elmira
City/State: Columbia, MD
Comments: I only remember, riding the train from St. Louis to Memphis Tennessee with my family and smelling the fried chicken that was served in the diner. We had a train pass until we turned 18. There were seven children.

Registrant ID: 3762
Name: Willie Sparks
City/State: Little Rock, AR
Position: Dining Car Waiter
Years of Service: 1935-1961
Submitter's Name: Aletha
City/State: Oakland, CA

Registrant ID: 3765
Name: Marvin R. Sparks Sr.
City/State: IL
Railroad: Santa Fe, Burlington
Position: Porter In Charge
Years of Service: 1940 to 1969
Submitter's Name: James E.
City/State: Oak Park, IL
Comments: I traveled with my father from Chicago to Sacramento to experience what he did to support our family. It was the most insightful experience of my life.

Registrant ID: 3771
Name: Chester C. Spaulding
City/State: Savannah, GA
Position: Sleeping Car Porter
Years of Service: 1945-1960
Submitter's: Johnnie Mae
City/State: Savannah, GA

Registrant ID: 3772
Name: Eugene Spearman
City/State: Chicago, IL
Position: Sleeping Car Porter
Years: Circa 1920's-1940's
Submitter's Name: Lila
City/State: Chicago, IL
Comments: Eugene Spearman
(June 6, 1893-July 25, 1976)
Found one of his Pullman
company identification cards,
I.D. pin, 25 years of service pin
and retirement pin.

Registrant ID: 3773
Name: U.S. Spearman
City/State: Wesleyville, PA
Railroad: New York Central RR
Position: Dining Car Waiter
Years of Service: 34 Years
Submitter's Name: Denise
City/State: Erie, PA
Comments: Worked Wesleyville
Roundhouse retired Oct 22,
1956

Registrant ID: 3779
Name: Susan Spencer
City/State: Columbus, OH
Railroad: Pullman Company
Position: Baby Cook
Years of Service: 1942-44

Registrant ID: 3776
Name: John J. Spencer
Railroad: Pullman Company

Position: Porter
Years of Service: 1922-1957
Submitter's Name: David
Spencer

Registrant ID: 3775
Name: John Spencer
City/State: Evanston, IL
Railroad: California Limited
Position: Pullman Porter
Years of Service: Early 1940's
Submitter's Name: Normandie
City/State: Chicago, IL
Comments: My grandfather
used to take me on his run when
I visited my father in California. I
lived with he and my
Grandmother in Evanston, Il.

Registrant ID: 3774
Name: James Spencer
City/State: Martinsville, VA
Years of Service: 1940's 1950's
Submitter's Name: Ruth
City/State: Owings Mills, MD
Comments: My uncle is
deceased. He worked during the
1940's and 1950's. I was a little
girl during the 50's and I
remember him coming home on
the weekends and how happy my
aunt was to see him.

Registrant ID: 3777
Name: Lemuel Spencer
City/State: Floyd, VA
Railroad: Norfolk and Western
Position: Pullman Porter
Submitter's Name: Vanessa
City/State: Roanoke, VA

Registrant ID: 3780
Name: Anderson Springfield
City/State: Chicago, AL

Railroad: Illinois Central
Position: Porter
Years: Circa 1944-1950
Submitter's Name: Patricia
City/State: Chicago, IL
Comments: My Father is deceased. He frequently spoke of meeting and speaking with Cardinal Stritch during one of his trips. This meeting resulted in a conversation which was instrumental in getting his children enrolled in Chicago's parochial school system.

Registrant ID: 3781
Name: D.E. Springs
Position: Pullman Porter
Years of Service: Over 25
Comments: He was also a B.S.C.P union member.

Registrant ID: 3783
Name: Dennis Spurell, Sr.
City/State: San Antonio, TX
Railroad: Southern Pacific, MO & Decatur
Position: Sleeping Car Porter
Submitter's Name: Dennis
City/State: San Antonio, TX

Registrant ID: 3784
Name: John Square
City/State: Tyler, TX
Railroad: Cotton Belt
Position: Blacksmith
Submitter's Name: Kashan
City/State: Oakland, CA
Comments: Relative deceased

Registrant ID: 3785
Name: Edward Sryder
City/State: Chicago, IL

Railroad: Chicago Line
Position: Dining Car Waiter
Years of Service: 1940
Submitter's Name: Delain J
City/State: Chicago, IL
Comments: Deceased Brother

Registrant ID: 3786
Name: George Stallings
Position: Pullman Porter
Years: 1930's-1950's
Submitter's Name: Carla
City/State: Eustin, FL
Comments: He was my cousin

Registrant ID: 3787
Name: William F. Stanfield
City/State: AR
Railroad: Union Pacific out of Chicago & El Reno Oklahoma
Position: Pullman Porter
Years of Service: 1950-1960
Submitter's Name: Wyethia
City/State: Los Angeles, CA
Comments: I was a little girl when my father worked on the railroad. He passed away on March 15th 1990. He was also a Korean War Veteran.

Registrant ID: 3788
Name: Clauzell Stanley
City/State: Buffalo, NY
Railroad: L & N Railroad
Position: Cook & Waiter
Years of Service: 1941-1976
Comments: Enjoyed working for the railroad in spite of those times. I worked mostly on the company Presidential Car and later as an office worker when I became older. Retired from L&N after about 35 years of service.

Registrant ID: 3789
Name: Edgar Stanley
City/State: AL
Position: Pullman Porter
Years of Service: 1940 -1965
Submitter's Name: Sylvia
City/State: New Orleans, LA

Registrant ID: 3791
Name: Charlie Stantton
City/State: IL
Position: Porter
Years of Service: 1930-1958
Submitter's Name: Shirley
City/State: Chicago, IL

Registrant ID: 3792
Name: Verna Staples, Sr.
City/State: Washington, DC
Railroad: Southern Railroad
Position: Pullman Porter
Years of Service: 1928-1961
Submitter's Name: Rosa Nell
City/State: Washington, DC
Comments: During his travels on the railroad and being an African American man, Mr. Staples had to get a pass in order to travel on the streets of Florida. During World War II, he traveled with the Troop Trains transporting military personnel from one post to another.

Registrant ID: 3793
Name: Harry Starks
City/State: Philadelphia, PA
Railroad: Pennsylvania
Position: Pullman Porter
Years of Service: 1930-1958
Submitter's Name: Priscilla D.Christina, & Allison
City/State: Stockbridge & Los Angeles & Arnold, GA & MD

Comments: Priscilla states: My father was one of the original members of the Brotherhood. A. Philip Randolph used to come to our house when I was a little girl while he was in Philadelphia. Christina Writes: My mother told me many stories about my grandfather's experiences on the railroad. She also told me about Mr. Randolph coming to her house as they organized the union. My grandmother's sister's husband Leander Williams was also an original member. When he worked as a Porter he was sometimes the Porter-In-Charge.

Registrant ID: 3794
Name: Arthur J. Starr
City/State: Los Angeles, CA
Railroad: Union Pacific
Position: Porter
Submitter's Name: Edwina
City/State: Los Angeles, CA

Registrant ID: 3795
Name: Savoy Steed
City/State: Memphis, TN
Railroad: Illinois Central Railroad
Position: Porter
Years of Service: 1957-1991

Registrant ID: 3799
Name: John Steele
City/State: AL
Submitter's Name: Beverly
City/State: Detroit, MI

Registrant ID: 3798
Name: James Vernon Steele
City/State: AL
Railroad: Illinois Central

Position: Pullman Porter
Years of Service: Early 1900's
Submitter's Name: Carla
City/State: Florence, MS
Comments: James Vernon Steele is my great-grandfather (maternal) who is father to my grandfather, Porter Washington Steele, who I also entered into the registry. I cannot provide any details beyond this, i.e. date of birth, years of service or further experiences.

Registrant ID: 3797
Name: Homer Steele
City/State: AL
Railroad: Illinois Central
Position: Pullman Porter
Years of Service: 1930's through the late 1940's (approx.)
Submitter's Name: Carla
City/State: Florence, MS
Comments: Homer Steele is my great uncle (maternal), brother to my grandfather, Porter Washington Steele, and son of James Vernon Steele, all of whom worked on the railroads and all of whom I am adding to the registry.

Registrant ID: 3796
Name: Costerroma Steele
City/State: Oroville, CO
Railroad: Western Pacific Rail Road-California Zephyr
Position: Pullman Porter
Years of Service: 10 years
Submitter's: Jo, Kenneth, & Alice
City/State: Oroville, Chiu, & Oakland, CA

Comments: My father's route was San Francisco, Ca to Chicago, IL, three days there a one night sleep over and three days back. 'He worked on the California Zephyr. On that route winter temperatures would range from the low fiftes to below zero. The trip through the Feather River Canyon would be unbearable.

Registrant ID: 3801
Name: William Steele
City/State: Memphis, TN
Railroad: Illinois Central
Position: Sleeping Car Porter
Years of Service: 1917 to 1943
Submitter's Name: William
City/State: Pasadena, CA
Comments: My Grandfather was very proud of his job and what he did even when things were not the greatest. He worked more than 30 years at this and when he passed on, my Grandmother got his benefits and free pass to travel which we used always.

Registrant ID: 3803
Name: Virgil Steen
Position: Sleeping Porter
Years of Service: 1929-1969
Submitter's Name: Purnell
City/State: Denver, CO

Registrant ID: 4109
Name: Virgil Steen
City/State: Denver, CO
Position: Porter
Years of Service: 1929-1969
Submitter's Name: Punnell
City/State: Denver, CO
Comments: DOB 11/14/1902

Registrant ID: 3805
Name: Robert Lee Stephens
City/State: Philadelphia, PA
Railroad: Pennsylvania RR
Position: Waiter
Years of Service: 1935-1950
Submitter's Name: Marilyn
City/State: Norfolk, VA
Comments: Robert Lee Stephens, the youngest son of the Late Orange Stephens and Parry Lee (Johnson) Stephens, was born on December 10, 1919 in Morgan County, Georgia. He graduated from Washington High School.

Registrant ID: 3806
Name: Victor W. Stephens
City/State: Bellevue, WA
Railroad: Northern Pacific Railroad
Position: Dining Car Waiter
Years of Service: 1949-1952
Submitter's Name: Linda
City/State: Phoenix, AZ
Comments: My father passed away June 2000. He did not talk much about this time of his life. But I grew up thinking that my daddy could do just about anything. He could cook and clean and always was a food server at most church and social events that my parents were envoled with.

Registrant ID: 3807
Name: Lott Sterling
City/State: Wheaton, IL
Railroad: He worked for many, but ended on the Union Pacific
Position: Pullman Porter
Years of Service: 1920's-60's
Submitter's Name: Cynthia
City/State: Columbia, MD

Registrant ID: 3809
Name: Fred Stevensen
City/State: AL
Position: Porter
Years of Service: 1937-1940
Submitter's Name: Everett
City/State: Newport News, VA

Registrant ID: 3811
Name: John Stevensen
City/State: Markham, IL
Railroad: Chesapeake Ohio
Position: Carmen
Years of Service: 31
Submitter's Name: Shirley
City/State: Chicago Ridge, IL

Registrant ID: 3810
Name: Claude Stevensen
City/State: Columbus, OH
Railroad: Sea Board
Position: Pullman Porter
Years of Service: 1950 - 1970
Submitter's Name: Claude
City/State: Columbus, OH

Registrant ID: 3812
Name: William Stevensen
City/State: Pleasantville, NJ
Railroad: B & O
Position: Conductor Out of Philadelphia
Years of Service: 1930's
Submitter's Name: Edith
City/State: Pleasantville, NJ
Comments: Cousin Passed in 50's, Very fair could have passed as a white man, but didn't, but he wore different uniform, Called out stops

Registrant ID: 3813
Name: Howard Stevensen
City/State: Chicago, IL
Railroad: Santa Fe
Position: Waiter
Years: 1930s through 1950s
Submitter's Name: Audrey
City/State: Lansing, MI
Comments: He was my uncle. He used to take my cousins and I down to the yards in Chicago have us board either the Super Chief or El Capitan. We kids used to have a great time running through the trains, and visiting the beautiful dining cars. Many times when he came off of his run he would bring fresh crab and other goodies for us to feast on. After his career on the road he became president of the waiter's union in Chicago for many years. There is a surviving son (my cousin) Howard Stevenson Jr. who lives in Johannesburg, South Africa.

Registrant ID: 3820
Name: Shalon Stewart
City/State: Frederickson, VA
Position: Hair Stylist
Years of Service: 4 Years
Submitter's Name: India
City/State: Frederick, VA

Registrant ID: 3815
Name: Ben Stewart
City/State: AL
Position: Sleeping Car Porter
Years of Service: 50 years
Submitter's Name: Ben Jr.
City/State: Ft. Worth, TX
Comments: Son of a Porter

Registrant ID: 3816
Name: John Stewart
City/State: Jacksonville, CA
Position: Pullman Porter
Years of Service: 1930-50
Submitter's Name: Saramae
City/State: Inglewood, CA

Registrant ID: 3817
Name: Lonnie Stewart
City/State: Chicago,, IL
Position: Pullman Porter
Years: Late 40's to the 1960's
Submitter's Name: Yvonne
City/State: Kansas City, KS
Comments: My grandfather, Lonnie Stewart, was a Black Pullman Porter. He lived in Chicago, Ill. when I was growing up in Kansas City, Ks. He was my mother's dad. Grandfather. He was born in 1900.

Registrant ID: 3814
Name: Albert Stewart
City/State: IL
Railroad: Illinois Central
Position: Pullman Porter
Years of Service: 1935-1972
Submitter's Name: Janet
City/State: Las Vegas, NV

Registrant ID: 3819
Name: Robert D. Stewart
City/State: St Louis, MO
Railroad: Missouri Pacific
Position: Pullman Porter
Years of Service: 1930's-1969
Submitter's Name: Barbara S.
City/State: St Louis, MO

Registrant ID: 3821
Name: Floyd Stockey
City/State: Berkeley, CA

Railroad: Southern Pacific
Position: Pullman Porter
Years of Service: 40-50 yrs.
Submitter's Name: Loyci
City/State: Bellevue, WA
Comments: Floyd Stockey migrated to Calif. from Louisiana in 1917, in the first black migration, to work as a Pullman Porter with Southern Pacific. He was stationed at the Oakland Depot & generally ran on the road 3 days and was off for 4 days. He retired in 1966. One of the perks of being a porter was that you were allowed to keep all of the magazines & books that people left on your train run. In this way, our family regularly read all the popular magazines of that era & developed an unquenchable thirst for learning. As far as I know, all of the small & elite cadre of Berkeley's Porters from tht are now dead.

Registrant ID: 3822
Name: Charles Stone
City/State: New York, NY
Railroad: Pennsylvania
Position: 4th Cook to Chef
Years of Service: 1925-1966
Submitter's Name: Floralee
City/State: Seabrook, MD
Comments: I am the widow of Charles Stone. He worked on the Pennsylvania railroad from until his retirement in 1966.

Registrant ID: 3824
Name: Herbert Stoute
City/State: Cincinnati, OH
Railroad: B&O Rail Road
Position: Waiter Dining Car

Submitter's Name: Jeanne
City/State: Englewood, NJ
Comments: Herbert Stoute was my Uncle. He was born in Barbados in 1887 and died in Cincinnati in 1983. I know very little about him as he had little contact with his family. The information above is from his 1937 application for a Social Security Number.

Registrant ID: 3826
Name: Samuel Strart Streaty
City/State: San Diego, CA
Railroad: Northern Pacific
Position: Sleeping Car Porter
Years of Service: In 1930's
Submitter's Name: Pearlie
City/State: San Diego, CA
Comments: Several of his brothers were all Sleeping Car Porters, Grandfather.

Registrant ID: 3827
Name: James Streaty
City/State: Jeffersonville, IN
Years of Service: Circa 1880 to 1910
Submitter's Name: Konrad
City/State: Arlington, TX

Registrant ID: 3829
Name: Grover W. Strickland
City/State: Chattanooga, TN
Railroad: Pullman Co./Louisville
Years of Service: 1947-1953
Submitter's Name: Mariane
City/State: Chatanooga, TN
Comments: Father deceased

Registrant ID: 3828
Name: David T. Strickland

City/State: Cherry Hill, NJ
Position: Porter
Years of Service: Retired 1958
Submitter's Name: Walker D
City/State: Cherry Hill, NJ
Comments: He retired in 1958

Registrant ID: 3831
Name: Sephus Strickland
City/State: IL
Railroad: Northwestern RR
Position: Porter and one of the first Black Conductors
Years of Service: 1943-1967
Submitter's Name: Judy
City/State: Palos Hills, IL
Comments: Sephus was my grandfather.

Registrant ID: 3832
Name: David Stricklin
City/State: Pontiac, IL
Railroad: Alton RR
Position: Pullman Porter
Years of Service: 1933-1960
Submitter's Name: James
City/State: Chicago, IL
Comments: My uncle David's run on the Alton RR was between Chicago, Illinois and Saint Louis, MO.

Registrant ID: 3833
Name: Estell "A.E. Strode
Years of Service: 51 years
Submitter's Name: William
City/State: Denver, CO
Comments: Laid track on Central Pacific. Flagman on Pacific Limited Ellis, Ks. to Kan. City MO.

Registrant ID: 3835
Name: Wilbur Strong

City/State: Chicago, IL
Railroad: Illinois-Central
Position: Porter
Years of Service: 25 years
Submitter's Name: Carol
City/State: Chicago, IL
Comments: Worked as a Porter on the I.C. lines. Usually worked the route from Chicago to Florida

Registrant ID: 3834
Name: Colonel Strong
City/State: Dallas, TX
Railroad: KATY. ATS&F
Position: Pullman Porter
Submitter's Name: Harold
City/State: Wichita, KS

Registrant ID: 3836
Name: Joseph Strothers
City/State: Indianapolis, IN
Railroad: Pennsylvania
Position: Pullman Porter
Submitter's Name: Linda
City/State: Chicago, IL

Registrant ID: 3837
Name: Joseph Strowder
City/State: Washington, DC
Railroad: Seaboard Railroad
Position: Waiter and the first African-American Steward
Years of Service: l938-l968

Registrant ID: 3838
Name: James Sullivan
City/State: Portland, OR
Railroad: Union Pacific/Southern
Position: Waiter
Years of Service: 1923-1959
Submitter(s): Elaine
City/State: Springs, Colorado

Comments: James was my uncle "Sunny" is what we called him. My maternal grandmother's brother. He and his wife Aunt Mabel never had any children and he doted on his and nephews. I remember riding the train one time and I got to see him.

Registrant ID: 3839
Name: Edward Summers
City/State: AL
Railroad: Pennsylvania RR
Position: Redcap
Years of Service: over 20 years
Submitter's Name: Dolores
City/State: North Babylon, NY
Comments: My father, Edward Summers, who is deceased was a proud Redcap for Pennsylvania Station for over 20 years.
My father was very proud and humble in his position. It was a great job for an African American to have at that time.

Registrant ID: 3840
Name: Frank Summers
City/State: GA
Railroad: The Southern – and the Cresant
Position: Chef
Years of Service: 1954-1970
Submitter's Name: Tressie
City/State: Washington, DC

Registrant ID: 3842
Name: Mathew Sutton
Railroad: B & O
Position: Waiter in Charge
Years of Service: 1931 - 1962
Submitter's Name: Margaret
City/State: Cincinnati, OH

Registrant ID: 3843
Name: Frank Swain
Position: Pullman Porter
Years of Service: Over 25
Comments: Union member.

Registrant ID: 3844
Name: Jessie Swain
City/State: MI
Railroad: Southern Pacific
Position: Dining Car Waiter
Years of Service: Mid 20's- 40's
Submitter's Name: Jacqueline
City/State: Detroit, MI

Registrant ID: 3845
Name: Charles M. Swain
City/State: Bethlehem, PA
Position: Dinning car Waiter
Years of Service: Circa 1935
Submitter's Name: Lynn
City/State: Bethlehem, PA
Comments: Worked on the Wabash Line in St Louis

Registrant ID: 3846
Name: James Swain
City/State: NY
Railroad: Pennsylvania RR
Position: Pullman Porter
Submitter's Name: Mary
City/State: New York, NY
Comments: Deceased 2001

Registrant ID: 3848
Name: Woody James Syhacker
City/State: Fairview Heights, IL
Railroad: Illinois Central
Years of Service: 1960-1970
Submitter's Name: Bobby
City/State: Fairvien Heights, IL
Comments: Woody was my father

Registrant ID: 3851
Name: William B. Sykes
City/State: Chicago, IL

Registrant ID: 3850
Name: Joseph Sykes
City/State: St Paul, MN
Railroad: Northern Pacific
Position: Head-Dining Car
Years of Service: 1942-1958
Submitter's Name: Leora
City/State: San Francisco, CA
Comments: Deceased

Registrant ID: 3852
Name: William Symms
City/State: Jacksonville, FL
Railroad: Seaboard
Position: Cook
Years of Service: 1920's
Submitter's Name: Esther
City/State: Cape Coral, FL

Registrant ID: 3853
Name: Henry Syms
City/State: Newton, MA
Position: Supply handler -
Commissary
Years of Service: 1946 until the
company closed
Submitter's Name: Gertrude
City/State: Dorchester, MA

Registrant ID: 3854
Name: Charlie Syvick
City/State: New Orleans, LA
Years of Service: 1925-1936
Submitter's Name: M.W
City/State: Chicago, IL

Registrant ID: 3855
Name: Anthony T.
City/State: New York, NY
Position: Baker

Registrant ID: 3857
Name: Thomas Talley
City/State: Van Buren, AR
Railroad: Missouri-Pacific
Position: Porter
Years of Service: 20 yrs
Submitter's Name: Everett
City/State: Phoenix, AZ
Comments: My father (listed
above)at the time of this
submission is our oldest
remaining family member. It is
my great-grandfather,(who is
now deceased) that worked on
the railroad. My father is not
sure of the length of his
grandfather's employment but
his run was from Little Rock
Arkansas to Coffeyville Kansas.

Registrant ID: 3858
Name: Allen Tannahill
Position: Pullman Porter
Years of Service: 25 Plus
Comments: B.S.C.P.union
member

Registrant ID: 3859
Name: Alfred Tanner
City/State: New York, NY
Railroad: From Grand
Central to Chicago
Position: Pullman Porter
Years of Service: 1928-1955
Submitter's Name: Joy
City/State: New York City, NY

Registrant ID: 3860
Name: Herman Tapp
City/State: Belleried(NE), AL
Railroad: Union Pacific
Position: Services Attendant
president car service
Years of Service: 1916-1938

Submitter's Name: Aujuran
City/State: Belleried, NE

Registrant ID: 3861
Name: Harold Paul Tardy, Sr.
City/State: Pittsburgh, PA
Position: Pullman Porter
Years of Service: 20+ yrs.
Submitter's Name: Linda Tardy
City/State: Pittsburgh, PA
Comments: My grandfather worked between Pittsburgh and New York.

Registrant ID: 3863
Name: Nathan Tate
City/State: Chicago, IL
Position: Porter
Submitter's Name: Regina

Registrant ID: 3862
Name: James Walter Tate
City/State: Baltimore, MD
Railroad: Pennsylvania
Position: Pullman porter
Yearse: Circa 1920-1950
Submitter's Name: Pauletta
City/State: Baltimore, MD
Comments: I don't remember too much. I just know he worked for Pennsylvania RR. My grandmother was able to go to NC free in the summer on the RR. My grandfather passed in 1963. I remember seeing a picture of him at the "Brotherhood" members meeting.

Registrant ID: 3869
Name: Doris Taylor
City/State: Jersey City, NJ
Position: Sleeping Car Porter
Registrant ID: 3866
Name: Clarence Taylor

Position: Pullman Porter
Years of Service: Over 25
Comments: He was a member of the union.

Registrant ID: 3871
Name: Eugene Taylor
City/State: Queens Village, NY
Railroad: Pullman Company
Position: Pullman Porter
Years of Service: Over 25

Registrant ID: 3877
Name: Leonard H. Taylor
City/State: Montgomery, AL
Position: Pullman Porter
Years of Service: 1946
Submitter's Name: Rogers

Registrant ID: 3884
Name: Willis Taylor
City/State: Oakland, CA
Submitter's Name: Karen
City/State: Berwyn, PA
Comments: Born approx 1869

Registrant ID: 3873
Name: Jesse Taylor
City/State: Buffalo, NY
Railroad: New York Central
Position: Pullman Porter
Years of Service: 1928---196?
Submitter's Name: Willetta
City/State: Buffalo, NY
Comments: Did not think this would be historical information. Jesse Taylor was my father.

Registrant ID: 3880
Name: Prentiss Taylor
City/State: Chicago, IL
Railroad: Milwaukee Road
Position: Sleeping Car Porter
Years of Service: 1934-71

Submitter's Name: Peter
City/State: Chicago, IL

Registrant ID: 3876
Name: Joseph Taylor
City/State: AL
Railroad: B&O
Position: Dining Car Waiter And Air Knocker
Years of Service: Nov. 1936-1973
Submitter's Name: Laura
City/State: Crestline, OH
Comments: B&O Railroad - Willard, Ohio - until death in 1973. He also traveled to Cumberland, Maryland for

Registrant ID: 3883
Name: Walter Taylor.
City/State: Jacksonville, FL
Railroad: Seaboard
Position: Porter
Years of Service: 1925-1968
Submitter's Name: Kathryn
City/State: Ford, WA
Comments: My father worked 43yrsand enjoyed his job. He never spoke of any mistreatments.

Registrant ID: 3870
Name: Ernest Taylor
Railroad: N.Y. Central/Burlington
Position: Chef
Years of Service: 1940's
Submitter's Name: Edith
City/State: Galesburg, IL

Registrant ID: 3882
Name: Roscoe C. Taylor
City/State: Baltimore, MD
Railroad: B&O Railroad
Position: Red Cap and Pullman Porter
Submitter's Name: Gwendolyn

City/State: Highland Park, NJ
Comments: Roscoe Taylor was my grandfather, and he died August 1980. He worked for B&O Railroad, and then Pennsylvania Railroad before retiring in the late 50's. I am not sure of the exact period, but I know that he was employed by the railroad when I was a child.

Registrant ID: 3865
Name: Chester Taylor
Submitter's Name: Marquerito
City/State: Louisville, KY

Registrant ID: 3872
Name: Henry William Taylor
City/State: Memphis, TN
Railroad: Marshall City, MS
Position: Railroad Hand
Years of Service: 1870
Submitter's Name: Rochelle
City/State: Memphis, TN
Comments: I found his name listed in the 1870 census record in the town of Lamar, in Marshal County, Mississippi. He was the son of a white plantation owner and a slave.

Registrant ID: 3875
Name: Joseph Taylor
City/State: New York, NY
Submitter's Name: Donald
City/State: New York, NY

Registrant ID: 3874
Name: John A. Taylor
City/State: Newport, NY
Position: Porter
Years of Service: 1930's-1950
Submitter's Name: Helen
City/State: Newport, NY

Registrant ID: 3881
Name: Robert Taylor
City/State: Harlem, NY
Railroad: Whatever was going through North Carolina (Hamlet)
Years of Service:
Circa 1920-s to 1950's or
Submitter's Name: Andrenna
City/State: Queens Village, NY

Registrant ID: 3878
Name: Nathaniel Oliver Taylor
City/State: TX
Railroad: The Illinois Central and the New York Central
Position: Dinning Car Waiter and Dinning Car Steward
Years of Service: 1940-1970
Submitter's Name: Theodore V
City/State: Sacramento, CA
Comments: Nathaniel worked out of St Louis Mo, then out of Chicago , then out of Cleveland. Nathaniel worked on the Twentieth Century Limited to New York.

Registrant ID: 3886
Name: William Taylor Sr.
City/State: Rocky Mount, NC
Railroad: Unknown
Submitter's Name: Larry
City/State: Greensboro, NC

Registrant ID: 3888
Name: Gladwin L. Teague
Railroad: New Haven Railroad
Position: Porter and a Dining Car Attendant
Submitter's Name: Gladwin
City/State: Highland Park, MI
Comments: Father

Registrant ID: 3887
Name: Edwin Teague
City/State: Highland Park, MI
Railroad: New Haven Railroad
Position: Porter and a Dining Car Attendant
Submitter's Name: Gladwin
City/State: Highland Park, MI
Comments: Grandfather Not sure about the dates.

Registrant ID: 3890
Name: Romis Tees
City/State: Oak Park, CA
Submitter's Name: Amy
City/State: Oak Park, CA

Registrant ID: 3892
Name: Felix R. Terrell
Railroad: Illinois Central
Position: Brakeman
Years of Service: 1922 -1965
Submitter's Name: Janice
City/State: Middletown, DE
Comments: I believe he was one of the first African-American brakemen.

Registrant ID: 3893
Name: Walter R. Terry
City/State: Latham, MD
Railroad: Seaboard Coastline
Position: Pullman Porter
Years of Service: 1932-1969

Registrant ID: 3894
Name: James Thames
City/State: AL
Railroad: Illinois Central
Position: Dining Car Waiter
Years of Service: 1948-1973
Submitter's Name: Lauren
City/State: Chicago, IL

Comments: My grandfather was James Thames, who is now deceased. He worked as a dining car waiter after World War II, and earned a very decent living for his family. His route went from Chicago to New Orleans. We are very proud as a family of his accomplishments.

Registrant ID: 3895
Name: Edward Thigpen
City/State: New Orleans, LA
Railroad: Illinois Central
Position: Porter
Years : Mid 1930's –40's
Submitter's Name: Patricia
City/State: New Orleans, LA

Registrant ID: 3920
Name: Porter Thomas
Railroad: Pennsylvania
Years of Service: 40-50 Years
Submitter's Name: Madonna

Registrant ID: 3910
Name: Love P. Thomas
City/State: Chicago, IL
Railroad: Illinois Central
Position: Waiter and
Dinning Car Waiter
Years of Service: 1946-1948

Registrant ID: 3900
Name: Clarence Thomas
City/State: Los Angeles, CA
Railroad: Southern Pacific Road
Position: Dining Car Waiter
Years of Service: 1946 - 1951
Comments: In 1946 I was very glad to have a job to support my family we were not treated very good but we needed our jobs.

Registrant ID: 3898
Name: Charles Thomas
City/State: Jackson, MS
Railroad: Illinois Central
Position: Pullman Porter
Years of Service: 1943-1961
Submitter's Name: Dorothy P.

Registrant ID: 3924
Name: Shadd D. Allen Thomas
City/State: Denver, CO
Railroad: Union Pacific-Santa Fe
Position: Pullman Porter
Years of Service: 1942-1948
Submitter's Name: Tremy

Registrant ID: 3902
Name: Claude Thomas
Submitter's Name: Carla

Registrant ID: 3917
Name: Ondre Thomas
City/State: ID
Railroad: A.B. and C Railroad
and the Atlanta-West Point
Position: Private Car Cook
Years of Service: 20's,30's.40's
Submitter's Name: Ondrea
City/State: Atlanta, GA
Comments: As told to me by my mother Mrs. Julia, and Aunt Dorothy:"Dad (Ondre Thomas) was an employee of F.H. Hill and later of the A.B. & C Railroad and the Atlanta West Point Railroad as Private Dining Car Cook under Messrs. O. T. Nelson, C.A. Wickersham and S.R. Young. He was Mr. Charles Wickersham's private porter and cook. Mr. Wickersham was the president of the Atlanta and West Point Railroad. The train

Dad rode, came through College Park and on to Alabama.

Registrant ID: 3926
Name: Walter Thomas
City/State: Columbus, OH
Railroad: Pennsylvania
Position: Pullman Porter
Years of Service: 1946-1958
Submitter's Name: Joan
City/State: Baltimore, MD

Registrant ID: 3913
Name: Noah Todd Thomas
City/State: IL
Submitter's Name: Barbara H.
City/State: Chicago, IL

Registrant ID: 3908
Name: John Thomas
City/State: Chicago, IL
Railroad: Pullman Railcar Co.
Position: Pullman Porter
and a Red Cap
Submitter's Name: June
City/State: Chicago, IL
Comments: John Thomas is now deceased. His wife, who is also deceased, Pearl Thomas was my grandmother. My mothers name was Johnie Pearl Thomas, she is also deceased.

Registrant ID: 3927
Name: William Jerome Thomas
City/State: Chicago, IL
Railroad: The Empire Builder, Amtrak
Position: Pullman Porter
Years of Service: 1938 - 1958
Submitter's Name: Velma
City/State: Chicago, IL
Comments He died in 1958.

His wife is still living at his old address in Chicago listed above. Her name is Fannie Thomas and she is 92 years old. He has two surviving children.

Registrant ID: 3925
Name: Sylvester L. Thomas
City/State: AL
Railroad: Santa Fe
Position: Pullman Porter
Years of Service: 1964
Submitter's Name: Cheryl
City/State: Chicago, IL
Comments: He was proud of what he did. Never mentioned anything negative about people he encountered. He considered it an opportunity to better his life and mine.

Registrant ID: 3921
Name: Robert Thomas
City/State: Houston, TX
Railroad: Union Pacific
Position: Pullman Porter
Years of Service: 45 Years
Submitter's Name: Paula
City/State: Houston, TX

Registrant ID: 3923
Name: Rupert Thomas
City/State: Kansas City, MO
Railroad: Union Pacific
Position: Waiter
Years of Service: 1947-1955
Submitter's Name: Artie
City/State: Kansas City, MO
Comments: African Americans could not eat the same meals they served. They also could not have lunch until everyone was served. The conductor of the train would throw away the good

food to prevent the waiters from having it.

Registrant ID: 3897
Name: Alfred C. Thomas
City/State: Kansas City, MO
Position: Porter
Years of Service: 1941-1960's
Submitter's Name: Alfred C.
City/State: Kansas City, MO

Registrant ID: 3906
Name: George Thomas
City/State: Wilmington, NC
Position: Porter
Years of Service: 1900-1925
Submitter's Name: Sherry
City/State: Laurelton, NY

Registrant ID: 3909
Name: John Henry Thomas
City/State: Columbus, OH
Position: Custodian
Years of Service: 1952-1964
Submitter's Name: Paulus S.
City/State: London, OH

Registrant ID: 3929
Name: Willie Thomas
City/State: Tampa, FL
Railroad: Union Station
Position: Pullman Porter
Submitter's Name: Mary
City/State: Pennsauken, NJ
Comments: Was Porter for Mary McLeod Bethune

Registrant ID: 3931
Name: William Albert Thomas
City/State: IL
Position: Pullman Porter
Years of Service: 1915-1935

Submitter's Name: Barbara
City/State: Chicago, IL
Comments: Both of my relatives died before I was born and, I do not have any additonal information.

Registrant ID: 3937
Name: Grady Clyde
City/State: NY
Railroad: Southern Pacific
Position: Pullman Porter Overnight from New York City to southern states and west to Chicago
Years of Service: 1946-1949
Submitter's Name: Patrice
City/State: Arlington, VA
Comments: My uncle, Grady Clyde Thomason, who was my mother's brother, was very proud of his position. He never complained. He considered himself lucky to have a job that provided steady income.

Registrant ID: 3939
Name: George Thompkins
City/State: Washington , DC
Railroad: Pullman Company
Position: Sleeping Car Porter and later also workrd as a Red Cap
Years of Service: 1929-1946
Submitter's Name: Stephanie
City/State: Upper Marlboro, Maryland

Registrant ID: 3960
Name: Luther Thompson
Position: Pullman Porter or Dining Car Waiter
Submitter's Name: Elizabeth

Registrant ID: 3962
Wesley James Thompson
City/State: Brentwood, NY
Railroad: Atlantic Coas-
Eastern Seaboard
Position: Chef
Years of Service: 1948-1989
Submitter's Name: Cornie
City/State: Brentwood, NY
Comments: Retired from Amtrak

Registrant ID: 3940
Name: Alexander
City/State: Chicago, IL
Railroad: Santa Fe
Position: Porter
Years of Service: 1945-1965
Submitter's Name: Betty
City/State: Chicago, IL

Registrant ID: 3947
Name: Franklin Thompson
City/State: AL
Railroad: Pennsylvania Railroad
and Amtrak
Position: Dining Car Waiter
Years of Service: April 12, 1928
to December 24, 1977
Submitter's Name: Pamela
City/State: Columbia, MD

Registrant ID: 3949
Name: George Elbert Thompson
City/State: Kansas City, MO
Railroad: Frisco
Position: Waiter and
Head Waiter
Years of Service: 1920s -60s
Submitter's Name: Debora
City/State: Dublin, OH
Comments: My grandfather
(George E. Thompson) was born
in the 1890s and was hired when

he was in his teens. I remember
him stating he started very
young because he was tall and
looked older. I believe when he
originally began with the railroad
he was under age.

Registrant ID: 3941
Name: Arthur Thompson
City/State: AL
Railroad: Atlantic Coast Line
Position: Switchman, and
Fireman
Years of Service: 1905 - 1930
Submitter's Name: Aiyanna
Yasmeen and Gwendolyn
City/State: Encino California
and Reisterstown, 'MD
Comments: My Great-grandma.
He died in 1930.

Registrant ID: 3956
Name: Lazarus Thompson
City/State: NC
Railroad: Southern
Position: Chef and Dining Car
Waiter
Years of Service: 1900-1940
Submitter's Name: Mary
City/State: Fletcher, NC
Comments: As a young man,
Mr. Thompson migrated from
Newberry, SC to the valley areas
of McDowell County, NC. He
married and moved to the
mountain town of Asheville, NC,
and purchased property while he
continued to work on the
railroad traveling up and down
the Saluda Mountains into South
Carolina. The property they
purchased in the late 30's is still
owned by our family.

Registrant ID: 3959
Name: Leon Bernard (known as L.B.) Thompson
City/State: AL
Railroad: Union Pacific
Position: Sleeping Car Porter
Submitter's Name: Tammy
City/State: Los Angeles, CA
Comments: My great grandfather was active in the Brotherhood of Sleeping Car Porters - Los Angeles division. He served as president as well as the Secretary/Treasurer. Posthumously, he was designated the 1st Negro Pullman Conductor in the state of California.

Registrant ID: 3961
Name: Theodore Thompson
City/State: Los Angeles, CA
Railroad: Union Pacific
Position: Porter
Years of Service: 1948
Submitter's Name: Leora
City/State: Los Angeles, CA

Registrant ID: 3942
Name: Charlie Thompson
City/State: OR
Railroad: Southern Pacific
Position: Pullman Porter
Years of Service: 30 Years
Submitter's Name: Mattie
City/State: Oklahoma City, OK

Registrant ID: 3946
Name: Frank Thompson
Railroad: Northern Pacific
Years of Service: 32 Years
Submitter's Name: Joan
City/State: St. Paul, MN

Registrant ID: 3950
Name: James Thompson
City/State: Watervliet, NY
Railroad: Union Station Albany
Submitter's Name: Anna B.
City/State: Troy, NY

Registrant ID: 3964
Name: John Thompson
City/State: Lorain, OH
Position: Railroad Laborer
Years of Service: 1945-1955
Submitter's Name: John
City/State: Lorain, OH

Registrant ID: 3967
Alice E .Thompson-Jackson
City/State: Bronx, NY
Position: Pullman Porter
Years of Service: 1946-1948
City/State: Bronx, NY
Comments: He was Secretary, A Philip Randolph's Office, Harlem, N.Y.C.

Registrant ID: 3969
Name: Jesse Thornhill
City/State: Detroit, MI
Position: Pullman Porter
Years of Service: 1925-1935
Submitter's Name: Thornhill B

Registrant ID: 3970
Name: Ralph Thornton
City/State: Chicago, IL
Position: Sleeping Car Porter
Years of Service: unknown start until 1963
Submitter's Name: Theresa
City/State: Chicago, IL

Registrant ID: 3971
Name: Revered Lenill
City/State: Peoria, IL

Railroad: Rock Island Railroad,
Peoria Turniball,
Toledo Ohio & Western
Position: Track Maintenance,
Machine Operator,
Years: May 18, 1953 - 1982
Submitter's Name: Rose
City/State: Peoria, IL

Registrant ID: 3978
Name: Julius A.Thurston
City/State: Oakland,, CA
Railroad: Western Pacific
Position: Pullman Porter
Years of Service: In the
50's/uncertain
Submitter's Name: Queen E.
City/State: Oakland, CA
Comments: I have submitted
this information for my brother
and my father/Hartie, my uncle
James, himself and my brother
in-law Willie

Registrant ID: 3977
Name: Hartie
City/State: CA
Railroad: Western Pacific
Position: Sleeping Car Porter
Years of Service: Approx 30 yrs
Submitter's Name: Queen E.
City/State: Oakland, CA
Registrant ID: 3979
Name: Franklin Tilford
City/State: Chicago, IL

Registrant ID: 3980
Name: Austell Tiller
City/State: Thomasville, NC
Railroad: Silver Metro out of
New York
Position: Chef
Submitter's Name: Bridget
City/State: Philadelphia, PA

Registrant ID: 3981
Name: Irma M. Tillery
City/State: Cincinnati, OH
Position: Pullman Porter
Years of Service: 1917-1964
Submitter's Name: David D.
City/State: AL

Registrant ID: 3982
Name: George Tillman
City/State: Chicago, IL
Railroad: Pullman Rail Car
Company and Amtrak
Position: Pullman Porter and
Car Manager
Years: 1940's-thru the 1960's
Submitter's Name: Rene
City/State: Chicago, IL
Comments: Mr. Tillman is my
Grandfather

Registrant ID: 3983
Name: Edward
City/State: Santa Monica, CA
Railroad: Southern Pacific and
Union Pacific
Position: Dining Car Waiter
Years of Service: 1942-47
Comments: I was employed
during the summers while
attending college before army
service and after discharge from
the service. In 1942. Quite a few
of my trips were carrying armed
services personnel, some to the
South. The rest of the trips were
in the sate of California and state
of Oregon. In 1947 all of my trips
were in northern states.

Registrant ID: 3989
Name: David S. "Moon" Tindall
City/State: Houston, TX
Position: Pullman Porter

Submitter's Name: Eva M.
City/State: Kyle, TX

Registrant ID: 3990
Name: Coultley "Dock" Tindall
City/State: Columbia, SC
Railroad: Pullman Company
Position: Cook
Years of Service: 20yrs
Submitter's Name: Jean

Registrant ID: 3993
Name: Marion Tobias
City/State: MS
Railroad: Illinois Central
Position: Train Porter
Years of Service: 35 yrs
Submitter's Name:
Herbert/Jean
City/State: St. Louis , MO

Registrant ID: 3994
Name: William Henry Tolbert
City/State: GA
Position: Porter
Years of Service: 1920-1945
Submitter's Name: Emerson
City/State: Saint Mountain, GA

Registrant ID: 3996
Name: Lonnie Torrance
City/State: NY
Railroad: Pennsylvania Terminal
Position: Cook.
Years of Service: 1926- 1960's
Submitter's Name: Gwendolyn
City/State: Savannah, GA

Registrant ID: 4005
Name: Henry Townsend
City/State: Chicago, IL
Position: Waiter and a Porter

Submitter's Name: Mable S.
City/State: Chicago, IL

Registrant ID: 4006
Name: James Tours Travis
City/State: St. Louis, MO
Railroad: Pullman Co. **Position:**
Pullman Porter and Attendant
Years of Service: Unknown, His
last issued ID badge was issued
4-27-53
Submitter's Name: Janice
and 'Marsha
City/State: St. Louis , MO
Comments: he worked out of
Union Station, in St. Louis.

Registrant ID: 4007
Name: Percy L Travis, Sr.
City/State: St. Louis., MO
Railroad: Pullman Co.
Position: Sleeping Car Porter
Years of Service: 42 Years
Submitter's Name: Percy L.
City/State: St. Louis , MO
Comments: Father

Registrant ID: 4008
Name: Paul Trebble
Railroad: Milwaukee & St. Paul
Position: Dining Car Waiter &
Bartender
Years of Service: Start date
unknown to 1968
Submitter's Name: Constance
City/State: Whitecloud, MI

Registrant ID: 4009
Name: Thomas Trice
City/State: Chicago, IL
Position: Dining Car Waiter
Years of Service: 1943-1956

Registrant ID: 4010
Name: John A. Trimble
City/State: AL
Railroad: Chicago North
Position: Porter
Years of Service: 1937-1967
Submitter's Name: Marybelle
City/State: Chicago, IL

Registrant ID: 4011
Name: Clarence Tripp
City/State: Cleveland, OH
Railroad: Cleveland District
Position: Porter
Years of Service: unknown
Submitter's Name: Jewel
City/State: Cleveland, OH
Comments: My grandfather last day of service was 1/10/1942

Registrant ID: 4015
Name: John M. Tubbs
City/State: Chicago, IL
Position: Pullman Porter
Years of Service: 20yrs
Submitter's Name: Colleen
City/State: Chicago, IL

Registrant ID: 4016
Name: Wilbur Tubbs
City/State: Chicago, IL
Railroad: Denver Zephyr, South Wind, Sunset Limited
Position: Dining Car Waiter
Years of Service: 1940-1960
Submitter's Name: Edna
City/State: Chicago, IL

Registrant ID: 4017
Name: Robert Craig Tucker
City/State: Roanoke, VA
Years of Service: 1900-1932
Submitter's Name: Wallace
City/State: Detroit, MI

Registrant ID: 4018
Name: Taft Tumlin
City/State: Brooklyn, NY
Railroad: Seaboard
Position: Pullman Porter
Years of Service: 25 - 30 years
Submitter's Name: Anita
City/State: Old Bridge, NJ

Registrant ID: 4019
Name: Frank M.Tuner, Jr.
City/State: Port Charlotte, FL
Position: Club care attendant
Years of Service: 1942-1957
Submitter's Name: Frank M
City/State: Port Charlotte, FL

Registrant ID: 4020
Name: Carthage Turner
City/State: Kansas City, KS
Position: Tractor Operator
Years of Service: 1946-1976

Registrant ID: 4021
Name: Carthageb Turner
City/State: Kansas City, Kansas
Railroad: Pullman Company
Position: O.P.E
Years of Service: 1946-1976

Registrant ID: 4030
Name: Edward Turner
City/State: Merrillville, IN
Railroad: Union Pacific
Years of Service: 1942-1978

Registrant ID: 4043
Name: Melvin Turner
City/State: Chicago, IL
Position: Pullman Porter
Years of Service: Aprox 2 Years

Registrant ID: 4042
Name: Marcus Payne Turner

City/State: Chicago, IL

Registrant ID: 4028
Name: David Hamilton Turner
Railroad: New Haven Hartford
Position: Dining Car Waiter
Years of Service: 1929-1967
Submitter's Name: Deborah
City/State: NY

Registrant ID: 4040
Name: John Henry Turner
City/State: Oakland, CA
Railroad: Southern Pacific RR
Position: Chef Cook, Waiter, Chair Car Porter, Red Cap
Years of Service:Circa 190- 50
Submitter's Name: Anthony
City/State: Antioch, CA
Comments: Began with Southern Pacific Railroad in Chicago, Ill. to California. Began in the position of a Chef Cook, then to a Waiter, then Chair Car Porter and retired as a Red Cap. Met President Franklin Delano Roosevelt at the Southern Pacific Mole at the 7th Street.

Registrant ID: 4038
Name: John C. Turner
City/State: AL
Position: Porter
Years of Service: 1940's
Submitter's Name: Jacqueline
City/State: Calumet City, IL

Registrant ID: 4035
Name: James Herbert Turner
City/State: Cincinnati, OH
Position: Pullman Porter
Years of Service: 30 plus years
Submitter's Name: Regina
City/State: Cincinnati, OH

Comments: Daughter

Registrant ID: 4048
Name: Willis J. Turner
City/State: Pine Bluff, AR
Railroad: St. Louis Southwestern Railway, "The Cotton Belt."
Position: Stowman
Years of Service: 1942-1972
Submitter's Name: Gladys T.
City/State: Dayton, OH
Comments: He retired after thirty years of service. He experienced racism and discrimination but survived the indignities. The railroad allowed him to make a decent living for his family.

Registrant ID: 4029
Name: Earl Turner
City/State: Springfield, OH
Position: Porter
Years of Service: 1950's
Submitter's Name: Lisa
City/State: Houston, TX

Registrant ID: 4045
Name: Moses Sr. Turner
City/State: New Orleans, LA
Position: Pullman Porter
Years of Service: 1940's
Submitter's Ida Lorraine and Linda
City/State: Minneapolis, MS
Comments: Uncle

Registrant ID: 4032
Name: James Turner
City/State: Ogden, UT
Railroad: Union Pacific
Submitter's Name: Brenda
City/State: Ogden, UT
Comment: James was my father

Registrant ID: 4022
Name: Clint Turner
City/State: Roanoke, VA
Railroad: Norfolk & Western
Position: Dinning Car Waiter
Years : 1940 thru 1950
Submitter's Name: Robert
City/State: West Haven, CT
Comments: His route was on the train called the Power Tan Arrow his run was from Norfolk to Cincinnati. He met a lot of famous people while working and would get their autograph for my mother.

Registrant ID: 4027
Name: David Turner
City/State: Bronx, NY
Railroad: New Haven RR
Position: Dining Car Waiter
Years: Circa 1926 - 1967
Submitter's Name: Nancy
City/State: White Plains, NY
Comments: Prior to the New Haven RR, my dad worked on the Erie Lackawanna. That was before his marriage in 1926. He once told me he worked with Malcolm (Little) X and got him to open his first savings account. He was on the RR during their 'glory years' and often served movie stars and musicians.

Registrant ID: 4051
Name: Frank M. Turner Jr.
City/State: Port Charlotte, FL
Position: Club Car Attendant
Years of Service: 1942-1957

Registrant ID: 4052
Name: William Turney
City/State: Baltimore, MD

Railroad: Santa Fe Railroad
Position: Pullman Porter
Years of Service: 40 Years
Submitter's Name: Clarissa
City/State: Baltimore, MD

Registrant ID: 4053
Name: Louie A. Tyson
City/State: AL
Railroad: Pennsylvania
Position: Porter
Years of Service: Unknown
Submitter's Name: Vernon P
City/State: Fremont, CA

Registrant ID: 4055
Name: Neal Underhill
City/State: New York, NY
Position: Pullman Porter
Submitter's Name: Joan
City/State: Beechhurst, NY

Registrant ID: 4065
Name: William Underwood
City/State: Covington, KY
Railroad: Illinois Central
Submitter's Name: Mary
Comments: Co-founder of NY a Heritage task force Northern KY African Heritage Task force

Registrant ID: 4063
Name: Richard B. Underwood
City/State: MA
Railroad: Boston& Maine
Position: Red Cap
Years of Service: 1940's-1960's
Submitter(s): Joseph J. Jr.
City/State: Everett, MA
Comments: Like many Black men of that day , he was educated but unable to obtain a suitable position, thus he was

forced to work for the railroad to survive.

Registrant ID: 4062
Name: Joseph J. Sr.Underwood
City/State: MA
Railroad: Boston & Maine
Position: Red Cap
Years of Service: 1938-1960's
Submitter(s): Joseph J. Jr.
City/State: Everett, MA
Comments: Worked as a Red Cap while holding a Degree from West Virginia State College.

Registrant ID: 4059
Name: John W.Underwood
City/State: MA
Railroad: Baltimore/Ohio
Position: Pullman Porter
Years of Service 1890's-1930's
Submitter(s) Joseph J. Jr
City/State: Everett, MA

Registrant ID: 4069
Name: Sears E. Upchurch
Railroad: Atlantic Coastline RR
Position: Cook
Years of Service: 1921-1933
Submitter's Name: Barbara
City/State: Philadelphia, PA

Registrant ID: 4068
Name: Irvin Upchurch
Railroad: Atlantic Coastline
Position: Cook
Years of Service: 1920-1930
Submitter's Name: Barbara
City/State: Philadelphia, PA

Registrant ID: 4071
Name: Mae Upperman
City/State: Malden, MA

Position: My grandfather lived in Jersey City and in Asbury Park, New Jersey
Years of Service: Early 1900's
Comments: Unfortunately, my grandfather died in the late 1940's. He used to tell us about doing our jobs with dignity. He was a very stately tall man.

Registrant ID: 4080
Name: William Upshaw
City/State: Indianapolis, IN
Railroad: Super Chief
Position: Porter/Waiter
Years of Service:1930's-1950's
Submitter's Name: Beatrice M.

Registrant ID: 4076
Name: Milton Edward
City/State: Chicago, IL
Position: Sleeping Car Porter
Years of Service: 1942-1965
Submitter's Name: Sandra
City/State: Chicago, IL
Comments: Daughter

Registrant ID: 4082
Name: Alfred Upshaw
City/State: Glenwood, IL
Position: Porter
Submitter's Name: Karen A
City/State: Glenwood, IL
Comments: Grandfather Deceased

Registrant ID: 4083
Name: Marshall Upson
City/State: Longview, TX
Railroad: Amtrak
Position: Dinning Car Waiter, Coach Car Porter
Years of Service: 1974-1979

Comments: I enjoyed working on the railroad, the passengers were great.

Registrant ID: 4085
Name: Rayfield Sr. Van
City/State: E. St Louis, Il
Railroad: Pullman Company
Position: Porter
Years of Service: 1931-1966
Submitter's Name: Jackson

Registrant ID: 4086
Name: Elbert VanDyke
City/State: Austin, TX
Railroad: Southern Pacific and Missouri Pacific
Position: Pullman Porter and Dining Car Waiter
Years of Service: 1944
Submitter's Name: Thomas
City/State: Austin, TX
Comments: He loved the railroad and talked about it all the time"

Registrant ID: 4088
Name: Louis Varnado
City/State: New Orleans, LA
Railroad: Illinois Central
Position: Pullman Porter
Years of Service: 1937-1956
Submitter's Name: Clyde-Linda
City/State: New Orleans, LA

Registrant ID: 4089
Isaac Cephus Varnedore, Sr.
Position: Cook/Waiter
Years of Service: 1920's
Submitter(s): Isaac Cephus
City/State: Detroit, MI

Registrant ID: 4091
Name: Robert Vaughan

City/State: Buffalo, NY
Railroad: New York Central (Pullman Company)
Position: Pullman Porter
Years of Service: 1924 ?-1969
Submitter's Name: Bonnie
City/State: Buffalo, NY

Registrant ID: 4093
Name: Elvin Munroe
City/State: Cleveland, OH
Railroad: Tennessee Coal Iron And Railroad Company
Position: Pullman Porter
Years: 8 years, 1937-1945
Submitter's Name: Sylvia J.
City/State: Hudson, OH
Comments: Tennessee Coal Iron & RR Comp., Jan 1937-Sept. 1945, 1939 Fairfield Steel Works, Dept. The Yard, Manufacturing Division 1943,, Tenn. Iron & Steel, left the company as a Pullman Porter 1945. Mr. Elvin Munroe Vauss SR.

Registrant ID: 4096
Name: Lemuel Veland
City/State: Chicago, IL
Railroad: SantaFe
Position: Waiter
Years of Service: 1959-1975
Submitter's Name: Catherine
City/State: Chicago, IL
Comments: Lemuel (Prince) Veland traveled from Chicago to California on many occasions. We had on various trips traveled together, and met many of my current friends, who still reside in California, and with whom we have kept communication for all these years. I'm his wife and have many loving memories of

our many travels. I'm 83 years old and continue to work because I want to. I re-live so many memories of us each day traveling across country.

Registrant ID: 4098
Name: William Vernell Flowers
City/State: Chicago, IL
Railroad: NYC-Burlington-and Amtrak
Pullman Porter and Conductor
Years of Service: 1936-72
Submitter's Name: Silvia
City/State: Chicago, IL
Comments: He was my Father

Registrant ID: 4103
Name: Howard
City/State: Syracuse, NY
Railroad: Crescent City From Louisiana
Position: Porter
Years of Service: 1960
Submitter's Name: Louis
City/State: Syracuse, NY

Registrant ID: 4108
Name: Harvey Oscar Vick, Sr.
City/State: AL
Railroad: Illinois Central (City of New Orleans and City of Miami
Position: Dining Car "Waiter
Years of Service: 1939-1971
Submitter's Name: Sybil
City/State: Louisville, KY
Comments: My grandfather, who passed away on February 24, 1997, worked for over 30 years on the IC Railroad. He held the title of "Waiter in Charge" for most of that time and was on the road sometimes 4-5 days a week. He lived in South Fulton, TN.

Registrant ID: 4104
Name: Clarence Vincent
City/State: Baldwin, MI
Position: Trackman
Years of Service: 1951-1987
Submitter's Name: Gwendolyn
City/State: Milwaukee, IL

Registrant ID: 4117
John "Sonny" William Wade
City/State: AL
Railroad: Norfolk & Southern
Position: Waiter
Years of Service: 1935-1941
Submitter's Name: James W
City/State: VA

Registrant ID: 4116
Name: James Henry Wade
City/State: Roanoke, VA
Railroad: Norfolk & Southern
Position: Cook
Years of Service: 1940-1943
Submitter's Name: James W.
City/State: Roanoke, VA

Registrant ID: 4114
Name: David Jackson Wade
City/State: AL
Railroad: Norfolk & Southern
Position: Cook
Years of Service: 1939-1952
Submitter's Name: James W.
City/State: Roanoke, VA

Registrant ID: 4121
Name: Jesse Wafer
City/State: AL
Position: Pullman Porter
Years of Service: 1941-1944
Submitter's Name: Bernard J.
City/State: Chicago, IL

Registrant ID: 4127
Name: R.L.Waford Sr.
City/State: VA
Position: Porter
Years of Service: 1942-1957
Submitter's Name: Roy L.
City/State: Portsmouth, VA

Registrant ID: 4129
Name: Nathaniel Waiters
City/State: Brenham, TX
Railroad: Santa Fe
Position: Seeping Car Porter
Service: 1946-1960
Submitter's Name: Albert
City/State: Temple, TX
Comments: My father died 1974

Registrant ID: 4132
Name: Edward Alpheus Walden
City/State: Bressler Steelton, AL
Railroad: Pennsylvania
Position: Pullman Porter
Submitter's Name: Ruth S.
City/State: Harrisburg, AL
Comments: My father and his
brothers were all Pullman
Porters on the Pennsylvania
Railroad. They were: Mr. Pearl
Hedgeman Walden uncle) Mr.
Daniel Preston Walden uncle)
Mr. John Lewis Walden uncle

Registrant ID: 4134
Name: Carl Walker
Railroad: El Paso
Submitter's Name: Lawrence

Registrant ID: 4171
Name: Willie H.
City/State: St. Louis, MO
Position: Waiter
Years of Service: 1939-1944

Registrant ID: 4153
Name: Lars Walker
City/State: TX
Railroad: T&P Railroad
Years of Service: 14 Years
Submitter's Name: Lawrence

Registrant ID: 4150
Name: Joseph Walker
City/State: Atlanta, GA
Position: Porter
Submitter's Name: Sharron
City/State: Atlanta, GA

Registrant ID: 4140
Name: James Walker
City/State: Atlanta, GA
Railroad: The Crescent and The
Seaboard Coastline
Position: Pullman Porter
Years of Service: 1940's
Submitter's Name: Anwar
City/State: Atlanta, GA

Registrant ID: 4139
Name: Henry Walker
City/State: NY
Position: Sleeping Car Porter
Years of Service: 10+ years
Submitter's Name: Wendy
City/State: Brooklyn, NY
Comments: Henry Walker is my
maternal grandfather. He
passed on more than 20 years
ago. Yet, even as a youngster I
recall him sharing stories of his
travels.

Registrant ID: 4156
Name: Lars Walker
City/State: Buffalo, TX
Railroad: TP RR
Submitter'(s): Lawrence Lars
City/State: Buffalo, TX

Comments: Retired 1977 worked for 14years

Registrant ID: 4161
Name: N. Courtney Walker
City/State: Chester, PA
Railroad: Pennsylvania Line
Years of Service: Over 42 yrs
Submitter's Name: Jeanette
City/State: Chester, PA
Comments: My uncle was the Sec/Treasurer of the BSCP (Pennsylvania) local.

Registrant ID: 4157
Name: Luther Walker
City/State: AL
Railroad: Chesapeake and Ohio
Position: Waiter and Steward
Submitter's Name: Celeste
City/State: Cincinnati, OH

Registrant ID: 4164
Name: Wesley J. Walker
City/State: Cincinnati, OH
Railroad: Baltimore & Ohio, And Southern
Position: Pullman Porter
Years of Service: 1940's
Submitter's Name: Linda M.
City/State: Cincinnati, OH

Registrant ID: 4146
Name: James Walker
Position: Porter
Years of Service: 1915-1948
Submitter's Name: Shirley
City/State: Hinesville, GA

Registrant ID: 4159
Name: Luther Walker
City/State: Cincinnati, OH
Railroad: C&O and Chesapeake
Position: Pullman Porter

Years of Service Circa 1953 -68
Submitter's Name: Cynthia
City/State: Liberty Township, OH

Registrant ID: 4143
Name: James Walker
City/State: N/A,
Position: Porter
Years of Service: 1945-1950's
Submitter's Name: Audrey
City/State: Matinez, GA

Registrant ID: 4167
Name: Willie Walker
City/State: Midway, FL
Railroad: CSX
Position: Trackman
Years of Service: 1930-42
Submitter's Name: Allene
City/State: Midway, FL
Comments: My Grandfather Willie Walker, worked for the railroad for many years. He retired from the railroad.

Registrant ID: 4162
Name: Nathaniel Walker
City/State: Minneapolis, MN
Railroad: Great Northern, Milwaukee Road
Position: Pullman Porter
Years of Service: 1942-1979
Submitter's Name: Karla
City/State: Minneapolis, MN
Comments: My grandfather had two runs. He either went to Chicago/Detroit or he went to Seattle-Banff. I remember him talking about the Vista Dome Limited and that the trip to Banff was the most scenic trip he had ever made.

Registrant ID: 4136
Name: Charles Walker
City/State: Maryland, AL
Position: Dining Car Waiter
City/State: Mitchellville, MD

Registrant ID: 4147
Name: Joe Walker
City/State: Nashville, TN
Position: Porter
Years of Service: 1942
Submitter's Name: John
City/State: Nashville, TN

Registrant ID: 4163
Name: Troy Walker
City/State: Seattle, WA
Railroad: AT&SF Railroad
Amtrak
Position: Waiter Supervisor
Years of Service: 1943 –82
Submitter's: Thomas Henry
City/State: Seattle, WA
Comments: Worked as waiter on
the Santa Fe and transferred to
Waiter-Supervision when Amtrak
started.

Registrant ID: 4174
Name: Frederick Wall, Jr.
City/State: San Diego, CA
Railroad: Amtrak/National
Railroad Passenger Corporation
Position: tendant/Sleeping Car,
Coach & Dining Car
Years of Service: 1996

Registrant ID: 4175
Name: Weslely "Bubba" Wallace
City/State: Buffalo, NY
Position: Porter
Years of Service: 1950-1963
Submitter's Name: John
City/State: Elizebeth City, NC

Registrant ID: 4177
Name: Edward Lee Wallace Sr.
City/State: Chicago, IL
Railroad: C&EI
Position: Dining Car Porter
And Waiter
Years of Service: 1940-1955
Submitter's Name: Arthur
City/State: Fort Washington, MD
Comments: Edward was my
father

Registrant ID: 4178
Name: Maxie Walker
City/State: St. Louis, MO
Railroad: Missouri Pacific
Position: Waiter
Years of Service: 1950-1970
Submitter's Name: Maxine
City/State: St. Louis , MO
Comments: Daughter of a Porter

Registrant ID: 4179
Name: Kellis Walters
City/State: MS
Position: Porter
Submitter's Name: Marilyn
City/State: Grand Blanc, MI
Comments: My great-
grandfather was a Porter on the
railroad in the late 1800's and
the early 1900's.

Registrant ID: 4180
Name: Cleveland F. Walters Sr.
City/State: Libertyville, TX
Position: Labor
Years of Service: 1950's
Submitter (s): Cleveland F.
City/State: Dayton, TX

Registrant ID: 4183
Name: Harvey Walton
City/State: Belleville, IL
Railroad: L&M or B&O

Position: Sleeping Car Porter
Submitter's Name: Deborah
City/State: Beleville, IL
Comments: My father retired in 1961. For 32 years he worked out of the St Louis Union Station

Registrant ID: 4184
Name: Hughie Walton
City/State: AL
Railroad: L & M or B & O
Position: Pullman Porter
Years of Service: 32 Years
Submitter's Name: Deborah A
City/State: Bellevilee, IL
Comments: Father retired in 1961 for 32 years Worked out of St Louis Union Station

Registrant ID: 4187
Name: Ossie Walton
City/State: Glenside, PA
Railroad: Pennsylvania RR
Position: Waiter, and Chef cook
Years of Service: 1924-56
Submitter's Name: Frederick
City/State: Bryn Mawr, PA
Comments: He enjoyed his experiences. He was able to travel from New England to Virginia. He also traveled from Philadelphia to New York. Deceased.

Registrant ID: 4185
Name: James Walton
City/State: Los Angeles, CA
Railroad: Southern Pacific
Position: Chair Car Porter
Years of Service: 1934-1972
Submitter's Name: Pamela
City/State: Washington, DC
Comments: My father is James W. Walton. His brother also worked on the railroad, same capacity, (Smith Walton) 1933-1978. Both my father and uncle are now deceased but I rode many times on the train and loved it. My mother has a lifetime pass and may be contacted.

Registrant ID: 4182
Name: Gus Walton
City/State: Kansas City, MO
Railroad: Union Pacific
Position: Pullman Porter
Years of Service: late 40's- 60's
Submitter's Name: David
City/State: Woodstock, GA

Registrant ID: 4188
Andrew Charles Warbington Sr.
City/State: Bronx, NY
Railroad: Amtrak
Position: Red Cap
Years of Service: 1947-1983
Submitter's Name: Katherine
City/State: New York, NY
Comments: Andrew Charles Warbington loved working for the railroad. Working for the railroad benefited him and his family in many ways. His wife and children were allowed to travel anywhere in the United States.

Registrant ID: 4189
Name: Lorn Ward
City/State: Lafayette, AL
Position: Car Cleaner
Submitter's Name: Emily
City/State: LaFayette, AL

Registrant ID: 4191
Name: Sherman Ware
City/State: Jersey City, NJ

389

Railroad: New York Central
Position: Pullman Porter
Years of Service: 1929 - 1969
Submitter's Name: Patricia
City/State: Colonia, NJ
Comments: My dad was hired in Thomasville, Ga. to move to the New York area for employment, but he lived in New Jersey. He worked for the Pullman Company for forty years. His final assignment was the run from New York Mont Haven Yard to Los Angeles. This run took him away from home for 10 days. Four days to get there, two-day layover and four days for the return trip. What a great time we had upon each of his returns.

Registrant ID: 4192
Name: John E. Ware, Sr.
City/State: St. Louis, MO
Position: Pullman Porter
Years of Service: 1942-1958

Registrant ID: 4193
Name: William Cullen Ware, Sr.
Railroad: B & O Railroad
Position: Cook
Submitter's Name: Annetta
City/State: East Orange, NJ

Registrant ID: 4194
Name: Benny Warren
City/State: Irving, MI
Railroad: Memphis ,IN
Position: Porter
Years of Service: 1940-1970
Submitter's Name: Billie
City/State: Irving, MI

Registrant ID: 4195
Name: William Henry

City/State: lived in Poynor, TX
Railroad Southern Pacific-Santa FE **Position:** Porter
Years of Service: 1927 - 1934
Submitter's Name: Kamara
City/State: Los Angeles, CA

Registrant ID: 4197
Name: Samuel Warrick
City/State: VA
Comments: He was my grandfather

Registrant ID: 4198
Name: Harvey Wartman
City/State: Baltimore, MD
Railroad: B&O
Position: Pullman
Years of Service: See below
Submitter's Name: Renee
City/State: Woodstock, MD
Comments: I don't know when my father began working for the railroad but, when he died in 1970 he was still employed by the B&O.

Registrant ID: 4204
Name: William Washington
City/State: Texarkana, AR
Railroad: T&P
Position: Foreman
Years of Service: 1899-1950
Submitter's Name: Helen E.W.
City/State: Charlotte, NC

Registrant ID: 4203
Name: Handy Washington
City/State: Chicago, IL
Submitter's Name: James
City/State: Chicago, IL

Registrant ID: 4201
Name: Ernest T. Washington

City/State: Baldwin Park, CA
Railroad: Southern/Union Pacific
Position: Head Chief
Years of Service: 1923-1959
Submitter's Name: Elaine
City/State: Colorado Springs, CO
Comments: My grandfather is now deceased, however, you wouldn't think so, to hear my Aunts talk about their father, my grandfather with a vivid memories. He used to pass through Nebraska, and now my Aunt Ruby his daughter now lives in Grand Island, Ne. In 1993 she was the Nebraska and National Mother of the Year.

Registrant ID: 4205
Name: William A. Washington
City/State: Fayetteville, NC
Railroad: NY Central
Position: Chef/Cook
Years of Service: 1940-1960
Submitter's Name: Josephine
City/State: Faylterville, NC
Comments: Father

Registrant ID: 4202
General Phinigan Washington
Railroad: Pullman Co.
Position: Pullman Porter
Submitter's Name: Patricia

City/State: Philadelphia, PA
Comments: My great grandfather, General Phinigan Washington, graduated from Meharry Medical School in 1895 and while he was in medical school, he worked on the railroad. We know he worked out of Chicago during the

summers to finance his medical school expenses.

Registrant ID: 4199
Name: Charles Washington
City/State: CA
Railroad: Southern Pacific
Position: Waiter
Submitter's Name: Yvette
City/State: Vallejo, CA
Comments: He liked his job and was good at it.

Registrant ID: 4200
Name: Daley Washington
City/State: Wichita, KS
Railroad: Southern Pacific
Position: Cook/Waiter
Years of Service: 1958
Submitter's Name: Gail
City/State: Wichita, KS
Comments: He was scheduled on the trains that went thru Shawnee, Oklahoma; and through Tutenkari, New Mexico, and on from there. Not exactly sure of the entire route.

Registrant ID: 4212
Name: Roy Watford
City/State: Portsmouth, VA
Position: Porter
Years of Service: 35 years
City/State: AL

Registrant ID: 4213
Name: Eugene Watkins
City/State: Gary, IN
Years of Service: 1933
Submitter's Name: Joseph
City/State: Chicago, IL

Registrant ID: 4215
Name: Horace Watkins

City/State: Berkeley, CA
Railroad: Worked out of
Memphis, Tenn.
Position: Porter
Years of Service: 1944 -1946
Submitter's Name: Cora
City/State: El Sobrante, CA

Registrant ID: 4214
Name: George Watkins
City/State: Lexington, KY
Position: Pullman Porter
Submitter's Name: George
City/State: Lexington, KY

Registrant ID: 4217
Name: Henry Watson
City/State: AL
Railroad: L& N Railroad
Position: Track Layer
Submitter's Name: Kimberly
City/State: Detroit, MI
Comments: My grand father
retired before my brother and I
were born. My mom told me he
worked 30 years at the railroad
and he lived to be 92 years old.

Registrant ID: 4216
Name: Dennis C. Watson
City/State: IL
Railroad: Santa Fe
Position: Pullman Porter
Years of Service: 1935-1970
Submitter's Name: Patricia
City/State: Evanston, IL

Registrant ID: 4218
Name: Charles Watson Jr.
City/State: Bladensburg, MD
Railroad: Amtrak
Position: Chair-Car Attendant
Years of Service: 46 years
Submitter's Name: Cheryl

City/State: Bladensburg, MD
Comments: My father began his
duty on the Silver Meteor from
New York to Miami, Florida until
the last five (5)years of his
career. I was fortunate and
proud to occasionally ride the
east coast with my dad. I
appreciated how he conducted
himself through humiliation.

Registrant ID: 4220
Name: Caroline Watson-Pickens
City/State: St. Louis, MO

Registrant ID: 4222
Name: Morris J.Watts
City/State: AL
Railroad: Penn. Railroad
Position: Porter
Submitter's Name: Ronald F.
City/State: NJ

Registrant ID: 4221
Name: Ernest Watts
Position: Chef
Years of Service: Prior to 1929
Submitter's Name: Joyce
City/State: Alton, IL

Registrant ID: 4223
Name: Lee B. Watty Sr.
City/State: Oakland, CA
Years of Service: Circa
1940's-50's
Submitter's Name: Lee B.
City/State: Stockton, CA
Comments: Father lived in
Oakland Ron Delums (CA
congressman's) uncle was CL
Delums local union president of
the Oakland Chapter of the
BSCP and John Iverson , John
Faust and James Farist.

Registrant ID: 4224
Name: Rona Wave
City/State: Louisville, KY

Registrant ID: 4225
Name: Olden C. Way
City/State: Newark, NJ
Railroad: Pennsylvania RR
Submitter's Name: Sandra
City/State: Copperas Cove,, TX
Comments: Olden C. Way was
my great-grandfather. I often
heard stories of him having
worked with the railroad

Registrant ID: 4226
Name: Roberta Wearer
City/State: Detroit, Mt
Railroad: Pullman Company

Registrant ID: 4230
Name: Herbert B.Webb
City/State: Chicago, IL
Railroad: Santa Fe
Position: Dining Car Waiter
Years of Service: 1914 to 1933
Submitter's Name: Doris L.
City/State: Chicago, IL

Registrant ID: 4229
Name: Charlie Webb
City/State: Marshall, TX
Railroad: Texas and Pacific
Position: Pullman Porter
Years of Service: 1946-1958
Submitter's Name: Mary
City/State: Denver, CO
Comments: Uncle Charlie
started working for Texas and

Pacific in 1939 as a station
worker and after a stint in the
Army he joined the ranks of the
Pullman Porters. He was a

stately and proud member of the
this team of invaluable workers.

Registrant ID: 4228
Name: Albert L Webb
City/State: Cleveland, OH
Position: Loader
Years of Service: 1924-1955
Submitter's Name: Anna M.
City/State: Euclid, OH

Registrant ID: 4232
Name: Wellington Webb
Railroad: N W Railroad
Position: Pullman Porter
Submitter's Name: Zella
City/State: Homewood, IL

Registrant ID: 4231
Name: Luman Sidney Webb
City/State: New Orleans, LA
Railroad: Southern pacific
Porter and Dining Car Waiter
Submitter's Name: Daniel
City/State: Sioux City, IA
Comments: Luman was my
fathers first cousin. He worked
the City Of New Orleans. He died
in the mid 70s.

Registrant ID: 4233
Name: Osar J. Webb Sr.
Position: Sleeping Car Porter
Registrant ID: 4234
Name: Wellington Webs
Railroad: NW Rail Road
Position: Porters
Years of Service: 1930-1940

Registrant ID: 4237
Name: Milton P. Webster
City/State: Chicago, IL
Submitter's Name: Jean

City/State: Chicago, IL
Comments: First international VP of the BSCP Union.

Registrant ID: 4235
Name: Benjamin Webster
City/State: CA
Railroad: Southern Pacific
Position: Pullman Porter
Years of Service: 1941 - 1958
Submitter's Name: Saundra
City/State: Palo Alto, CA
Comments: Benjamin Webster began his career in New Orleans, LA in 1941 and was transferred to Oakland, CA in 1954. He was married to Emma Louise McDaniel-Webster and they had seven children. Daniel, Benjamin, Saundra, Willie, Wilburt, Mary and Lenora.

Registrant ID: 4238
Name: Harry Webster Harper
City/State: Indianapolis, IN
Position: Chief of the Red Cap
Years of Service: 1911-1966
Submitter's Name: Wester Jones

Registrant ID: 4239
Name: Jerry Weiss
City/State: Niles, IL
Railroad: Pullman Company
Years of Service: 1964

Registrant ID: 4240
Name: Charles Nathanial Wells
City/State: Mt. Pleasant, IA
Railroad: Chicago or Minneapolis
Position: Porter
Submitter's Name: Linda
City/State: Burlington, IA

Comments: Charles Nathaniel Wells was my uncle. he would return to Mt. Pleasant, LA - the place of his birth and share his tales of being a Porter on the train. I was very young and didn't really appreciate the significance of his contribution to Black History.

Registrant ID: 4241
Name: Samuel Demar Wells
City/State: New York, NY
Position: Porter
Years of Service: 1932-1960's
Submitter's Name: Juanita
City/State: New York, NY
Comments: He was my uncle

Registrant ID: 4242
Name: Wilbert Wells
City/State: St. Louis, MO
Railroad: Wabash Railroad
Position: Freight loader
Years of Service: 1950's
Submitter's Name: Patricia
City/State: St. Louis , MO

Registrant ID: 4245
Name: Mack C. Westbrook
City/State: Chicago, IL
Railroad: Panama L and D Line
Position: Sleeping Car Porter
Years of Service: 44 Years
Submitter's Name: Agnes
City/State: Chicago, IL
Comments: My father

Registrant ID: 4247
Name: John Westbrooks
Submitter's Name: Maxwell
City/State: Bronx, NY

Registrant ID: 4246
Name: Hazel Westbrooks
City/State: Bronx, NY
Railroad: Penn Railroad
Position: Dining Car
Submitter's Name: Maxwell
City/State: Bronx, NY

Registrant ID: 4250
Name: Thomas Hart Weston
Railroad: Missouri Pacific
Position: Pullman Porter
Years of Service: 30 Years
Submitter's Name: Rosemary
City/State: Florissant, MO

Registrant ID: 4251
Name: Norman Whatley
City/State: PA
Position: Handler
Years of Service: 1938-1942
Submitter's Name: Audrey
City/State: Willow Grove, PA

Registrant ID: 4252
Name: Walter Wheeler
City/State: IL
Railroad: New York Central
Position: Club Car Attendant
Years of Service: 1937-1970
Submitter's Name: Walter
City/State: Chicago, IL
Comments: My father worked for the NYC until it became Amtrak and died on the road in 1970. The union was notified by the company before my mother was that my father had a heart attack and died.

Registrant ID: 4259
Name: Earl C. White
City/State: Bowling Green, KY
Position: Pullman Porter

Years of Service: Retired in the 1960's

Registrant ID: 4258
Name: Clyde A. White
City/State: Chicago, IL
Position: Porter
Years of Service: Circa 1924-1940's
Submitter's Name: BeBe

Registrant ID: 4253
Name: David W. White
City/State: Cadmen, SC
Railroad: Pullman Company
Position: Kmart-Stick
Years of Service: 5yrs

Registrant ID: 4263
Name: Hosea White
City/State: Los Angeles, CA
Railroad: Union Pacific
Position: Dining Car Waiter
Years of Service: 1942 / 1950
Comments: I passed for 21 years of age although I was only 16 when I was employed by the Union Pacific Railroad in Kansas City Mo. I was sent to Ogden Utah where I worked as a Dining Car Waiter running to Los Angeles California. I fell in love with L.A. immediately and transferred.

Registrant ID: 4255
Name: Aaron Oscar White
City/State: St. Louis, MO
Railroad: Frisco
Years of Service: 1920-1930's
Submitter's Name: Kimberly
City/State: Burbank, CA

Comments: From what I've been told, my grandfather, Aaron Oscar White, was president of the Pullman Porter's Union local in St. Louis, MO. His wife, Susie, was very active in assisting the local, from what I've been told. As far as his experiences, I don't have any information.

Aaron Oscar White

Registrant ID: 4265
Name: John W. White
City/State: AL
Railroad: Southern Pacific
Position: Cook
Submitter's Name: Jennie B
City/State: AL
Comments: A Friend

Registrant ID: 4271
Name: William Tyler White
City/State: Richmond, VA
Railroad: Phoebe Snow
Position: Chef

Years of Service: Not sure, but it was before 1954
Submitter's Name: Beverly
City/State: Atlanta, GA

Registrant ID: 4268
Name: Preston White
City/State: Cincinnati, OH
Railroad: L & N
Position: Assistant Cook
Years of Service: 30 - 35 yrs.
Submitter's Name: Gwen
City/State: Cincinnati, OH
Comments: He enjoyed working on the Railroad for 35 years; he always dreamed in traveling around the U.S., and he fulfill his dreams working on the railroad.

Registrant ID: 4266
Name: Lee White White
City/State: IL
Railroad: Chicago/ Northwestern
Position: Porter and Bartender
Years of Service: 28 Years
Submitter's Name: Julie
City/State: Evanston, IL
Comments: My father was (born 1910) and worked for 28 years on the railroad until he was furloughed- as did my father's older brother (born 1894) (my uncle) and my uncle's son. They both told stories of the fight to get the union started and of all the prejudice they faced.

Registrant ID: 4256
Name: Aron White
City/State: DC
Railroad: B&O
Position: Pullman Porter

Years of Service: 1945
Submitter's Name: Ann W.
City/State: Hyattsville, MD

Registrant ID: 4270
Name: William Jr. White
City/State: Lexington, KY
Position: Dining Car Waiter
Years of Service: 1941-1942
Submitter's Name: Beulah W.
City/State: Lexington, KY

Registrant ID: 4264
Name: John White
City/State: Washington, DC
Railroad: Southern
Position: Chef/Pullman Porter
Years of Service: 1923 – 1973
Submitter's Name: Pamela
City/State: San Francisco, CA
Comments: Both of my uncles
worked on the railroad as well
as many others that I grew up
with. Alphonso Chisolm and my
uncle John White worked
together for many years. Both
are deceased.

Registrant ID: 4269
Name: Richard Hervey White
City/State: St. Louis, MO
Railroad: Pullman Company
Position: Pullman Porter
Years of Service: 39 Years
Submitter's Name: Marilyn
City/State: St. Louis , MO
Comments: I remember daddy-
having lots of scary stories
replete with newspaper articles
to back them up. I remember
little gifts he brought home also,
like a Canadian dollar for my
brother and, maps of the United
States and abroad and always
books.

Registrant ID: 4267
Name: Marcellus White
City/State: MO
Railroad: Position: Porter
Years of Service: 1940's
Submitter's Name: Bernardino
City/State: Sunnyvale, CA
Comments: He was my father.
died 1953. My grandmother
(May Age - now deceased) housed
railroad men

Registrant ID: 4257
Name: Charles White
City/State: Temple Hills, MD
Railroad: Seaboard Airline
Position: Freight Handler
Years of Service: 1942 -1963
Submitter's Name: Janet
City/State: Temple Hills, MD
Comments: This was my Dad's
first job, and his entire RR career
was in Hamlet, North Carolina.
At the "Transfer Shed" in Hamlet,
NC he was the lead Freight
Caller/Handler and had two to
three employees working under
him.

Registrant ID: 4272
Name: La Valle White Sr.
City/State: Berkeley, CA
Railroad: Southern Pacific
Position: Dining Car Waiter
Years of Service: Late
1930's to 1973
Submitter's Name: La Valle
City/State: San Leandro, CA

Registrant ID: 4273
Name: Samuel White Sr.

City/State: St Louis, MO
Railroad: Terminal Railroad
Position: Porter, diesel porter,
Years of Service: 1930's- 1955
Submitter's Name: Cynthia
City/State: St. Louis , MO
Comments: I am doing
genealogy research on my family.
My grandfather Sam Sr. and his
son Sam Jr. both worked for The
Terminal Railroad. I needed
information to find out where in
Tennessee that he came from.
This was my starting point.

Registrant ID: 4274
Name: Robert Whiteside
City/State: Indianapolis, IN
Position: Dinner Car Waiter
Years of Service: 1937 - 1965
Submitter's Name: Davis
City/State: Indianapolis, IN
Comments: He worked on the Red
eye from Chicago to Indianapolis.

Registrant ID: 4275
Beaufort Nathaniel Whitfield
City/State: Chicago, IL
Railroad: Based out of Chicago
and worked all over the country
Position: Pullman Porter
Years of Service: 1936 - 1970
Submitter's Name: Lucy L.
City/State: Chicago, IL
Comments: Beaufort N.
Whitfield was my father and died
December 1970. I am grateful
that you have taken up the
cause of documenting the
employee's as this is a part of
our history.

Registrant ID: 4277
Name: Eddie H. Whitfield

Railroad: Chesapeake & Ohio
Years of Service: 1930's-1950's
Submitter's Name: Edda
City/State: Detroit, MI

Registrant ID: 4278
Name: Otto Whiting
City/State: IL
Position: Pullman Porter
Years of Service: 1930's
Submitter's Name: Lynn
City/State: Brooklyn, NY

Registrant ID: 4279
Arthur Brown (A. B.) Whitlock
City/State: Gary, IN
Railroad: Illinois Central
Position: Waiter
Years of Service: 1910-1917
Submitter's Name: Elmyra
City/State: Sun Valley, CA

Registrant ID: 4280
Name: Archie Wigfall
City/State: MD
Position: Car Cleaner
Years of Service: 1925-1951
Submitter's Name: Lillie
City/State: Takama Park, MD

Registrant ID: 4281
Name: Russell Wiggington Sr.
City/State: KY
Railroad: Louisville & Nashville
(L& N) Railroad
Position: Red Cap
Years of Service:Circa 1919-67
Submitter's Name: Lawrence
City/State: Louisville, KY
Comments: My grandfather
worked for the L&N railroad for
48 years in Louisville, KY. This
allowed him to come in contact
with people from all around the

world. He used his wages plus tips to provide for his wife and three children, two of whom are college graduates.

Registrant ID: 4282
Name: Joe Nathan Wiggins
City/State: Sanford, FL
Railroad: Seaboard Coastline, Amtrak
Position: Track & yard motorcar driver, etc.
Years of Service 1940's -70's
Submitter's Name: Ella
City/State: Winter Springs, FL

Registrant ID: 4283
Name: Thomas Wilcox
City/State: AL
Position: Pullman Porter
Years of Service: 1945-1955
Submitter's Name: Pamela
City/State: Moreno Valley, CA
Comments: My fondest memory of my father's experience as a Porter was when my mother and I would travel by train to Texas, where my family is from, my father was adamant about us eating in the dining car and ensuring that we had enough money to do so. His words were "I get so tired of seeing black folks with a shoebox full of chicken and a pound cake I don't know what to do. He was so comical.

Registrant ID: 4284
Name: Jasper Wilder
City/State: Chicago, IL
Railroad: Santa Fe Railroad
Position: Pullman Porter
Yearse: 1920's -- 1941

Submitter's Name: Sylvia
City/State: Takoma Park, MD
Comments: My Grandfather worked under A. Philip Randolph, who came to his home in Chicago.

Registrant ID: 4286
Name: Deon Wiliams
City/State: Roseville, CA
Submitter's Name: Brenda M
City/State: Rosevelle, CA

Registrant ID: 4287
Name: Clarence A. Wilkes
City/State: NY
Railroad: New York Central
Position: Dining Car Waiter
Years of Service: 1941-1957
Submitter's Name: Helen
City/State: Port St. Lucie, FL
Comments: My father loved his job. He had no choice in his departure from the railroad, it was due to the lack of runs. He died loving the work and the company of his co-workers. He always stated that his co-workers were refined and educated men who took their jobs seriously.

Registrant ID: 4288
Name: Benjamin (B.J.) Wilkins
Railroad: Pennsylvania
Position: Porter
Years of Service: 1929-1969
Submitter's Name: Danice
City/State: Cary, NC
Comments: He did not like traveling with the President on board. Couldn't get his work done because the secret servicemen liked having Doris

Duke on board. (She was a good tipper, and always treated him with dignity.

Registrant ID: 4289
Name: Willie E. Wilkins
City/State: CA
Railroad: Western Pacific
Position: Pullman Porter
Submitter's Name: Queen E.
City/State: Oakland, CA
Comments: Willie was my brother

Registrant ID: 4290
Name: Huckaby William
City/State: Teague, TX
Position: Railroad Worker
Years of Service: 1916 +
Submitter's Name: Mary
City/State: Fairfield, CA

Registrant ID: 4333
Raymond Bernard Williams
Railroad: Southern Pacific
Years of Service: Until 1963

Registrant ID: 4297
Name: Cecelia Williams
City/State: Cleveland, OH
Railroad: Pullman Company
Position: Sleeping Car Porter

Registrant ID: 4314
Name: James G. Williams
Railroad: Pullman Company
Position: Laborer
Years of Service: 47.5 years
Submitter's Name: Lee W

Registrant ID: 4306
Name: Grayce Williams
Railroad: Penn. Railroad
Position: Pantry

Years: 3yrs 1943-46
Submitter's Name: Grayce

Registrant ID: 4308
Name: Howard J. Williams
Railroad: Pennsylvania RR
Position: Dining Car
Waiter- in Charge
Years of Service: 1943-1961
Submitter's Name: Grayce
Comments: Husband

Registrant ID: 4329
Name: Louis Clyde Williams
Position: Porter
Years of Service: 1937-1957
Submitter's Name: Ward

Registrant ID: 4332
Name: Morteir Williams
Position: Porter
Years of Service: 1937-1957
Submitter's Name: Ward

Registrant ID: 4324
Name: Leander Williams
City/State: Wilmore, PA
Railroad: Penn Railroad
Position: Pullman Porter
Years of Service: 1926-1961

Registrant ID: 4325
Name: Leroy Williams.
City/State: TX
Position: Waiter
Submitter's Name: Jessica
City/State: TX
Comments: My uncle (by marriage) was a waiter. He was a very proper gentleman, well-spoken and an impeccable dresser. He lived in Houston, Texas.

Registrant ID: 4330
Name: Luther Williams
City/State: Aurora, CO
Position: Porter
Years of Service: 1930-1962
Submitter's Name: Sandra
City/State: Aurora, CO

Registrant ID: 4321
Name: Josepheus Williams
City/State: Virginia Beach, VA
Position: Baggage Man
Submitter's Name: June
City/State: Baltimore , MD
Comments: My family members relate that my great,great uncle, Josepheus Williams, born 1876 in Princess Anne Co.(Virginia Beach, VA), along with his nephew, William Newton Williams, Jr. founded the Williams & Williams Transfer Co. and were the first baggage-men.

Registrant ID: 4335
Name: Richard Williams
City/State: Baltimore, MD
Railroad: B & O Railroad
Position: Porter to President Daniel Willard
Years of Service: 1893-1912
Submitter's Name: Linda
City/State: Bordentown, NJ

Registrant ID: 4339
Name: Travis Simeon Williams
City/State: Laurelton Queens, NY
Position: Attendant
Years of Service: 1945-1948
Submitter's Name: Ms. Rene
City/State: Brooklyn, NY

Registrant ID: 4292
Name: Alexander Williams
City/State: AL
Position: Porter
Years of Service: Circa1901-14
Submitter's Name: Donna
City/State: Chicago, IL
Comments: My grandfather was born in Barbados in 1883. He worked as a Pullman Porter after he immigrated to Pittsburgh, PA from Barbados at approximately 17 or 18 years of age. His run was between Pittsburgh and Cleveland, Ohio.

Registrant ID: 4331
Name: Monroe Williams
City/State: Chicago, IL
Railroad: Illinois Central Railroad
Position: Porter
Submitter's Name: Sharon
City/State: Chicago, IL

Registrant ID: 4342
Name: Willie Williams
City/State: TX
Railroad: Texas Pacific
Position: Section Gang Laborer
Years of Service: 1910-1940
Submitter's Name: Jesse D.
City/State: Dallas, TX
Comments: Worked in East Texas and Louisiana border

Registrant ID: 4294
Name: Anderson Williams
Position: Pullman Porter
Years of Service: Early 1900's - Retired 1943
Submitter's Name: Naomi E.
City/State: Denver, CO

Registrant ID: 4295
Name: Antonio Williams
City/State: Denver, CA
Railroad: Rio Grande, California Zephyr
Position: Waiter, Porter
Years of Service: Circa 1949-79
Submitter's Name: Frances
City/State: Denver, CO
Comments: Dad was a hard working man and was dearly loved by all his family members, friends as well as his co-workers. He had a good rapport with the passengers.

Registrant ID: 4303
Flemon Douglas Williams
Railroad: Southern Railroad
Position: Pullman
Years of Service: 40's-50's
Submitter's Name: Joy
City/State: East Cleve, OH

Registrant ID: 4299
Name: Clarence Louis Williams
City/State: Oakland, CA
Railroad: Southern Pacific
Years of Service: During depression
Submitter's Name: E
City/State: El Cerrito, CA

Registrant ID: 4341
Name: William Williams
City/State: Jersey City, NJ
Position: Red Cap
Years of Service: 1923-1945
Submitter's Name: Mrs. Wilhelmina
City/State: Elkins Park, PA

Registrant ID: 4320
Name: John Williams

City/State: Brooklyn, NY
Position: Pullman Porter
Years of Service: About 1932
Submitter's Name: Thelma B.
City/State: Jamaica, NY

Registrant ID: 4334
Name: Richard Williams
City/State: AL
Railroad: The line that traveled from Chicago to the West
Position: Pullman Porter/Waiter
Years of Service: 1937-1941
Submitter's Name: Anita
City/State: Lake Ridge, VA
Comments: It appears that my father joined the railroad as a Pullman Porter after graduating from Pearl High School, Nashville, TN. I remember him describing his travels on the railroad. After his tenure with the railroad he joined the US Navy in 1944.

Registrant ID: 4298
Name: Charles E. Williams
City/State: Markham, IL
Railroad: Baltimore & Ohio
Years of Service: 1900-1945
Submitter's Name: Sheryl
City/State: Markham, IL
Comments: Grandfather

Registrant ID: 4311
Name: J.C. Williams
City/State: MN
Railroad: Burlington North Coast
Position: Waiter
Years of Service: After World War I until 1948
Submitter's Name: Audrey
City/State: Matteson, IL

Comments: Uncle worked until he retired. His brother was Matthew Miller from New York Central.

Registrant ID: 4296
Name: Caldrich Williams
City/State: Jamaica, NY
Railroad: Pennsylvania RR
Position: Pullman Porter
Years of Service: 1930's
Submitter's Name: Tani
City/State: Middletown, NY
Comments: My grandfather was a dedicated, hard worker and so were his friends that worked the railroad. It wasn't until my adult years that I realized that what I thought were acts of submission on his part when working were really acts of heroism and survival in a racist world.

Registrant ID: 4340
Name: Will Williams
City/State: Monrovia, CA
Railroad: Union Pacific
Position: Dining Car Waiter
Years of Service: 1919 to 1968
Submitter's Name: Sarah
City/State: Morro Bay, CA
Comments: My father was better known as "Salty Dog", he route was from Los Angeles to Chicago. Our family has many stories about the railroad it was our life. We have a letter Franklin Roosevelt wrote to my father before he was president.

Registrant ID: 4301
Earnest Sylvester Williams
City/State: Mt Vernon, NY
Railroad: New Haven Line

Position: Sleeping Car Porter
Submitter's Name: Dr. Gwendolyn
City/State: Mt. Vernon, NY
Comments: My father was born September 11, 1908

Registrant ID: 4304
Name: Fred Williams
City/State: AL
Railroad: Seaboard Railroad
Position: Waiter
Years of Service: 1950's
Submitter's Name: Verdelle
City/State: New York, NY

Registrant ID: 4307
Name: Horace Williams
City/State: AL
Railroad: Union Pacific
Position: Waiter
Years of Service: 1944-1970
Submitter's Name: Marcellus
City/State: Oakland, CA

Registrant ID: 4326
Name: Leroy Williams
City/State: So. Ozone Par, NY
Position: Pullman Porter
Years of Service: 1943-1960
Submitter's Name: Louise
City/State: S. Ozone Prk., NY

Registrant ID: 4318
Name: John Williams
City/State: TX
Position: Pullman Porter
Years of Service: 1920-57
Submitter's Name: Johnet
City/State: Sacramento, CA
Comments: John Williams was my grandfather and is now deceased. His run was from Houston Texas to New York. He

retired in 1957. My mother has always told me that because of his job on the railroad she doesn't remember any affect of the stock crash on our family.

Registrant ID: 4300
Name: Earl Williams
City/State: Seattle, WA
Position: Porter
Submitter's Name: Marjorie
City/State: Seattle, WA
Comments: He died of cancer.

Registrant ID: 2939
Name: Otis Bill
City/State: Jacksonville, FL
Railroad: Seaboard Coast Line
Years of Service: 1955 - 1978
Submitter's Name: Bartricia
City/State: Sherman Oaks, CA
Comments: I just remember stories my grandfather (now deceased) would tell about how proud he was of his job to work for the railroad. He was very passionate about it.

Registrant ID: 4317
Name: John Williams
City/State: Spartanburg, SC
Railroad: Southern
Position: Cook & Porter
Submitter's Name: Deborah
City/State: Spartern Burg, SC
Comments: Grandfather

Registrant ID: 4310
Name: Hubert, Sr.Williams
City/State: AL
Railroad: Wabash and Norfolk and Western
Position: Pullman Porter
Years: Early 1920's - 1965

Submitter's Name: Hubert, Jr.
City/State: St. Louis , MO
Comments: My father ran between St. Louis and Chicago for approximately 30 of the 40+ years that he worked as a Pullman Porter.

Registrant ID: 4315
Name: Jesse Pedro Williams
City/State: Tampa, FL
Railroad: Seaboard
Position: Pullman Porter
Years of Service: 1926-1969
Submitter(s): Ethel
City/State: Stamford, CT

Registrant ID: 4322
Name: Lang Williams
City/State: Pittsburgh, PA
Position: Pullman Porter
Submitter's Name: Shawn
City/State: Stone Mountain, GA
Comments: Lang Williams was is my great grandfather. He was born 1877 and died in 1954.

Registrant ID: 4312
Name: James E. Williams
City/State: Hawthorne, FL
Railroad: Tallahassee, Florida
Position: Dining Car Waiter and a Porter
Submitter's Name: Kathryn N.
City/State: Taunton, MA
Comments: I just thought it was important to add my grandfather's name to your registry. Everyone in my mother's immediate family are all deceased now; Grandma Wobble who lived in Hawthorne, FL and who raised James E.Williams,

and my grandmother Beatrice (Vaughn) Williams.

Registrant ID: 4293
Name: Ananise James Williams
City/State: Morrow, LA
Railroad: Texas & Pacific
Position: Track Maintenance
Years of Service: 30+years
Submitter's Name: Wilbert Ben
City/State: Urbandale, IA
Comments: My father was injured severely while working on the railroad in 1960 or 61. He was transferred to the Railroad Hospital in Marshall, Texas and was kept there for quite some time.

Registrant ID: 4305
Name: George W. Williams
City/State: Yonkers,, NY
Railroad: New York Central
Position: Dinning Car Waiter
Years 33 years of service worked until 1960's
Submitter's Name: Melvin
City/State: Washington, D.C.,
Comments: At the time of this submission his surviving widow, Mrs Annie Mae Williams is (age 98) Melton (son) of MR. Williams, livres in Yonkers. Mr. Williams also had a son who was George M. Williams (My father), who also worked for the railroad.

Registrant ID: 4337
Name: Robert Williams
City/State: Woodridge, IL
Railroad: North Western
Position: Pullman Porter
Years of Service: 20 years
Submitter's Name: Jacqueline
City/State: Woodridge, IL

Registrant ID: 4313
Name: James Edward Williams
City/State: NY
Railroad: New York Central Pennsylvania Rail lines
Position: Pullman Porter
Years of Service: 1940-1969
Submitter's Name: Orlando
City/State: Yellow Springs, OH

Registrant ID: 4343
James "Chief Jim" Williams
City/State: New York, NY
Railroad: Grand Central Station New York city.
Position: Chief of Red Caps
Years of Service:1930's - 40's
Submitter's Name: Dorothy
City/State: New Haven, CT
Comments: He was a fine gentleman and well respected.

Registrant ID: 4344
Name: George Williams Jr.
City/State: St. Louis, MO
Railroad: Missouri pacific New York central
Position: Dining Car Waiter
Years of Service: October, 1942-February, 1943 to 1953
Submitter's Name: Gregory
City/State: Atlanta, GA
Comments: Waited on Eleanor Roosevelt and Duke Ellington. Started as bottle boy on Missouri Pacific then began working as a Dinning Car Waiter.

Registrant ID: 4345
Name: William Williams Jr.
City/State: Virginia Beach, VA
Position: Baggage Man
Submitter's Name: June
City/State: Baltimore, MD

Registrant ID: 4346
Name: Naomi E. Williams Price
City/State: Denver, CO
Position: Pullman Porter
Years of Service: 1900's - 1943
Submitter: Mr. Anderson
City/State:

Registrant ID: 4349
Name: ILL.. Williams Sr.
City/State: Roxbury, MA
Railroad: New Haven
Position: Pullman Porter
Years of Service: 1926 - 1995
Comments: My dad spent 39 years working as a Pullman Porter and had fond memories about his career on the road after his retirement.

Registrant ID: 4347
Name: Harold J Williams Sr.
City/State: Berkeley, CA
Railroad: Santa Fe, Southern Pacific, Amtrak
Position: Pullman Porter
Years of Service: 1943 - 1971
Submitter's Name: Harold J
City/State: Charlotte, NC
Comments: As a member of the Brotherhood of Sleeping Car Porters, my father, the late Harold "Bill" J. Williams, Sr. participated in the famous railroad strike of 1963, which was ended by an executive order signed by President Kennedy.

Registrant ID: 4350
Name: Leonard Williams Sr.
City/State: Chicago, IL
Railroad: Illinois Central
Position: Sleeping Car Porter

Years of Service: 1938-1969
Submitter's Name: Milton
City/State: Chicago, IL

Registrant ID: 4351
Name: Richard Williams Sr.
Position: Porter
Years of Service: 1920-1961
Submitter's Name: Richard
City/State: New Orleans, LA

Registrant ID: 4350
Name: Raymond B. Williams Sr.
City/State: Harvey, LA
Position: Pullman Porter
Years of Service: 1924-1969
Submitter's Name: Arthur C.
City/State: San Antonio, TX

Registrant ID: 4351
Logan Jacob Williams Sr.
City/State: Roxbury, MA
Railroad: Boston
Position: Pullman Porter
Submitter's Name: Lutisha
City/State: Lexington, KY

Registrant ID: 4352
Name: Leonard Williams Sr.
City/State: Chicago, IL
Railroad: Pullman Company
Submitter's Name: Dorothy
City/State: Chicago, IL

Registrant ID: 4353
Willie Mae Williams Fields
City/State: Chicago, IL
Railroad: Super Chief
Position: Maid
Years of Service: Circa 25 to 30 Yrs
Submitter's Name: Gloria
City/State: St. Paul, MN
Comments: She was my aunt. I remember she ran from Chicago to Los Angeles, California.

Registrant ID: 4354
Name: Eli Williamson
City/State: Buffalo, NY
Railroad: Pullman Railcar Co.
And Penn Central and Amtrak
Position: Cook
Submitter's Name: Lorraine A.
City/State: Buffalo, NY
Comments: My father retired
from the railroad. We still have a
brass ash tray that was given to
him from the Pullman Service.

Dennis Williamson

Registrant ID: 4354
Name: Dennis Williamson
City/State: Blair, SC
Railroad: Pullman Rail Car Co.
Position: Trackman

Years of Service: 1909-1924
Submitter's Name: Jacqueline
City/State: Washington, DC

Registrant ID: 4356
Name: John "Sonny" Willis
Position: Waiter
Years of Service: 1939-1965
Submitter's Name: James W.
City/State: Roanoke, VA

Registrant ID: 4358
Name: Richard C. " Willis
City/State: Chicago, IL
Railroad: Pennsylvania
Position: Pullman Porter
Years of Service: Hired 1937

Registrant ID: 4357
Name: George " Willis
Railroad: Burlington
Position: Chef
Submitter's Name: Joan
City/State: Detroit, MI

Registrant ID: 4361
Name: Hollis Wilson
City/State: AL
City/State: AL

Registrant ID: 4362
Name: June Wallace Wilson
City/State: Brooklyn, NY
Railroad: Penn
Position: Pullman Porter
Submitter's Name: Mary
Catherine
City/State: Anchorage, AK
Comments: Unsure of dates of
employment circa late 1940s-50s.

Registrant ID: 4359
Name: Amos " Willison
City/State: SC
Railroad: Southern Railways
Position: Trackman
Years: Circa-1920's -died 1927
Submitter's Name: The Wilson
City/State: Elmont, NY

Registrant ID: 4361
Name: James Bob Wilson
City/State: Jacksonville, FL
Position: Pullman Porter
Submitter's Name: Rhonda
City/State: Jacksonville, FL
My father was born 9-29-14

Registrant ID: 4363
Name: McKinley Wilson
City/State: Montgomery, AL
Position: Pullman Porter
Years of Service: 1940-50
Submitter's Name: Lillian
City/State: Montgomery, AL

Registrant ID: 4360
Name: Augustus Henry Wilson
City/State: NY
Position: Waiter-Porter
Years of Service: 1935-1948
Submitter's Name: Diane E.
City/State: New York, NY

Registrant ID: 4361
Name: Benjamin Wilson
City/State: IL
Railroad: Baltimore & Ohio
Position: Dining Car Waiter
Submitter's Name: Charlaine
City/State: Oak Park,, IL
Comments: He used to talk about all the interesting people he served, including many celebrities, i.e., Lucille Ball

before she married Desi. Some were very kind and spoke to the waiters like old friends if they traveled often. Others weren't so friendly.

Registrant ID: 4364
Name: Sydney Wilsoni Smyre
Position: Pullman Porter
Years of Service: 1912-1947
Submitter's Name: Randolph
City/State: Clinton, MD

Registrant ID: 4366
Name: Fred Winfield

Registrant ID: 4365
Name: Fred Winfield
Railroad: N W Railroad
Position: Porter
Submitter's Name: Zella
City/State: Homewood, IL

Registrant ID: 4368
Name: Chester Winfield
City/State: Washington, DC
Railroad: Seaboard
Position: Waiter
Years of Service: 1950's
Submitter's Name: Card
City/State: Washington, DC

Registrant ID: 4369
Name: Henry Winfrey
City/State: Indianapolis, IN
Railroad: Pennsylvania Railroad
Position: Porter
Years of Service: 1928-1940
Submitter's Name: Delores
City/State: Indianapolis, IN
Comments: Have several ticket stubs, uniform and suitcase used to travel

Registrant ID: 4370
Name: Herbert Winn Winsmore
City/State: Tucumcari, NM
Railroad: Southern Pacific
Position: Dining Car Waiter,
Pullman Porter
Years of Service: Approximately
1935- 1955
Submitter's Name: Barbara
City/State: Kansas City, MO
Comments: Reverend Winn was
my uncle by marriage. I don't
know a lot about him because I
lived in California and saw my
aunt infrequently, and
Rev Winn even less frequently.
His wife, Jessie Morrow Winn,
was my father's oldest sister.

Registrant ID: 4371
Name: Norman
City/State: Washington D. C.
Position: Pullman Porter
Submitter's Name: Marry
City/State: Glen Burnie, MD
Comments: My Aunt Mrs.
Florence Slaughter in
Washington D.C

Registrant ID: 4372
Name: Dr. Eric Winston
City/State: Wilberforce, OH
Railroad: Santa Fe
Position: Dining Car
Years of Service: 1963, 64, 65
Comments: My three years on
the railroad were the most
fascinating years of my life. I
have gone from elementary
school through to a PhD degree
and I can still say I learned more
about life, and people from my
railroad experience than I did in
any class.

Registrant ID: 4373
Name: Matthew B. Wise
City/State: Galesburg, IL
Railroad: Burlington Northern
Railroad formly C B& Q railroad
Position: 1st baggage handler
2nd materials manager
Years of Service: 30 years.
started 1945 retired 1980.
Submitter's Name: Wendy B.
City/State: Rock Island, IL

Registrant ID: 4373
Name: David Withers
City/State: Pelham, NC
Railroad: Pullman Co.
Position: Pullman Porter
Years: Retired back in the 30's
Submitter's Name: Alisa
City/State Ft. Washington, MD
Comments: David was my
grandfather. He worked most of
his life as a Pullman Porter. He
made a good living because they
had a beautiful home in Pelham
North Carolina and my mother
was able to attend Virginia Union
Seminary.

Registrant ID: 3371
Name: William Ruford Wofork
City/State: Nashville, TN
Position: Porter
Years of Service: 1900-1955
Submitter's Name: Beulah
City/State: Nashville. TN

Registrant ID: 4374
Name: Robert L Wood
City/State: Louisville, KY
Railroad: Pullman Company
Position: Porter
Years : 9/19/43-1953

Registrant ID: 4374
Name: Paul L.Wood
City/State: St. Paul, MN
Railroad: Great Northern--
Burlington Northern
Position: Waiter, Lounge Car
Attendant, Steward, and
Management Position
Years: 30 years retired in 1976
Submitter's Name: Paula V.
City/State: Chicago, IL
Comments: My Dad, Paul L.
Wood, has registered with you.

Registrant ID: 4375
Name: Chester A. Woodard
City/State: TX
Submitter's Name: Nolan E.
City/State: CA

Registrant ID: 4377
Name: Robert Woodard
City/State: Los Angeles, CA
Railroad: Union Railroad
Position: Pullman Porter
Years of Service: 47 years
Submitter's Name: Donna
City/State: Los Angeles, CA
Comments: My Dad, once was
pushed off the moving train by a
soldier. The train was traveling
between Wichita, Kansas and
Denver, Colorado. This happened
in 1959 or 1960. He couldn't
sue nor could he miss work.

Registrant ID: 1946
Name: Elmer Woodard
City/State: Tyler, TX
Railroad: Pullman Co.
Position: Pullman Porter
Submitter's Name: Kashan
City/State: Oakland, CA

Registrant ID: 4378
Name: James Woodhouse
City/State: Chicago, IL
Railroad: Santa Fe
Position: Pullman Porter
Years of Service: 1939 to 1969
Submitter's Name: Irene
City/State: Chicago, IA
Comments: My father actually
started around 1933 but was
laid off and then returned
around 1939.

Registrant ID: 4379
Name: Samuel Woodhouse
City/State: Chicago, IL
Railroad: Illinois Central and
Rock Island
Position: Pullman Porter
Years of Service: 1948-1960
Submitter's Name: John
City/State: Mattson, IL
Comments: My grandfather is a
retired Pullman Porter. He
pasted away in 1977. March
1896 December 1977. He made
beds, clean shoes, and service
the customer. The listed address
is the address where he lived
during his employment.

Registrant ID: 4383
Name: Earl Woods
City/State: Gary, IN
Position: Dining Car Steward
Years of Service: 1945-1986

Registrant ID: 4383
Name: Isaiah B. Woods
City/State: Poplar Bluff, MO
Railroad: Missouri Pacific
Position: Pullman Porter
Years of Service: 1940's-50's
Submitter's Name: Charlene

410

City/State: Baltimore, MD
Comments: My grandfather was a proud member of the Brotherhood of Sleeping Car Porters. He was unjustly terminated sometime in the 1950's. I remember his letter writing campaign to A. Philip Randolph and legal efforts to regain his job. I recall many conversation.

Registrant ID: 4382
Name: Columbus Woods
City/State: Memphis, TN
Position: Pullman Porter
Submitter's Name: Christopher
City/State: Brooklyn, NY
Comments: My grandfather was born in approximately 1887. My late father's birth certificate (dated January 1926) listed his employment as Pullman Porter.

Registrant ID: 4384
Name: Ray Woods
City/State: Fulton, AR
Position: Railroad
Years of Service: 1926-1969
Submitter's Name: Elbert C.
City/State: Detroit, MI

Registrant ID: 4381
Name: Clyde/Arthur
City/State: Fairmont, CA
Railroad: Santa Fe Railroad
Position: Pullman Porter
Submitter's Name: Joyce
City/State: Fairmont, CA

Registrant ID: 1945
Name: Willie Woods
City/State: Tyler, TX
Railroad: Cotton Belt

Position: Car Painter Helper
Submitter's Name: Kashan
City/State: Oakland, CA
Comments: Relative deceased

Registrant ID: 4384
Name: Walter Woods
City/State: AL
Railroad: Georgia Pacific
Position: Porter & Waiter
Years of Service: 1938
Submitter's Name: John
City/State: Riverside, CA
Comments: My father Walter Woods & my uncle Harold Norris both worked on the railroad lines from Ohio to Chicago and as well as to Georgia & Alabama. They worked during the time when they had no civil rights! As we know of today.

Registrant ID: 4386
John Wesley Woolridge, Sr.
City/State: Chicago, IL
Railroad: Santa Fe
Position: Waiter
Years of Service: 1962-1969
Submitter's: Barbara Ann
City/State: Calumet City, IL

Registrant ID: 4387
Name: Rufus Thomas Wooten
City/State: San Antonio, TX
Railroad: Caty Main
Position: Waiter
Years of Service: 1943-1945
City/State: San Antonio, TX

Registrant ID: 2211
Name: Rufus Thomas Wooten
City/State: San Antonio, TX
Railroad: Caty Main
Position: Waiter 1943-1945

City/State: San Antonio, TX

Registrant ID: 4388
Name: Henry A. Wortham, Jr.
City/State: Baltimore, MD
Railroad: Erie-Lackawanna
Con Rail
Position: Cook
Years of Service: 40 plus.
Submitter's Name: Renee
City/State: Bronx, NY
Comments: Mr. grandfather,
Henry A. Wortham Sr. worked for
the railroad in early 1930's as a
Cook.

Registrant ID: 4389
Name: Henry A. Wortham, Sr.
City/State: Baltimore, MD
Railroad: Erie-Lackawanna/Con
Rail
Position: Station Master, Porter,
Baggage Handler
Years of Service: 40 plus.
Submitter's Name: Renee
City/State: Bronx, NY
Comments: My father, Henry A.
Wortham, Jr., retired after 40
plus years. of service and was
also He was the recording
Secretary for the BSCP union.

Registrant ID: 4390
Name: Driver R.. Wright
Position: Pullman Porter
Years of Service: Over 25
Comments: B.S.C.P.

Registrant ID: 4398
Name: Thomas Wright
City/State: New York, NY
Railroad: Pennsylvania Railroad
(presently Amtrak)
Position: Railroad Chef

Years of Service: January 29,
1928 March 21, 1978
Comments: Cooked for many
celebrities and personal chef for
the President of Conrail.
Registrant ID: 4391
Name: Ernest Wright
City/State: MS
Railroad: Passed thru Chicago
and Los Angeles
Position: Pullman Porter
Years of Service: 1930's-40's
Submitter's Name: George
City/State: Boston, MA
Comments: He was my uncle
(mother's brother) and my
Christmas present each year
were things that he had collected
on the train.

Registrant ID: 4395
Name: Mary Emma Wright
City/State: New York, NY
Railroad: Pennsylvania Railroad
Pullman Car Division
Position: Car Cleaner
Years of Service: Circa 1948
Submitter's Name: Frances
City/State: Bronx, NY

Registrant ID: 4394
Name: John J. Wright
City/State: Louisville, KY
Position: Waiter
Years of Service: 1936-40
Submitter's Name: Sandra
City/State: Louisville, KY

Registrant ID: 4396
Name: Russell A. Wright
City/State: McLean, VA
Railroad: Pullman Porter
Years of Service: 1943-1974
Submitter's Name: Denise W.

City/State: McLean, VA

Registrant ID: 4393
Name: John Wright
City/State: Washington, DC
Position: Porter
Years of Service: 1944-55
Submitter's Name: Rev Eugene
City/State: North, SC
Comments: Brother

Registrant ID: 4392
Name: J. Wright
City/State: Philadelphia, PA
Position: Porter
Submitter's Name: Christine
City/State: Philadelphia, PA

Registrant ID: 4399
Name: Richard Wright Jr.
City/State: GA
Railroad: The Central of Georgia
Position: Dining Car Waiter and Assistant to President
Years of Service: 55 Years
Submitter's Name: Jocelyn
City/State: Port St. Lucie, FL
Comments: My grandfather started as a teenager. During my childhood, I recall that he was a valet or assistant to the president of the railroad line, Mr. Calloway. My grandfather traveled in the president's car.

Registrant ID: 4993
Name: Leon Wynn
City/State: Toronto, Ontario, NE
Submitter's Name: Phillip
City/State Farmington Hills, MI
Comments: Leon was my maternal grandfather. He died circa 1982. He last resided in

Toronto, Ontario, and retired from the imperial oil company. He was born circa 1916 and resided in Memphis Tennessee.

Registrant ID: 4995
Name: Winnie W. Wynne
City/State: Indianapolis, IN
Position: Porter
Years of Service: 1941-1969
Submitter's Name: Emery D
City/State: Indianapolis,, IN

Registrant ID: 4994
Name: Marion Wynne
City/State: Buffalo, NY
Railroad: Lehigh Valley
Position: Porter/waiter
Years: May 6, 1931
Submitter's Name: Wesley
City/State: Philadelphia, AL
Comments: Father

Registrant ID: 4996
Name: Clarence Yelverton
City/State: AL
Railroad: Chicago Northwestern
Position: Pullman Porter
Years of Service: 10 Years
Submitter's Name: Brenda
City/State: Chicago, IL

Registrant ID: 4999
Name: Ernest Young
Railroad: Pullman Company
Position: Pullman Porter
Years of Service: 1955-1990
Submitter's Name: Canton

Registrant ID: 4998
Name: Calvin James Young
City/State: New York, NY
Railroad: Penn Central
Position: Pullman-Porter

Years of Service: 1884-1924
Submitter's Name: Toni-Kim &
Yvonne, Julia
City/State: Bronx, NY
Comments: He was our
grandfather

Registrant ID: 5000
Name: John Logan Young
City/State: Buffalo, NY
Railroad: New York Central
Position: Sleeping Car Porter
Years of Service: 1923-1968
Submitter's Name: Barbara
City/State: Cheektowaga, NY

Registrant ID: 3952
Name: James Young Thompson
City/State: Buena Park, CA
Railroad: Union Pacific
Years of Service: 20yrs
Submitter's Name: May L
City/State: Buena Pk, CA
Comments: One Daughter, Betty

Registrant ID: 5002
Name: Eugene Young, Jr.
City/State: Dallas, TX
Position: Pullman Porter
Submitter's Name: Eugene
City/State: Dallas, TX
Comments: I am glad to know
that this museum exists, I am
the grandson of a Pullman Porter
who died in 1998 at the age of
89.

Registrant ID: 2462
Name: Roscoe Young, Sr.
City/State: NY
Railroad: New York Central
Position: Pullman Porter
Years of Service: 1925-1960
Submitter's Name: William R.

City/State: Bronx, NY

Registrant ID: 5003
Herman Wesley Young, Sr.
City/State: Richmond, VA
Railroad: Chesterpeak & Ohio
Position: Pullman
Porter/Conductor
Submitter: Mrs.Loney
City/State: Richmond, VA

References

Arnesen, E. (2001). *Brotherhoods of Color: Black Railroad Workers and the Struggle for Equality.* Cambridge, MA: Harvard University Press.

Grossman, J.R. (1991). *Land of Hope: Chicago, Black Southerners and the Great Migration.* Chicago, IL: University of Chicago.

Perata, D. (1996). *Those Pullman Blues: An Oral History of the African-American Railroad Attendant.* New York, NY: Twayne Publications.

Reef, C. (March 2001). *A. Philip Randolph: Union Leader and Civil Rights Crusader.* African-American Biographies. Berkeley Heights, NJ. Enslow Publishers, Inc.

Tye, L (2004). *Rising from the Rails: Pullman Porters and the Making of the Black Middle Class.* New York, NY. Henry Holt and Company.

Suggested Readings:

Brailsford R. Brazeal produced the first formal history of the organization in *The Brotherhood of Sleeping Car Porters: Its Origin and Development* (New York: Harper and Brothers, 1946); to be followed by William H. Harris, *Keeping the Faith: A. Philip Randolph, Milton P. Webster, and the Brotherhood of Sleeping Car Porters, 1925-1937* (Urbana: University of Illinois Press, 1977) and *The Harder We Run: Black Workers Since the Civil War* (New York: Oxford University Press, 1982); Patricia and Frederick McKissack's, *A Long Hard Journey: The Story of The Pullman Porter* (New York: Walker, 1989); David D. Perata, *Those Pullman Blues: An Oral History of the African-American Railroad Attendant* (New York: Twayne, 1996); Beth Tompkins-Bates, *Pullman Porters and the Rise of Protest Politics in Black America, 1925-1945* (Chapel Hill: University of North Carolina Press, 2001); and Larry Tye, *Rising from the Rails: Pullman Porters and the Making of the Black Middle Class* (New York: Henry Holt and Company, 2004). Also, E. Franklin Frazier's *The Negro Family in Chicago* (Chicago: University of

Chicago Press, 1929) cemented the image of the Pullman Porter as an individual of high status in black society. In addition, a fictional account that resonates with the vividity of the actual experience of the Pullman Porter was presented in historian and former porter, J.A. Rogers' *Superman to Man* (Rpt., New York, 1957; Chicago: 1917).

Illustrations and Photo Credits

38 top, CHS Prints and Photographs Collection; 40, from *The Messenger,* (January 1926), courtesy of The Newberry Library; CHS Library; 42 top, *"No. 9:" The Story of the First Pullman Car* (1924), CHS Library; 42 bottom, CHS, ICHi-26271; 43 top, CHS, ICHi-12867; 43 bottom, courtesy of the City of Chicago, Department of Development and Planning, Landmarks Division; 44, CHS, ICHi-20821; 46, from *The Messenger,* (July 1926), courtesy of The Newberry Library; 48 top, from *The Messenger* (September 1925), courtesy of The Newberry Library; 48 bottom, from *The Bulletin,* (vol. 1, no. 8), courtesy of The Newberry Library; 49, CHS, ICHi-21783; 50, CHS Archives and Manuscripts Collection, BSCP papers; 16 left, CHS, ICHi-25676; 53, CHS, ICHi-25389; 55, CHS, ICHi-22353; 57 top, CHS, ICHi-22642;

REGISTRY SECTION

A. Philip Randolph Pullman Porter Museum Photo Archives:

Persons identified by family members
Cover Page Photo Collage
Robert Harris (Far Left)
(Upper Right Group) L to R 2nd from left Vernon Lee Miller

417

About the Author

For more than a decade Lyn Hughes has made an immeasurable contribution helping to generate interest in urban historic and cultural heritage preservation. Hughes is a strong advocate of the notion that these valuable but overlooked tools can be used to help rebuild community and cultural pride on a national scale, particularly in urban communities; by generating a combined interest in History, the Arts, Cultural Heritage Tourism and Historic Preservation. An Anthology Of Respect is yet another effort in a series of her pursuits, to accomplish that goal.

Hughes' work and research as an urban-cultural heritage preservationist and an activist holds international recognition, and she has begun conducting research to support the position of a need for the development of uniform cultural policy. She is currently completing her doctoral dissertation on the topic, which she believes will further support that position. However, her most prominent accomplishment is being Founder of the A. Philip Randolph Pullman Porter Museum, located in Chicago Illinois; the first museum in the United States dedicated to the contributions of African Americans to America's Labor movement.

www.aphiliprandolphmuseum.org.

If you, or someone you know, worked in the railroad industry
between 1867-1969, and they are not listed in this first edition please
fill out this card so that you, or they, can be listed in the second
edition of the Pullman Porters National Historic Registry of African
American Railroad Employees.

Name of the person being registered   Position held   Railroad Line if known

Years Worked   Is the person being registered living or deceased?

Where did the person live while working for the railroad?

Please tell us your name   Your relationship to the registrant

Your email address   Phone Number

Your mailing address   City   State   Zip Code

Please complete and mail this insert back to:
A. Philip Randolph Pullman Porter Museum
P O BOX 6276
Chicago, IL 60680-6276
Doing do indicates you have given us permission to include its contents in future

CPSIA information can be obtained at www.ICGtesting.com
Printed in the USA
LVOW11s1739140616

492540LV00027B/47/P

9 780979 394126